AF586318

Operation Z

Jacques Baud

Operation Z

Max Milo

Max Milo, Paris, 2022
www.maxmilo.com
ISBN: 978-2-31501-064-6

Sommaire

Introduction

On 18 May 2022, George W. Bush sparked hilarity around the world by castigating

> *the one-man decision to launch a totally unjustified and brutal invasion of Iraq... I mean, of Ukraine.*

This Freudian slip illustrates and underlines the absurdity of the Western attitude towards Russia. On the one hand, it accepts and supports the crimes of the Western powers and, on the other, it applies a barrage of sanctions against Russia that border on the absurd.

Three months earlier, on 24 February 2022, Vladimir Putin, speaking on Russian television, announced his decision to intervene militarily in Ukraine at the request of the republics of Donetsk and Lugansk, whose independence he had recognised three days earlier. The Western world, shocked, began to rain down sanctions on Russia and Belarus. Ukraine is neither a member of the European Union nor of NATO, but since 2014 its regime has been under Western protection. Resolving crises by force is rarely the right solution. The Russians know this as well as we do. So was Vladimir Putin's decision the right one? In unison, the Westerners answer in the negative, but their unanimity stems from a reading of events that conveniently combines a form of negationism and revisionism aimed at taking into consideration only what confirms their prejudices. In addition to the political lies, there is also the media illusion, as our media outlets have contributed to the confusion by painting a reality that is far from the facts.

But the way we understand the crisis determines our strategy for getting out of it.

The aim of this book is to provide precise, factual and nuanced information, which will facilitate a calmer view of this crisis. Not everything is black; not everything is white. The truth lies in the shades of grey. The biased and extremist discourse tends to make the least discordant information appear favourable to Russia. It is time to remember what popular wisdom has been saying since the dawn of time: there are always two relevant points of view in a conflict.

Readers with an exclusively Westernist perspective will judge this book as «Putinian» or even «Putinolite». On the contrary, those who seek a better understanding of the crisis in order to find a path towards dialogue will find this book to be peace-friendly and therefore ultimately pro-Ukraine.

To understand the inconsistent way in which the West has responded to the Ukrainian crisis, one need only ask why this conflict - and Russia in particular - are more reprehensible than those we initiated before.

The illegal and illegitimate invasions of Afghanistan, Iraq, Libya or Syria by Western countries have not been met with sanctions or condemnation. American or Polish disabled athletes have not been deprived of the Paralympics; British cats have not been excluded from cat shows; Polish, German, American, British,

French or Lithuanian weightlifters have not been condemned for crimes they did not commit personally; British, American or Swiss tennis players have not been forced to condemn their governments in order to participate in a tournament, Chopin's «Polish girls» have not become «Iraqi girls», and the atrocities of the Polish military have not been condemned, etc.

With the Russian operation, it seems that, all of a sudden, the West has created a conscience, but one that functions - as we shall see - in a very selective and variable geometry manner...

Methodology

In order to counterbalance the radical, simplistic and under-informed discourse that hinders understanding of the conflict and favours the recitation of an anti-Russian vulgate to the detriment of informational objectivity, my approach is different from that of the media that respect neither the Munich Charter nor the most elementary journalistic deontology - among which are Swiss Radio-Television, France 5 or LCI. It is also different from those who fight the propaganda of one party by using the propaganda of the other (and often of the extreme right), such as heidi.news. My aim is to combat the propaganda of each party by examining its own information and therefore its own contradictions. Therefore, I will use exclusively Western and Ukrainian sources (governmental side), as well as those from the Russian opposition.

The lack of diversity in the French-speaking media landscape has led me to take most of my sources from the Anglo-Saxon mainstream media, which are often more honest than their French-speaking counterparts, even if they remain fiercely opposed to Russia.

1. Fundamentals and perceptions

The way the Western community has reacted to the Ukrainian crisis shows that the nature of the conflict is singular. While Western countries (and my detractors) have accepted and even applauded the massacre of Arab populations without ever condemning or sanctioning the perpetrators, this crisis has unleashed passions. With a foolishness and hatred rarely seen in history, Russia has been fought on all fronts, in a low, often thoughtless and totally unnecessary manner.

The crisis results from the convergence of three types of factors.

1.1. The emotional and cultural level

The first factor is emotional and cultural. It can be summed up by a feeling that is quite widely shared in the West, which some call «Russophobia». In Ukraine, it has been developing since the beginning of the 20th century and is reminiscent of the old fear of «Judeo-Bolshevism» which inspired the ultra-nationalist paramilitary militias. In the West, it feeds on the confusion maintained by many self-proclaimed experts and our media between Russia and the USSR. It explains the sometimes irrational character of sanctions that seem more interested in satisfying old grudges than in achieving a concrete objective, such as the exclusion of Russian cats from cat shows or the embargo on certain typefaces in Russia (!).

It is not unimportant that some current Western political leaders have a family history that seems to prevent them from having the necessary hindsight to manage in a calm manner. This is the case of Chrystia Freeland, Canadian Minister of Foreign Affairs, Ursula von der Leyen[1], President of the European Commission, Olaf Scholz, German Chancellor, Anthony Blinken, US Secretary of State or Victoria Nuland, US Under Secretary of State for Political Affairs[2]. All of them - for totally different reasons - have a partisan view of Russia that illustrates and explains our temptation to treat this conflict differently from all other previous conflicts.

In a way, the very passionate and irrational dimension that the conflict has taken in the West could be explained - at least in part - by the revenge of grandchildren for their grandparents. Largely of Generation X, European politicians do not seem to have the intellectual maturity to deal with complex issues[3]. As a result, they tend to deal with issues that are too demanding for their limited intelligence with their guts. Their political action is guided more by emotion and ideology than by reflection. In contrast, more experienced personalities

1.Peter Kuras, 'The Aristocratic Ineptitude of Ursula Von Der Leyen', Foreign Policy, 30 April 2021

2.»Yiddish and the Ukrainian-Jewish roots of the new U.S. Secretary of State», Ukrainian Jewish Encounter, 30 November 2020

3.Rachel Elbaum, «European Shift: Generation of Young Leaders Sweeps To Power Across Continent», NBC News, 17 October 2017 (https://www.nbcnews.com/news/world/european-shift-generation-young-leaders-sweeps-power-across-continent-n811351)

such as Henry Kissinger[4], Oskar Lafontaine and Jürgen Habermas encourage - alas in vain - current leaders to take a step back[5].

1.2.The strategic level

1.2.1.The Russian perspective

Victims of several invasion attempts in two centuries (1812, 1918-1922 and 1941-1945, not to mention the 1917 Revolution, instigated by Germany), the Russians have retained a deep distrust of Westerners, whose unfortunate tendency to start wars is no longer in evidence. June 1941 is still very much in the memory, and the Russians do not want to experience such a situation again.

The Russian perception of their environment has two dimensions that the West tends to amalgamate, in order to support a narrative more favourable to Ukraine.

The first is the strategic dimension, which we will see below, and which is Russia's permanent quest to be surrounded by a neutral and non-hostile zone. This is why, even during the Cold War, the USSR was content to have neutral Finland on its northern border and Romania (which was not part of the Warsaw Treaty, and where there was no Soviet military presence). Similarly, it maintained cordial relations with Iran, as the Shah's policy - although close to the US - was to maintain equidistance with both superpowers. Like the USSR, Russia does not need

4.Timothy Bella, «Kissinger says Ukraine should cede territory to Russia to end war», The Washington Post, 24 May 2022 (https://www.washingtonpost.com/world/2022/05/24/henry-kissinger-ukraine-russia-territory-davos/)

5.Philip Oltermann, «German thinkers' war of words over Ukraine exposes generational divide», The Guardian, 6 May 2022 (https://www.theguardian.com/world/2022/may/06/german-thinkers-war-of-words-over-ukraine-exposes-generational-divide)

to be surrounded by a 'zone of influence' but by a 'zone free of influence'. That is why it did not see NATO's eastward expansion as hostile. It was only after the US withdrawal from nuclear disarmament treaties and the installation of missiles in the former Eastern Bloc countries that Russia perceived a danger in the early 2000s.

The second dimension is more cultural and emotional. The break-up of the USSR left Russian minorities, established for several generations in now independent countries, but whose populations were hostile to Russians. The countries of Eastern Europe and the Caucasus have nationalisms that have never really been able to express themselves since the beginning of the 20th century, and this probably explains resentment and absolutist behaviour towards their ethnic minorities today. The result has been a sense of responsibility for Russia - and for the Russian people in particular - for these 'abandoned' communities. This is also reflected in Vladimir Putin's sense that 'the collapse of communism was the greatest catastrophe of the 20th century': he does not regret the system (his policies are the opposite), but the consequences of this collapse on the Russian population.

This dimension is essential for understanding relations between Russia and its neighbours since 1990. It is what has determined Russia's commitment to the implementation of the Minsk Agreements since 2015. It also explains why Vladimir Putin maintains - and even increases - his popularity in Russia, despite the effect of sanctions.

It should also be remembered that even Alexei Navalny, who is seen by some in the West as Vladimir Putin's main opponent, has said that if he were in power he would not return Crimea to Ukraine[6]. This is what the West does not want to understand

6.Anna Dolgov, «Navalny Wouldn't Return Crimea, Considers Immigration Bigger

and has not understood, which is why they thought that imposing sanctions on Russia would cause the «regime» to collapse.

1.2.2. The American perspective

Despite the end of the Cold War, the US has not given up on weakening Russia. Taking advantage of Russia's structural weakness and a still developing China, the United States has enjoyed an advantage that has allowed it to impose itself on the international scene. This strategy began with a gradual withdrawal from the arms control agreements signed during the Cold War: the ABM Treaty (2002), the Open Skies Treaty (2018) and the Intermediate-range Nuclear Forces (INF) Treaty (2019).

In order to maintain its dominant position, the US seeks to isolate Russia. No conspiracy here!This strategy is spelled out in two documents prepared in 2019[7] by the RAND Corporation[8]. They describe exactly the situation we see today: a form of 'strategic mobbing' aimed at alienating Russia from the international community and causing its collapse. It is a similar strategy that the United States is applying to China, which explains China's resistance to following the West in condemning Russia.

This strategy also includes the fragmentation of Russia and the physical destruction of the Russian state by causing it to break up. The idea is not new and was revived by the US State

Issue Than Ukraine», The Moscow Times, 16 October 2014 (https://www.themoscowtimes.com/2014/10/16/navalny-wouldnt-return-crimea-considers-immigration-bigger-issue-than-ukraine-a40477)

7. James Dobbins, Raphael S. Cohen, Nathan Chandler, Bryan Frederick, Edward Geist, Paul DeLuca, Forrest E. Morgan, Howard J. Shatz, Brent Williams, 'Extending Russia: Competing from Advantageous Ground', RAND Corporation, 2019; James Dobbins & others, 'Overextending and Unbalancing Russia', RAND Corporation, (Doc Nr RB-10014-A), 2019

8. The RAND Corporation is a think tank created in 1948 by the Pentagon to advise the US government on strategic issues.

Department, which organised a conference on the issue in June 2022, in the framework of the Helsinki Commission. This is a far cry from what the media call Vladimir Putin's «paranoia».

As Robert Wade of the London School of Economics notes, the US has long been looking for a way to provoke a Russian attack on Ukraine[9]. He thus confirms what Oleksei Arestovich said in March 2019, as we shall see. But implementation is more a matter of belief and fantasy than strategy. The West, led by the Americans, has an image of a weak Russia, incapable of mobilising forces for a crisis. Their «strategy» is based on what the Anglo-Saxons call «wishful thinking». It is therefore often out of step with the reality of the facts, and requires an adjustment of the discourse:

- In March, the first stated objective was regime change[10], using sanctions to cause the collapse of the Russian economy. The narrative was that Ukraine was holding up better than the Russians had expected, and their defeat was predicted; the rouble collapsed and the economy with it; anti-war protests grew in Russia. Joe Biden even talks about the fact that Putin «should not stay in power»[11].

9.Robert H. Wade, «Why the US and Nato have long wanted Russia to attack Ukraine», London School of Economics, 30 March 2022 (https://blogs.lse.ac.uk/europpblog/2022/03/30/why-the-us-and-nato-have-long-wanted-russia-to-attack-ukraine/)

10.Sam Blewett, 'Joe Biden calls for regime change in Moscow as he likens invasion to WW2 horrors', The Independent, 26 March 2022 (https://www.independent.co.uk/news/uk/joe-biden-vladimir-putin-ukraine-moscow-warsaw-b2044743.html)

11.Ashley Parker, Tyler Pager & Marianna Sotomayor, «Biden at war: Inside a deliberate yet impulsive Ukraine strategy», The Washington Post, 7 April 2022, (https://www.washingtonpost.com/politics/2022/04/07/biden-war-ukraine/)

- By the end of April, the US objective is to weaken Russia so that it is no longer able to restore its capabilities[12]. The strategy is to «isolate Russia from the rich democracies[13] «.
- In June, seeing that previous strategies had not worked, US objectives were reduced to providing arms to Ukraine to consolidate its position in negotiations[14].

Thus, in less than three months, the objective of a regime overthrow in Moscow associated with a victory for Ukraine is replaced by the search for a firmer negotiating position. The Europeans are content to follow. In short, starting from false premises, the action of the West goes from failure to failure, demonstrating that they have no real strategy and no coherence in action.

1.3.The operative level

NATO expansion is of course essential to understanding Russia's position, but it is not the cause of its intervention in February 2022. On this point, the Russians have always favoured a political resolution. It is likely that, without the conditions that led to the 24 February offensive, the problem would have been resolved around a negotiating table.

12.Sarakshi Rai, «Pentagon chief says US wants to see Russia 'weakened'», The Hill, 25 April 2022 (https://thehill.com/policy/defense/3462190-pentagon-chief-says-us-wants-to-see-russia-weakened/)
13.Olivier Knox, «The U.S. has a big new goal in Ukraine: Weaken Russia», The Washington Post, 26 April 2022 (https://www.washingtonpost.com/politics/2022/04/26/us-has-big-new-goal-ukraine-weaken-russia/)
14.Anastassia Fedyk, «Op-Ed: Why more weapons will help Ukraine and Russia negotiate a lasting truce», Los Angeles Times, 12 June 2022 (https://www.latimes.com/opinion/story/2022-06-12/ukraine-russia-war-negotiations-peace-strategy)

In a video filmed on 18 March 2019, Volodymyr Zelensky's advisor Oleksei Arestovich cynically explains that conditions had to be created to force Russia to attack Ukraine[15]. This confession illustrates the perfidy of the West towards Ukraine because, as Volodymyr Zelensky notes in an interview on CNN[16], his country has been instrumentalised to satisfy the US objectives set out in 2019.

However, to understand this operative level, it is necessary to look back at the events of 2014 and contextualise them.

15.»Predicted Russian - Ukrainian war in 2019 - Alexey Arestovich», YouTube, 18 March 2022 (https://youtu.be/1xNHmHpERH8)

16.Chandelis Duster, «Zelensky: 'If we were a NATO member, a war wouldn't have started'», cnn.com, 20 March 2022

2. The historical context

2.1. The post-Cold War era

In 1990-1991, the hope generated by the end of communism was very real for the new Russian leaders. In July 1991, with the dissolution of the Warsaw Treaty, they saw the opportunity to reflect on a new security architecture on the European continent. The Soviets/Russians never claimed or wanted a dissolution of NATO as a reciprocal of the dissolution of the Warsaw Treaty, contrary to what Caroline Roux claims[17], and the West never promised to do so, as General Vincent Desportes claims on France 5[18]. On the contrary, Russia has joined NATO's Partnership for Peace (PfP).

Russia was very attached to the OSCE (created on the initiative of the USSR) and cherished the idea of a collective security

17.Caroline Roux in the programme «C dans l'air» on 25 January («Ukraine: Russian or American one-upmanship? #cdanslair 25.01.2022», France 5/YouTube, 26 January 2022 (20'20")

18.»NATO increases tensions in Europe, with General Vincent Desportes - C à Vous - 28/02/2022 «, France 5/YouTube, 28 February 2022 (01'15")

system based on it, which would bring together European and North American countries. The Russian leaders, who had seen the damage caused by communism, thought that a security architecture based on power relations was outdated and dreamed of a more cooperative system. This was the idea of a «common European home», which Mikhail Gorbachev had launched in 1989, borrowing Charles De Gaulle's idea of a «Europe from the Atlantic to the Urals».

There was nothing absurd about this idea, as Manfred Wörner, then Secretary General of NATO, pointed out in his speech on 17 May 1990:

> *The main task of the next decade will be to build a new European security structure, including the Soviet Union and the Warsaw Pact countries. The Soviet Union will have an important role to play in building such a system. If you look at the current situation of the Soviet Union, which has practically no allies left, then you can understand its justified wish not to be forced to leave Europe.*[19]

The creation of the North Atlantic Cooperation Council (NACC) by NATO at the end of 1991 was enthusiastically welcomed by the authorities and public opinion in Russia. The idea of continental security cooperation was very popular and did not exclude the possibility of NATO membership. Discussions in this direction took place in October 1993 between Boris Yeltsin and the American Secretary of State Warren Christopher, who remained reserved:

19. Dave Majumdar, "Newly Declassified Documents: Gorbachev Told NATO Wouldn't Move Past East German Border", The National Interest, 12 December 2017

We will in due course consider the question of membership as a longer-term possibility. There will be an evolution, based on the development of a habit of cooperation, but over time.[20]

Documents recently released by Britain show that this idea has been described as a «joke» and rejected by Western chancelleries[21]. Indeed, in the logic of 1949, NATO's raison d'être is to place its members under the nuclear protection of the United States. However, the United States did not see the coexistence of the two main nuclear powers in the same alliance as a good idea. It was partly for this reason that General de Gaulle withdrew France from the Alliance's integrated command in 1966.

At first glance, the Russian idea seems far-fetched. But in reality, Russia's leaders are visionary. They are thinking of international security based on cooperation, not confrontation, along the lines of the OSCE.

But the West has no intention of changing the European security architecture. The collapse of the communist system, the success of the Gulf War (1991) and the role of the West in the Balkan crisis have shown the Americans the advantages of a unipolar world.

NATO's reaction did not meet the expectations of the Russian population. In June 1994, the Russian government joined NATO's newly created Partnership for Peace, against the advice of its public opinion. In 1997, in order to give the illusion that it wants to develop cooperation with Russia, NATO laid the foundations

---

20. Warren Christopher's internal memorandum on his 22 October 1993 interview with Boris Yeltsin (declassified 8 May 2000) quoted in Dave Majumdar, 'How Bill Clinton Accidentally Started Another Cold War', The American Conservative, 18 October 2017

21.Chris York, «A Secret Plan To Let Russia Join Nato Was Dismissed As 'Farcical', Declassified Papers Reveal», The Huffington Post, 31 December 2019.

for the NATO-Russia Council (NRC), created in 2002. The NRC aims to maintain a dialogue with Russia so that NATO's expansion is not perceived as a threat. In fact, as Bill Clinton summarised it, it is a way of not implementing promises made to the leaders of the former USSR:

> *What the Russians get out of this exceptional agreement that we are offering them is the opportunity to sit in the same room with NATO and join us whenever we all agree on something, but they have no way of stopping us from doing something that they don't agree with. They can show their disapproval by leaving the room. And as a second great advantage, they get our promise that we will not put our military affairs with their former allies, who will now be our allies, unless we wake up one morning and decide to change our minds.*[22]

For the Eastern European countries, the situation is somewhat different. In their minds, membership of the European Union and NATO often go hand in hand: it is a question of ensuring their development in security, in an approach that is more opportunistic than philosophical. For them, the values of democracy and human rights remain, despite everything, very secondary. Thus, despite some constitutional and legal safeguards, their intelligence services have essentially remained security services that largely retain the legacy of their communist predecessors. This is evidenced by their participation in the CIA torture programme, which does not seem to move the European Union in the least! Similarly, their willingness to follow the US into Afghanistan and

22. James Goldgeier and Michael McFaul, Power and Purpose: US Policy toward Russia after the Cold War, Washington D.C., 2003, pp. 204-205

Iraq was motivated more by the modernisation of their armies than by humanistic values.

They have earned the label of 'new Europe' from Donald Rumsfeld[23]. They played a major role in creating the political migration crisis by intervening alongside the United States in the Middle East, then refusing to accept the consequences and relying on the countries of 'old Europe' to deal with it.

2.2.NATO expansion

Often presented as a fanciful rumour propagated by Russia[24], Western assurances of non-expansion of NATO are attested to by numerous declassified documents made public in December 2017 by the National Security Archive at George Washington University[25].

In the early 1990s, Switzerland considered whether to join continental institutions such as the European Union and NATO. Anxious to preserve its neutrality, it consulted these institutions and the members of the Security Council in order to assess the possible implications of such membership. In this context, I was involved in dialogue with the highest Russian foreign and defence authorities at the time, which gives me a more accurate picture of the Russian perception than we have today.

23. Mark Baker, "U.S.: Rumsfeld's 'Old' And 'New' Europe Touches On Uneasy Divide", RFE/RL, 24 January 2003

24.Nato enlargement and Russia: myths and realities (www.nato.int/docu/review/2014/Russia-Ukraine-Nato-crisis/Nato-enlargement-Russia/FR/index.htm)

25. "Declassified documents show security assurances against NATO expansion to Soviet leaders from Baker, Bush, Genscher, Kohl, Gates, Mitterrand, Thatcher, Hurd, Major, and Woerner", National Security Archive, Washington D.C., 12 December 2017.

In 2021, NATO Secretary General Jens Stoltenberg expressed[26] - quite logically - the Alliance's position that 'there was never a promise that NATO would not expand eastwards after the fall of the Berlin Wall'[27].This claim remains widespread among self-proclaimed experts on Russia, such as Bruno Tertrais of the Foundation for Strategic Research (FRS)[28], Isabelle Mandraud on France 5[29] or Nicolas Gosset of the Royal Higher Institute for Defence (IRSD) on RTBF[30], who explain that there were no promises because there was no treaty or written agreement. The argument is a bit simplistic.

It is true that there are no treaties or decisions of the North Atlantic Council (NAC) that embody such promises. But this does not mean that they have not been made, nor that they have been made out of flippancy!

Today we have the feeling that the USSR, having «lost the Cold War», no longer had a say. This is not correct. As the winner of the Second World War, the USSR had a de jure right of veto over German reunification. Western countries were therefore obliged to obtain her agreement, in exchange for which she demanded a commitment to non-expansion of NATO. It should not be forgotten that, at this stage, the USSR still existed! The March 1991 referendum will show that there is no question of dismantling it. It is therefore not in a weak position and has no reason not to demand a counterpart to its agreement to reunification.

26.»Conversation on ''The Future of NATO", nato.int, 25 March 2021 (updated 29 March 2021)

27. «NATO enlargement and Russia: myths and realities", NATO Review, 2014

28. https://twitter.com/BrunoTertrais/status/943152395273539584

29.Isabelle Mandraud in the programme «C dans l'air» of 11 January 2022 («Poutine rêve d'URSS, l'Ukraine sous tension #cdanslair 11.01.2022», France 5/YouTube, 12 January 2022) (24'06")

30.Nicolas Gosset in the programme «QR l'actu», 21 February 2022

This was expressed by Hans-Dietrich Genscher, German Foreign Minister, in his speech on 31 January 1990 in Tutzing (Bavaria), reported by the American Embassy in Bonn:

> *Genscher warned, however, that any attempt to extend [NATO's] military reach into the territory of the German Democratic Republic (GDR) would block German reunification.*

German reunification had two major consequences for the USSR: the withdrawal of the Soviet Group of Forces in Germany (SGF), the most powerful and modern contingent outside its territory, and the disappearance of an important part of its protective «glacis». In plain language, this meant that NATO was moving ipso facto closer to the Soviet border.

With the Warsaw Treaty still in force and NATO doctrine unchanged, it was legitimate for the USSR to fear for its security. This is why Genscher states:

> *The changes in Eastern Europe and the German unification process must not «undermine Soviet security interests». Therefore, NATO should exclude «expansion of its territory to the east, i.e. to get closer to the Soviet borders».*[31]

Mikhail Gorbachev therefore very quickly - and very legitimately - set conditions on his agreement, prompting James Baker, the US Secretary of State, to immediately begin discussions with him. On 9 February 1990, in order to calm his concerns, Baker declared:

---

31. https://nsarchive.gwu.edu/document/16112-document-01-u-s-embassy-bonn-confidential-cable

Not only for the Soviet Union but also for other European countries, it is important to have guarantees that, if the United States maintains its presence in Germany within the framework of NATO, not one inch of NATO's current military jurisdiction will spread eastwards.[32]

Promises were therefore made simply because the West had no alternative to obtain the USSR's approval, and without promises, Germany would not have been reunified. Gorbachev accepted German reunification only because he had received assurances from President George H.W. Bush and James Baker, Chancellor Helmut Kohl and his Foreign Minister Hans-Dietrich Genscher, British Prime Minister Margaret Thatcher, her successor John Major and their Foreign Secretary Douglas Hurd, President François Mitterrand, but also from CIA Director Robert Gates and Manfred Wörner, the then Secretary General of NATO[33].

Thus, on 17 May 1990, in a speech in Brussels, Manfred Wörner declared:

The fact that we are prepared not to deploy a Nato army beyond German territory gives the Soviet Union a strong guarantee of security.[34]

---

32. Record of Conversation between Mikhail Gorbachev and James Baker, 9 February 1990 (National Security Archive, The George Washington University, Washington DC) (https://nsarchive2.gwu.edu//dc.html?doc=4325680-Document-06-Record-of-conversation-between)

33. "Declassified documents show security assurances against NATO expansion to Soviet leaders from Baker, Bush, Genscher, Kohl, Gates, Mitterrand, Thatcher, Hurd, Major, and Woerner", National Security Archive, Washington D.C., 12 December 2017.

34. Dave Majumdar, "Newly Declassified Documents: Gorbachev Told NATO Wouldn't Move Past East German Border", The National Interest, 12 December 2017

In February 2022, in the German magazine Der Spiegel, Joshua Shifrinson, an American political scientist, revealed a document dated 6 March 1991, classified as SECRET, drawn up at the end of the meeting of the political directors of the foreign ministries of the United States, Great Britain, France and Germany. He reports the words of the German representative, Jürgen Chrobog:

> *We made it clear in the 2+4 negotiations that we would not extend NATO beyond the Elbe. So we cannot offer NATO membership to Poland and others.*

The representatives of the other countries also accepted the idea of not offering NATO membership to the other Eastern countries. Raymond Seitz, American representative states:

> *We have made it clear to the Soviet Union - in the 2+4 talks and elsewhere - that we will not benefit from the withdrawal of Soviet troops from Eastern Europe.* [35]

Secondly, whether or not there is a paper trail, there was a deal simply because a deal was inevitable. Now, in international law, a «promise» is a valid unilateral act that must be respected («promissio est servanda»). Those who deny this today are simply individuals who do not know the value of a given word. But it is true that such principles are not worth much in front of a New York lawyer...

The problem is that the West - and the Americans in particular - saw the fall of communism as «their victory», which they wanted to be total, and that Russia therefore had nothing

35.Klaus Wiegrefe, «Neuer Aktenfund von 1991 stützt russischen Vorwurf», Der Spiegel, 18 February 2022

more to say. In reality, the West did not «win» the Cold War, the communist system «lost» it: it was unsustainable and collapsed of its own accord. As Brent Scowcroft, George Bush (Sr.)'s National Security Advisor, said:

> *In the end, we did not take any action. We just let it happen.*[36]

Nevertheless, the American «hawks» saw an opportunity to destroy Russia completely. Robert M. Gates, former director of the CIA (1986-1993), reveals in his memoirs that Richard Cheney, then Secretary of Defense, was seeking to destroy Russia:

> *When the Soviet Union collapsed at the end of 1991, Dick [Cheney] wanted to see the dismantling not only of the Soviet Union and the Russian empire, but of Russia itself.*[37]

Thus, Vladimir Putin's repeatedly expressed perception of a West seeking to dismantle Russia is far from being an expression of «Putin paranoia», as Jean-Eric Schoettl, former Secretary General of the Constitutional Council in France, puts it[38]. The proposed US discussion on the 'decolonisation of Russia'[39]

36.Casey Michel, 'To avoid more senseless bloodshed, the Kremlin must lose what empire it still retains', The Atlantic, 27 May 2022 (https://www.theatlantic.com/ideas/archive/2022/05/russia-putin-colonization-ukraine-chechnya/639428/)
37.Robert M. Gates, Duty: Memoirs of a Secretary at War, Knopf Doubleday, 2014, p. 97.
38.Jean-Eric Schoettl, «Have we contributed to the worst-case scenario?», Revue politique et parlementaire, 28 February 2022 (https://www.revuepolitique.fr/avons-nous-concouru-au-scenario-du-pire/)
39.Casey Michel, 'Decolonize Russia', The Atlantic, 27 May 2022 (https://www.theatlantic.com/ideas/archive/2022/05/russia-putin-colonization-ukraine-chechnya/639428/)

shows that their determination to dismember Russia has only grown since 1991[40].

At that time, China was not yet a rival, and the US sought to prevent Russia from rising up and challenging its leadership. Therefore, during the 'Yeltsin decade', despite good relations with the Clinton administration, there is no significant Western development or investment in Russia. Instead, the country fell prey to unbridled capitalism led by unscrupulous oligarchs, who stripped the country bare and encouraged the rule of mafias. In the early 2000s, these oligarchs fled to Israel and Britain with huge fortunes.

The fine promises of 1990-1991 were soon forgotten. The countries of the 'new Europe' joined the Atlantic Alliance from 1999. For today's primary anti-Russians, the West has in good faith fulfilled all its obligations, and what has not been written has not been said... This is not the opinion of Robert M. Gates, who declared in July 2000:

> *At a time of particular humiliation and difficulty for Russia, the acceleration of NATO's eastward expansion, when Gorbachev and others were led to believe that this would not happen - at least not quickly - has, I think, probably not only worsened the relationship between the United States and Russia, but made it much more difficult to work constructively with them.* [41]

Note here the phrase «were led to believe», which indicates that there was bad faith on the part of the United States from the beginning. Mikhail Gorbachev's mistake was to believe in the

---

40. https://www.csce.gov/international-impact/events/decolonizing-russia

41.Robert Gates, University of Virginia, Miller Center Oral History, George H.W. Bush Presidency, July 24, 2000, p. 101 (http ://web1.millercenter.org/poh/transcripts/ohp_2000_0723_gates.pdf)

good faith of the Western democracies and not to ask them for written assurances...

The West did not keep its word. At first, Russia does not see this as a direct threat: it understands that for its neighbours, membership of the European Union and NATO often go hand in hand to ensure secure development.

The withdrawal of the United States from the ABM Treaty in 2002, and the Bush administration's subsequent discussions with Eastern European countries to install missiles, triggered Russian mistrust. This explains the firmness of Vladimir Putin's speech in Munich in 2007, in which he recalled the assurances given to Mikhail Gorbachev in 1990-1991, ruling out NATO expansion to the East. But the West still refuses to understand and the following year's announcement of an «intensified dialogue» with Ukraine and Georgia with a view to their admission further strains relations between Russia and NATO.

So the Russians are right to question the West's word and intentions today[42]. In the event of a rapprochement with Russia, we have already lost all credibility, as Stephen F. Cohen, Professor of Russian and Slavic Studies at New York University, notes. Cohen, Professor of Russian and Slavic Studies at New York University[43].

2.3.The indivisibility of security

The problem today is that the legitimate security concerns of European countries are bringing American nuclear power closer

42.Philippe Descamps, «Quand la Russie rêvait d'Europe - «L'Otan ne s'étendendra pas un pouce vers l'Est», Le Monde Diplomatique, September 2018, pp. 10-11

43.»Stephen F. Cohen: NATO expansion and Russia», YouTube/Carnegie Council for Ethics in International Affairs, 2 June 2010

to the Russian border, increasing the likelihood of nuclear war in the event of increased tension. However, the principles accepted by OSCE members clearly state that the security of one state cannot be achieved at the expense of others. Therefore, Russia calls on NATO to stop its expansionist policy or reform itself.

Clearly, Russia cannot interfere in Alliance decisions and cannot have a veto over NATO enlargement. However, membership in the Alliance is not simply the result of a state's will. It is supposed to meet two criteria.

The first comes from NATO's founding act - the Washington Treaty - itself. Its Article 10 states:

> *The Parties may, by unanimous agreement, invite to accede to the Treaty any other European State which is likely to further the principles of this Treaty and to contribute to the security of the North Atlantic area. Any State so invited may become a Party to the Treaty by depositing its instrument of accession with the Government of the United States of America. The Government of the United States of America shall inform each of the Parties of the deposit of each instrument of accession.*

In other words, countries are «invited» insofar as they can «contribute to the security of the North Atlantic region». In other words, the criterion is not the security of individual countries, but the collective security of the region. This is what the «new Europe» countries have not understood. Moreover, it means that potentially every country in the Euro-Atlantic area can be a member, but the decision is at the discretion of the Alliance, which is under no obligation to accept every country that wishes to join.

In June 2022, at the Madrid Summit, countries were ecstatic after NATO formally invited Finland and Sweden to join the Alliance. In reality, the Alliance had only invited these two countries to apply. They will have to pass through the Turkey-defined pitchforks to get the votes they need to join.

The second criterion, which has some relation to Article 10 above, is the indivisibility of security. This is a principle that has been accepted by OSCE members and was sealed in the Istanbul Document (1999)[44] and the Astana Declaration (2010):

> *The security of each participating State is inextricably linked to that of all the others.* [45]

The security of one country cannot be achieved at the expense of another. However, when NATO - and in particular the United States - deploys armaments, thereby reducing the warning and early warning times of a neighbouring country (in this case: Russia), this principle is not respected.

Until now, the acceptance of the new NATO members was done in euphoria and without any strategic reflection, because Russia and China were weak. Today the situation is radically different. The problems of one country can quickly become those of the whole Alliance, as in 1914. The Ukrainian crisis has highlighted the risks to NATO itself of ill-considered expansion.

This was emphasised by Vladimir Putin on 7 February 2022 in Moscow during his press conference with Emmanuel Macron. The problem is that our 'experts' do not listen to what they are told. As Richard Sakwa, Professor of Russian and European Politics at the University of Kent, puts it:

44. https://www.osce.org/files/f/documents/0/2/39570.pdf
45. https://www.osce.org/files/f/documents/b/3/74987.pdf

A real geopolitical paradox is that NATO exists to manage the risks created by its own existence. [46]

In 2002, when the United States withdrew from the ABM Treaty and began negotiations with Poland, the Czech Republic and Romania to install dual-use (anti-ballistic and nuclear) launchers, the Russians perceived a direct threat. This was expressed by Vladimir Putin in Munich in 2007.

2.4.The nuclear issue

In 1945, the USSR had won the race to Berlin and emerged from the war victorious, but unlike the West, it was bled dry. For some of its Western allies, such as Winston Churchill in Great Britain or certain American generals such as George Patton, this would be an opportunity to continue the war towards Moscow. Stalin was thought to have similar intentions towards the Atlantic... In any case, a certain wisdom prevailed and the Cold War began.

The historical tendency towards expansion that is attributed to Russia today is fundamentally an attribute of the Marxist thinking that guided Soviet policy. In this scheme, the USSR saw itself as the spearhead of the class struggle and engaged in a permanent and systemic war with the West, which was part of a historical process. Until Stalin's death, the USSR's strategic military thinking was dominated by the idea that its security would only be guaranteed by a victory of socialism over capitalism, and that

46. Daniel McLaughlin, 'Familiar chill blows through Russia but it has also changed for the better', The Irish Times, 18 December 2021

the confrontation between the two systems was inevitable. Soviet strategists spoke of the principle of «the inevitability of war».

However, according to American documents, even during the Cold War, it seems that the Soviets had no intention of invading Europe[47] :

> *Recently declassified Soviet documents, articles and minutes of meetings indicate that the Soviet leadership had no intention of invading Europe.* [48]

> *However, the experiences of the First and Second World Wars raised fears that the West would invade the territory of the USSR if it appeared militarily weak.*[49]

In 1949, the USSR acquired nuclear weapons. This led to the creation of NATO in the same year, with the aim of placing Western Europe under the US nuclear umbrella. At this stage, there was no talk of tactical nuclear weapons and nuclear warfare was mainly envisaged at the strategic level. The concern of the two nuclear powers is to avoid being pushed into a conflict that would pit them directly against each other and into a nuclear exchange, which would result in Mutual Assured Destruction (MAD).

47.Dr. Mahir J. Ibrahimov, Mr. Gustav A. Otto & Col Lee G. Gentile, Jr, «Cultural Perspectives, Geopolitics & Energy Security of Eurasia: Is the Next Global Conflict Imminent?», US Army Command and General Staff College Press, Fort Leavenworth, 2017 (https://www.armyupress.army.mil/Portals/7/combat-studies-institute/csi-books/cultural-perspectives.pdf)

48.Raymond Garthoff, Deterrence and the Revolution in Soviet Military Doctrine, The Brookings Institute, Washington D.C., 1990, p. 11

49.Vladislav Zubok, The Kremlin's Cold War: From Stalin to Khrushchev, Harvard University Press, Boston, 1997, p. 20

This is why the Russians and Americans sought to maintain a «neutral» space between them. In 1952, the accession of Greece and then Turkey brought NATO to the border of the USSR and alarmed the Soviets. But the decisive step was the entry of the Federal Republic of Germany (FRG) into NATO on 8 May 1955. The following week, it led to the creation of the Warsaw Treaty Organisation (WTO), also known as the Warsaw Pact.

Contrary to what the so-called experts on our TV sets say, the VTO is not about creating a 'sphere of influence'. In fact, the Eastern European countries were already ruled by communist parties that were often worse than their Soviet counterparts and were kept in a tight grip by Moscow. The aim of the Warsaw Treaty was to create a «buffer zone» («glacis» or Vorfeld in German), which was not intended to «stop» an aggressor, but to slow him down in order to give the Soviet Army time to get into battle order and counter-attack. In other words, the purpose of VTO is to give more space to a conventional conflict in order to prevent it from going nuclear too quickly.

Since the late 1960s, technological developments have allowed for the miniaturisation of nuclear weapons. As a result, the range of available weapon systems allows the intensity of a nuclear exchange to be varied.

To avoid reaching nuclear holocaust (MAD) too quickly, doctrines were developed to control the transition of a nuclear engagement from the tactical to the strategic level. On both sides of the Iron Curtain, similar mechanisms were adopted to graduate the use of nuclear weapons from the tactical to the strategic level.

This is what NATO calls the «flexible response». It is intended to send a clear signal to the Soviets that the United States will not move directly and automatically to a strategic nuclear exchange. Indeed, despite its evolution over time and technology, the US nuclear strategy retains one constant element: keeping the use of nuclear weapons off US soil.

The geostrategic situation of the United States and Russia is deeply asymmetric. The US can reach Russian territory with tactical/operational nuclear weapons, while Russia can only reach US soil with strategic weapons.

In other words, in the event of a major conflict, in order to avoid a strategic nuclear exchange that would affect its territory, the United States would seek to keep a nuclear conflict in the European theatre. To do so, it would carefully avoid directly hitting Russian national soil, so as not to trigger a «strategic duel» with Russia. Thus, this asymmetric situation became asymmetric: Russia could use low-intensity nuclear weapons in Europe, and the United States could only respond by striking its allies.

Therefore, from the late 1970s onwards, the United States deployed tactical and theatre nuclear weapons in Europe. In this way, they turned it into a potential nuclear battlefield. This triggered the peace and anti-nuclear movement in Germany and Northern Europe.

The Baltic States, Poland or even countries like Sweden, Finland or even Switzerland, who think that NATO could provide them with additional security, are sadly mistaken because the Americans will never sacrifice Washington, New York or Los Angeles to protect Helsinki or Stockholm. In any case, they would not engage in a strategic nuclear duel with Russia without going through a tactical and operational nuclear phase that would first destroy the European countries.

During the Cold War, the Warsaw Treaty provided a space for a conventional phase in the event of a conflict in Europe. With its disappearance and NATO's move eastwards, this space has disappeared. As a result, Russia has changed its doctrine of engagement, which allows it to use nuclear weapons more quickly. This situation is the result of two phenomena that took place in parallel in the early 2000s: the expansion of NATO and the denunciation of disarmament treaties by the United States in 2002.

What is astonishing is that Westerners seem not to have perceived this risk. NATO's advance has been seen as a geographical success, but no strategic conclusions have been drawn. By moving closer to the Russian border, NATO is also removing an early warning capability.

Therefore, Russia sees NATO on its doorstep - and in particular in Ukraine - as an existential threat. This has absolutely nothing to do with NATO's defensive vocation - or not - because the Alliance runs exactly the same risk, as the Ukrainian crisis of December 2021-February 2022 illustrates.This is what Vladimir Putin tries to explain in his press conference on 7 February 2022, following Emanuel Macron's visit to Moscow. Amusingly enough, this is what Sweden and Finland have not understood: in the event of war, these countries could be nuclearised first as a pre-emptive measure...

2.5.The 2007 Munich speech

On 10 February 2007, Vladimir Putin gave a speech to world experts at the Munich Security Forum, which is generally considered to be a major turning point in Russian security policy, marking Russia's return to control. The astonishment and heated reactions from the West launched a veritable demonisation of Vladimir Putin. Western disbelief is rooted in the concealment of two major facts: the eastward enlargement of NATO combined with the progressive abandonment by the United States of the normative framework of international security.

In 2001, George W. Bush decided to unilaterally withdraw from the ABM Treaty in order to deploy anti-ballistic missiles (ABMs) in Eastern Europe. The ABM Treaty was intended to limit the use of defensive missiles[50]. Its rationale was to exploit the deterrent effect of the risk of mutual destruction by allowing the protection of decision-making bodies by a ballistic shield in order to preserve a negotiating capacity. Thus, it limited the deployment of anti-ballistic missiles to specific areas, notably around capital cities, and prohibited it outside national territories.

In 2007, the Americans were in the midst of negotiations with the Czechs and Poles to deploy these missiles, officially to protect themselves from the Iranian threat. By doing so, they are breaking the strategic balance guaranteed by the ABM Treaty and creating a new situation for conflict in Europe.

Not only does Vladimir Putin see this as a risk to Russia's security, but he also notes that the United States is increasingly disregarding international law in order to pursue a unilateral policy. This explains his tone in Munich.

Indeed, the United States has gradually withdrawn from all Cold War arms control agreements: the ABM Treaty (2002), the Open Skies Treaty (2018) and the Intermediate-range Nuclear Forces (INF) Treaty (2019). This trend has continued under Trump and Biden with the withdrawal from the Joint Comprehensive Plan of Action (JCPOA) with Iran (May 2018), the 1955 Treaty of Amity, Commerce and Consular Rights (October 2018), the 1961 Optional Protocol to the Vienna Convention on Diplomatic Relations concerning the Compulsory Settlement of Disputes (October 2018), the Universal Postal Union (October

50. https://www.armscontrol.org/factsheets/abmtreaty

2018), UNESCO (January 2019), the World Health Organisation (July 2020), etc. Europeans whine when Trump withdraws from the Paris Agreements (November 2020), without noticing that the whole system of international law is being called into question.

In 2019, Donald Trump justified his withdrawal from the INF Treaty by an alleged violation by the Russian side. As the Stockholm International Peace Research Institute (SIPRI) notes, the Americans never provided any evidence of these violations[51]. In fact, they were seeking to get out of the agreement in order to install their AEGIS missile systems in Poland and Romania, officially intended to intercept Iranian ballistic missiles. But two facts cast doubt on the Americans' good faith:

- The first is that there is no indication that the Iranians are developing intercontinental range ballistic missiles[52], as Michael Ellemann of Lockheed-Martin told a US Senate committee[53].
- The second is that these systems use Mk41 launchers, which can launch either anti-ballistic (defensive) or nuclear (offensive) missiles. The Radzikowo site in Poland is 800 km from the Russian border and 1,300 km from Moscow.

In February 2022, after the meeting between Vladimir Putin and Emmanuel Macron, Patrick Cohen, on France 5, was astonished by the Russian president's talk of nuclear war and stated

51.Dr Tytti Erästö & Dr Petr Topychkanov, «Russian and US policies on the INF Treaty endanger arms control», SIPRI, 15 June 2018

52.Dr Tytti Erästö, «Europe's Overlooked Missile Defence Dilemma», European Leadership Network, 20 July 2017

53.Statement of Mr. Michael Elleman - Iran's Ballistic Missile Program - Before the U.S. Senate Committee on Banking, Housing, and Urban Affairs, International Institute for Strategic Studies, 24 May 2016

that the systems deployed in Europe were purely defensive[54]. He repeats what the Bush and Trump administrations said.

But even if this is theoretically true, it is technically and strategically false. For the doubt invoked for their installation is the same doubt that the Russians could legitimately have in the event of a conflict. This presence in the immediate vicinity of Russia's sanctuary territory could indeed lead to a nuclear conflict.

For in the event of a conflict, the Russians would not know the nature of the missiles loaded into the systems. With no early warning, they would have no time to determine the nature of a fired missile and would be forced to respond pre-emptively with a nuclear strike. This is why Vladimir Putin says that European countries could be drawn into a nuclear conflict without even wanting to.

In nuclear jargon, a distinction is made between «preventive» and «pre-emptive» strikes. Pre-emptive strikes aim to destroy an adversary's nuclear potential. The latter aim to prevent the firing of a ready-to-go device. This distinction comes from English, but is rarely used in French, where they are grouped under the term «préventives».

2.6.The role of minorities

It has become common for the «experts» on our television screens to affirm, like Jean-Dominique Giuliani, President of the Robert Schuman Foundation, on France 5 that «Russia wants to have a zone of influence in the Baltic countries or in Poland»[55].

54.Patrick Cohen in the programme «C à vous» of 8 February 2022 («Ukraine: is de-escalation possible? - C à vous - 08/02/2022», France 5/YouTube, 8 February 2022)

55.Jean-Dominique Giuliani in the programme «C dans l'air» of 25 January

This «sounds good» but it is false. Not only has Russia never claimed such a zone, neither openly nor secretly, but neither its Strategic Concept of National Security 2000[56], nor its National Security Strategy of Russia 2021[57] mention this notion once.

On the other hand, Russia has always felt a sense of responsibility towards those Russians who found themselves reduced to minorities overnight in the new countries that emerged from the break-up of the USSR. These countries have established cultural mechanisms for granting citizenship to their inhabitants, but minority rights fall far short of what one might expect. Countries like Georgia, Estonia, Latvia, Lithuania[58] or Ukraine have never had a democratic tradition and treat Russian minorities with disdain.

It is often forgotten that the Baltic States and Ukraine were briefly «liberated» from the Soviets by the Nazis. Western revisionist commentators and journalists conveniently «forget» that the armed struggle against the USSR was waged until the 1960s by NATO-supported clandestine networks[59], created as early as 1944 from networks set up with ex-Waffen-SS officers.

This explains why, in the Baltic States, 'de-Sovietisation' has been to the detriment of the Russian-speaking minority of their

(«Ukraine: Russian or American one-upmanship? #cdanslair 25.01.2022», France 5/YouTube, 26 January 2022 (19'02"))

56. https://www.bits.de/EURA/natsecconc.pdf

57. https://carnegiemoscow.org/commentary/84893

58.»CIA Torture in Lithuania: Time for a Full Investigation», Human Rights Monitoring Institute, 3 September 2014 (https://www.liberties.eu/en/stories/cia-torture-lithuania/1803)

59.Cristina Maza, «Veterans of World War II-Era Nazi SS Special Forces March in Latvia As Europe Experiences Wave of Far-Right Nationalism,» Newsweek, March 19, 2018; Cnaan Liphshiz, «Jewish community protests after plaque honoring SS officer unveiled in Estonia,» The Times of Israel, June 30, 2018; Paul Kirby, «Lithuania monument for 'Nazi collaborator' prompts diplomatic row,» BBC News, May 8, 2019.

population. In Latvia and Estonia, where Russian speakers make up 20-25% of the population, they have the status of 'non-citizens' (in Lithuania, they enjoy a more liberal status and have access to Lithuanian nationality). The hatred of Russia - largely fuelled by the West - goes so far that Ukraine refuses to license the Russian vaccine Sputnik V[60] and is reduced to «hoping» to receive it from another country[61] !

As a result, these countries, which have no respect for their Russian-speaking minorities (with our blessing), fear that Russia will invoke the UN's «responsibility to protect» (R2P) to intervene to their rescue[62]. The cultural genocide that we like to invoke to condemn China in relation to the Uighurs obviously does not apply to countries that forbid their own nationals to honour the soldiers who died for the victory against the Third Reich...

2.7.The Ukrainian question

2.7.1.Ukraine's rapprochement with Europe

EU defenders claim that Russian foreign policy is guided by the fact that «Putin hates the European Union» and «supranational constructs», and that he aims to «humiliate the European Union», as it is his «public enemy number one»[63].

60.»Ukraine formally bans registration of Russian COVID-19 vaccines, Reuters, 10 February 2021.

61.Natalia Zinets, 'Ukraine hopes to get some COVID-19 vaccines from other states', Reuters, 8 February 2021.

62. www.un.org/en/genocideprevention/about-responsibility-to-protect.shtml

63.Marion Van Renterghem in the programme «C dans l'air» of 19 January 2022 («Ukraine: can war be avoided? #cdanslair 19.01.2022», France 5/YouTube, 20 January 2022 (9'35") (https://youtu.be/owOJJKRYQZs?t=577); Jean-Dominique Giuliani in the programme «C dans l'air» of 25 January («Ukraine: Russian or

This myth stems from a simplification of the sequence of events that led to the Mayan crisis in 2013-2014. Vladimir Putin was credited with refusing to allow Ukraine to sign an agreement with the European Union.

However, Russia and its leaders have always been aware of their economic weaknesses. As a result, they have never tried to compete with Europe or the United States. Since the Tsarist era, Russia has never managed to develop an industrial base equivalent to that of Europe or Asia, and it knows it. In the post-Cold War era, Russia has seen itself as complementary to Europe, not its equal.

This is why the deluge of sanctions it has suffered since February 2022 only partially affects it: Europe is dependent on it for its raw materials, while Asia supplies it with its consumer products.

Secondly, it is important to remember that the Ukrainian population was not unanimously in favour of an agreement with the European Union. In November 2013, a poll conducted by the Kyiv International Institute of Sociology (KIIS) showed that it was then split «50/50» between an agreement with the European Union and a customs union with Russia[64].

Like President Yanukovych, many believe that the Ukrainian economy is structurally adapted to the Russian market. With an industrial base that complements that of the former USSR countries, it is not ready to face the very competitive European market. A too rapid rupture of commercial links with Russia would weaken its own economy. This will be confirmed by what happens next.

American one-upmanship? #cdanslair 25.01.2022», France 5/YouTube, 26 January 2022 (19'27")

64.»Poll: Ukrainian public split over EU, Customs Union options, Kyiv Post, 26 November 2013

For its part, Russia is not opposed to an agreement between Ukraine and the European Union, but it seeks to maintain its economic relations with its main historical partner. This is why it is proposing a tripartite working group, the aim of which would be to reconcile Ukraine's desire to join the European Union while preserving its ties with Russia. According to Mykola Azarov, the Ukrainian Prime Minister, studies showed that this proposal did not conflict with the European proposal[65] and that it was therefore possible to have a solution that satisfied Ukrainian interests.

However, José Manuel Barroso, then President of the European Commission, refused and asked Ukraine to choose[66]. The Ukrainian government therefore asked the European Union to delay the signing of the agreement in order to better study the implications of the agreement with the European Union on its relations with Russia and to better prepare its economy for this situation. He states:

There is no alternative to reforms in Ukraine and no alternative to European integration (...). We are going down this road and not changing direction. [67]

The then Ukrainian Prime Minister confirms:

I can say with full knowledge that the process of negotiating the Association Agreement is continuing and that the

65. «Azarov: Ukraine could cooperate with Customs Union and EU, Kiyv Post, 17 December 2012

66.»Barroso reminds Ukraine that Customs Union and free trade with EU are incompatible», ukrinform, 25 February 2013

67.»Ukraine has no alternative but European integration - Yanukovych», Interfax-Ukraine, 21 November 2013

work of bringing our country closer to European standards is not stopping for a single day. [68]

This suspension is clearly only temporary[69], but it is presented by the Western press and the Ukrainian opposition as a refusal to move closer to Europe under Russian pressure[70]. Ukrainian public opinion, which had been promised visas or salary increases, was quickly polarised and its discontent instrumentalised: this was the beginning of the Maïdan events.[71]

It is therefore the European Union that has created the tensions between Ukraine and Russia, as Arnaud Dubien notes in Le Monde :

Ukraine is a very fragmented country with multiple identities and cannot make a clear-cut choice, either in favour of the West or Russia. One of Brussels' mistakes was to ask it to do so and to turn its back on Russia, a suicidal option for the country. [72]

The Europeans have deliberately pushed Ukraine towards suicide. In the Washington Post, Henry Kissinger, National

---

68.»Ukraine says still wants historic pact with EU», Hürriyet Daily News/AFP, 28 November 2013

69.»Ukraine 'still wants to sign EU deal'», aljazeera.com, 29 November 2013

70.AFP, 'Ukraine renounces association agreement with EU', Libération, 21 November 2013; Lucas Roxo, 'Why Ukraine says no to Europe', Radio France/Franceinfo, 29 November 2013 (updated 2 May 2014); RTL/AFP, 'Ukraine still refuses to sign agreement with EU', RTL.fr, 29 November 2013; Pascal Boniface in 'Explain to me... La situation en Ukraine', YouTube, 31 October 2019

71.»Ukraine protests after Yanukovych EU deal rejection», bbc.com, 30 November 2013

72.Comments by Arnaud Dubien, director of the Franco-Russian Observatory, funded by the Franco-Russian Chamber of Commerce in «UE-Ukraine : «Moscou a remporté une nouvelle bataille géopolitique»», Le Monde.fr, 22 November 2013

Security Advisor under Ronald Reagan, notes that the European Union «helped turn a negotiation into a crisis[73] «. Ironically, the new government that emerged from Euromaidan will be forced to take the same time for reflection that Yanukovych had hoped for, and will only be able to sign the agreement with the European Union in 2017!

As researcher Frederico Santopinto of the Group for Research and Information on Peace and Security (GRIP) in Brussels puts it, Russia was not opposed to an agreement with the EU, but not at the expense of its relationship with Ukraine. It was the EU that refused the coexistence of two agreements: European diplomacy saw Ukraine as a border between East and West, while Russia saw it as a bridge[74]. As it will do in 2022, European diplomacy has failed to take into account three factors that are of key concern to Ukraine.

- Eastern European countries have - whether they like it or not - cultural, economic and historical links with Russia. This is particularly true of the former republics of the USSR (such as the Baltic States, Belarus and Ukraine), which have large Russian-speaking minorities and whose industries were largely complementary to Russia's.
- The EU has not succeeded in integrating the Eastern countries into a common European spirit. These countries have been brutally plunged into a European culture of tolerance and cooperation, slowly forged since the Second World War. However, not only do these countries of the 'new Europe' not have a democratic tradition, but they do not have the same values as the western part of

73. Henry A. Kissinger, "How the Ukraine Crisis Ends", The Washington Post, 5 March 2014

74.Federico Santopinto, «From free trade to the Ukrainian crisis - The EU facing its mistakes», GRIP, Brussels, 14 April 2014

the EU. In the Baltic States and Ukraine, hatred of the Soviets has turned into hatred of the Russians, which is conveniently exploited by the US. Unlike the rest of Europe, they still see the Third Reich as a liberator. The use of torture, social issues (abortion, LGBT, etc.), their unconditional alignment with American foreign policy, do not show a deep attachment to European values.

- The EU struggles to bring together the individual interests of its members into a coherent approach and a genuine common foreign policy. As a result, Germany, France and sometimes Italy often have to represent Europe's voice informally. The Ukrainian crisis and the economic crisis resulting from its decisions show that Europe gathers more around a common hatred than around common interests.

2.7.2.Euromaidan and the militarisation of the conflict

The Maidan revolution is broken down into several sequences, with different actors. Today, those who are driven by hatred of Russia are trying to merge these different sequences into one «democratic impulse». A way to validate the crimes committed by Ukraine and its neo-Nazis.

At first, the population of Kiev, disappointed by the government's decision to postpone the signing of the treaty, gathered in the streets. There was no mention of revolution or change of power, but a simple expression of discontent. Contrary to what the West claims, Ukraine is deeply divided on the question of rapprochement with Europe. A poll conducted in November 2013 by the Kyiv International Institute of Sociology (KIIS) shows that it was split exactly «50/50» between an agreement with the European Union and a customs union with Russia[75]. In the south

75.»Poll: Ukrainian public split over EU, Customs Union options, Kyiv Post, 26 and east of the country, industry is strongly linked to Russia. People fear that an agreement that excludes Russia will kill their jobs. This is what will happen.

At this stage, it does not appear that Ukrainians were generally hostile to Russia. But the situation is quickly being co-opted by the US, which is working behind the scenes to exploit the popular momentum and instrumentalise it to tighten the noose on Russia[76].

In 2014, I am at NATO and I am observing the Ukrainian crisis from the inside, so to speak. From the outset, it is clear that the situation is being fuelled by the West. Videos show that the coup plotters are supported by armed men speaking in English with an American accent... The German magazine Der Spiegel mentions the presence of mercenaries from the firm Academi (formerly Blackwater, of sinister memory in Iraq and Afghanistan)[77]. The Bundesnachrichtendienst (BND) apparently informs the German government. I inform my diplomatic contacts at the OSCE... but this will soon be forgotten.

A telephone conversation between Victoria Nuland, then Assistant Secretary of State for Europe and Eurasia, and Geoffrey Pyatt, the US ambassador to Kiev, revealed by the BBC, shows that the Americans themselves selected the members of the future Ukrainian government, in defiance of the Ukrainians and Europeans. This conversation, which became famous thanks to Nuland's famous «F*** the EU!», testifies to the fact that the European Union was only a doormat in this affair[78].

November 2013

76.David R. Marples, «Comparing Ukraine's Maidan 2004 with Euromaidan 2014», www.e-ir.info, 14 July 2017 (https://www.e-ir.info/2017/07/14/comparing-ukraines-maidan-2004-with-euromaidan-2014/)

77.»Ukrainische Armee bekommt offenbar Unterstützung von US-Söldnern», Der Spiegel, 11 May 2014

78.A transcript of this conversation is available on the BBC website («Ukraine crisis: Transcript of leaked Nuland-Pyatt call», BBC News, 7 February 2014)

In order to present this revolution as democratic, the real 'hand of the West' was cleverly masked by the imaginary hand of Russia. By claiming that the rebellions in Donbass and Crimea were the result of Russian intervention, it is hidden that a large part of the population did not approve of the overthrow of the government, which was both illegal and illegitimate. For the same reason, the ultra-nationalism of the coup plotters was systematically downplayed, as was the legitimacy of the claims of the Russian speakers who were accused of being agents of Moscow.

The beginning of the Euromaidan events was popular and good-natured. But just after an agreement was reached with the demonstrators to hold elections at the end of 2014 and have a democratic transition[79], the players change. Ultra-nationalists and other neo-Nazis supported by the West take over. The signed agreement is not respected and violence breaks out. Far from being the expression of a democratic revolution, it was the work of radical groups from the west of Ukraine (Galicia), who were not representative of all Ukrainians. They were the ones who overthrew President Yanukovych.

So Euromaidan was popular but not democratic. In May 2022, during a conference in Switzerland, a far-right journalist called out to me: «What is popular is democratic!» In fact, he was stating the principle of populism which is at the origin of the fascism that inspired the Ukrainian neo-Nazis, as we will see later. Indeed, a former participant in the Mayan events warns that «this revolution reflects the rise of fascism»[80].

79.Ian Traynor, «Ukraine protests: end nears for Viktor Yanukovych despite concessions», The Guardian, 21 February 2014 (https://www.theguardian.com/world/2014/feb/21/ukraine-protests-viktor-yanukovych-election)
80. https://www.youtube.com/watch?v=REKHrhfQQOc

As L'Obs reminds us, the 2014 Maidan revolution is nothing more than a coup d'état, led by the United States with the support of the European Union[81]. In December 2014, George Friedman, president of the US geopolitical intelligence platform STRATFOR, said in an interview with the Russian magazine Kommersant:

> *Russia defines the event that took place at the beginning of this year [in February 2014] as a coup organised by the US. And in truth, it was the most blatant [coup] in history.* [82]

Unlike European observers, the Atlantic Council, which is very supportive of NATO, was quick to note that the Maidan revolution was hijacked by certain oligarchs and ultra-nationalists[83]. It notes that the reforms promised by Ukraine have not been carried out and that the Western media have remained on a «white/black» narrative, without any critical spirit.

Thus, what Raphaël Glucksmann calls a «democratic revolution» is nothing more than a coup de force, carried out without any legal basis, against a government whose election had been qualified by the OSCE as «transparent and honest» and having «offered an impressive demonstration of democracy»[84]. Subsequently, the

81.Pierrick Tillet, «Le coup d'état ukrainien a bien piloté par les États-Unis : la preuve», L'Obs, 25 January 2017 (updated on 11 March 2014)
82.»La politique-système des USA en Ukraine mise à nu», Le Club Mediapart, 24 January 2015 (https://blogs.mediapart.fr/danyves/blog/240115/la-politique-systeme-des-usa-en-ukraine-mise-nu)
83.Maxim Eristavi, «Ukraine Is in the Middle of a Counterrevolution Again. Is Anyone Paying Attention?», Atlantic Council, 29 March 2017 (https://www.atlanticcouncil.org/blogs/ukrainealert/ukraine-is-in-the-middle-of-counterrevolution-again-is-anyone-paying-attention/)
84.»Ukraine: OSCE recognises the proper conduct of the election», Le Monde.fr/AFP, 8 February 2010

democratically elected President Yanukovych was convicted of «high treason» for having defended the constitutional order[85].

Far from being democratic, the coup d'état that concluded the events of Mayan is not unanimous among the Ukrainian people, either in its content or in its form. The nationalists are taking over the regional governments in the north of the country, while in the south the loyalists want to maintain constitutional order.

2.7.3. The rise of right-wing extremism in Ukraine

2.7.3.1. Vocabulary

Since 2014, in order to legitimise their support for the new regime in Kiev and the fight against Russia, the West has been at pains to minimise the importance of the far right in Ukraine. They cover up the crimes committed since 2014 against the population of Donbass in order to challenge Vladimir Putin's objective of «denazification».

The mention of 'neo-Nazis' in the Ukrainian regime is systematically dismissed as Russian propaganda by media, journalists and politicians who promote neo-Nazi and Russophobic ideas. As the American media outlet The Hill notes, this is not simply Russian propaganda[86].

It is important to understand the terms used. Indeed, the term «ultra-nationalist», often used to describe Ukrainian extremists, is only partially relevant. It refers to Ukrainians in the west of the country who seek to create a «pure» Ukraine, i.e. free of all non-Ukrainian minorities.

---

85. Indra Ekmanis, «Presidents aren't immune to treason convictions. Just look to Ukraine', The World, 10 October 2019

86. Lev Golinkin, «The reality of neo-Nazis in Ukraine is far from Kremlin propaganda», The Hill, 9 November 2017

The foreign volunteers were probably not 'nationalists' or 'ultra-nationalists'. Their motives are obviously very diverse, but there is the constant of a fight for a white Europe. The Europe envisaged here has nothing to do with the EU, which most Ukrainian paramilitaries reject. It is a 'racially pure' Europe, united by a natiocratic ideal.

The term 'Nazi' refers to National Socialism (Nazism), a doctrine that takes us back to the 1930s in Germany. Without going into detail, it combines nationalism and socialism into a 'compact' ideology, postulating that the main obstacle to the application of both is the presence of Jews in German society. It is a coherent doctrinal system.

What is described as 'neo-Nazism' is not a compact, constructed doctrine. It is more of a social phenomenon than a political doctrine in the strict sense. It is a heterogeneous collection of ideologies that combine hatred of everything and everyone in a kind of theatrical representation of violence, associating Nazi symbolism. There are individuals who see in the hatred of the other a glorification of their conception of the nation.

It is paradoxical that essentially nationalist movements have such international collaboration. The answer lies in the approach itself. The foreign fighters who engage with the Ukrainian far-right movements are not fighting for Ukraine but for the «Idea of Nation». In other words, they are fighting for the principle of power given to the nation. This is why, alongside Nazi symbols, one finds white supremacist symbols, such as the Celtic cross.

The term «neo-Nazi» is therefore somewhat misleading. Despite appearances, «neo-Nazis» are not the descendants of «Nazis». Rather, they are the second cousins of consanguineous marriages, who share the same brutality. The link of kinship appears clearly through the «Idea of

Nation», described in four principles by Andriy Biletsky, founder of the AZOV movement:

- The nation has an ethnic basis, defined by blood.
- The interest of the nation is superior to that of the individual.
- Society is structured around an ethnic hierarchy and power is held by members of the ethnic elite.
- The members of this nation constitute an elite group of full citizens, while the others are 'second class citizens'.

In fact, the Idea of Nation is a common theme in many extreme right-wing movements. It is symbolised by an 'N' crossed by a capital 'i', which is nothing but the inverted representation of the Wolfsangel rune found in Nazi symbolism.

The Wolfsangel and the «Idea of Nation».

Figure 1 - The Idea of Nation, a concept represented on the logos of the North American supremacist movement «Aryan Nation» (left) and the Svoboda movement in Ukraine (centre), as well as its derivatives. On the right, the emblem of the 2nd SS Panzer Division «Das Reich», which liberated Kharkov in 1943.

Despite snippets of far-right doctrines gleaned from both sides, the label 'neo-Nazi' expresses more a lifestyle than a coherent political doctrine. This is why some journalists who claim to be 'left-wing' - especially those who accuse others of being conspiratorial - relay the message of Ukrainian neo-Nazis.

The objective of denazifying the Ukrainian threat in the Donbass, as stated by Vladimir Putin on 24 February 2022, caused the media to react. They explain that the Ukrainian government cannot be Nazi because Volodymyr Zelensky is himself Jewish and, moreover, the main neo-Nazi party in parliament has just over 2% of the vote.

This is a somewhat simplistic argument, as the reality is more complex. Since the 1930s, the ambiguous links between Judaism and Zionism have led to counter-intuitive relations between the Jewish community and the European far-right regimes. This is the same phenomenon that we observe today between Ukrainian neo-Nazis and the Jewish community, which is alarming the international Jewish community, a concern that has gone unnoticed - and even contested - in France, not in the Anglo-Saxon world, as The Jewish Chronicle points out[87].

Figure 2 - Emblems of the Praviy Sektor's Uda Company (left) and the 'Jewish Company' of the Ukrainian Volunteer Army (UDA) (right), both wearing the red and black colours of the Ukrainian neo-Nazi movement. They are composed of ultra-nationalist Jews. The Ukrainian nationalist movement adopted many elements of the Third Reich's doctrine, but not officially antisemitism.

87.Sam Sokol, «Row after Ukrainian Jewish leader 'defends' Nazi collaborators», The Jewish Chronicle, 25 May 2018

The apparent ambiguity about the collaboration between Ukrainian nationalists and the Third Reich - especially in the massacre of Jewish civilians in the Ukraine - is probably explained by the fact that our view emphasises the Jewish character of the victims, whereas the Ukrainians of the time saw them as partisans who threatened the German rear in areas with a largely Jewish population. All this does not detract from the criminal nature of these organised massacres, but it could explain that they were not dictated by anti-Semitism, but by the desire for reprisals. This is not much better, but it explains the logic.

In other words, there is a difference between Ukrainian militants and the Nazis of the Third Reich. This is reflected in the names «neo-Nazis» or «Ukrainian-Nazis».

We will therefore use the following vocabulary for the Ukrainian context.

Ultra-nationalists want a Ukraine dominated by Ukrainians, i.e. the people of north-western Ukraine between Lvov and Kiev. They do not necessarily seek to expel other communities but to limit their constitutional rights.

Neo-Nazis fight for the supremacy of the «white, Christian West». They hate the Russians «and their friends», especially the Serbs. They admire the Third Reich and its symbolism, but do not have an intellectual reading of its doctrine and implications. They are guided more by hatred of others and aspire to an ethnically 'pure' Ukraine. Which, by the way, could translate into a Ukraine geographically reduced to its «Ukrainian-Ukrainian» part. Their motivation - and their volunteers - are generally associated with similar movements that have developed in Europe, especially since the early 2000s, and which seek to «return Europe to the Europeans».

2.7.3.2. A composite ideology born of history

The Ukrainian far right emerged at the beginning of the 20th century with European nationalisms. The western part of Ukraine was then part of the Austro-Hungarian Empire. The latter was dismembered after the First World War: Galicia and Volhynia were given to Poland, while the centre and east of present-day Ukraine went to the Soviet Union. The nationalist movements continued to live underground. The interwar period was marked by the extraordinary interweaving of nationalist struggles in this region, which saw the emergence of various forms of fascism.

Today, the word 'fascism' is almost automatically associated with Nazism. But in the 1920s, Italian fascism was a model. Unlike Nazism, anti-Semitism was not the central element; it would become important in the late 1930s as part of the collaboration between Italy and Germany, but it was a peripheral and opportunistic aspect of the ideology. For example, in the mid-1930s, Fascist Italy housed a Betar military unit, which had grown out of the revisionist Zionist movement, at the naval academy in Civitavecchia[88].

At that time, fascism defined itself as the 'true' expression of the popular will as opposed to democracy, which was seen as corrupted by oligarchies and private interests. This is why it was so successful in the 1920s and 1930s throughout Europe. In fact, it is the equivalent of what we call 'populism' today. So it was this model that inspired the beginnings of Ukrainian nationalism.

Then as now, Ukrainian ultra-nationalists are deeply antisemitic. But unlike the Nazis, whose anti-Semitism was a doctrinal

---

88. «Betar Naval Academy», Wikipedia (en.wikipedia.org/wiki/Betar_Naval_Academy); Alain Dieckhoff, The Invention of a Nation: Zionist Thought and the Making of Modern Israel, C. Hurst, 2003; Eric Kaplan, The Jewish Radical Right: Revisionist Zionism and Its Ideological Legacy, University of Wisconsin Press, 2005

element, the Ukrainian fascists hated Jews more because of their links to Soviet power than because of doctrine.

The strip stretching from the Black Sea to the Baltic Sea is an area with a historically important Jewish presence. It is also in this area that European antisemitism developed most vigorously. It is no coincidence that the founders of the State of Israel, such as Ben Gurion, Golda Meir and Moshe Dayan, came from this area. It is therefore quite logical to see its representatives in the structures of the Soviet socialist republics.

The «founding» element of Ukrainian antisemitism is the «Holodomor» (holod: hunger; mor: plague). It is believed to have caused between 4 million and 7 million deaths in 1932-33 and is considered in Ukraine to be genocide, often compared to the Jewish 'holocaust'. Despite its magnitude, which makes it perhaps the largest massacre in history, it remains largely ignored in the West, and its character as 'genocide' is disputed, in part to challenge the presence of antisemitism in Ukraine. Whatever the reality, the over-representation of Jews in the Communist Party leadership and among the NKVD cadres[89] has left the Ukrainian imagination with the feeling that they orchestrated the Holodomor. The result is a deep-seated hatred that targets both the Moscow leadership and the Jews. In 2021, the Jerusalem Post reported that the Ukrainian far right was demanding an apology from Israel for the Holodomor and the crimes of communism[90].

89.Timothy Snyder, professor at Yale University, estimates the proportion of Jews in the NKVD at 40 per cent and more than 50 per cent in the leadership of the Communist Party in the years 1920-2030 (Timothy Snyder, Bloodlands: Europe Between Hitler and Stalin, 2010); Tumshis M.A., Zolotarev V.A., Евреи в НКВД СССР. 1936 1938 гг. Опыт биографического словаря, Russian Foundation for the Promotion of Education and Science, Moscow, 2017.

90.Cnaan Liphshiz, «Far-right protesters in Ukraine demand Israel apologize for communism», The Jerusalem Post, 8 January 2021

Today, although not a 'doctrine', violent antisemitism is growing alarmingly in Ukraine[91].

In the framework of Operation BARBAROSSA, on 30 June 1941, the Third Reich granted independence to the western part of Ukraine, relying on the Organisation of Ukrainian Nationalists (OUN-B) led by Stepan Bandera[92]. The latter had been convicted in Poland for planning the assassination of the Polish Minister of the Interior in 1934. After the occupation of Poland in 1939, he was released by the Germans who 'put him back in the saddle'. The OUN-B thus formed the core of the Ukrainian government in Lvov. Under the authority of Stepan Bandera, the Ukrainian Insurgent Army (UPA) was created and took over from the OUN-B. Together with other Ukrainian nationalist movements, the UPA formed a sort of fifth column that protected the Wehrmacht's logistical lines against attacks by pro-Soviet partisans. It was in the context of this struggle that the Ukrainians distinguished themselves by committing massacres against the civilian and Jewish populations that supported the pro-Soviet partisans.

Nazi Germany's short-lived support for Ukrainian independence between 1941 and 1945 drew recognition from Ukrainians in the west of the country. They formed the 14th SS Grenadier Division «1. Galician», whose emblem is still used today by Ukrainian nationalists[93]. At the same time, the 2nd SS Panzer Division «Das Reich», infamous in France for the massacre of Oradour-sur-Glane, is revered in Ukraine. It was this division that

91. Lev Golinkin, "Violent Anti-Semitism Is Gripping Ukraine - And The Government Is Standing Idly By", The Forward, 20 May 2018 ;

92.Stepan Bandera (1909-1959). A hero of the Ukrainian resistance against the USSR at the head of the Organisation of Ukrainian Nationalists (OUN) and a notorious collaborator of the Nazis during the Second World War, he became the symbolic figure of the Maïdan events in 2014.

93. David Pugliese, "Canadian government comes to the defence of Nazi SS and Nazi collaborators but why?", ottawacitizen.com, 17 May 2018

liberated Kharkov from the Red Army in 1943 and its emblem inspired the emblem of today's Azov regiment[94].

From the end of the Second World War, the West sought to destabilise the USSR, which it saw as a threat. They supported the Baltic and Ukrainian insurrectionary movements, which remained after the Second World War, led by former members of the SS and the Nazi «Werewolf» networks.

It was in this context that the UPA continued its struggle against Moscow. Until the early 1960s, it carried out guerrilla operations in Ukraine with the material support of the American (Operation AERODYNAMIC), British (Operation VALUABLE) and French (Operation MINOS) secret services[95]. Thanks to Kim Philby, a mole in the British Secret Intelligence Service (MI-6), the KGB managed to neutralise these resistance movements. On 15 October 1959, it eliminated Stepan Bandera the day after a coordination meeting with the German secret service (BND) to intensify clandestine operations in Ukraine.

In Ukraine, the struggle against Soviet rule predates the Nazi occupation. What we perceive as 'collaboration' with the Nazis is understood in Ukraine as 'resistance' against the Soviets. The same phenomenon can be found among the French volunteer fighters of the SS Charlemagne division or among the Belgians of the SS Wallonie brigade. In short, Ukrainian ultra-nationalism today is a kind of ideological «mille-feuille» that brings together in a historical hatred of the Russians the anti-Bolshevism of the 1920s, the anti-Semitism of the 1930s resulting from the Holodomor and the anti-Sovietism of the 1940s-1990s.

94.Alec Luhn, 'Preparing for War With Ukraine's Fascist Defenders of Freedom', Foreign Policy, 30 August 2014.

95.Roger Faligot & Pascal Krop, La Piscine - Les Services Secrets français 1944-1984, Seuil, 1985, pp. 100-104.

However, there is an ideological rapprochement between Ukrainian 'social nationalism' and 'national socialism', which is reflected in the integration of racial theories. Andriy Biletsky, founder of the AZOV movement and leader of the National Corps, explains Ukrainian 'racial social nationalism':

All our nationalism is nothing (...) if it is not based on the foundation of blood, the foundation of race (...) Traditional (post-war, post-Soviet) nationalism is characterised by (...) declaring that the Nation is a linguistic, cultural or territorial-economic phenomenon. Of course, we do not reject the importance of spiritual and cultural-linguistic factors, as well as territorial patriotism. But our deep conviction is that these are only products of our Race, of our Racial nature. If Ukrainian spirituality, culture and language are unique, it is simply because our racial nature is unique. If Ukraine is an earthly paradise, it is only because our Race has made it a paradise.

Therefore, the treatment of our national organism must begin with the racial cleansing of the nation. And then a healthy national Spirit will be reborn in a healthy racial body, and with it the culture, the language and everything else. In addition to the question of purity, we must also pay attention to the question of the fullness of the Race. Ukrainians are part (and one of the peaks) of the European White Race. They form the Creator-Race of a great civilisation, of the highest human achievements. The historic mission of our Nation in this crucial century is to lead and direct (sic) the White

Nations of the whole world in the last crusade of its existence. A campaign against Semitic-led inhumanity.[96]

Although it is close to Nazi ideology, this set of ideas lacks the coherence of it. Thus, it justifies the label of «neo-Nazi» or «Ukrainian-Nazi» given to Ukrainian militant ultra-nationalists. This explains why our media - mainly those who share the same ideologies - and our governments[97] try to «whitewash» Ukrainian extremism.

To support the 2014 coup and maintain pressure on Russia, the West relied on Ukrainian nationalism whose epicentre is in the Lvov region (Galicia) in the west of the country. They use the militants of Oleh Tyahnybok's Svoboda party and its armed wing, Praviy Sektor (Right Sector). Today, the party seems to have lost its importance and the institutional far right has become a very small minority. But this is misleading, because the militias remain a tool of choice for the West, as we shall see.

This explains the remarkable rise of antisemitism and Holocaust denial in Ukraine since the events of Mayan. In 2014, Andriy Biletsky, founder of the AZOV movement and several far-right movements, deputy in the Rada between 2014 and 2019, declared:

The historic mission of our nation at this critical moment is to lead the white races of the world in a final crusade for survival (...). A crusade against Semitic-led subhumans. [98]

96.Український соціальний націоналізм. - Харків: «Патріот України», 2007 (https://web.archive.org/web/20080409023834/http://www.patriotukr.org.ua/index.php?rub=stat&id=267)

97.Antisemitism in Ukraine, DIDR-OFPRA, 7 January 2015

98.Tom Parfitt, «Ukraine crisis: the neo-Nazi brigade fighting pro-Russian separatists», The Telegraph, 11 August 2014 (https://www.telegraph.co.uk/news/

Relaying the words of Luke Harding[99] (a British journalist known for his plagiarism and anti-Russian bias), *Conspiracy Watch* (a French organisation linked to British influence in Europe) sees the *Svoboda* and *Praviy Sektor* groups as «*only a very small fraction of the Maidan activists*» who «*cannot be equated solely with 'fascist' or 'neo-Nazi' groupings*[100] « This is a bit simple. In April 2018, 50 US congressmen petitioned the US State Department to urge the Ukrainian and Polish governments to take action against :

> *a rise in the glorification of Holocaust-era leaders across Europe, including in Hungary, Slovakia, Romania and the Baltic States. This is a worrying trend that must be met with a firm response from our government.* [101]

Since Euromaidan, as I have observed myself during my visits to Ukraine, in every street demonstration one sees in abundance the flags of far-right Svoboda movements and portraits of Stepan Bandera[102]. In 2018, the Ukrainian parliament even established an official day to celebrate his memory[103]. While our media claims that the paramilitaries were 'denazified' long ago, the American media NBC News disagrees:

---

worldnews/europe/ukraine/11025137/Ukraine-crisis-the-neo-Nazi-brigade-fighting-pro-Russian-separatists.html)

99.Luke Harding, «Kiev's protesters: Ukraine uprising was no neo-Nazi power-grab», The Guardian, 13 March 2014

100.Hélène Roudier and Philippe de Lara, «Étienne Chouard has got it all wrong on Ukraine, here's why», conspiracywatch.info, 21 November 2018

101.»Congress members urge US stand against Holocaust denial in Ukraine, Poland», The Times of Israel, 25 April 2018

102. Max Blumenthal, "Is the U.S. Backing Neo-Nazis in Ukraine?", AlterNet, 24 February 2014

103. Cnaan Liphshiz, "Ukraine celebrates Nazi collaborator, bans book critical of pogrom leader", The Times of Israel, 27 December 2018

Equally worrying, neo-Nazis are among some of the growing ranks of Ukrainian volunteer battalions. They are seasoned after fighting some of the toughest street battles against Moscow-backed separatists in eastern Ukraine after Putin's 2014 invasion of Crimea. Among them was the Azov Battalion, founded by an avowed white supremacist who claimed that Ukraine's national goal was to rid the country of Jews and other inferior races. In 2018, the US Congress stipulated that its aid to Ukraine could not be used «to provide weapons, training, or other assistance to the Azov Battalion». Despite this, Azov is now an official member of the Ukrainian National Guard.[104]

Ukraine practices torture on a regular basis, but the West remains very discreet about it. Our media and authorities do not want to give the wrong role to Ukraine[105], while, according to the Dutch media Raamoprusland.nl :

The ongoing war against the Russian-led insurgency in eastern Ukraine is causing fundamental human rights abuses under the guise of security measures. [106]

104.Allan Ripp, «Ukraine's Nazi problem is real, even if Putin's 'denazification' claim isn't», NBC News, 5 March 2022 (https://www.nbcnews.com/think/opinion/ukraine-has-nazi-problem-vladimir-putin-s-denazification-claim-war-ncna1290946)

105.Alisa Sopova, «U.N. Suspends Torture Inquiry in Ukraine», The New York Times, 26 May 2016 (https://www.nytimes.com/2016/05/27/world/europe/un-suspends-torture-inquiry-in-ukraine.html?_r=0)

106.»Western press dismisses Ukrainian reforms too soon», Raam op Rusland, 13 June 2016 (https://www.raamoprusland.nl/dossiers/oekraine/achtergrond/171-westerse-media-oordelen-te-snel-over-oekraine)

In October 2021, the Jerusalem Post[107] expressed concern about a study published in September by the Institute for European, Russian, and Eurasian Studies (IERES) at George Washington University, which showed that Canada, the United States, France, and Britain are training extreme right-wing groups in Ukraine at the Hetman Petro Sahaidachny National Military Academy[108].

The ideology that has developed in Ukraine revolves around a few markers, which constitute the common ground of groups with different histories. One of these is the constitution of a state stretching from the Baltic to the Black Sea, reminiscent of seventeenth-century Poland, and intended to counter Russia. This is the Polish Intermarium project[109], which is opposed - in substance - to the European project.

On 3 March 2022, the Anti Defamation League (ADL) notes that neo-Nazism is part of the Ukrainian national discourse and highlights the Western contradictions around Vladimir Putin.For example, Swiss politician Claude Ruey states on his Facebook account that «the European neo-Nazi far right is overwhelmingly pro-Putin». This is not the opinion of the ADL, which quotes the media outlet The American Futurist:

> *if you are NS [national socialist] and you support Putin who is literally invading a country with the stated reason of destroying NS [national socialist] groups like the Azov Battalion, then you are a fucking retard.*[110]

107.»Western countries training far-right extremists in Ukraine - report», Jerusalem Post, 19 October 2021

108.Oleksiy Kuzmenko, «Far-Right Group Made Its Home in Ukraine's Major Western Military Training Hub», Institute for European, Russian, and Eurasian Studies (IERES) Occasional Papers, no. 11, September 2021

109.Emil Avdaliani, «Poland and the Success of its 'Intermarium' Project», moderndiplomacy.eu, 31 March 2019

110.»White Supremacists, Other Extremists Respond to Russian Invasion of

Another focus of this ideology is the feeling that the 'white race' is threatened (by Russians, by Islam, by Jews, etc.)[111]. According to the ADL, the far-right narrative against the Russian offensive is that Vladimir Putin is under the control of Jewish oligarchs, hence his nickname 'Jewtin'.

This explains the veneration of various Ukrainian far-right groups for the Norwegian Anders Behring Breivik (author of the Utoya massacre on 22 July 2011), whom they see as a hero of the «white and Christian» West. According to a Norwegian researcher, Breivik was inspired in particular by a journalist described as a «Swiss-French conspiracy theorist», who works with certain media outlets that have «blacklisted» me in Switzerland[112].

Here we are at the antipodes of the values and concepts that have guided Europe since 1945. This is why our media remain strangely silent in the face of the crimes of the Ukrainian neo-Nazis.

2.7.3.3. The Western Bleaching Campaign

Western propaganda seeks to hide these incestuous relations in order to give a democratic image of Ukraine, in the face of Vladimir Putin's «dictatorship». Thus, on France 5, Jean-Dominique Giuliani asserts that Vladimir Putin created these Ukrainian extreme right-wing movements, which then «turned» against him[113] ! A reasoning worthy of the great hours of Pravda!

Ukraine, adl.org, 3 March 2022 (https://www.adl.org/resources/blog/white-supremacists-other-extremists-respond-russian-invasion-ukraine)

111.Raphaël Liogier, «The myth of the Arab-Muslim invasion», Le Monde diplomatique, May 2014, pp. 8-9

112.Mattias Gardell, «Crusader Dreams: Oslo 22/7, Islamophobia, and the Quest for a Monocultural Europe», Terrorism and Political Violence, 26:129-155, 2014 (https ://www.qub.ac.uk/Research/GRI/mitchell-institute/FileStore/Filetoupload,818003,en.pdf)

113.Jean-Dominique Giuliani in the programme «C dans l'air» of 25 January 2022 («Ukraine: Russian or American one-upmanship? #cdanslair 25.01.2022», France

The West seeks to minimise the extremist nature of these groups, which it trains, arms, protects and whose crimes it authorises by its silence. They are the «spearhead» of Ukrainian nationalism and the backbone of the determination to fight Russia.

In fact, in order not to delegitimise the antagonism between Ukraine and Russia, the flow of neo-Nazi volunteers from France, Britain and Canada, as well as the nationalist and far-right character of the Ukrainian government, are systematically concealed in the Western media, while the pro-Nazi tendencies of the militants are presented as Russian propaganda in the Western media[114].

Interviewed in Le Monde, on the links of the Belarusian opponent Roman Protassevitch with the «Ukrainian Nazis of the AZOV battalion», Isabelle Mandraud explains:

> *Since the term «Nazi» is used by the Russian authorities to describe anyone who contradicts their views, and is used ad nauseam in propaganda, I think that is enough to close this issue.*[115]

As always with the media, which is more propaganda than information, it is necessary to qualify. One can of course discuss the term «Nazi», but the fact remains that the AZOV regiment is certainly ultra-nationalist, violent, anti-Semitic, and displays former Nazi symbols. Its members have been guilty of numerous abuses against the (Ukrainian) civilian population of the areas in which they are

5/YouTube, 26 January 2022 (30'10")

114.Joshua Keating, «In Ukraine, fascists versus Nazis?», Slate.fr, 22 February 2014; «Russia is winning the propaganda war. Except in France», slate.fr, 2 June 2014

115.Isabelle Mandraud, «Avion détourné par la Biélorussie, sanctions de l'Union européenne : nos réponses à vos questions», Le Monde, 28 May 2021

deployed[116]... all qualities that Ms Mandraud apparently associates with propaganda. Fortunately, her view is not shared by the West Point Military Academy's Center for Counterterrorism[117], the Jerusalem Post, or the Simon Wiesenthal Center[118], which describe the AZOV group as «Nazi» and castigate the support it receives from the West.

The fact is that in late 2014-early 2015, the crimes committed by these fanatical units (including the massacre of civilians in Mariupol by detachments of the AZOV unit in the summer of 2014) and criticism from the international community prompted the Ukrainian authorities to erase their brutality. As a result, in October 2014, these units were forced to leave the frontline or integrate into the armed forces. In August 2015, the AZOV regiment changed its logo by removing the «black sun», a symbol used by the SS in the Second World War and by the European far right, but it still retains the inverted «Wolfsangel» which means «Idea of Nation». But this 'denazification' is only superficial. It is not accompanied by changes in doctrine or leadership. Individuals like Andriy Biletsky or Dmitro Yarosh remain in charge, and there is no indication that they have changed their beliefs or doctrine[119].

On 16 December 2020, only two countries rejected the UN resolution to combat the glorification of Nazism: the USA and Ukraine. In January 2021, the European Jewish Congress

116.Oren Dorell, «Volunteer Ukrainian unit includes Nazis», USA Today, 10 March 2015

117.Tim Lister, «The Nexus Between Far-Right Extremists in the United States and Ukraine», Combating Terrorism Center, Vol. 13, No. 4, April 2020

118.Cnaan Liphshiz, «Hundreds march with torches in tribute to Nazi collaborator in Ukraine», The Jerusalem Post, 4 January 2021

119.Oleksiy Kuzmenko, «The Azov Regiment has not depoliticized», Atlantic Council, 19 March 2020 (https://www.atlanticcouncil.org/blogs/ukrainealert/the-azov-regiment-has-not-depoliticized/)

condemned the inclusion of former collaborators of the Nazi occupiers in the memory project launched by the Ukrainian authorities[120]. Indeed, the dominant ideology in the western part of the country is clearly ultra-nationalist, with a complex mix of right-wing extremism[121], neo-Nazism, antisemitism and Zionism.

Like its neighbours in the 'new Europe', Ukraine has a very special relationship with Nazism and its atrocities. Unlike France, the Ukrainian far right prides itself on having fought the Soviets from the 1930s until the end of the Cold War. Its collaboration with the Nazis is part of the national narrative and explains - even excuses - the crimes against the Jews, who are seen as a kind of collateral damage. Rightly or wrongly, they are seen as having participated in the organisation and conduct of the crimes committed during the Soviet era against the Ukrainian population.

This is why, in order to maintain a certain coherence in the discourse on Ukraine, we have to hide the disturbing aspects. The result is a totally schizophrenic attitude towards the Ukrainian crisis, which gives us a reading of events that is less fair, less moral and less ethical than it seems.

Symptomatically, on 24 February 2022, pro-AZOV 'posts' were re-authorised on Facebook[122]. Until then, the platform placed the group in the same category as the Islamic State and other terrorist movements. This shows that Westerners are not fighting for values, but against Russia.

The complexity of our relationship with the Ukrainian far right is illustrated by the vocal activism of some Western politicians, such as Chrystia Freeland, Canadian Minister of Foreign Affairs,

---

120.»Nazi collaborators included in Ukrainian memorial project», European Jewish Congress, 22 January 2021

121.Josh Cohen, «Ukraine's neo-Nazi problem», Reuters, 19 March 2018

122.Sam Biddle, «Facebook Allows Praise of Neo-Nazi Ukrainian Battalion If It Fights Russian Invasion», The Intercept, 24 February 2022

or Ursula von der Leyen[123], President of the European Commission, both of whom - coincidentally - have family backgrounds active in the Third Reich in Central and Eastern Europe. Anthony Blinken, US Secretary of State, and Victoria Nuland, US Under Secretary of State for Political Affairs, former foreign policy advisor to Dick Cheney, both come from Ukrainian Jewish emigration[124] with a very nationalistic outlook on the situation. In January 2021, the American media Salon, which is close to the Democratic Party, deplored the inclusion of Victoria Nuland in the Biden team[125].

Not all these politicians are Nazis. But they obviously have a very partisan view of the situation in Ukraine, which works in favour of the ultra-nationalists and - above all - against Russia. Their actions have only escalated the tensions between Ukraine and Russia since 2014.

Moreover, Ukrainian nationalism is not only directed against Russian-speaking minorities, but also affects the Romanian[126] and Magyar minorities, causing tensions with Budapest[127]. This (also) explains Viktor Orban's rapprochement with Russia and the fact that, in February 2022, he declared that his country would not supply arms to Ukraine.

As in the rest of the «new Europe», democratic aspirations dominate in Ukraine, but unfortunately they are heavily tainted by

---

123.Peter Kuras, 'The Aristocratic Ineptitude of Ursula Von Der Leyen', Foreign Policy, 30 April 2021

124.»Yiddish and the Ukrainian-Jewish roots of the new U.S. Secretary of State», Ukrainian Jewish Encounter, 30 November 2020

125.Medea Benjamin, Nicolas J.S. Davies & Marcy Winograd, «Who is Victoria Nuland? A really bad idea as a key player in Biden's foreign policy team', Salon, 19 January 2021

126.»Preşedintele Ucrainei Petro Poroşenko a promulgat controversata Lege a Educaţiei, care restricţionează predarea în limba minorităţilor naţionale», news.ro, 25 September 2017

127.»Hungary Protests Ukrainian Military Moves, 'Death List' Of Dual Citizens», RFE/RL, 11 October 2018

nationalism, even ultra-nationalism, anti-Russian sentiments and anti-Semitism, especially in the western part of the country. It is no coincidence that the abolition of the law on official languages was the first act of the Euromaidan authorities; provoking the conflict in Donbass and the desire for secession of the Crimean population. More recently, the law giving different constitutional rights to «ethnic Ukrainians» and «Ukrainians of foreign origin[128] « smacks of «Nuremberg laws».

2.7.4.Armed confrontation

The first legislative act of the post-coup parliament, on 23 February 2014, was the abolition of the 2012 Kivalov-Kolesnichenko law, which established the Russian language as an official language on a par with Ukrainian.

The next day, Astrid Thors, OSCE High Commissioner on National Minorities, warned the new Ukrainian government against «quick decisions that could lead to an escalation of the situation» in a context where «languages are a divisive issue»[129]. This decision - taken by unelected authorities - is the starting point for demonstrations throughout the south of the country, demanding a return to equal rights for minorities. Coming from all categories of the population, it is a spontaneous and poorly organised citizen movement: housewives in shopping bags rub shoulders with farmers and workers.

Initially, overwhelmed, the Kiev authorities sent in the army, but the army was made up of conscripts, some of whom fraternised with the protesters and joined them. In August 2015, the Russian opposition website Meduza mentioned 8,000 defectors from the Ukrainian

---

128.»Принят Закон «О коренных народах Украины»», rada.gov.ua, 1er July 2021 (https://www.rada.gov.ua/ru/news/Novosty/Soobshchenyya/211516.html)
129. http://www.osce.org/hcnm/115643

army to the rebels[130]. Therefore, volunteer units from ultra-nationalist and neo-Nazi movements are hastily formed and sent to the front. But the Western media that support them will never mention them.

The result is brutal repression, which pushes the demonstrators to organise themselves.

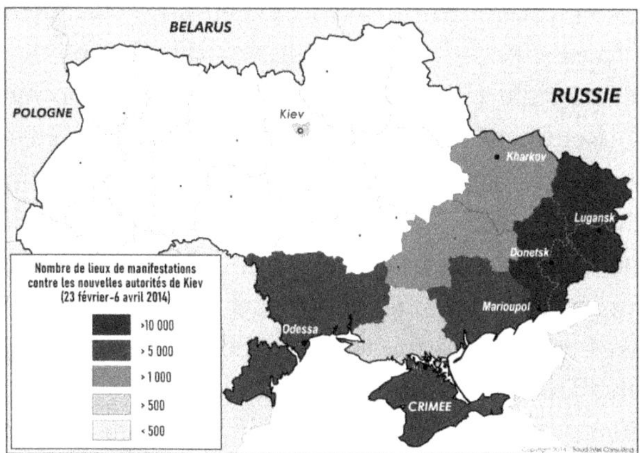

Figure 3 - Number of demonstration sites in Ukraine after the repeal of the official language law. The outline of what would later be called 'Novorossiya', which may well be the area taken by Russia in its 2022 offensive, can be seen.[131]

With the weapons of the defecting soldiers, the populations created popular militias and the conflict became militarised. Against units equipped with tanks, artillery and aviation, the rebels use highly mobile tactics, with successive skirmishes turning government weapons against the armed forces. The

130.»8 thousand Ukrainian officers have defected to the separatists», meduza.io, 14 August 2015 (https://meduza.io/en/news/2015/08/14/8-thousand-ukrainian-officers-have-defected-to-the-separatists)

131.»Meet the people behind Novorossiya's grassroots defeat», Euromaidan Press, 13 August 2015 (https://euromaidanpress.com/2015/08/13/meet-the-people-behind-novorossiyas-grassroots-defeat/)

conflict is gaining momentum. On 16 September 2014 the rebel groups regroup to form the «Novorossiya Joint Forces»[132].

Foreign volunteers are coming to reinforce the popular resistance in the Donbass. Not surprisingly, there are Russian Orthodox nationalists (Russian National Unity) and Serbian nationalists (Detachment «Jovan Sevich»); a detachment of the Russian far-left party «Other Russia»; Russian activists of the European far-right (Eurasian Youth Union); Russian nationalist activists (Regiment «Varyag»). These groups were used as a pretext by Ukrainian and Western propaganda to claim - even today - that 'neo-Nazis' are on Putin's side. However, unlike their governmental counterparts, these militias were neither perpetuated nor integrated into the republican forces.

The Western media were very discreet about some unexpected volunteers. Thus, we find representatives of the Magyar minority militants («Saint-Stephan» Legion), militants of the Polish extreme right-wing organisation «Phalange», Spanish militants of the extreme anti-fascist left-wing «Carlos Palomino» and a battalion of Israeli militants «Aliya».

The resistance in the southern part of Ukraine is therefore extremely eclectic and, unlike the pro-government forces, is very far from representing a particular ideology. Indeed, in the Donbass republics, the cultural and identity issue is very clear and widely shared among the population. Unlike government forces that seek to take away a community's rights, this community seeks to preserve its own. This is why the Russian-speaking resistance is very robust and does not need to resort to fanatical militias like the Kiev government.

132.»Террористы сообщили, что объединились в совместную «армию»», Украинская правда, 16 September 2014 (https://www.pravda.com.ua/rus/news/2014/09/16/7037979/index.amp)

After the signing of the Minsk Agreements in February 2015, the Kiev government decided to perpetuate the far-right militias that had effectively supplanted the regular armed forces, thanks to their fanaticism. The self-proclaimed People's Republics of Donbass, on the other hand, do not have the means to maintain their volunteer fighters. They will therefore go back to their respective countries and their groups will be quickly disbanded, making way for inexpensive popular militias formed from reservists (rather like the Swiss model).

In 2022, the Donbass militias, composed essentially of 'citizen-soldiers', are bearing a very large share of the fighting, especially in the Donbass region and in Mariupol. They are very combative, but less experienced than the Russian forces. The Western media have understood this and systematically talk about «Russian troops», without mentioning that the Donbass militias are popular structures. This makes it possible to say that the «Russian military» does not have the required expertise, etc., etc.

Forces Unifiées de Nouvelle Russie (octobre 2014) (1)

Commandement

Lieutenant-Général Ivan Korsun

 Bataillon "Voskhod" « Serguiy » *Env. 300*	 Bataillon Humanitaire «Novorossiya» ? *200 hommes*	 Bataillon Spécial «Kalmius» Sergueï Petrovskiy *1000 hommes*
 1e Groupe Tactique Bataillonnaire «Somali» « Givi » *?*	 Bataillon «Steppe» ? *Env. 300 hommes*	Bataillon de Service de Sécurité ? *200-500 hommes*
 Brigade Spéciale «Vostok» Aleksandr S. Khodakosvski *2500 hommes*	  Brigade Mécanisée «Oplot» Aleksandr Sakhartchenko *2500 hommes*	 Bataillon Féminin «Rus'» Mansour *300 personnels*
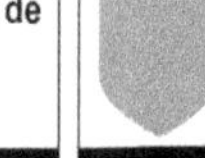 Groupement de Combat « Strelkov » Igor Girkin (« Strelkov ») *2000 hommes*	  Groupement de Combat «Bes» Igor Bezler *700-1000 hommes*	  Armée Orthodoxe Russe Mikaïlo Verin *350 hommes*
Brigade de Slavyansk ? *?*	  Division des Mineurs Konstantin Kuzmin *?*	 Bataillon «Sparta» « Motorola » *?*
 1er Bataillon de Slavyansk ? *?*	 2e Bataillon de Slavyansk ? *?*	 Bataillon «Artem» « Mongol » *Env. 300 hommes*

Forces Unifiées de Nouvelle Russie (octobre 2014) (2)

Forces de l'ex-Armée Interarmes du Sud-Est

Contingents de volontaires étrangers

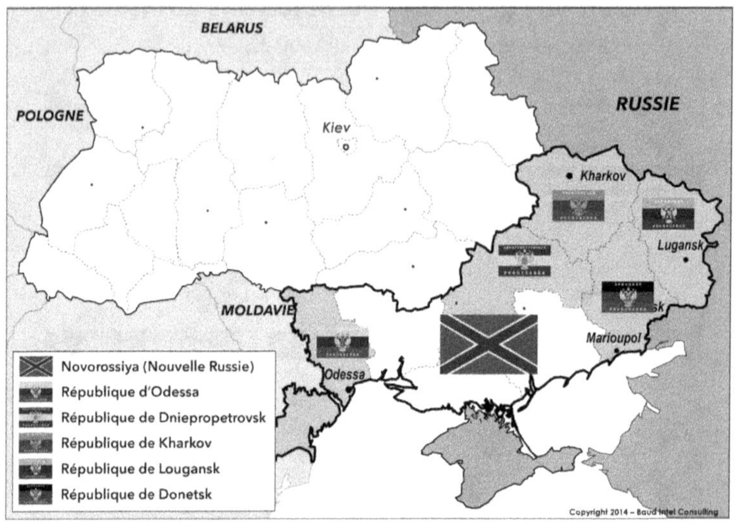

Figure 4 - While our media only mention the Donbass (whose geographical location lends credence to the narrative of a Russian intervention), the whole of southern Ukraine is in flames. In September 2014, groups from the South-Eastern Joint Army and the Donbass People's Militia joined forces to form the «Novorossiya Joint Forces». At this stage, these groups have proclaimed people's republics in the provinces of Odessa, Dnepropetrovsk, Kharkov, Lugansk and Donetsk. Other armed groups are resisting in the other southern provinces. The strong black line indicates the outline of Novorossiya.

Our media remain very discreet about the linguistic origin of the conflict. There are several reasons for this. The first is that it would contradict the official narrative that the regime change in Kiev was democratic and had massive popular support. The second is that the media, inspired by the neo-Nazi and Ukrainian supremacist narrative, do not want to admit that an ethnic problem is at the root of the conflict. The third is that this explanation would overshadow the narrative of Russian instigation 'jealous' of Ukrainian democracy.

In July 2019, the International Crisis Group (funded by several European countries and the Open Society Foundation) notes:

The conflict in eastern Ukraine began as a popular movement. (...)

The demonstrations were organised by local citizens claiming to represent the Russian-speaking majority in the region. They were concerned both about the political and economic consequences of the new government in Kiev and about the government's later abandoned measures to prevent the official use of the Russian language throughout the country.[133]

For this reason, the Minsk Agreements of September 2014 and February 2015 emphasise a solution of regional autonomy, particularly in the area of language, rather like the Swiss model. But this idea of preserving regional particularities does not suit the new leaders who want a Ukraine whose unity is not achieved through diversity, but through «purity».

In April 2019, the Rada passes a law establishing Ukrainian as the state language. It stipulates, among other things, that websites must use the Ukrainian language by default and that online political campaign materials must be in Ukrainian only. These provisions do not apply to foreign media that use English and European Union (EU) languages or to indigenous languages, such as Crimean Tatar. Russians are not considered an indigenous population[134].

133. Rebels without a Cause: Russia's Proxies in Eastern Ukraine, International Crisis Group, Europe Report N° 254, 16 July 2019, p. 2

134. https://freedomhouse.org/country/ukraine/freedom-net/2021

Storming of regional administrations in January-February 2014

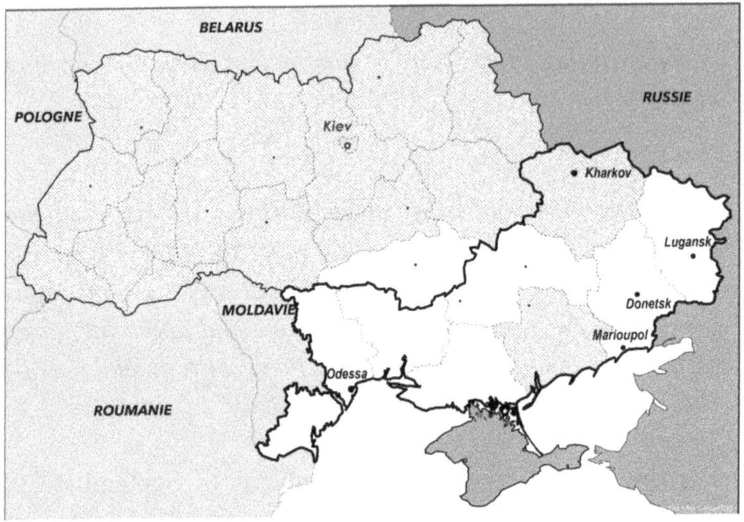

Figure 5 - Map of the occupation of regional administrations between 23 January and 26 February 2014. It appears that the regime change follows the language border rather schematically. It is a phenomenon concentrated in the northwest of Ukraine. The map shows that the coup - far from being democratic - literally split the country in two. As an indication, in strong line, the perimeter of what the rebels call «Novorossiya» (New Russia). [Source: Wikipedia[135]]

The map of events clearly shows a North-South division of the country. Western propagandists will try to hide this division, in order to support the discourse of a united Ukraine in favour of the «coup» on the one hand, and on the other hand, to put the responsibility for the conflict on Russia. Indeed, since the people are united, only Russia can be the cause of the opposition!

In 2022, after Vladimir Putin announced that one of the objectives of the offensive in Ukraine was to 'de-Nazify' the threat to the

135. https://en.wikipedia.org/wiki/2014_Euromaidan_regional_state_administration_occupations

people of Donbass, the Western discourse took the opposite view and tried to downplay the importance of neo-Nazis[136]. The result is a vast whitewashing campaign led by the militant Western far right[137]. It reached its peak after mid-May 2022, after the surrender of the Mariupol fighters, whose tattoos betray the true nature of those on whom the Kiev authorities rely.

It does not appear that Western influence has helped moralise Ukraine's handling of the Donbass conflict. In 2014, poorly advised by NATO military, Ukraine waged a war that could only lead to its defeat: it treated the people of Donbass and Crimea as enemy foreign forces, and made no attempt to win the 'hearts and minds' of the autonomists. Instead, its strategy has been to punish the people even more, as the West did in Afghanistan, Iraq or Libya, with the idea that they would rebel against their leaders.

This is why there are so many civilian victims. In her report of 17 October, Caroline Roux refers to the 14,000 victims of the conflict «including many civilians» suggesting that they are the work of «enemy separatist brothers backed by their Russian neighbours[138] «. What she carefully avoids saying is that - according to the UN - more than 80% of civilian casualties are the result of Ukrainian strikes. According to the UN, in the period from 1 October 2019 to 30 March 2020 alone, 84.4% of civilian casualties

136.Tara John & Tim Lister, «A far-right battalion has a key role in Ukraine's resistance. Its neo-Nazi history has been exploited by Putin', CNN, 30 March 2022 (https://edition.cnn.com/2022/03/29/europe/ukraine-azov-movement-far-right-intl-cmd/index.html)

137.Korine Amacher, «Where does the Russian obsession with a 'Nazi' Ukraine come from?», Heidi News, 11 March 2022 (updated 14 March 2022) (https://www.heidi.news/articles/d-ou-vient-l-obsession-russe-d-une-ukraine-nazie)

138.Caroline Roux in the programme «C dans l'air» of 17 October 2021 («Poutine, maître du jeu #cdanslair 17.10.2021», France 5/YouTube, 18 October 2021) (59'40")

are from Ukrainian artillery shelling[139]. The table in Figure 65 shows the figures for a wider period. As can be seen, the Ukrainian government is massacring its own people with the help, funding and advice of the military of NATO, the countries of the European Union that defend its values. As Jean-Yves Le Drian, Minister of Foreign Affairs, would say: «The absence of a reaction is tantamount to a guarantee»[140]...

Civilian victims of the Donbass war (2018-2021)

	On the territory of the self-proclaimed republics	In government-controlled territory	In the 'no man's land	Total	Change compared to previous year (in %)
2018	128	27	7	162	-41.9 %
2019	85	18	2	105	-35.2 %
2020	61	9	0	70	-33.3 %
2021	36	8	0	44	-37.1 %
Total	310	62	9	381	
%	81.4	16.3	2.3	100.0	

Figure 6 - Ukraine has not applied any of the rules of counterinsurgency to combat the desire for autonomy. By attacking its own citizens as if they were enemies, the Kiev government has alienated the people of Donbass [Source: «Conflict-related civilian casualties in Ukraine», United Nations Human Rights Monitoring Mission In Ukraine, Office of the High Commissioner for Human Rights, 31 December 2021 (updated 27 January 2022)[141]]

In 2014, Ukraine closed the Crimean Canal, which provided 82% of the peninsula's water supply[142] : a move that violated

139. UN Country Team Ukraine, "Conflict-related civilian casualties in Ukraine, March 2020", Reliefweb, 9 April 2020

140.»Aeroplane diverted by Belarus: «The absence of reaction from Russia is worth guaranteeing», says Jean-Yves Le Drian», francetvinfo.fr, 26 May 2021

141. https://ukraine.un.org/sites/default/files/2022-02/Conflict-related civilian casualties as of 31 December 2021 (rev 27 January 2022) corr EN_0.pdf

142.»Situation of human rights in the temporarily occupied Autonomous Republic of Crimea and the city of Sevastopol (Ukraine)», UN Human Rights Council,

international humanitarian law and deeply alienated the Russian-speaking population, but which no one in the West puts into the equation.

Moreover, the UN High Commissioner for Human Rights has repeatedly criticised the Ukrainian government for repeated and serious human rights violations on its territory, including in the Donbass Republics, which it claims as part of Ukraine[143]. In truth, European and American support for the Mayan revolution was never intended to help Ukraine, but to decouple it from Russia, and thus weaken it. The West simply instrumentalised Ukraine against Russia, just as it instrumentalised Taiwan against China.

Thus, the economic situation, which the strengthened links with Europe - proclaimed by the Maïdan revolutionaries - were supposed to improve, is only getting worse[144].

In 2013-2014, the West did not realise that for a variety of reasons, Ukraine was being carried at arm's length by Russia, through direct aid and privileged purchases. The break with Russia sought by the nationalists had the effect of cutting Ukraine off from its main support, which has not been replaced by the Europeans.

After Maidan, Ukraine was counting on the European Union for its economic prosperity. But its products, which were adapted to the Eastern European market in nature and quality, were not really adapted to the European market. Its agricultural products are facing competition from European products that no longer find outlets in Russia. The same phenomenon affects its industrial production, which is closely linked to Russia. Flagship Ukrainian industries,

---

25 September 2017 (A/HRC/36/CRP.3)

143.»Civic Space and Fundamental Rights in Ukraine - 1st November 2019 to 31 October 2021», UN HCHR, 15 December 2021

144.»Ukraine-EU Agreement: How Beneficial is Ukraine-EU Agreement?», EurAsian Times, 1er September 2017

such as the aircraft manufacturer Antonov[145] and the Nikolayev shipyards on the Black Sea, have gone bankrupt[146]... Since 2014, we have seen a gradual deindustrialisation of Ukraine. Today, Ukraine is the only former republic of the USSR with a GDP lower than that of the communist era. According to a survey by Interfax Ukraine, about 70% of Ukrainians think that the country is on the wrong track[147].

Moreover, no one seems to care much about Ukraine itself. The EU-Ukraine free trade agreement served the political interests of the US more than the welfare of the Ukrainian people. In 2022, no one is willing to fight for Ukraine: even the Americans have declared that they will not deploy troops in Ukraine[148]. In reality, they knew perfectly well that the «Russian threat» was fake: that is why they made no commitments to Ukraine and made threats that they cannot carry out in case of an offensive (which they knew was highly unlikely).

2.7.5. The Crimea

History of events concerning the Crimea

Date	Official narrative	Part of history hidden by the Western media
20/01/1991		In a referendum (the first in the USSR), the Crimeans accepted by 93.6%[149] that the peninsula be detached from Ukraine and attached to Moscow.

145.Article «Antonov (aeronautics)», Wikipedia

146. «Ukraine has lost the shipyard that built the corvette "Vladimir the Great", metallurgprom.org, 29 June 2021

147. «Some 69% of Ukrainians call economic situation bad, 32% expect it to deteriorate - poll", Interfax-Ukraine, 9 February 2021

148.Derek Saul, «Biden Says 'No Intention' To Deploy U.S. Troops In Ukraine-Here's What The U.S. Is Prepared To Do Instead», Forbes, 25 January 2022

149. NdA: with a participation of 81.3% of the population.

Date	Official narrative	Part of history hidden by the Western media
12/02/1991		The Autonomous Soviet Socialist Republic of Crimea (ASSR Crimea), abolished in 1945, is re-established by the Supreme Soviet of the Ukrainian SSR[150].
17/03/1991	In a referendum, the Soviet population accepts the continuation of the USSR.	
01/12/1991	The Ukrainian population accepts by referendum to become independent from Moscow.	
23/12/1991	The USSR is dissolved.	
17/03/1995		Ukraine abolishes the Crimean constitution, overthrows Yuri Mechkov, President of Crimea, by force and annexes the peninsula.
06/03/2014		The Crimean Parliament decides to hold a referendum to choose between remaining in Ukraine or requesting annexation to Moscow.
10/03/2014		The Crimean authorities ask the OSCE to send observers to the referendum[151].
16/03/2014	The referendum to demand the attachment of Crimea to Moscow is held.	

On the basis of UN Resolution 68/262, the «international community» considers the annexation of Crimea to Russia illegal[152] and illegitimate[153]. The Budapest Treaty (1994), which guaranteed the territorial integrity of Ukraine, the Russian military intervention to take over the institutions and the illegitimacy

150. Article «1991 Crimean referendum», Wikipedia (accessed 27 November 2021).
151. «Crimea invites OSCE observers for referendum on joining Russia», Reuters, 10 March 2014.
152.»Resolution adopted by the General Assembly on 27 March 2014», UN General Assembly, 1er April 2014 (A/RES/68/262)
153.John B. Bellinger III (interviewed by Jonathan Masters), 'Why the Crimean Referendum Is Illegitimate', Council on Foreign Relations, 16 March 2014

of the referendum organised by the Crimean authorities in 2014 are invoked to justify this judgement.

The secession of Crimea is always presented as a Russian-organised 'coup de force', justified by the fact that the peninsula is populated by Russians[154]. An honest examination of recent history requires a more nuanced look than what Western propagandists and revisionists tell us. What has led to this situation is that, prior to 2014, the law was not respected, either by the Soviets or by the Ukrainians. On several occasions, the Crimeans overwhelmingly expressed their desire to be governed by Moscow[155].

2.7.5.1. Ukraine's territorial integrity and the Budapest Memorandum (1994)

Firstly, it should be recalled that the transfer of Crimea to Ukraine in 1954 was not legal. Despite the approval of the Presidium of the Supreme Soviet on 19 February 1954[156], it was not approved by the Supreme Soviet of the USSR, the Supreme Soviet of the Russian Republic or the Supreme Soviet of the Republic of Ukraine. Officially presented as a gift to Ukraine on the occasion of the 300th anniversary of its ties with Russia, the transfer seems to have been motivated by Khrushchev's personal interest in having Ukraine's support in the Politburo, as Mark Kramer of the Wilson Center explains[157]. This cession was never perceived as legitimate by the Crimean population, which had

154.Pascal Boniface in «Explain to me... The situation in Ukraine», YouTube, 31 October 2019

155. Note: A chronology of the relationship between Crimea and Ukraine is provided by the UN High Commissioner for Refugees, for the interested reader: «Chronology for Crimean Russians in Ukraine», Minorities at Risk Project/Refworld.org, 2004

156. https://digitalarchive.wilsoncenter.org/document/119638

157.Mark Kramer, «Why Did Russia Give Away Crimea Sixty Years Ago?», Cold War International History Project e-Dossier No. 47, Wilson Center, 2014

never been under the authority of Kiev before. It illustrates the dysfunctions of the communist system of the time, which strangely seem to meet with the approval of today's 'experts'!

On 20 January 1991, before the independence of Ukraine and before the dissolution of the USSR, the Crimeans were asked to choose between staying with Kiev or being administered by Moscow. The question on the ballot paper was :

> *Do you support the restoration of the Autonomous Soviet Socialist Republic of Crimea as a subject of the Soviet Union and a member of the Union Treaty?*[158]

This was the first referendum on autonomy in the USSR. The Crimeans accepted by 93.6%[159] to no longer depend on Kiev and to be attached to Moscow. The Autonomous Soviet Socialist Republic of Crimea (ASSR Crimea), abolished in 1945, was thus re-established on 12 February 1991 by the Supreme Soviet of the Ukrainian SSR[160].

On 17 March, Moscow organised a referendum on the continuation of the USSR, which was accepted by Ukraine. By accepting the continuation of the USSR, Ukraine ratifies the status of Crimea, thus confirming that it is dependent on Moscow and no longer on Kiev. At this stage, Ukraine was not yet independent. It was not until December 1991 that Ukraine held «its» referendum for independence. The participation of the Crimeans was then low because they were already autonomous and no longer felt concerned.

158.Original text: «вы за воссоздание крымской автономной советской социалическая республики как субъекта ссp и участника союзного договора?»
159.NdA: with a participation of 81.3% of the population.
160.Article '1991 Crimean referendum', Wikipedia (accessed 27 November 2021)

Ukraine became independent more than six months after Crimea declared its sovereignty on 4 September. On 26 February 1992, the Crimean parliament proclaimed the «Republic of Crimea» with the agreement of the Ukrainian government, which granted it the status of a self-governing republic. On 5 May 1992, Crimea declared its independence and adopted a constitution[161]. The city of Sevastopol, which was directly managed by Moscow under the communist system, is in a similar situation, having been incorporated by Ukraine in 1991 outside the law. The following years were marked by a tug of war between Simferopol and Kiev, which wanted to keep Crimea under its control.

On 5 December 1994, by signing the Budapest Memorandum, Ukraine gave up the nuclear weapons of the former USSR that remained on its territory, in exchange for «its security, independence and territorial integrity[162] «. At this stage, Crimea considers that it is - de jure - no longer part of Ukraine. Therefore, it considers that it is not concerned by this treaty. But Kiev feels strengthened by the memorandum. On 17 March 1995, it abolished the Crimean constitution by authority, sent its special forces to forcibly remove Yuri Mechkov, president of Crimea[163], and de facto annexed the Republic of Crimea[164]. The population takes to the streets to demand that Crimea be returned to Russia. An event that was hardly reported by the Western media.

161.On 6 May, it is clarified that Crimea is part of Ukrainian territory.
162.Article «Budapest Memorandum», Wikipedia (accessed 27 November 2021)
163.»Ukraine Moves To Oust Leader Of Separatists», The New York Times, 19 March 1995 (https://www.nytimes.com/1995/03/19/world/ukraine-moves-to-oust-leader-of-separatists.html)
164. James Rupert, "Striking at Separatists, Ukraine Abolishes Crimea's Charter, Presidency", The Washington Post, 18 March 1995; Research Directorate, Immigration and Refugee Board, Canada "Chronology of Events March 1994 - August 1995", refworld.org, 1er March 1996

Crimea is then governed in an authoritarian manner by decrees from Kiev. This situation led the Crimean Parliament to formulate a new constitution in October 1995, which re-established the Autonomous Republic of Crimea. This new constitution was ratified by the Crimean Parliament on 21 October 1998 and confirmed by the Ukrainian Parliament on 23 December 1998. These events and the concerns of the Russian-speaking minority led to the signing of a Treaty of Friendship between Ukraine and Russia on 31 May 1997. Fearing a secession of Crimea, Ukraine included the principle of the inviolability of borders in exchange - and this is important - for a guarantee of «the protection of the ethnic, cultural, linguistic and religious originality of national minorities on their territory.[165]

However, on 23 February 2014, not only did the new authorities in Kiev emerge from a coup d'état that had nothing to do with the constitution and were therefore not elected, but, by repealing the law on official languages, they no longer respected this guarantee of the 1997 treaty. The Crimeans therefore took to the streets to demand the 'return' to Russia that they had obtained thirty years earlier.

On 4 March, during his press conference on the situation in Ukraine, a journalist asked Vladimir Putin if he was considering Crimea joining Russia. He replied:

> *No, we do not envisage this. In general, I believe that only the residents of a given country who are free to decide in safety can and should determine their future. If this right has been granted to the Kosovo Albanians, if this has been made possible in many parts of the world, then no one is excluding the right of nations to self-determination, which, as far as I*

165. https://apps.dtic.mil/dtic/tr/fulltext/u2/a341002.pdf

know, is laid down in several UN documents. However, we will not under any circumstances provoke such a decision and will not fuel such feelings.[166]

Renewed in 2010, the agreement between Ukraine and Russia for the stationing of troops in Crimea and Sevastopol ran until 2042. Russia therefore had no reason to claim the territory at that stage.

On 6 March, the Crimean Parliament decided to hold a popular referendum to choose between remaining in Ukraine or reques-ting annexation to Moscow. After an unambiguous vote, the Crimean authorities asked Moscow to be attached to Russia[167]. Thus, Crimea regains the status it had acquired by referendum before Ukraine's independence in January 1991.

Russia's so-called «special operation», denounced by the West, is in fact the result of repeated violations of the rights and interests of the Crimean people by the Soviets and then by the Ukrainian government (with Western complicity) since 1954.

Already in 2014, Ukrainians and Westerners are claiming violation of the Budapest Memorandum. To which the supporters of Russia and the Crimeans retort that:

a) In 1994, Crimea, as a de jure independent entity, was not covered by the Budapest Memorandum;

(b) By abolishing the Kivalov-Kolesnichenko Law of 2012, which made Russian an official language, Ukraine failed to comply with the 1997 Treaty of Friendship, which required it to protect minority rights, and that this decision was taken

166.»Vladimir Putin answered journalists' questions on the situation in Ukraine», kremlin.ru, 4 March 2014 (http ://en.kremlin.ru/events/president/news/20366)

167.Cordélia Bonal, «En Crimée, 95 % des votants en faveur d'un rattachement à la Russie», Libération, 16 March 2014 (https://www.liberation.fr/planete/2014/03/16/en-direct-referendum-decisif-en-crimee_987472/)

without following the normal legislative process by an unelected government.

On 19 February 2022, Anka Feldhusen, the German ambassador in Kiev, threw a spanner in the works by stating on the television channel Ukraine 24 that the Budapest Memorandum is not legally binding[168]. This is also the American position, as can be seen on the website of the American embassy in Minsk[169].

Lawyers can debate this issue, but it shows that the case for the illegality of the Crimea affair is much less clear-cut than our editorialists claim, and that it has been 'hyped' to maintain tension with Russia, leading to the war of 2022.

A close examination of the Western narrative on the 'annexation' of Crimea shows that it is based exclusively on the claims of the Kiev government, which rewrites history and obscures facts that might contradict its version[170].

2.7.5.2. The myth of Russian aggression

The myth of Russian aggression is inextricably linked to the myth of 'little green men arriving in numbers on the peninsula'[171], suggesting an invasion by Russia. By invoking sometimes

---

168.»German Ambassador on the Budapest Memorandum: no legal obligations», perild.com, 19 February 2022 (https://youtu.be/xoWczhVimYE)

169. http://minsk.usembassy.gov/budapest_memorandum.html

170.Michael Kofman, Katya Migacheva, Brian Nichiporuk, Andrew Radin, Olesya Tkacheva & Jenny Oberholtzer, «Lessons from Russia's Operations in Crimea and Eastern Ukraine», Rand Corporation, 2017 (https://www.rand.org/content/dam/rand/pubs/research_reports/RR1400/RR1498/RAND_RR1498.pdf)

171.Caroline Roux in the programme «C dans l'air» of 17 October 2021 («Poutine, maître du jeu #cdanslair 17.10.2021», France 5/YouTube, 18 October 2021) (56'25")

«special forces»[172], sometimes mercenaries from the «Wagner» company[173], a narrative has been created.

Our belief that Russia 'invaded a part of a sovereign state militarily by force', as military expert Pierre Servent claims on France 5[174], is intended to give legitimacy to the coup that the West had just supported in Kiev.

It is a fable that originated in NATO - where I used to work - and that plays with words to turn an engagement that is perfectly in line with the agreements between Russia and Ukraine into a special operation. However, the engagement of Russian troops in Crimea does not correspond in form, tactics or structure to that of their special forces. The latter is a field I know well and on which I wrote a book[175] (which has been translated into Ukrainian[176]).

As soon as the abolition of the Official Languages Act was announced, the south of the country was set ablaze. The Crimeans took to the streets. Among them were about 4,000 hunters or members of shooting societies and 15,000 members of the territorial reserve, who took up arms and occupied the regional parliament in Simferopol. Together they form the 'self-defence' units, which are mentioned in March 2014 by Foreign Minister Sergei Lavrov and Vladimir Putin[177].

172.Alan Malcher, «Russian Spetsnaz - Ukraine's Deniable 'Little Green Men'», moderndiplomacy.eu, 10 May 2015

173.»Ukraine, Mali: what are the Wagner militias doing? Leçon de géopolitique - Le Dessous des cartes», ARTE/YouTube, 26 January 2022

174.Pierre Servent in the programme «C dans l'air» of 11 January 2022 («Poutine rêve d'URSS, l'Ukraine sous tension #cdanslair 11.01.2022», France 5/YouTube, 12 January 2022) (26'50")

175.Jacques Baud, Les Forces spéciales de l'Organisation du Traité de Varsovie, L'Harmattan, 2002

176. https://constitutions.ru/wp-content/uploads/specnaz.pdf

177.»The Changing Story Of Russia's 'Little Green Men' Invasion», RFE/RL, 25 February 2019

These civilians are supplemented by military personnel from the Ukrainian forces. At the beginning of 2014, the Ukrainian army was still composed of a majority of conscripts, recruited and organised in a territorial manner: in Crimea, the majority of the military is Russian-speaking. Thus, when the government ordered them to suppress the demonstrations, 20,000 of the 22,000 Ukrainian military personnel stationed in Crimea refused to intervene against their compatriots and rallied to the demonstrators, as Ivan Vinnik, a deputy in the Kiev Rada, later confirmed[178]. They tore off their Ukrainian insignia to avoid confusion and became what the West nicknamed «little green men» and identified as Russian special forces. In addition to these soldiers, there are about 15,000 Russian-speaking members of the police, the Security Service (SBU) and the border guards[179], who also refuse to confront their «brothers». This makes a total of about 35,000 defectors.

As for the Russian military in Crimea, the Status of Forces Agreement (SOFA) signed in 2010 with Ukraine (and valid until 2042) capped their presence at 25,000 men, and only 20,000 to 22,000 are actually stationed on the peninsula. In the event of a crisis, the agreement allowed them to deploy to various strategic points on the peninsula (such as the airport), in order to provide an umbilical cord with Russia. These soldiers do not wear unit insignia on their combat uniforms, as is customary in the Russian armed forces (e.g. in Afghanistan).

---

178. Евгений Мураев и Иван Виник, народные депутаты, в «Вечернем прайме» телеканала «112 Украина», 4 August 2016 (https://112.ua/video/evgeniy-muraev-i-ivan-vinnik-narodnye-deputaty-v-vechernem-prayme-telekanala-112-ukraina-04082016-206216.html)

179. "Ukrainian defectors in occupied Crimea sidelined, relocated", www.unian.info, 5 October 2017

When Ukrainian nationalist paramilitaries began to violently clash with Crimean self-defence militias, the Russian military stepped in, invoking the principle of «responsibility to protect» (R2P).

Thus, neither in Donbass nor in Crimea was there a Russian invasion in 2014. In fact, the terms «intervention» and «invasion» are played back and forth to cast doubt on the real presence of Russians in eastern Ukraine[180]. For, despite their repeated allegations, the West has never provided any concrete evidence confirming a Russian «invasion» or even a «landing» of special forces! In fact, they have sought to hide the illegitimacy of a coup d'état that they largely supported and which is at the origin of the events in Crimea.

Some commentators, such as Arnaud Dubien[181], saw this as a «pledge», i.e. a territory that could be monetised in a negotiation, which was clearly not the case.

2.7.5.3. The illegitimate nature of the March 2014 referendum

Allegations that the 2014 vote was «*totally manipulated*» are based on the very high level of acceptance and are totally gratuitous[182]. Of course, it cannot be ruled out that there was fraud: the organisation, the counting, the proper functioning in each polling station, etc. have not been subject to international verification. So anything is possible, even if some countries hold referendums regularly - like Switzerland - and do not need international

180.Wikipedia, Article «Russian military intervention in Ukraine (2014-present)» (accessed 15 May 2019)

181.Arnaud Dubien, «Putin's power grab in Crimea is part of a desire to bargain», Le Monde, 3 March 2014 (updated 4 March 2014)

182.Michel Eltchaninoff in the programme «C dans l'air» of 17 October 2021 («Poutine, maître du jeu #cdanslair 17.10.2021», France 5/YouTube, 18 October 2021) (1h33'30")

verification, while others - like France - simply ignore results they do not like. That said, anything is possible.

Nevertheless, the 96.77%[183] acceptance is consistent with the 93.6% obtained in January 1991 and seems to be confirmed by a *Gallup* poll of April 2014[184]. Moreover, such results are not exceptional, as we saw in Kosovo in 1991 (99.98%[185]) or in the Falkland Islands in 2013 (99.8%[186]). So these accusations are nothing more than an artificial construction, based on hypotheses, which rule out the existence of a previous referendum, in order to imagine a plot hatched by Russia... thus meeting the definition of conspiracy!

Moreover, it is carefully avoided that on 10 March 2014, the Crimean authorities asked the OSCE to send observers for the referendum[187], but the organisation refused on the pretext that it was unconstitutional[188]. This will become a regular tactic for the Western community, and in particular for the European Union: refusing to go and observe elections and then declaring them illegitimate...

My contacts in the OSCE tell me that the Americans are now exerting significant pressure within the organisation. So, not only did the OSCE completely ignore the existence of a previous perfectly legal and legitimate referendum in Crimea, but it literally gave a blank check to regime change in Kiev. For the

183.Article «2014 Crimean referendum», Wikipedia (accessed 27 November 2021)
184. http://www.bbg.gov/wp-content/media/2014/06/Ukraine-slide-deck.pdf
185.Article '1991 Kosovan independence referendum', Wikipedia (accessed 27 November 2021)
186.Article 'Falkland Islands status referendum', Wikipedia (accessed 27 November 2021)
187.»Crimea invites OSCE observers for referendum on joining Russia, Reuters, 10 March 2014
188.»OSCE Chair says Crimean referendum in its current form is illegal and calls for alternative ways to address the Crimean issue», osce.org, 11 March 2014

coup was illegal in every respect and violated the constitutional order, while the Western involvement was contrary to the UN Charter and the Helsinki Final Act. In this situation, therefore, the Crimeans simply took advantage of the situation to return to the situation that Ukraine had been deprived of for more than 20 years, thus implementing the provisions of Article VIII of the Helsinki Final Act.

When Barak Obama says at the United Nations that «*it could happen to any of your* countries[189] «, he knows what he is talking about: at the end of the 19th century, the US illegally annexed Hawaii. It is still a dispute between the indigenous people and Washington. Some even dispute the notion of 'annexation' and prefer to say that Hawaii is a kingdom under US military occupation[190]. With the ironic consequence that if international law were respected, Barak Obama (a native Hawaiian) would - technically speaking - probably not have had the right to run in the presidential election[191] !... Proving Donald Trump right (but for the wrong reasons)[192] ! However, whereas in Crimea, it was at the request of the Crimean population that Russia agreed to annex the peninsula; in Hawaii, the Americans took over the islands by force before unilaterally deciding to annex them to the US territory.

Do as I say, not as I do!

189.Programme «C dans l'air» of 17 October 2021, («Poutine, maître du jeu #cdanslair 17.10.2021», France 5/YouTube, 18 October 2021) (57'58")

190. Keanu Sai Ph.D., "The Illegal Overthrow of the Hawaiian Kingdom Government," NEA Today, April 2, 2018; Keanu Sai (Ph.D.), "The U.S. Occupation of the Hawaiian Kingdom," NEA Today, October 1er 2018; https://en.wikipedia.org/wiki/Legal_status_of_Hawaii

191.NdA: Before his election, Obama was subjected to a smear campaign about his birthplace: bad people claimed he was born in Kenya, but nobody argued about Hawaii. Trump continued to claim that he was not an American...

192.NdA: Donald Trump claimed that Obama was a native of Kenya.

2.7.6. The Donbass crisis

As in Crimea, the abolition of the Kivalov-Kolesnichenko law on official languages on 23 February 2014 is a bombshell throughout the south of the country. From Odessa to Kharkov, Russian speakers are taking to the streets because the decision is not only illegitimate, it is illegal: the new authorities were not elected and the decision violates the 1997 treaty between Russia and Ukraine.

The repression of these demonstrations was brutal and bloody, but the West remained very discreet about these exactions. They tried to show that the regime change was democratic and widely supported by the Ukrainian population.

In order to legitimise the coup d'état led by ultra-nationalists and neo-Nazis in Western Ukraine, the Western narrative has to adapt: the repression of these riots hardly appears in our media, and this opposition is reduced to Russian influence in the Donbass and an imaginary Russian 'invasion', explained by Vladimir Putin's 'ambitions'.

In 2014, I was at NATO at the time and I noticed that the reports we received came from Poland and did not match the information from the OSCE. It was obvious that they were trying to exaggerate the events and give them an international dimension. But even within NATO, I am «only» Swiss, and therefore technically a «partner» and not an «ally»: my warnings are politely dismissed in favour of a more forceful discourse.

In a resolution adopted in September 2014, the European Parliament speaks of «direct military intervention», ceasefire violations «mainly by regular Russian troops» and claims that Russia has «increased its military presence on Ukrainian territory»[193]. This is obviously not true: the allegations come from

193.European Parliament resolution of 18 September 2014 on the situation in

Polish intelligence services, but have never been confirmed by OSCE monitors. As is often the case, the European Parliament accuses and then sanctions without any facts to confirm its accusations. So much for the rule of law!

In June 2015, in an interview with Corriere della Sera, Petro Poroshenko claimed that Russia had deployed 200,000 troops to Ukraine[194]. Then, in September, before the United Nations General Assembly in New York, he stated that

> *we are forced to fight the trained and armed troops of the Russian Federation. Heavy weapons and military equipment are concentrated in the occupied territories in such quantities that the armies of the majority of UN member states could only dream of them.*[195]

On 19 November 2016, at the NATO Parliamentary Assembly in Istanbul, the presence of 75 Russian military units in Ukraine was mentioned[196]. In fact, the accusations made by President Petro Poroshenko are simply being repeated.

The result is an official discourse - blindly served up by 'experts' of all stripes - that the situation in Crimea and the conflict in Donbass are consequences of Russian policy.

In reality, nothing was observed at all.

On 29 January 2015, General Viktor Muzhenko, head of the Ukrainian General Staff, admitted that there were no Russian

---

Ukraine and the state of EU-Russia relations (2014/2841(RSP), Strasbourg, 18 September 2014

194.Giuseppe Sarcina, «Ukraine's Poroshenko: «Putin the Pact-Breaker»», Corriere della Sera, 30 June 2015

195.Programme «C dans l'air du 02-10-2015: Syria: Putin Attacks», YouTube/ France 5, 10 November 2015 (46'10")

196. «The 75 Russian military units at war in Ukraine", Euromaidan Press, 23 November 2019

troops on Ukrainian soil and that only individual Russian fighters had been observed[197]. His assertion was confirmed in October 2015 by General Vasyl Hrytsak, head of the Security Service (SBU), who then stated that since the beginning of the fighting in eastern Ukraine, only 56 Russian servicemen had been observed[198]. In fact, Ukrainian troops have captured young Russians (wearing uniforms dating from the war in Afghanistan) who came to join the Donbass insurgents in solidarity during their holidays. A similar phenomenon was already observed during the war in the Balkans, when young Swiss men went to Bosnia on weekends to «do the shooting» with their prescription weapons! This is exactly the same as the Ukrainian soldiers of the (French) Foreign Legion, who are trying to reach their country to fight in March 2022[199].

Meanwhile, in Security and Human Rights Monitor, Alexander Hug, Deputy Head of the OSCE Observer Mission, states that

> *It [is] very difficult to verify who owns the tank because Russia and Ukraine use largely the same equipment. Often the military equipment used by the rebels is the same equipment that was previously used by the Ukrainian army because the*

---

197. «No Russian Troops in Ukraine says Kiev General, YouTube, 1er February 2015

198. «SBU says 56 Russians in military actions against Ukraine since conflict began», Interfax-Ukraine/Kiyv Post, 10 October 2015 (https://www.kyivpost.com/article/content/war-against-ukraine/sbu-registers-involvement-of-56-russian-in-military-actions-against-ukraine-since-military-conflict-in-eastern-ukraien-unfolded-399718.html); "Only 56 Russians Fought in Ukraine- says Ukraine's State Security (SBU)", YouTube, 7 February 2016

199.»Some soldiers of the Foreign Legion authorized to go to countries bordering Ukraine», Le Figaro, 2 March 2022

rebels have taken over their equipment. So we are in a difficult position to verify who owns or operates the equipment. [200]

In 2018, he admitted to Foreign Policy magazine that the OSCE has made no observations confirming the presence of Russian troops in Ukraine[201]. Moreover, the American observation satellites, which are said to be able to read registration numbers from space, remain very discreet...

Accusations of Russian intervention in Ukraine are based on the rebels' armament, which appears to match that of Ukrainian troops. In 2014, when I was responsible for countering the proliferation of small arms at NATO, I monitored the appearance of new weapons among the rebels to determine whether Russia was supplying them. In fact, we find that the appearance of heavy weaponry among the rebels can systematically be associated with the disappearance of a unit of the Ukrainian army: Russian-speaking servicemen - and sometimes entire units - suddenly switch to the rebel side.

The «experts» go to great lengths to find photos of weapons that were never in the Ukrainian army, in order to demonstrate Russia's involvement. But they fail to mention that the weapons in question were indeed in the Ukrainian Security Service (SBU), whose agents also went over to the rebel side!

So there is no evidence that Russia was involved in the Donbass conflict at this stage. Moreover, if this had been the case,

200.Stephanie Liechtenstein, «Interview with Alexander Hug: Special Monitoring Mission is the eyes and the ears of the international community in Ukraine», Security and Human Rights Monitor, 8 September 2014 (https://www.shrmonitor.org/interview-alexander-hug-special-monitoring-mission-eyes-ears-international-community-ukraine/)

201. Amy Mackinnon, "Counting the Dead in Europe's Forgotten War", Foreign Policy, 25 October 2018

we would certainly have had satellite images of these troops. But nothing...

By the end of 2021, the Americans had not been short of satellite images showing Russian troops near the Ukrainian border. Yet they have not released any satellite images of Russian contingents deployed in the Donbass between 2014 and 2022, or even of logistical convoys to support these contingents!

Map published by the Washington Post (3 December 2021)

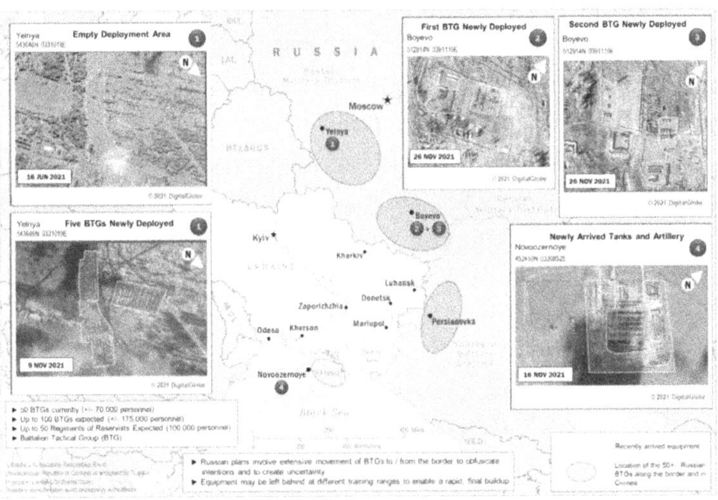

Figure 7 - US intelligence map of Russian forces deployed around Ukraine in December 2021. There are no Russian troops in the Donbass. Western politicians - notably the US, France and Britain - have systematically lied about this to justify the lack of progress in implementing the Minsk Agreements. France has failed to play its role as guarantor of the agreements and has turned a blind eye to Ukrainian strikes against the civilian population of Donbass. This is what will push the Russians to the offensive on February 24, 2022. [Source: Washington Post]

The only satellite image produced by Nato that was supposed to demonstrate the presence of the Russian army in Ukraine was a picture of 4 (!) «Russian» armoured howitzers[202]. However, not only is this not military imagery (which could have provided more accurate information), but these vehicles have not been formally identified as Russian. They are only assumed to be Russian, as Nato could see no other possible explanation. In reality, it was the rebel battalion «KALMIUS», formed by Russian-speaking Ukrainian servicemen who «switched» to the side of the autonomists with their Russian-origin weapons, and which was operating in August 2014 in the area covered by the photo[203].

Obviously, the passage of entire Ukrainian army units to the rebel side contradicts the idea that the Mayan revolution is popular... Besides, since August 2014, it seems that NATO has not found any other photos to publish!

Clearly, the claims that the Russian army has been operating in the Donbass since 2014 are just rumours, based on hot air. But they were enough to impose sanctions against Russia, confirming that the sole purpose of Western intervention in Ukrainian internal affairs was to destabilise Russia.

2.8. The Minsk Agreements

The first talks leading to the Minsk Agreements were held in Geneva in April 2014 between John Kerry, Catherine Ashton, Sergei Lavrov and Andriy Deshchytsia, foreign ministers of the United States, the European Union, Russia and Ukraine. There

202.»NATO releases satellite imagery showing Russian combat troops inside Ukraine», 28 August 2014, (http://www.nato.int/cps/en/natohq/photos_112202.htm)

203.Confidential source

was clear talk of a resolution to Ukraine's internal conflict[204], including constitutional changes inspired by federalism[205].

In May 2014, armed repression of protests prompted the population in some areas of the Donetsk and Lugansk regions of Ukraine to hold referendums to adopt the Act of Self-Determination of the Donetsk People's Republic (approved by 89%) and the Act of Self-Determination of the Lugansk People's Republic (approved by 96%). The state media France 24[206] and Radio-Télévision Suisse[207] speak of «independence» referendums, but this is false: they are referendums of «self-determination» or «autonomy» (самостоятельность). Thereafter, those who seek to add fuel to the fire will continue to talk about «separatists» and «separatist republics». This is disinformation designed to mislead public opinion.

Following these referenda, the two republics wrote to Vladimir Putin asking to be «integrated» into Russia[208]. But he did not accede to their requests.

After its defeat in Ilovaisk in August 2014, the Ukrainian government had to invent the excuse of a Russian intervention to justify Western propaganda and hide the undemocratic nature of the regime change. This defeat forced the Ukrainians to accept the first Minsk I Agreements (September 2014). Agreements that Kiev immediately broke after signing them, in order to launch

204. «Foreign Minister Sergey Lavrov 's statement following his talks with German Foreign Minister Frank-Walter Steinmeier», Permanent Mission of the Russian Federation to the European Union, 18 April 2014
205. «Transcript: Kerry and Ashton on April 17 Geneva deal on Ukraine», The Washington Post, 17 April 2014
206.»Eastern Ukraine prepares to vote on its 'independence'», France 24, 10 May 2014
207. https://pages.rts.ch/la-1ere/programmes/le-journal-du-matin/5822909-le-journal-du-matin-du-12-05-2014.html
208. https://iz.ru/news/570657

a large-scale offensive called «Anti-Terrorist Operation» (ATO) against the rebel forces. The ATO will totally undermine the Minsk I agreements. Supported and advised by NATO officers, the Ukrainian army suffered another crushing defeat in Debaltsevo in February 2015. This led Ukraine to enter into the Minsk II Agreements (February 2015). Minsk II follows on from the Geneva Declaration of April 2014 and confirms the internal nature of the conflict in Donbass.

But the Ukrainian government will systematically refuse to implement the agreement, which is the subject of a UN Security Council resolution. It claims that the implementation of these agreements would condemn the very existence of Ukraine.

This narrative is supported by commentators who seek to fan the flames of hatred by labelling the rebels as «separatists» or «independentists» who seek to challenge the integrity of Ukraine. They are liars because, at this stage, the Russian-speaking people of Donbass are neither seeking to separate from Ukraine nor to be independent. They only want a form of autonomy that allows them to use their language and their particularities. It is no coincidence that the first discussions on an agreement for Donbass took place under the aegis of the OSCE, which was then chaired by Switzerland. Swiss diplomats suggested a solution based on the Swiss model.

As stated in the Minsk Agreements, the Donetsk and Luhansk Republics of Ukraine are defined as «parts of the territory of Ukraine», and there is no question of their «separation». This is why the implementation of these agreements is based exclusively on negotiations between the Kiev government and «representatives of certain areas of the Donetsk and Luhansk regions» (Articles 9, 11 and 12). It should be noted that in the text of the agreements, the name «Luhansk» is in Ukrainian and not in Russian (Lugansk), which means that the regions are on Ukrainian and not Russian territory and that there is no question of separating them from Ukraine.

The agreements state that their implementation is a matter for Kiev, which is logical since it is a matter of its internal structure and sovereignty. Naturally, this major change in the structure of the Ukrainian state requires a change in the constitution, which must necessarily be initiated by Kyiv. At no time did the Ukrainian authorities initiate this reform process. They have simply never started to put in place the legal framework for the implementation of the agreements.

In Europe, where support for Ukrainian ultra-nationalists and the far right is very strong, the idea that the Minsk Agreements were agreed between Russia and Ukraine prevails. This is a lie, regularly repeated by some «fire brigade experts»[209].

But beyond the ignorance of the 'experts', this is largely what explains the ineffectiveness of European diplomatic action in resolving the crisis. Thus, on 12 October 2021, during the EU-Ukraine summit, Ursula von der Leyen declared:

> *We fully support the position of President Zelensky's government. And we call on Russia to assume its responsibilities as a party to the conflict.* [210]

209.Pascal Boniface, in «Russia/United States: Europe is not at the negotiating table, it is on the menu», YouTube, 10 January 2022 (https://youtu.be/IJyjEcuR-0v4?t=203)

210.Statement by President von der Leyen at the joint press conference with President Michel and President Zelensky following the EU-Ukraine Summit, European Commission, 12 October 2021 (https://ec.europa.eu/commission/presscorner/detail/fr/statement_21_5222)

She has a reputation for not knowing her files well, so nothing really surprising. But she is not the only one, because on France 5, François Hollande says that he negotiated the Minsk Agreements in the belief that Russian troops were in the Donbass, whereas it was well known at the time that this was not the case[211].

In reality, the agreement was between the Ukrainian government and the rebel forces in Donbass. So on the one hand, France and Germany were the guarantors of the agreement on the Ukrainian side, while on the other hand, Russia was the guarantor of the Russian-speaking autonomists. Russia only played a facilitating role, as the Ukrainian government refused to talk to representatives of the autonomist entities.

The problem is that the Ukrainian side refused to negotiate with the representatives of the autonomists, so the Russian ambassador had to sign as guarantor of the commitments made by the representatives of the two self-proclaimed republics.

The next problem, which will lead to the Russian offensive in 2022, is that the two Western guarantors have not kept their word. Instead of urging Kiev to implement the agreements, they have chosen to side with Kiev in an attempt to replace the Minsk Agreements with bilateral negotiations between Moscow and Kiev.

Unable to respect their word and their signature, European leaders are burying their heads in the sand. For it has long been known that it is the Ukrainians who refuse to implement the Agreements, as the Washington Post points out[212] :

> *According to diplomats close to the matter, a major obstacle was Kiev's opposition to negotiating with the pro-Russian*

211/ Programme «C dans l'air» of 17 October 2021 («Poutine, maître du jeu #cdanslair 17.10.2021», France 5/YouTube, 18 October 2021) (1h02'43")

212.John Hudson & David L. Stern, 'Facing maximum pressure from Russia, Zelensky refuses to blink at the negotiating table', The Washington Post, 11 February 2022

separatists, with whom they have been in a deadly but low-intensity conflict for the past eight years.

This was confirmed by Angela Merkel in June 2022, who confessed that the signing of these agreements was simply a way for Ukraine to buy time «to become what it is today»[213]. Ukraine never intended to implement the Minsk Agreements, and the French and Germans never intended to encourage it to do so.

The duplicity of the French and German governments has led to confusion, as in Ursula von der Leyen's address to the EU-Ukraine summit on 12 October 2021[214] :

We fully support the position of President Zelensky's government. And we call on Russia to assume its responsibilities as a party to the conflict.

As usual, Ursula von der Leyen knows little about the issue, which is good news for the French government, which, since François Hollande and Laurent Fabius, has understood nothing about the situation.

This will become very clear in June 2022, with the publication of the telephone conversation between Emmanuel Macron and Vladimir Putin of 20 February 2022[215]. It shows that by

213.Alistair Walsh & Rina Goldenberg, «Angela Merkel opens up on Ukraine, Putin and her legacy», DW News, 7 June 2022 (https://p.dw.com/p/4CMeH)

214.Statement by President von der Leyen at the joint press conference with President Michel and President Zelensky following the EU-Ukraine Summit, European Commission, 12 October 2021

215.»We don't care about the separatists' proposals!»: quand Emmanuel Macron téléphonait à Vladimir Poutine pour éviter la guerre en Ukraine «, franceinfo / AFP, 25 June 2022 (https://www.francetvinfo.fr/monde/europe/manifestations-en-ukraine/on-s-en-fout-des-propositions-des-separatistes-quand-emmanuel-macron-telephonait-a-vladimir-poutine-pour-eviter-la-guerre-en-ukraine_5220382.html) declaring «We don't care about the separatists' proposals», Emmanuel Macron was not aware of the content of the Minsk Agreements mentioned during the conversation and for which he was supposed to be the guarantor! For the very purpose of the agreements was to force Kiev to enter into a dialogue with the autonomist republics. It was therefore precisely their proposals that Zelensky was supposed to hear, but which he refused to do.

On 17 October 2021, faced with the deceitful declarations of French diplomacy, Sergei Lavrov, Russian Minister of Foreign Affairs, decided to publish the diplomatic correspondence on the discussions in progress. This procedure, unusual in diplomatic practice, has the merit of highlighting Western insincerity. Indeed, we discover that France and Germany refuse to mention an «internal conflict in Ukraine» and reject the idea of «establishing a direct dialogue between Kiev, Donetsk and Lugansk».

As early as 2014, the Ukrainian government stopped all economic aid, funding (for the reconstruction of cities and infrastructure, restoration of services, etc.), payment of social benefits (pensions, allowances, etc.) and banned all banking activity in the autonomous areas.

This is why the Minsk Agreements provide for Kiev to restore these services (Article 8) with the help of Paris and Berlin. But since Kiev refuses to talk to representatives of the Donbass and neither France nor Germany has played its part in encouraging Ukraine to fulfil its obligations, nothing has been done. Nature abhors a vacuum, so the Russian government took steps to help the people of Donbass. On 15 December 2014, it created the «Interdepartmental Commission for the Provision of Humanitarian Aid to the Affected Areas in the Southeast of the Donetsk and Luhansk Regions». Thus, gradually, Russian companies and banks are now providing the services that Kiev no longer provides.

Furthermore, without sources of income, pensioners and the needy no longer receive any assistance or pensions from the Ukrainian government. Therefore, on 24 April 2019, Vladimir Putin signed a decree allowing the issuance of Russian passports to Donbass residents, entitling them to social benefits from Russia.

While in 2015-2016 Ukraine was still buying heating coal from the Donbass republics, the Ukrainian government closed the borders and trade in 2017[216], pushing the Donbass population to trade goods with Russia. This led Vladimir Putin, on 15 November 2021, to issue a decree temporarily abolishing (until the resolution of the conflict between the «areas of the Donetsk and Luhansk regions of Ukraine on the basis of the Minsk Agreements») customs duties on certain products with the autonomist areas[217]. As for former President Poroshenko, who had authorised this trade with the autonomist republics in order to allow the population to keep warm, he was indicted for «treason» at the request of President Zelensky in early 2022[218]. So much for the democracy that Vladimir Putin fears.

The Ukrainian government has done with its own people exactly what the European Union is doing with Belarus or Russia:

---

216. "Donbas coal blockade: 5 things you need to know", Ukraine Crisis Media Center, 21 February 2017; Oleg Varfolomeyev, "Coal Smuggled From Ukraine's Occupied Donbas Ends up in Poland", The Jamestown Foundation, Eurasia Daily Monitor, Volume 14, No. 128, 12 October 2017

217.Decree of the President of the Russian Federation of 15/11/2021 No. 657 «On providing humanitarian support to the population of certain areas of the Donetsk and Lugansk regions of Ukraine» (http://ips.pravo.gov.ru:8080/default.aspx?pn=0001202111150030)

218.Andrew E. Kramer, «Court in Ukraine Declines Request to Arrest Former President», The New York Times, 19 January 2022

it has driven them into the arms of their enemy. A child would see that this strategy is sterile, but it is largely maintained by France and Germany, which refuse to encourage Ukraine to implement the Minsk Agreements, as the interview with François Hollande shows. As Caroline Roux rightly says, it is a question of «countering Vladimir Putin»[219], not of finding a solution to the conflict.

For the Ukrainian government, the issue is not the improvement of the situation in Donbass, nor the well-being of its population, but the country's entry into NATO. This is why it invokes a terrorist situation, refuses to talk to the representatives of the autonomous republics of Donetsk and Luhansk and maintains the fiction of external aggression from Russia.

For all these reasons, the United States is beginning to see Ukraine as an increasingly troublesome partner, which could create a major crisis in Europe and permanently seal the alliance between Russia and China, its main rival. It is perhaps no coincidence that Ukraine is the main country targeted by the Pandora Papers, which are suspected to have originated from US intelligence services. But here again, Western propaganda prefers to focus on Russia. This is the case of Le Soir, in Belgium, which offers us a caricatural article[220]. One should not highlight the fact that one supports a state that does not respect human rights or the rule of law...

On the other hand, the West is not comfortable with a Mayan revolution that would be rejected by a significant part of the population, and is not comfortable with the defeat of Ukrainian forces, advised by NATO military. Blaming this situation on a military

219.Caroline Roux in the programme «C dans l'air» of 17 October 2021 («Poutine, maître du jeu #cdanslair 17.10.2021», France 5/YouTube, 18 October 2021) (1h00'33")

220.»Russia, Czech Republic, Chile... the many reactions to the Pandora Papers», lesoir.be, 4 October 2021

intervention by Russia is a convenient solution. For Ukraine, this external threat is a way of justifying its membership of NATO. This is why, since 2014, the Western strategy has been to consider Russia as one of the parties to the conflict in Donbass. This is a dialogue of the deaf, which explains why the negotiations of the Minsk Agreements were so long and laborious.

The central element preventing the implementation of the Minsk Agreements is the belief - widespread in France - that they «put an end to a war that had started between Russia and Ukraine», as Pascal Boniface says on his YouTube channel[221] and on France 5[222]. This is disinformation based on the allegation - never verified and never explained - that Russia had attacked Ukraine. Throughout the Ukrainian crisis of 2021-2022, there were stationings of military equipment on Russian territory, but no images of Russian troops in the Donbass for years. Therefore, one only has to read the text of the agreements to see that Russia is not mentioned.

As Pascal Boniface rightly notes, France and Germany played a leading role in the genesis of the Minsk Agreements, but they are now marginalised[223], as they put a lot of bad faith into helping Ukraine implement them. It is not surprising, therefore, that Vladimir Putin feels he is wasting time with partners who are not playing their part and that he prefers to «talk to God and not to his saints». Thus, if Putin addresses the American president directly, it is not because he hates Europe (as Marion Van Renterghem, a

221.»Russia/United States: Europe is not at the negotiating table, it is on the menu», Pascal Boniface/YouTube, 10 January 2022

222.Pascal Boniface in the programme «C dans l'air» on 25 January («Ukraine: Russian or American one-upmanship? #cdanslair 25.01.2022», France 5/YouTube, 26 January 2022 (1h02'08")

223.Pascal Boniface in the programme «C dans l'air» on 25 January («Ukraine: Russian or American one-upmanship? #cdanslair 25.01.2022», France 5/YouTube, 26 January 2022 (38'45")

columnist for L'Express, claims[224]), but simply because Europeans are not playing the role they claim.

One wonders whether French diplomats have read the Minsk Agreements. Apparently, it was after his telephone conversation with Vladimir Putin on 27 January 2022 that Emmanuel Macron realised his mistake and started working on a common position with Germany, which should have been done 7 years ago! Because between the end of 2021 and the beginning of 2022, no effort is made on the diplomatic level beyond visits that are more like posturing than negotiations.

It is to mask their weakness that Ukraine and France are trying to substitute the Minsk Agreements with the «Normandy format», which consists of the meeting of the German, French, Russian and Ukrainian heads of state. But we are talking about two different things. The «Normandy format» appeared fortuitously in 2014, on the occasion of the commemoration ceremonies of the June 1944 landings, and was envisaged as an instrument for monitoring the agreements, not for redoing the rules that Ukraine had not respected. They are therefore two different things: the Minsk Agreements are a way to resolve the conflict, while the «Normandy format» is only a means to enforce these agreements.

On 8 February 2022, President Macron is on an official visit to Kiev. According to Ukrainian MP Murayev, he expects Zelensky to guarantee that the situation in Donbass will not be resolved by force. But against all odds Zelensky will not give any guarantees. And for good reason: he is preparing an offensive against the autonomous republics.

224.Marion Van Renterghem in the programme «C dans l'air» of 19 January 2022 («Ukraine: can war be avoided? #cdanslair 19.01.2022», France 5/YouTube, 20 January 2022 (9'35")

The Minsk Agreements were intended to end the conflict in Donbass by granting autonomous status to the self-proclaimed republics, in order to guarantee their cultural specificities. In 2022, in order to justify the fact that Ukraine never even initiated a process of implementation, it is explained that Ukraine was «forced» to sign them, that it was a «diktat» from Moscow, that these agreements were aimed at endangering the Ukrainian state structure, or that their implementation had to be initiated by Moscow. This is simply not true.

Even today, official French and European rhetoric still considers Russia to be an actor in the conflict. It is the obsession with Russia's direct involvement that has led France and Germany to want to negotiate the Minsk Agreements with Vladimir Putin.

Even François Hollande participated in the genesis of these agreements by being convinced that Russian troops were in the Donbass[225]. Clearly, he has not understood the nature of these agreements. For neither Minsk I (5 and 19 September 2014) nor Minsk II (12 February 2015) involve Russia. Minsk I is an agreement in principle - accepted by «representatives of certain areas of the Donetsk and Luhansk regions» - and Minsk II takes up the elements of Minsk I and adds certain modalities of implementation, which are set out in a UN resolution (17 February 2015).

Moreover, on France 5, he uses the term «separatists»[226], a term widely used by Ukrainian propaganda, neo-Nazis and the militant far-right, alternating with «independentists»[227]. This is

225.Programme «C dans l'air» of 17 October 2021 («Poutine, maître du jeu #cdanslair 17.10.2021», France 5/YouTube, 18 October 2021) (1h02'43")

226.François Hollande in the programme «C dans l'air» of 17 October 2021 («Poutine, maître du jeu #cdanslair 17.10.2021», France 5/YouTube, 18 October 2021)

227.Pascal Boniface in «Explain to me... The situation in Ukraine», YouTube, 31 October 2019

not true, and Hollande should know this as he was one of the negotiators of the Minsk Agreements.

As the National Review puts it:

> *Although Ukrainian President Volodymyr Zelensky came forward to find a solution to the conflict with Russia, he could not get Ukraine to implement Minsk II. He faced fierce objections from Ukraine's far-right nationalist militias on the one hand, and from international foreign policy and press circles on the other. It turned out that no one was prepared to help Ukraine end the conflict. Or to help its president overcome ultra-nationalist resistance to do so*[228].

In other words, the Western guarantors of Ukraine (France and Germany) and our Russia-obsessed media have done the work of the Ukrainian far right[229].

228.Michael Brendan Dougherty, 'How to Lose Big in Ukraine', National Review, 24 June 2022 (https://www.nationalreview.com/2022/06/how-to-lose-big-in-ukraine/)

229.Andrian Prokip, «Implementing the Minsk Agreements Would Pose a Russian Trojan Horse for Ukraine, but There Is a Third Way», The Wilson Center, 7 December 2021 (https://www.wilsoncenter.org/blog-post/implementing-minsk-agreements-would-pose-russian-trojan-horse-ukraine-there-third-way)

3. The forces at work

3.1.The Ukrainian armed forces

3.1.1.Unrest in the Ukrainian armed forces

The overthrow of power by the ultra-nationalists in 2014 is not supported by the entire Ukrainian people. The revolutionaries came from the western part of Ukraine and by far do not represent the whole population. After the decisions of 23 February 2014 on official languages, rebellions broke out throughout the south of the country. The Ukrainian army was sent in to restore order and the situation became more violent. The army was largely composed of Russian speakers, who were torn between their duty as soldiers and their loyalty to their community, whose demands they shared. The repression of the demonstrations was not carried out willingly by the soldiers, who then tried to escape recruitment, committed suicide at the front or deserted to the rebels. The task of the armed forces is virtually impossible.

Moreover, the Ukrainian army, which has been made up of professionals since 2013, does not have enough manpower to respond to the situation. It is undermined by the corruption of its cadres and no longer enjoys the support of the population. According to a British Home Office report[230], during the March-April 2014 recall of reservists, 70% did not show up for the first session, 80% for the second, 90% for the third and 95% for the fourth.

On 1 May 2014, the new government ordered the conscription of young people between the ages of 18 and 25 in all parts of the country, including the southern regions[231]. Desertions to the rebel regions are becoming increasingly common. The problem became so serious that the Ukrainian parliament passed a law allowing officers to use their weapons against their men if they tried to desert[232]. In May 2022, an amendment to this law was proposed to the Rada[233], which called for the deletion of the phrase «without causing death». The proposal triggered deep indignation on social networks and was withdrawn[234]. But it shows that the same causes produce the same effects: Ukrainian conduct has only limited popular support and Western talk of Ukrainians' willingness to defend themselves is wishful thinking. Yet the proposal did not really change the existing legislation. Indeed, commanders are allowed to use their weapons «to stop a criminal offence, if it is impossible to stop it in any other way».

---

230. https://www.justice.gov/eoir/page/file/1008261/download

231.»Ukraine Enacts Compulsory Military Draft,» NBC News, 1er May 2014 (https://www.nbcnews.com/storyline/ukraine-crisis/ukraine-enacts-compulsory-military-draft-n94906)

232.Damien Sharkov, «Ukraine Passes Law Allowing Military to Shoot Deserters», Newsweek, 6 February 2015 (https://www.newsweek.com/ukraine-passes-law-shoot-deserters-304911)

233. https://itd.rada.gov.ua/billInfo/Bills/Card/39562

234.»The Rada will withdraw the bill on the murder of deserters», The News 24, 24 May 2022 (https://then24com/2022/05/24/the-rada-will-withdraw-the-bill-on-the-murder-of-deserters/)

In combat situations, according to the code of military discipline, these offences are: disobedience, resistance or threat to a leader, violence and desertion[235].

In October-November 2017, 70% of conscripts did not show up for the «Autumn 2017» recall campaign[236]. This is without counting suicides[237] and desertions[238] (often to the benefit of autonomists), which reach up to 30% of the workforce in the ATO area. Young Ukrainians refuse to fight in the Donbass and prefer to emigrate, thus contributing to the country's demographic deficit.

In October 2018, Ukraine's Chief Military Prosecutor Anatoly Matios stated that after four years of war Ukraine has lost 2,700 men out of combat in the Donbass: 891 due to illnesses, 318 in road accidents, 177 in other accidents, 175 by poisoning (alcohol, drugs), 172 as a result of careless handling of weapons, 101 as a result of breaches of security regulations, 228 due to murder and 615 by suicide[239]. In short, the situation is getting worse: the regular army is demoralised, deserters are numerous, young people refuse to attend recruitment sessions. As for the general staff, it was not prepared for such a situation, which was degrading to the benefit of the insurgents.

235.Anna StechenkoAnna Stechenko & Irina GamaliyIrina Gamaliy, «З Верховної Ради відкликали законопроєкт про розстріл дезертирів», lb.ua, 24 May 2022 (https://lb.ua/pravo/2022/05/24/517817_z_verhovnoi_radi_vidklikali.html)

236.»ВСУ заявили о 70% неявки во время осеннего призыва», ipress.ua, 13 December 2017 (https://ipress.ua/ru/news/v_vsu_zayavyly_o_70_neyavky_vo_vremya_osennego_pryziva_237367.html)

237.Mikhail Klikushin, «Why Are So Many Ukrainian Soldiers Committing Suicide?», The Observer, 30 June 2017 (https://observer.com/2017/06/ukraine-war-soldiers-suicide/)

238.Office français de protection des réfugiés et apatrides (OFPRA), Fact Finding Mission Report - Ukraine, May 2017, (https://www.refworld.org/docid/593a581b4.html) [accessed 24 May 2022]

239.»Названы небоевые потери ВСУ на Донбассе», vesti.ua, 27 October 2018 (https://vesti.ua/strana/309880-nazvany-neboevye-poteri-vsu-na-donbasse)

To deal with this disastrous situation, the Ukrainian authorities have a two-pronged approach:

- Requesting NATO's help in upgrading military careers to encourage young people to enlist. This is also the context in which I have been involved with Ukraine. The aim is to revitalise the Ukrainian army by making it more attractive. But this is a long-term activity, which does not allow us to respond to the urgency of the situation.
- Integrate the paramilitary formations of the extreme right-wing parties, considered more reliable and determined, into the armed forces. This is a short-term solution, adapted to the emergency of the moment.

3.1.2. The use of paramilitaries

In order to respond to the rising tension in the south of the country, the government decided to formalise the use of the ultra-nationalist and neo-Nazi far-right militias, which had made the Maidan events a success: they are ideologically more robust, more determined and more combative.

A series of volunteer units financed by oligarchs, such as Igor Kolomoyski (who would later promote the artistic and then political career of Volodymyr Zelensky), were formed, such as the battalions AÏDAR, AZOV, DNIEPR-1, DNIEPR-2 and DONBASS.

The problem is that these fanatical troops run the risk of getting out of control and taking on their own momentum[240]. This is what will happen, and it will take the help of our 'experts' and

240.Shaun Walker, «AZOV fighters are Ukraine's greatest weapon and may be its greatest threat», The Guardian, 10 September 2014 (https://www.theguardian.com/world/2014/sep/10azov-far-right-fighters-ukraine-neo-nazis)

other 'journalists' to whitewash the image of these unscrupulous troops.

The Russian offensive of February 2022 showed that the Ukrainian resistance is mainly carried by ultra-nationalist and neo-Nazi militias, including AZOV, AIDAR, KRAKEN and many others.

3.1.3. The role of volunteers

In France, more than in the rest of the world, the struggle of foreign volunteers in Ukraine evokes memories of the International Brigades (IB) during the Spanish Civil War (1936-1937). At the time, the IBs attracted the cream of European and American intellectuals and journalism. Today, the situation is very different. The foreign volunteers are very often small «hooligans» looking for an opportunity to translate into reality what they have «experienced» on their video screens. They have no great political ideals, or even no political culture at all. Their motivation is to go and «smash some Russian». As for intellectuals and journalists, the Frank Kappa or Ernest Hemingway have long since disappeared. They prefer to castigate those who try to calm opinions, and encourage others to go and fight on the basis of rumours propagated by Zelensky's neo-Nazi allies, sitting comfortably in front of their computers.

On 25 January 2022, on the programme «C dans l'air», Pascal Boniface relayed Washington[241] by saying that in the event of an attack on Ukraine, Russia would face strong resistance and lose the war[242]. However, once we move beyond conjecture, the

241.Amy Mackinnon & Jack Detsch, «Ukraine Ready to Fight to 'Last Drop'», Foreign Policy, 8 December 2021

242.Pascal Boniface in the programme «C dans l'air» of 25 January 2022 («Ukraine: Russian or American one-upmanship? #cdanslair 25.01.2022', France 5/YouTube, 26 January 2022 (56'46")

reality seems different. From 3 to 11 December 2021, the Kyiv International Institute of Sociology (KIIS) surveyed Ukrainians' willingness to resist a Russian invasion. It appears that only 50.2% of Ukrainians would resist in some way, of which only 33.3% (16.6% of the population) would be willing to take up arms. The majority of these are in the 50-59 age group. Paradoxically, the least willing to take up arms are the 18-29 year olds, who usually constitute the lifeblood of armies[243]. This means that Ukraine has a problem, and that the lyrical rhetoric about Ukrainian resistance is a lie that feeds Western self-persuasion.

The Ukrainians have understood this. As in 2014, the lack of will to fight against Russia is pushing the Ukrainian government to resort to volunteers. This is why on 27 February - three days after the start of the Russian offensive - Volodymyr Zelensky ordered the creation of the International Legion for the Territorial Defence of Ukraine and invited Western volunteers to join it. The decision was enthusiastically welcomed by European countries[244], who allowed[245] their citizens to go and fight in Ukraine, and even encouraged them to do so[246].

243.»Will Ukrainians resist Russian intervention: results of a telephone survey conducted on December 3-11, 2021», kiis.com.ua, December 2021

244.Austin C. Doctor, «Making the Most of Foreign Volunteers in Ukraine», War on the Rocks, 7 March 2022 (https://warontherocks.com/2022/03/making-the-most-of-foreign-volunteers-in-ukraine/)

245.Florent Coury, «Why I'm fighting in Ukraine - a Frenchman explains», euobserver.com, 3 March 2022 (https://euobserver.com/rule-of-law/154473)

246.»Ukraine conflict: Liz Truss backs people from UK who want to fight», BBC News, 27 February 2022 (https://www.bbc.com/news/uk-60544838)

Soon enough, volunteers were pouring in from 52 countries[247] and soon reached 20,000, according to the Ukrainian Foreign Minister[248].

Western journalists - who do not venture into Russian-speaking areas - show us young Ukrainians determined to fight in the Lvov or Kiev region.

Encouraged by the media's portrayal of a defeated Russian army, many of these young people set off imagining that they are going - literally - on a hunting trip. However, once there, they are disillusioned. Numerous testimonies confirm those of two British doctors who went to Ukraine as volunteers[249]. They all show that these 'amateurs' often end up as 'cannon fodder' without having any real impact on the outcome of the conflict[250]. The experience of recent conflicts shows that the contribution of foreign fighters only increases its brutality and lethality[251].

In early March 2022, 450 Islamist fighters from Hayat Tahrir al-Sham (HTS), including 300 Syrians and French, Belgians, Chechens, Uighurs and Tunisians, joined the ranks of volunteers

---

247.Lisa Abend, «Meet the Foreign Volunteers Risking Their Lives to Defend Ukraine-and Europe», Time Magazine, 7 March 2022 (https://time.com/6155670/foreign-fighters-ukraine-europe/)

248.Jackie Salo, «20,000 foreign volunteers have signed up to fight in Ukraine», New York Post, 6 March 2022 (https://nypost.com/2022/03/06/20k-foreign-volunteers-signed-up-to-fight-in-ukraine-officials/)

249.Jack Hardy & Nataliya Vasilyeva, «They wanted us for cannon fodder, say British medical volunteers 'tricked' into fighting for Ukraine», The Telegraph, 16 March 2022 (https://www.telegraph.co.uk/world-news/2022/03/17/wanted-us-cannon-fodder-say-british-medical-volunteers-tricked/)

250.Mohammad Al-Kassim, «Impact of foreign fighters on war in Ukraine will be minimal, experts say», The Jerusalem Post, 16 March 2022 (https://www.jpost.com/middle-east/article-701412)

251.Naureen C. Fink & Colin P. Clarke, «Foreign Fighters Are Heading to Ukraine. That's A Moment for Worry', Politico, 10 March 2022 (https://www.politico.com/news/magazine/2022/03/10/foreign-fighters-are-heading-to-ukraine-thats-a-moment-for-worry-00016084)

in Ukraine[252]. They come from the Idlib region, an area controlled and protected by the Western coalition in Syria (and where two Islamic State leaders were killed by the Americans). Apparently, the SVR, the Russian intelligence service, had announced this arrival a few days earlier[253].

Symptomatically, the volunteer presented by RTBF on the 7.30 pm news of 8 March 2022 was an admirer of the «Corps Franc Wallonie», the Belgian volunteer structure committed to the Third Reich, illustrating the type of audience attracted to Ukraine. In the end, one has to ask who won more in this case: Ukraine or Belgium!

For Swiss politician Claude Ruey, who criticised one of my Facebook posts, «Ukrainian volunteers are republicans». This is not the view of the Anti-Defamation League (ADL), which fights hate and anti-Semitism, and which notes that these volunteers are overwhelmingly supremacists who «also rail against non-white refugees resettling in 'white' Europe and offer support to a Ukrainian military wing with neo-Nazi ties»[254], and that they tend to fuel extremism. As some democratic commentators note, the contribution of these volunteers only adds misery to misery, in order to satisfy small European elites[255] and not Ukraine itself[256].

252.»Hundreds of Al-Qaeda militants arrive in Ukraine from Syria», The Cradle, 8 March 2022 (https://thecradle.co/Article/news/7669)

253.»Russia warns Washington is sending ISIS fighters to Ukraine», The Cradle, 4 March 2022 (https://web.archive.org/web/20220305103229/https://www.thecradle.co/Article/news/7541)

254.»White Supremacists, Other Extremists Respond to Russian Invasion of Ukraine, adl.org, 3 March 2022 (https://www.adl.org/resources/blog/white-supremacists-other-extremists-respond-russian-invasion-ukraine)

255.Arta Moeini, «How Western elites exploit Ukraine», UnHerd, 5 March 2022 (https://unherd.com/2022/03/how-western-elites-exploit-ukraine/)

256.Ruth Pollard, «Are Foreign Fighters a Blessing or a Curse for Ukraine?», Bloomberg, 11 March 2022 (https://www.bloomberg.com/opinion/articles/2022-03-11/are-foreign-fighters-a-blessing-or-a-curse-for-ukraine-in-russia-s-invasion)

Moreover, a US Department of Homeland Security intelligence memo dated 7 March 2022 already expresses concern about the return of volunteers who have left to fight in Ukraine[257] :

> *Ukrainian nationalist groups, including the Azov Movement, are actively recruiting racially or ethnically motivated extremist white supremacists to join various battalions of neo-Nazi volunteers in the war against Russia.*

The peculiarity of the volunteer combatant formations is that they are not all under the command of the Ukrainian armed forces, which may lead to different rules of conduct.

In early March 2022, on the Ukrainian channel Channel 24, journalist Fakhrudin Sharafmal quoted Nazi war criminal Adolf Eichmann, who advocated fighting a people starting with its children:

> *The Ukrainian armed forces cannot kill Russian children because the law of war prohibits it, and it is prohibited by various conventions, including the Geneva Convention. But I am not a member of the Armed Forces of Ukraine. And when I have the opportunity to shoot down Russians, I will certainly do so. Since you call me a Nazi, I adhere to the doctrine of Adolf Eichmann, and I will do everything in my power to ensure that you and your children never live on this earth, so that you can feel what it is like to kill innocent civilians and bear all the pain and suffering.* [258]

257.US Department of Homeland Security, US Borders and Customs Protection, Intelligence Note, 7 March 2022 (Document IN-NER-22-2507017) (UNCLASSIFIED/LAW ENFORCEMENT SENSITIVE)

258. https://twitter.com/Intent_B/status/1503848996955168772

The next day, after reactions on social networks, he apologised on the same channel for comments dictated by emotion[259]. In addition to the choice of reference, which seems to contradict a republican ideal, his remarks illustrate an essential problem posed by the use of volunteer combatants.

Figure 8 - Fakhrudin Sharafmal's statements on Ukrainian television went viral on social networks but were strangely forgotten by the Western mainstream media. Finally, the real difference with his Western counterparts is that he apologised.

As can be seen, the point of paramilitary forces is that - according to the Ukrainians - they are not subject to the same rules as the armed forces. Thanks to their blind support, the West accepts the war crimes committed on the Ukrainian side.

From May 2022, when the pressure of the Russian coalition was strong and Ukrainian regular units were surrendering in large numbers, volunteer units were used to force them to fight and to hunt down deserters. They play the same role as the political commissars in the Red Army during the Second World War, whose function was (also) to fight defeatism.

259. https://youtu.be/86HAMukxsjE

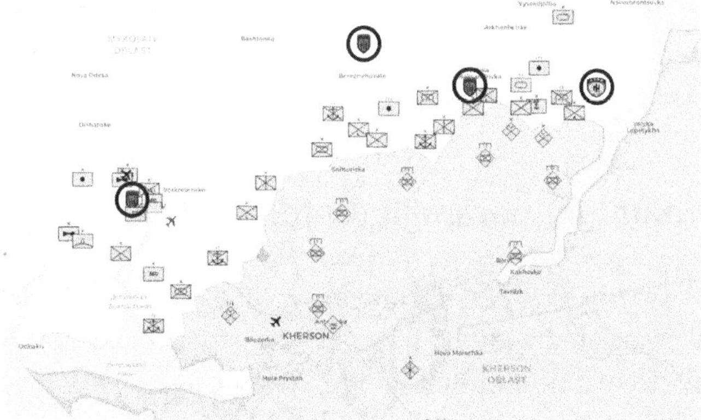

Figure 9 - Map of Ukrainian force deployment on 6 November 2022. After many unsuccessful attempts to break through to Kherson, the Ukrainian troops are demoralised. Under Western pressure Zelensky attempted a major offensive. In order to prevent formations from retreating, Ukraine deployed two companies and a battalion of the Ukrainian Volunteer Army (UDA) and a battalion of the AZOV brigade (black circles). The volunteers are tasked with fighting any units that attempt to withdraw. [Source: https ://militaryland.net/maps/deployment-map/].

3.1.4.National resistance

The forces leading the national resistance in Ukraine are of four kinds:

- the territorial defence troops of the Ministry of Defence (TerOborona);
- the territorial defence troops of the Ministry of the Interior, which include the National Guard units;
- independent volunteer formations, such as the Ukrainian Volunteer Army (UDA); and
- the fighters from the population, who fight independently at the local level in areas occupied by the Russian-speaking coalition forces.

The forces in the areas occupied by the Russian-speaking coalition are coordinated by the Special Operations Command of the Ukrainian armed forces.

3.2.Voluntary paramilitary forces

To varying degrees, Ukrainian volunteer paramilitary units are all associated with the far right. In Europe, the demonisation of sovereignist or anti-immigration parties has slowly made the notion of the 'far right' meaningless. What we mean here by this term has almost no connection with European parliamentary political parties. We are talking about a much deeper movement, whose nationalism has an ethnic dimension and which has grown alarmingly strong in recent years, not least because of immigration from the southern hemisphere. This is the case of Aube Dorée in Greece and Casapound in Italy.

Répartition des formations volontaires dans les forces armées ukrainiennes
(Liste non exhaustive)

Forces armées d'Ukraine
Forces du ministère de l'Intérieur
Forces du ministère de la Défense
Garde Nationale
Forces spéciales de la Milice (Police)
Forces de la Défense territoriale
Formations de l'armée ukrainienne
Formations indépendantes

Figure 10 - The integration of volunteer forces from political movements with different histories and ambitions has led to a very fluid organisation with sometimes unclear boundaries. The result was unclear subordinations that led to abuses and war crimes.

The following voluntary groups or movements share ideologies rooted in pre-war fascism and radical neo-Nazi nationalism. They all have military representation in the Ukrainian conflict.

3.2.1.Ukrainian National Assembly - Ukrainian National Self-Defence (UNA-UNSO)) (Українська Національна Асамьлея-Українська Наробна Самооборона - УНА-УНСо)

Figure 11 - UNA-UNSO logo, which uses the colour code of extreme right-wing nationalist movements: red and black.

UNA-UNSO (Українська Національна Асамьлея-Українська Наробна Самооборона (-УНА-УНСо) is one of the organizations-parent organisations of Ukrainian nationalism and the ultra-nationalist movements derived from it. It is an extreme right-wing nationalist paramilitary group mainly active in western Ukraine. It originated at the first conference of the Organisation of Ukrainian Nationalists (OUN) in Vienna on 3 February 1929. The OUN was then an umbrella organisation of various Ukrainian nationalist movements. It was the mainstay of the anti-communist resistance in Ukraine during the Second World War until the 1960s.

In 1991, the UNA-UNSO was reborn with the independence of Ukraine, from the Ukrainian National Assembly created on 30 June 1990.

During the civil war in Moldova (Transnistria) (2 March - 21 July 1992) UNA-UNSO fighters were engaged alongside the

Transnistrian army. Strongly anti-Russian, the UNA-UNSO also sent contingents to fight against Russia during the Chechen and Abkhazian (Georgian) wars in the 1990s[260].

It is formed as a political party. On 22 May 2014, it was renamed «Praviy Sektor» (Right Sector) and became a new party led by Dmitro Yarosh. On 7 April 2015, UNA-UNSO decided to return to the political scene, and formed a new party.

Today, it provides contingents of volunteers who form separate units, integrated into the Praviy Sektor forces

3.2.2.Freedom (Свобода - Svoboda)

Figure 12 - Svoboda logo from 1991 to 2003

Svoboda is a Ukrainian nationalist party established in 1991 as the Social-Nationalist Party of Ukraine (SNPU). It is conceived as a federation of various patriotic groups and associations of students and Afghanistan veterans. Originally, the party does not accept atheists or ex-communist party members. It is pan-Ukrainian in outlook and inspired by the works of Ukrainian nationalist Yaroslav Stetska.

260. https://warriors.fandom.com/ru/wiki/УНА-УНСО

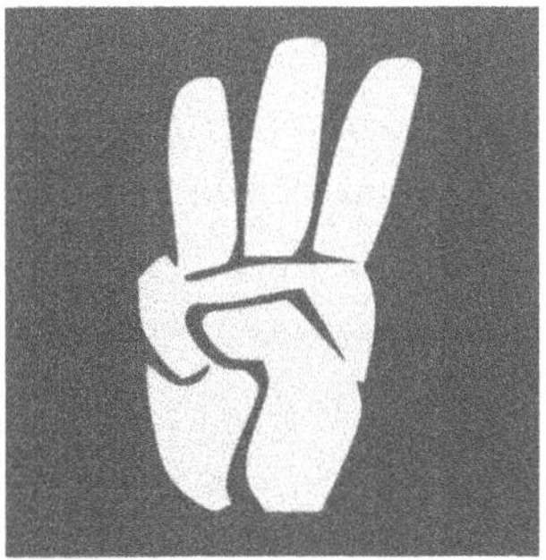

Figure 13 - Svoboda logo from 2003. The three fingers symbolise the trident (trizub), which is the Ukrainian national emblem.

In addition to its name - which evokes 'National Socialism' - the party quickly acquired a reputation associated with antisemitism and fascism. It claims the heritage of Stepan Bandera. In the second half of the 1990s, the party incorporated members of skinhead and similar groups, which damaged its reputation.

In 1993, the party organised «National Security Detachments» which paraded in black or camouflaged uniforms.

Politically, the party ran in regional parliamentary elections and won 10% of the vote in Lviv in 1994. In 1998, the election of its leader Oleh Tyahnybok to the Ukrainian Parliament led the party to moderate its positions.

In 1999, the PSNU activated a paramilitary component called Patriots of Ukraine. In 2004, it was officially disbanded, but remained within the «Right Sector», which brings together the extreme Ukrainian right.

On 12 December 2012, the European Parliament adopted a resolution on the situation in Ukraine which

> *Is concerned about the rise in nationalist sentiment in Ukraine, which has resulted in support for the «Svoboda»*

party, which is one of the two new parties entering the Verkhovna Rada; recalls that racist, anti-Semitic and xenophobic views are contrary to the fundamental values and principles of the European Union and therefore calls on the democratic parties in the Verkhovna Rada not to associate themselves with that party, nor to endorse or form a coalition with it [261]

In December 2013, Senator John McCain met with Svoboda party leader Oleh Tyahnybok and promised him financial support for the AZOV battalion, which was then the spearhead of the right-nationalist movement[262]. Ironically, after McCain's death in 2018, the Washington Post paid tribute to the 'champion of human rights' with a photo showing him alongside Tyahnybok[263], who had been refused entry to the United States in June 2013... for anti-Semitism[264] !

The Svoboda logo uses the «Wolfsangel» (hook) rune widely used in Nazi symbolism, inverted to form the «Idea of Nation» logo.

The Svoboda group advocates the recognition of the former combatants of the 14th Waffen SS Grenadier Division «Galicia», which was mainly composed of Ukrainian volunteer fighters, as national heroes. It should be recalled here that in addition to its support for the Third Reich during the war, Ukraine was the scene of fierce anti-communist resistance in the post-war years until the early 1960s, with the support of the Western secret services. In addition to regular

261.European Parliament resolution of 13 December 2012 on the situation in Ukraine (2012/2889(RSP))

262.Laurent Brayard, «Nazis in Ukraine: from the Nachtigall battalion to the Azov battalion», arretsurinfo.ch, 10 March 2015

263. Jennifer Rubin, «The human rights community lost a champion», The Washington Post, 27 August 2018

264. «Ultranationalist Ukrainian political party leaders banned from U.S.», Jewish Telegraphic Agency, 27 June 2013

contacts with members of the German neo-Nazi party (NPD), Svoboda received support from German authorities, including the German Development Cooperation (GIZ).[265] These factors led to the use of the term «fascist» by the pro-Russian community to describe the insurgents in Maidan Square in Kiev in November 2013-February 2014.

By adopting a posture of confrontation with Russia, the European Union has not only relayed the official discourse of the new Ukrainian authorities, but has also been led to support movements such as Svoboda[266]. Just as ironically, the French intellectual Bernard Henri-Lévy has become a defender of these neo-Nazi movements by following the same dynamic.

3.2.3.Patriot of Ukraine (Патріóт Украї́ни - *Patriot Ukraïni)*

Figure 14 - Logo of the Patriots of Ukraine

The Patriots of Ukraine (PU) is an ultra-nationalist Ukrainian organisation created in 2005 and officially registered on 17 January 2006. It was led by Andriy Biletsky. Its epicentre

265.Der Spiegel, No. 12/2014, 17 March 2014

266. http://www.euractiv.com/sections/global-europe/eus-acceptance-ukraines-radical-svoboda-party-shameful-301110

is in Kharkov, but it is also present in Kyiv, Zaporijia, Jytomyr and Poltava.

The PUs fight for a white race and a racially homogeneous 'white Europe'. Affiliated with the Ukrainian social-nationalist party, they aspire to national greatness and social justice. The PU advocates an alternative to democracy through natiocracy, according to the principles established by Nicholas Stsiborsky in the 1930s. These principles call for national solidarity (without social class or party), personal responsibility at all levels, as well as a social hierarchy based on quality and discipline, social control, self-management and self-governance.

Figure 15 - A variant of its logo takes the 'Wolfsangel' theme of the Svoboda party and transforms it into the Cyrillic letters P and U.

Since 2005, the PUs have been involved in «strong-arm» actions to secure political or cultural events with a political focus. The PUs supported Serbia during the declaration of independence of Kosovo.

3.2.4. Black Body (Чорний Корпус)

Figure 16 - Black Body logo

Formed in 2014 by activists from the AutoMaidan movement and the Patriots of Ukraine, this small formation of less than a hundred men at first quickly became a battalion called the «Black Corps».

The Black Corps operated mainly in the Kharkov and Mariupol sectors. Its fighters are hooded and dressed in black fatigues. Equipped with light weapons, they carry out raids against the Russian-speaking autonomists of the region.

The group has not been formally disbanded and appears to have merged with the AZOV group, which was formed shortly afterwards. In 2022, fighters wearing the Black Corps insignia are fighting alongside the AZOV formations, apparently in separate combat units.

3.2.5. Trident (Тризуб - ***Trizub)***

Figure 17 - The Trizub (Trident) is the Ukrainian national symbol. It is also the name of a movement inspired by the nationalist movements of the Second World War.

Also known as the All-Ukrainian Organization Trident in the name of Stepan Bandera - Всеукраїнська організація "Тризуб" імені Степана Бандери) this far-right paramilitary group is mainly active in the western part of the country and in Kiev. It was founded in 1993 by the Congress of Ukrainian Nationalists, itself composed of members of the fiercely anti-Russian OUN-B, which had collaborated extensively with the Third Reich during the Second World War and openly claims to be a legacy of Stepan Bandera.

The number of its fighters is not precisely known. They are integrated into the Ukrainian Volunteer Corps (DUK) of the Praviy Sektor, where they form small combat units.

3.2.6. *Right Sector* (Прáвий сéктор - ***Praviy Sektor***)

Figure 18 - Right Sector logo. It features the trident (Trizub), the Ukrainian national symbol, with the sword on a red and black background. It is surrounded by a string of Odal runes, once used as a symbol of the Third Reich's 'Office for Race and Settlement', whose function was to ensure the racial purity of SS members.

Praviy Sektor, which emerged in November 2013 during the Euromaidan events that led to the overthrow of Viktor Yanukovych's government, is a far-right political-military movement that is a kind of rival to the AZOV movement. Like other Ukrainian ultra-nationalist movements, it claims the spiritual and political heritage of Stepan Bandera. It was created as an umbrella organisation for ultra-nationalist groups of the Ukrainian right.

The backbone of the movement is its military element, the Ukrainian Volunteer Corps (Добровольчий Український Корпус) (DUK). Created on 17 July 2014, it is composed of combat and reserve units, distributed throughout in each oblast of the Ukrainian territory. Unlike the AZOV movement, DUK troops are not integrated into Ukrainian government structures.

The operational structure (order of battle) of the Praviy Sektor movement is not well known, largely because it evolves rapidly according to the needs of the war. It is an ideological reference for other neo-Nazi and ultra-nationalist groups. In its active operational structure, it incorporates armed groups from Svoboda, Trizub, Ukrainian National Assembly - Ukrainian National Self-Defence, Patriots of Ukraine, National Social Assembly, White Hammer and Carpathian Sich.

The Western press presents Secteur Droit as a nationalist grouping whose National Socialist intellectual heritage is minimised. Its anti-Semitic actions, for example, are largely ignored by our media.

Structure of the National Liberation Movement «Praviy Sektor

Mouvement de Libération Nationale

Corps des Volontaires Ukrainiens

Jeunesse de Droite

Parti Politique « Secteur Droit »

Service de Sécurité

Organe de propagande « Krila »

Figure 19 - Western media insist that it lost the parliamentary elections and is therefore not a force in Ukraine. In reality, it is a force that operates outside the country's political institutions and is one of the largest paramilitary forces in the country, but it does not appear on any official organisation chart.

The armed wing of Praviy Sektor is the Ukrainian Volunteer Corps (DUK) (Добровольчий Український Корпус - ДУК - Dobrovolchiy Ukraïnskiy Korpus). It is a militia whose purpose is to participate in the defence of the territorial integrity of Ukraine and its independence.

Figure 20 - Ukrainian Volunteer Corps (DUK) badge

The DUK defines itself as a «political and social movement» and not as the combat organ of a party. However, its mission, membership profile and structures are reminiscent of a military organisation. Its members must be over 18 years old and well trained.

Figure 21 - Deployment of DUK reserve companies. With the exception of the two self-proclaimed Donbass republics, every oblast in Ukraine has its own Praviy Sektor volunteer units. In addition to these territorial units, there are combat battalions.

3.2.7. Ukrainian Volunteer Army (Українська добровольча армія) ***(UDA)***

Figure 22 - Ukrainian Volunteer Army (UDA) badge. It follows the graphic codes of Praviy Sektor, but is a separate structure.

The Ukrainian Volunteer Army (UDA) was created by Dmytro Yarosh in December 2015, after he left the National Liberation Movement Praviy Sektor (PS). Removed from the leadership of the SP by some radical elements of the movement, he created a new political movement, ACTION, as well as the UDA, on the basis of the 5th and 8th infantry battalions on the one hand, and the medical battalion of the SP's Ukrainian Volunteer Corps (DUK) on the other.

Figure 23 - DUK intelligence service.

The UDA is headed by Dmytro Yarosh, placed by Russia on the wanted terrorist list for inciting Chechen Islamist movements to carry out terrorist actions against Russia during the Euromaidan in 2014. At the beginning of November 2021, he was appointed adviser to the commander-in-chief of the Ukrainian army. He resigned a month later to take over the command of the UDA. This international far-right militia is composed of Ukrainian and foreign volunteers. It is financed by the United States and some European countries. It is not part of the Ukrainian armed forces and operates autonomously, but coordinates its actions.

Summary structure of the Ukrainian Volunteer Army (UDA)

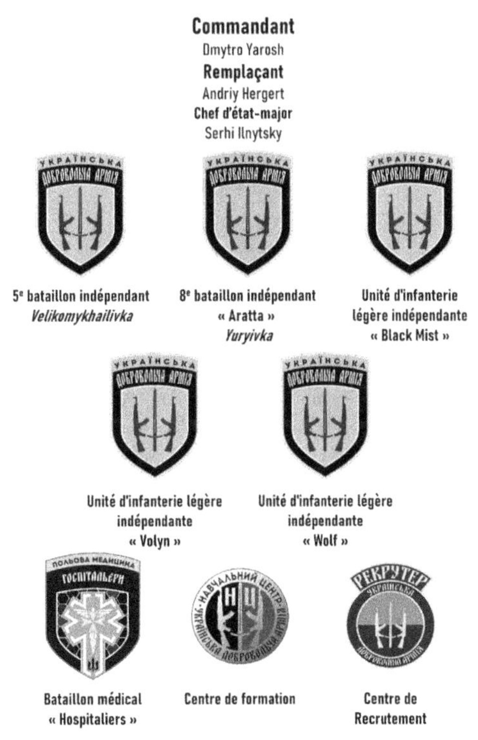

In 2015, unlike other far-right formations such as the AZOV units, the DUK refused to be legalised and enter the Ukrainian armed forces. The UDA units did the same. On 14 October 2018, the Ukrainian armed forces encounter coordination problems in the Donbass region. The Ministry of Defence therefore decides to exclude units that are not part of the armed forces from the front zone. The UDA therefore withdraws its battalions from the area of the anti-terrorist operation.

The UDA is mainly active in the west of the country and in Kiev, but its headquarters are located in Dnepropetrovsk (Dnipro), in the Russian-speaking part of the country. On 26 February 2022, Dmytro Yarosh announced that he had deployed three battalions (about 2,000 men) against the Russian attackers.

Figure 24 - The UDA's 'Jewish Company'. The UDA shares many extreme right-wing ideological elements with the Praviy Sektor, including the notion of ethnic distinction. It is not doctrinally antisemitic, which again demonstrates the ambiguous links between the far right and the Jewish community in Ukraine.

3.2.8. The AZOV Movement

Frequently mentioned in our media, AZOV is often reduced to a mere regiment, or even a battalion, by the pro-neo-Nazi, far-right, extremist-supremacist media. In reality, AZOV is a movement that includes :

- the Independent Special Purpose Detachment AZOV (armed branch);
- the National Corps (Natsionalnii Korpus) (political branch);
- the National Militia (Natsionalna Droujina) (police branch); and
- the Civil Corps (Tsyvilnyi Korpus «Azov») (propaganda branch).

The main components of the AZOV movement

Figure 25 - Often presented as a «regiment», AZOV is a much larger movement with branches throughout society.

3.2.8.1. The AZOV Special Purpose Independent Detachment (OZSP «AZOV»)

Figure 26 - Emblem of the battalion, regiment, and later OZSP AZOV. The change of logotype in 2015 corresponds to the idea of «denazifying» the unit, but it is not accompanied by any doctrinal change.

Created on 5 May 2014 in Berdiansk by Andriy Biletsky as the «Azov» Volunteer Battalion, from elements from the Patriots of Ukraine and Avtomaydan groups. It is integrated into the Special Police Patrol Service (BPSMOP) of the Ministry of the Interior. In 2008, Biletsky created the Social-National Assembly, another ultra-nationalist movement which he led until 2015.

On 17 September 2014, by order of the Ukrainian Minister of the Interior, the unit is reorganised and elevated to the rank of «AZOV special police regiment» of the Ministry of the Interior. On 11 November 2014, the regiment was transferred under the authority of the Ukrainian National Guard. It then fulfils the criteria of National Guard brigades. Although its strength is much larger than that of a regiment, the Western media still consider it a battalion. In May 2022, the surrender of nearly 2,500 of its fighters indicated that it was a formation larger than a brigade. It was probably to keep its size unclear that it was named the 'Independent Special Purpose Detachment AZOV' (OZSP AZOV) and referred to as 'Military Unit 3057' of the Ukrainian National Guard, the military unit number being a postal routing number used to conceal the actual designation of units. On 24 February 2022, two formations named «Special Operations Forces AZOV» (Сил Спеціальних Операцій АЗОВ) (SSO AZOV) in Kyiv and Kharkov were established.

It is a prestigious regiment that attracts Ukrainian and foreign volunteers. For example, Roman Protassevitch (arrested in Belarus after the RyanAir FR 4978 case, in May 2021) fought in the Donbass with the AZOV Regiment, in the Belarusian volunteer detachment PAGONIA, and was wounded in Shirokino in March 2015[267].

267.Oleksiy Rains, «Золоті мечі на шевронах ССО АЗОВ», censor.net, 30 May 2022 (https://censor.net/ru/blogs/3344770/zoloti_mechi_na_shevronah_sso_azov)

The OZSP «AZOV» was commanded by Andriy Biletsky (May-October 2014), Igor Mikhailenko (October 2014-August 2016), Maxim Zhorin (August 2016-September 2017), Denys Prokopenko (September 2017-May 2022) and Nadtochiy Nikita (since June 2022).

Figure 27 - Badge of the PAGONIA detachment of the AZOV regiment. It features the image of Kastous Kalinovski, a symbol of the struggle against Russia.

The symbolism of unity is based on the old Germanic rites used by the Third Reich. The most obvious is the Wolfsangel of the Svoboda party and the Patriots of Ukraine. Like the other runes, it is a much older symbol than Nazism. It is found on many emblems and coats of arms in northern Europe, but not in the Ukrainian tradition. The Wolfsangel is the rune of freedom and independence, a common thread in nationalist discourse in relation to Russia. This rune was the emblem of the 2nd SS Panzer Division that 'liberated' Kharkov from the Soviets in 1943. Here it is inverted to form the abbreviation of the 'Idea of the Nation', dear to the founders of the movement. The letter 'N' simultaneously becomes the rune of sacrifice. Among the symbols used by the Azov movement are the

«Black Sun», which is also the title of its magazine[268], and the rune of Odal, which evokes racial purity.

The OZSP AZOV is made up of Ukrainian and foreign volunteers from all countries, united by their extreme right-wing ideology. There are fighters of nineteen different nationalities, including French, Swiss and Americans.

The regiment has even been used by the government to eliminate opponents and journalists[269]. Already in 2014, the American magazine Newsweek stated that the AZOV militia was committing war crimes in Ukraine «in the style of the Islamic State»[270].

This is not a trivial phenomenon, as extremists trained and educated in this way could become a source of problems back home. In 2017, the FBI indicted four members of the AZOV regiment for training American far-right supremacist activists from the highly antisemitic Rise Above movement[271]. Despite several attempts by Congress to ban military aid to far-right militias, it was not until 2018 that the Pentagon stopped supporting the training of its fighters.

268.IK, «Баец атраду «Пагоня»: У выпадку ўварваньня мы будзем першымі, хто кінецца бараніць Беларусь», svaboda.org, 18 September 2015

269. pbs.twimg.com/media/E2UIHnIXsAAVSE7?format=jpg&name=large

270.»Баец атраду «Пагоня»: У выпадку ўварваньня мы будзем першымі, хто кінецца бараніць Беларусь», svaboda.org, September 18, 2015 (https://www.svaboda.org/a/27255566.html)

271. twitter.com\Volod_Ishchenko\status\1397509726641008643

Components of the AZOV

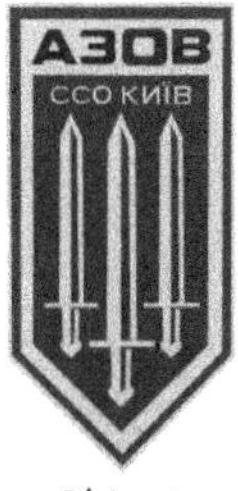

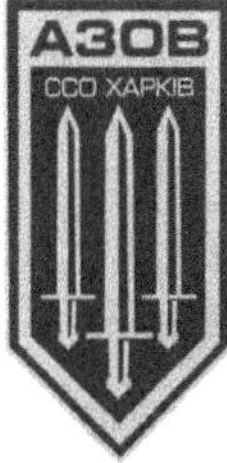

Figure 28 - Some units of the AZOV OZSP. The total number of units and personnel engaged under the AZOV banner is not known, but its numbers are far greater than those of the entrenched unit in Mariupol, which already numbered about 3,000. This is a much larger potential than the media reports, which seek to discredit the need to 'denazify' the Ukrainian threat to the people of Donbass.

In mid-May 2022, in order to quickly detect the most fanatical elements among the 2,500 or so AZOV fighters who surrendered in Mariupol, the Russian military stripped them naked. They look for Nazi-inspired tattoos. These images went around the world, lending credence to the Russian discourse that the Ukrainians were using neo-Nazi militants. A vast operation to 'whitewash' the image of Ukrainian paramilitaries is unleashed in our media.

For their part, the Ukrainians sought to smooth out the image of their elite units. On 24 May, new insignia appeared in Kiev, showing the three swords of Urzuf, an important place in Ukrainian nationalist mythology.

Figure 29 - Emblem of the AZOV units that appeared on 24 May 2022, depicting the three swords of Urzuf, in an attempt to soften the neo-Nazi image of the movement. Some saw this as a reminder of the Ukrainian national 'Trizub' (Trident).

The OZSP AZOV includes independent formations, such as the 226th reconnaissance-sabotage battalion 'KRAKEN', which operates in the Kharkov sector. This battalion alone is estimated to have about 1,800 men[272].

Figure 30 - Badge of the 226th Reconnaissance Sabotage Battalion KRAKEN, named after the mythical animal, and its sleeve badge.

272. https://archive.ph/mYUOU

3.2.8.2. National Corps (Natsionalnii Korpus)

Figure 31 - Logo of the National Corps of the AZOV movement.

The National Corps is the political branch of the AZOV movement. It was created on 21 December 2015, by Andriy Biletsky (founder of the AZOV battalion), but its existence materialised on 14 October 2016 through the merger of the groups «Chasni Spravi» and «Patriot Ukraïni». It is composed of former members of the AZOV battalion.

Its ideology is a combination of Ukrainian nationalism, economic nationalism, natiocracy and Euroscepticism.

The elements of his programme give the colour of his foreign policy:

2.3. Ukraine is the base of the Baltic-Black Sea Union of the new European unity. A new vector of Ukrainian geopolitics.

2.3.1. We feel part of European civilisation and do not want to join the Brussels bureaucracy. The priority of Ukrainian foreign policy is therefore to build a new community of European nations based on a harmonious combination of traditional values and innovative ideas.

2.3.2. The seed of a new European unity should be the construction of a community of countries located in the geopolitical space connecting the Baltic and Black Seas. It is with these countries that the Ukrainian state is building close and comprehensive relations (military, political, economic, energy, etc.).

3.2.8.3. National Militia (Natsionalna Droujina)

Figure 32 - Logo of the National Militia of the AZOV movement

The National Militia is the police branch of the AZOV movement. It is represented in all major cities in Ukraine. It is known for its heavy-handed actions against minorities, such as Roma and members of the LGBT community.

3.2.9. White Hammer (Білий Молот - Biliy Molot)

Figure 33 - Logo of the extreme right-wing militia Biliy Molot

This Ukrainian neo-Nazi group is closer to skinheads than to a political movement. It is driven more by anti-Russian sentiment than by a constructive project for Ukrainian society. Between November 2013 and February 2014, he took part in the events on Maidan Square in Kiev. He joined the Right Sector movement but was expelled in March 2014. Its leader, Vladislav Horanyn, an official of the new Ukrainian Ministry of the Interior, was at the time one of the cadres of the Ministry of Defence's AIDAR territorial defence battalion. Suspected of having participated in the murder of three policemen, he was arrested on 21 March 2014 and released on 4 April. On 18 June, he participated in an operation by the AIDAR battalion against autonomists in the town of Metalist, which ended in a complete fiasco.

3.2.10. Sich des Carpathes (Карпатська Січ - Karpatska Sich)

Figure 34 - Flags and emblems of the 'Sich des Carpathes' militia. The Germanic symbols of the radical right-wing and neo-Nazi international can be found alongside the Ukrainian national trident in its 1938-1939 version.

The «Carpathian Sich» (KS) was a Ukrainian nationalist organisation created in November 1938 by Stepan Rosokha, in order to resist Soviet control. It was then articulated in ten district commands with local sections and had its headquarters in Khust. Many of its members joined the German army during the Second World War.

In 2014, the group was resurrected with the events of Maïdan Square where it was engaged alongside ultra-nationalist and neo-Nazi militias. A volunteer battalion is formed under the command of Oleg Koutsne to fight the Russian-speaking rebellion in Donbass. Its members receive military training, but very few details are known about its organisation. The KS provides volunteers for the battalion, which is integrated into the Ukrainian armed forces.

Its doctrine is clearly associated with the radical far right, very close to the neo-Nazis. It is fiercely anti-European, advocates the emergence of a «European Man» and proclaims[273] :

> *We will not allow globalism, liberalism, capitalism, leftism, LGBT and femen activism and other types of perversions to peacefully exist and thrive in our land.*

The nightly meetings and ceremonies by torchlight are reminiscent of the rites of the SS of the Third Reich.

In 2022, the KS battalion was engaged in Irpin (near Butcha) and then in the Izyum sector in the west of the country. In June 2022, Kutsin was killed in a Russian strike on the command post near Dnepropetrovsk.

3.2.11.S14 (C14)

Figure 35 - Logo of the S14 movement.

The S14 is a movement present in many European countries. It is not specific to Ukraine. It is more neo-Nazi than nationalist and the American media The Atlantic Council calls it a «dangerous threat» to Ukraine.

273.Oleksiy Kuzmenko & Michael Colborne, «Ukrainian Far-Right Extremists Receive State Funds to Teach 'Patriotism',» Bellingcat, 16 July 2019.

It takes its name from a 14-word phrase: «We must ensure the existence of our people and a future for white children. According to the Anti-Defamation League (ADL) this slogan was created by David Lane, a member of the white supremacist group. It is based on the idea that the white race is destined to be overwhelmed by a «rising tide of colour» allegedly controlled and manipulated by the Jews.

He participated in the Mayan events and remains active in Ukraine. In 2018, it was receiving subsidies from the Ukrainian government for its «patriotic activities», although these often amounted to attacks on Roma settlements around Kiev. The group also sells its services to carry out strong-arm actions.

3.2.12. Misanthropic Division

Figure 36 - Flag of the Misanthropic Division.

The Misanthropic Division is more a movement than a defined group. Founded in Ukraine in 2013 by Russian and Ukrainian neo-Nazis, it campaigns for full independence for Ukraine, against the grip of Russia and the European Union. It has representatives in all Western countries. In February 2021, the German newspaper Die Zeit expressed concern about the collaboration between Ukrainian and German neo-Nazis. The latter were offering Ukrainian «fighters» rehabilitation stays in Saxony.

It campaigns for the defence of the 'white nation'. Its motto «Kill for Wotan» has nothing to do with the Norse god. Wotan stands for «Will of the Aryan Nation». Our media is very quiet about these antisemitic movements[274], which are targeting the Roma community[275] and LGBT[276] in Western Ukraine.

The Misanthropic Division is very close to the AZOV movement and is often described as one of its operational sections.

3.2.13. Tradition and Order (Традиція і - tsiya i Tradi - порядок ryadokol')

Figure 37 - Logo of the 'Tradition and Order' movement

«Tradition and Order» (TiP) is a far-right organisation founded in 2016 on the basis of the far-right group «Revanche», inspired by classical Italian fascism. Its members were associated with Mykola Kokhanivskyi's «OUN» battalion. After Euromaidan in 2014, its members of «Revanche» opposed the new government of Petro Poroshenko. In May 2015, several members of Revanche were arrested by the Ukrainian Security Service (SBU). TiP members are responsible for numerous attacks on the LGBT+

274.Damien Sharkov, «Ukrainian Nationalist Volunteers Committing 'ISIS-Style' War Crimes», Newsweek, 10 September 2014.

275.Tim Hume, «Far-Right Extremists Have Been Using Ukraine's War as a Training Ground. They're Returning Home,» Vice News, July 31, 2019

276. Max Blumenthal, "US-Funded Neo-Nazis in Ukraine Mentor US White Supremacists", consortiumnews.com, 17 November 2018

community, feminists and left-wing activists, against whom the organisation's activities are mainly directed. The head of the organisation until autumn 2021 was Bohdan Khodakovsky.

3.2.14.International Legion for Territorial Defence of Ukraine (Інтернаціональний легіон територіальної оборони України - ***Internatsionalny lehion terytorialnoï oborony Oukraïny)***

Figure 38 - Logo of the International Legion of Ukraine

The International Ukrainian Legion (Інтернаціональний легіон територіальної оборони України - Internatsionalny lehion terytorialnoi oborony Oukraïny) was established on 27 February 2022 by the Ukrainian government at the request of President Volodymyr Zelensky to fight the Russian invasion of the country. On 6 March 2022, Ukrainian Foreign Minister Dmytro Kuleba announced that more than 20,000 nationals[277] from 52 countries had already volunteered to fight in Ukraine[278].

277.Fredrick Kunkle & Serhii Korolchuk, «Ukraine's volunteer 'Kraken' unit takes the fight to the Russians», The Washington Post, 3 June 2022 (https://www.washingtonpost.com/world/2022/06/03/ukraine-kraken-volunteer-military-unit/)
278. https://nationalcorps.org/programm_nk/

3.2.14.1 Belarusian quota

Figure 39 - Emblem of the Belarusian Kastous Kalinovski Battalion (which became a regiment in May 2022) engaged on the side of Ukraine.

The creation of the Belarusian battalion within the Ukrainian Foreign Legion was announced on 9 March 2022. It is named after «Kastous Kalinovski», a hero of the fight against Russia in Poland. It has 200 to 300 volunteers in its ranks. It was officially formed on 25 March 2022 and engaged from 28 March in the Irpin-Butcha sector[279].

3.2.14.2. Canadian quota

Figure 40 - Canadian units in the International Legion: the Canadian Ukrainian Brigade and the Norman Brigade.

Canadians form one of the largest contingents in the Ukrainian Foreign Legion. The Canadian Ukrainian Brigade is reported to

279.Max Bearak, «A Belarusian battalion fights in Ukraine 'for both countries' freedom'», The Washington Post, 1er April 2022 (updated 26 April 2022) (https://www.washingtonpost.com/world/2022/04/01/ukraine-belarus-fighters-russia/)

have about 550 men[280], while the Norman Brigade is reported to have about 30 fighters[281]. Volunteers who returned to Canada reported the miserable conditions in which the foreigners fought. Often inexperienced, under-equipped, unfamiliar with the environment and poorly adapted to the local culture, they serve more as 'cannon fodder' for Ukrainian regular units[282].

3.2.14.3. Albanian contingent

Figure 41 - Emblem of the Albanian Third Position, whose militants are fighting in Ukraine. The 'Idea of Nation' symbol is characteristic of neo-Nazi and supremacist movements.

The Albanian Third Position (ATP) is the Albanian branch of a European neo-fascist movement. It is also present in France under the name «Troisième Voie». It advocates a left-wing approach on the economic and social level, and a very conservative approach

280.Tom Blackwell, «So many Canadian fighters in Ukraine, they have their own battalion, source says», National Post, 11 March 2022 (https://nationalpost.com/news/world/exclusive-so-many-canadian-fighters-in-ukraine-they-have-their-own-battalion-source-says)

281.Tom Blackwell, 'Incompetence or the realities of war? Turmoil for Canadian-led foreign battalion in Ukraine', National Post, 7 May 2022 (https://nationalpost.com/news/canada/turmoil-for-norman-brigade-canadian-led-foreign-battalion-in-ukraine)

282.Tom Blackwell, «Canadian infantry veteran enters 'living hell' in Ukraine to capture village from Russians», National Post, 5 April 2022 (updated 6 April 2022) (https://nationalpost.com/news/canada/living-hell-canadian-veteran-enters-chaotic-combat-in-ukraine-to-capture-village-from-russians)

on the societal level. It is a form of populism, very close to the fascism of the 1920s.

3.2.14.4 Russian contingent

Figure 42 - Insignia and blue and white flag (worn on the sleeve) of the 'Freedom of Russia' Legion.

The «Freedom of Russia» Legion is composed of Russian citizens opposed to the war against Ukraine. Its formation was announced in March 2022, and its creation was officially presented on 5 April 2022[283]. Its strength is not known, but it does not seem to have more than a few dozen fighters.

3.2.14.5. The Georgian National Legion

Figure 43 - Emblem of the Georgian National Legion

The Georgian National Legion is a formation of volunteer fighters whose members are part of the Georgian diaspora around

283.Amie Ferris-Rotman, 'The Russians Fighting Putin in Ukraine', Time Magazine, 8 April 2022 (https://time.com/6165422/russians-in-ukraine/)

the world: Austria, Australia, Croatia, France, Germany, Great Britain, Greece, Georgia, Mexico, Serbia and the United States. Formed in early March 2022, it had about 700 fighters by the end of the month[284]. It is reputed to be very brutal and made up of extremists - regardless of what Ukrainian officials say - responsible for numerous documented war crimes[285]. It is commanded by Mamuka Mamulashvili, who says: 'I speak for the Georgian legion, we will never take prisoners from the Russian soldiers. Not a single one of them will be taken prisoner»[286]. The Georgian National Legion is even said to be responsible for war crimes in the vicinity of Butcha on 30 March 2022, according to Ukrainian sources[287].

3.2.15. Territorial defence battalions

3.2.15.1. The «AÏDAR» battalion

Figure 44 - Emblems of Battalion 24 AÏDAR (left) and its branch OSKAR DIRLEWANGER (right). The symbolism of the skull and crossbones, used by the Third Reich for the SS and for the armoured units of the Wehrmacht, as well as the reference

284.Andy Blatchford, «Band of others: Ukraine's legions of foreign soldiers are on the frontline», Politico, 24 March 2022 (updated 25 March 2022) (https ://www.politico.com/news/2022/03/24/ukraine-legion-foreign-soldiers-00020233)
285.Alexander Rubinstein, «US lawmakers welcomed notorious Georgian warlord now boasting of war crimes in Ukraine», The Grayzone, 8 April 2022 (https://thegrayzone.com/2022/04/08/lawmakers-georgian-warlord-war-crimes-ukraine/)
286. https://twitter.com/RWApodcast/status/1511698257566654466
287. https://t.me/uniannet/42715

to the SS commander Oskar Dirlewanger, unambiguously lead us back to the Second World War. SS-Oberführer Dirlewanger had committed so many crimes as head of the Stary Dzików labour camp in Poland that he was relieved of his command by the SS hierarchy. Sent to Belarus, he led a brutal and ruthless struggle against the Soviet partisans as head of the 'Sonderkommando Dirlewanger'.

Since 2014, the AIDAR battalion has been infamous for its brutality in the Donbass. The difference between the Russian-speaking formations fighting in the Donbass and the governmental formations is that the former are from that region. The Ukrainian volunteers come from other regions and have no particular empathy for the local population. This explains the complete lack of a 'hearts and minds' strategy to fight the insurgency. The aim is not to win over the local population by seduction and thus suppress support for the rebels, as the British had done in Malaysia, for example, but to punish them. This is why Russian-speaking propaganda refers to them as 'reprisal battalions'.

In November 2022, after the withdrawal of the Russian troops, Ukrainian units took over and began a purge. Unsurprisingly, the emblem of the SS Dirlewanger Brigade, recycled for Ukrainian reprisal formations, appeared.

Figure 45: Insignia of the Waffen SS Brigade Dirlewanger, seen on the helmets of Ukrainian soldiers in Kherson. Also known as the 'Black Hunters', this brigade was dedicated to purge operations. While not suggesting the existence of a retaliation unit in the city, the insignia suggests the state of mind there. Apparently, the Ukrainian forces are carrying on this tradition to defend our values...

The West, which practiced the same methods in Afghanistan and Iraq, obviously does not condemn this brutal approach, which allows Vladimir Putin to use the term «genocide».

3.2.15.2. The OUN volunteer battalion

Figure 46 - Emblem of the voluntary movement of the Organisation of Ukrainian Nationalists (OUN). Its graphic code is the same as that of Praviy Sektor.

The battalion of the Organisation of Ukrainian Nationalists (Організація українських націоналістів) has its roots in the late 1920s. Its links with Praviy Sektor and the Ukrainian far right are strong.

Figure 47 - Emblem of the 14th SS Panzer Division 'Galicia' frequently observed demonstrations with the OUN battalion in western Ukraine.

The OUN is the mother of Ukrainian nationalist organisations. It originated in the western part of Ukraine and gave considerable support to the forces of the Third Reich in the struggle against the Soviets. The gradual fragmentation of the Ukrainian nationalist movement reduced its numerical potential. On the other hand, the OUN remained a reference and continued to enjoy great prestige in Ukraine. Its units are integrated into the Ukrainian Volunteer Corps (DUK) of Praviy Sektor.

4. Rising tensions

To explain the Russian intervention, the Cold War discourse is brought out, replacing «USSR» by «Russia». Thus, on France 5, Benoît Vitkine, Le Monde's correspondent in Moscow, attributes to Russia the desire to export «its model». However, since 1991, Russia has adopted our Western model. The idea that it is trying to convince us that «its model is better than ours» makes absolutely no sense.

The course of events as seen by the Western media

Date	Event
03/02/2021	Zelensky issues a decree banning eight opposition media outlets, including three TV stations (*112 Ukraine*, *NewsOne* and *ZIK*) [288] [289].
24/03/2021	Zelensky issues a decree[290] to reconquer Crimea, which implies taking over the Donbass. From then on, he strengthened his military presence in the south of the country and along the line of contact with the self-proclaimed Donbass republics. Several Western intelligence services note the signs of a Ukrainian offensive in the Donbass, including the deployment of demining assault systems.

288«Ukraine: Zelenskiy bans three opposition TV stations», dw.com, 3 February 2021 (https://p.dw.com/p/3ooET)

289«Ukraine: Zelenskiy bans three opposition TV stations», dw.com, 3 February 2021 (https://p.dw.com/p/3ooET)

290. https://www.president.gov.ua/documents/1172021-37533

Date	Event
19/01/2022	US Congress passes the *Ukraine Democracy Defense Lend-Lease Act of* 2022 (S.3522)[291] to provide arms to Ukraine for «*ongoing aggression*
11/02/2022	At a press conference, US President Joe Biden says that Russia will attack Ukraine on 16 February. The United States alerted its allies[292]. The British tabloid *Sun* even mentions an attack with 200,000 men (double the number of troops mentioned until then), and specifies that it will take place at 1 a.m.[293], while others announce 3 a.m.[294] !
12/02/2022	Representatives of the Lugansk People's Republic report to the *Joint Centre for Control and Coordination* (JCCC) meeting that there have been no ceasefire violations in the last 15 days.
14/02/2022	In a televised address, President Zelensky tells the international community: «If you, or anyone else, has any additional information regarding a 100% Russian invasion starting on the 16th, please pass on that information.»[295] The US State Department closes its embassy in Kiev, orders the destruction of computers and communications equipment[296] and moves its staff to Lvov, near the Polish border[297].

291. https://www.congress.gov/bill/117th-congress/senate-bill/3522

292. Alexander Ward & Quint Forgey, «Putin could attack Ukraine on Feb. 16, Biden told allies», Politico.com, 11 February 2022; «Biden tells allies Russia may attack Ukraine on February 16: Reports», WION, 12 February 2022 (https://www.politico.com/newsletters/national-security-daily/2022/02/11/putin-could-attack-ukraine-on-feb-16-biden-told-allies-00008344)

293. Nick Parker & Jerome Starkey, 'HIGH ALERT Russia set to invade Ukraine at any time with massive missile blitz and 200,000 troops, US intelligence claims', The Sun, 15 February 2022 (updated 16 February 2022)

294. Chris Hughes, 'Russian invasion of Ukraine set for '3am today' with missiles and tank attack', mirror.co.uk, 15 February 2022 (updated 16 February 2022) (https://www.mirror.co.uk/news/world-news/breaking-russian-invasion-ukraine-set-26232612)

295. Ellen Knickmeyer, Jim Heintz & Aamer Madhani, 'Ukraine's President: 'If You Have Information About a Russian Invasion, Please Forward That to Us', Time, 14 February 2022

296. John Hewitt Jones, «State Department orders destruction of IT equipment at Kyiv embassy», FedScoop, 14 February 2022

297. Laura Kelly, «US Embassy in Kyiv destroying documents as drawdown underway», The Hill, 14 February 2022

Date	Event
15/02/2022	The Duma formally asks Vladimir Putin to recognise the independence of the self-proclaimed Donbass republics. He did not respond.
15/02/2022	The media reported a «denial of service» cyber-attack that targeted major Ukrainian banks and institutions[298]. The next day, in the programme «*C dans l'air*», Alain Bauer, criminologist, explains it by a complex strategy of «*small touches*» by which Vladimir Putin would seek to make war without making war, the attack would be a message to indicate that the war would be made both on the ground and in cyberspace[299]. Yet on the same day, *Reuters* notes: «Cloudflare, a leading denial-of-service security firm based in San Francisco, said it has seen no evidence of «significant denial-of-service activity» in Ukraine against its data centres or customers there.»[300]
15/02/2022	President Zelensky announced that 16 February would be '*Unity Day*', defined by The *Times* of London as '*a new festival introduced as a mark of defiance against the* Russian *troops*'[301]. He called on the population to take to the streets en masse the following day. The Western media is preparing to film the event. *Reuters* even announced a «*live stream*» from Maidan Square in Kiev[302].
16/02/2022	The Reuters stream shows a hopelessly empty Maidan Square, which Internet users will quickly make fun of. In their daily report, the OSCE observers mention the gathering of 200 people in Kiev «in total»[303]. Clearly, Ukrainians are in no hurry to demonstrate their unity against Russia!

298. Maggie Miller, «Ukrainian Ministry of Defense websites hit by cyberattack», politico.com, 15 February 2022
299. Alain Bauer, in the programme «C dans l'air» of 16 February 2022 («Ukraine: mais à quoi joue Poutine? #cdanslair 16.02.2022', France 5/YouTube, 18 February 2022) (16'45")
300. «Ukraine defence ministry website, banks, knocked offline», Reuters, 15 February 2022
301. Catherine Philp, «Ukraine puts on a defiant Unity Day», The Times, 17 February 2022
302. https://nitter.net/UkrWarReport/status/1493681084084760578#m
303. https://reliefweb.int/sites/reliefweb.int/files/resources/2022-02-17 %20Daily %20Report_ENG.pdf

Date	Event
16/02/2022	The OSCE monitors record a significant increase in ceasefire violations along the line of contact. The number of explosions has increased tenfold and the map they produce shows that they are mainly affecting the civilian population of the Donbass. For Russia, this sharp increase in artillery fire is an indicator of the imminent launch of a ground offensive.
17/02/2022	Artillery fire intensifies further and reaches 20 times the «usual» level along the line of contact. The West immediately blames the «pro-Russians». A projectile that hit a kindergarten in Stanitsa Luganskaya was described as a «*false-banner*» attack by Boris Johnson and Jens Stoltenberg, NATO Secretary General[304]. In France, *La Dépêche* reported the event and quoted Boris Johnson, avoiding mentioning the expression «*false banner*» but turning the argument around and speaking of a provocation[305]. So would the rebels like the Ukrainian army to attack them? A quick examination of the scene after the incident shows that the location of the school in government territory tends to invalidate the idea of a false-banner attack, while the direction of impact tends to indicate that the shot came from the Ukrainian lines. The attribution of the shot to autonomist forces is all the less credible given that Ukrainian troops are preventing the OSCE monitors (SMM) from gaining access to the building, as they indicate in their daily report: «The MMS was only able to carry out its assessment at a distance of about 50m from the north-east façade and about 30m from the south-west façade of the damaged building, as a law enforcement officer did not allow the Mission access to the site on the grounds that an investigation was under way»[306] Naturally, no Western media reports this aspect of things, as it could confirm that the provocations are coming from the Ukrainian side. In reality, we don't know.
18/02/2022	President Joe Biden tells a press conference that he is convinced that Vladimir Putin has made his decision to attack Ukraine within days[307].

304. Heather Stewart, Dan Sabbagh & Patrick Wintour, 'Boris Johnson: Ukraine kindergarten shelling is false-flag operation', The Guardian, 17 February 2022; 'UK PM Johnson says Ukraine kindergarten attack a «false flag operation»', Euronews/Reuters, 18 February 2022
305. «Bombardment d'une école en Ukraine : ce que l'on sait de cette attaque qui a fait trois blessés», ladepeche.fr, 17 February 2022
306. https://www.osce.org/files/2022-02-18 Daily Report_ENG.pdf
307. «Citing U.S. Intelligence, Biden Says Putin Has Decided to Invade Ukraine», The New York Times, 18 February 2022 (updated 13 April 2022) (https://nyti.ms/36iLhfn)

Date	Event
18/02/2022	The Russian state broadcaster *RT* claims that Ukraine did not give the order to attack Donbass[308], showing that neither the Russians nor the Ukrainians want to increase tensions.
18/02/2022	The Ukrainian nationalist website *Information Resistance* announces a false-banner action against the ammonia depots of the Stirol company in Gorlivka[309]. Incidentally, on the same day, the Tass agency revealed that the militia of the Donetsk People's Republic (DPR) had intercepted two commandos «*speaking Polish*» and equipped with «*foreign weapons*». They were preparing to carry out attacks on the chlorine depot of a water treatment plant and on the ammonia depot of Stirol in Gorlivka[310]. Russian speakers attribute the operation to Ukraine, but it could have been carried out by a third actor.
18/02/2022	Faced with Western claims of an imminent attack, Oleksei Reznikov, the Ukrainian Defence Minister, stated before the Rada : «Ukraine believes that the probability of a major escalation of the conflict with Russia is low.»[311]
19/02/2022	President Zelensky attends the annual Munich Security Conference[312], although the Americans have advised against it because of the risk of a Russian attack[313]. He raises the possibility of Ukraine reneging on the Budapest Memorandum and nuclear armament.

308. «Ukraine says it hasn't ordered Donbass attack», rt.com, 18 February 2022
309. 24. «Окупанты минируют места хранения аммиака на заводе «Стирол»: данные группы ИС», Information Resistance, 18 February 2022 (https://sprotyv.info/news/okkupanty-minirujut-mesta-hraneniya-ammiaka-na-zavode-stirol-dannye-gruppy-is)
310. https://tass.ru/mezhdunarodnaya-panorama/13755607/amp
311. «Ukraine Estimates Probability of Major Escalation With Russia as Low Defence Minister», Reuters/USNews, 18 February 2022
312. «President's Office announces Zelensky's schedule for Munich Security-Conference», ukrinform.ua, 19 February 2022
313. Kylie Atwood, Phil Mattingly & Matthew Chance, «Biden administration urged Zelensky not to leave Ukraine and visit Munich», CNN, 19 February 2022

Date	Event
19/02/2022	The *Washington Post* confirms that there is no indication that Russia has decided to attack Ukraine: some European allies question the US belief that the Kremlin will launch hostilities, and say they have seen no direct evidence to suggest that Putin has taken such a course. In Munich, one European official told the Washington Post that «we have no clear evidence that Putin has made his decision and we have seen nothing to suggest otherwise. Another said that while the situation is serious, «at this stage we have no clear intelligence» that Putin has decided to invade the country. The officials said they had received little information about the sources and methods used by the US to reach their conclusions, which limits their ability to make an independent judgment about the weight to be given to Biden's claims that Putin made the decision to attack.[314]

From the Russian point of view, things are perceived a little differently, because since March 2021, their military intelligence services have been following the evolution of the Ukrainian reinforcement in southern Ukraine. The course of events is hardly mentioned in our media, which will later give the illusion that the Russian attack was a «thunderbolt in a blue sky».

The course of events as seen from Russia

Date	Event
15/02/2022	The Russian parliament (Duma), votes on a resolution asking Vladimir Putin «The Russian Federation has been asked to consider the issue of recognition by the Russian Federation of the Donetsk People's Republic and the Lugansk People's Republic as autonomous, sovereign and independent states.[315] Vladimir Putin refuses.»
15/02/2022	The Russian opposition website Meduza, reports that, during his press conference with Olaf Scholz, Putin indicated that the question of the independence of the republics is not on the agenda and that the priority of Russian policy remains the implementation of the Minsk Agreements[316].

314. Souad Mekhennet, Karoun Demirjian, Ellen Nakashima, John Hudson & Shane Harris, 'Zelensky rips the West for inaction as shelling makes Russia-Ukraine war seem increasingly imminent', The Washington Post, 19 February 2022

315. https://sozd.duma.gov.ru/bill/58243-8

316. «Мы должны вселать для решения проблем Донбасса». Путин - о

Date	Event
16/02/2022	OSCE observers report a significant increase in Ukrainian artillery activity against the Donbass[317]. For the Russians, this is an indicator of an imminent Ukrainian offensive.
18/02/2022	Civilians in the Donbass are beginning to be hastily evacuated away from the contact line and towards Russia.
19/02/2022	According to Reuters : «Two regions in eastern Ukraine where government and separatist forces have clashed since 2014 were hit by more than 1,400 explosions on Friday, observers from the Organization for Security and Co-operation in Europe (OSCE) said, pointing to an upsurge in shelling[318] «
21/02/2022	As the situation worsened for the civilian population of Donbass, President Vladimir Putin signed Russia's recognition of the independence of the two republics. At the same time, he signed «Treaties of Friendship, Cooperation and Mutual Assistance» with them. The same evening, he gave an unambiguous televised speech: «We want those who have seized and continue to hold power in Kiev to cease hostilities immediately. Otherwise, the responsibility for any further bloodshed will rest entirely on the conscience of the regime in power in Ukraine.»[319]
22/02/2022	The parliaments of Russia and the two republics of Donetsk and Lugansk ratified the treaties signed the day before. From then on, Russia has a formal legitimacy to militarily help the populations of Donbass.
23/02/2022	Faced with the intensification of Ukrainian strikes, which have increased 40-fold since 14 February, the Donetsk and Lugansk republics are requesting military assistance from Russia under the agreement signed on 21 February.
24/02/2022	Invoking Article 51 of the UN Charter on the right to collective defence, Vladimir Putin announces that he has decided to launch a military operation against Ukraine in order to neutralise the threat to the populations of Donbass.

предложении Госдумы признать независимость ДНР и ЛНР», meduza.io, 15 February 2022

317. «OSCE reports surge in number of explosions in east Ukraine, Reuters, 19 February 2022 (https://www.reuters.com/world/europe/osce-reports-surge-number-explosions-east-ukraine-2022-02-19/)

318. «OSCE reports surge in number of explosions in east Ukraine, Reuters, 19 February 2022 (https://www.reuters.com/world/europe/osce-reports-surge-number-explosions-east-ukraine-2022-02-19/)

319. «Address by the President of the Russian Federation, kremlin.ru, 21 February 2022 (http://en.kremlin.ru/events/president/news/67828)

Evolution of the number of explosions recorded by the OSCE in Donbass between 2020 and 2022

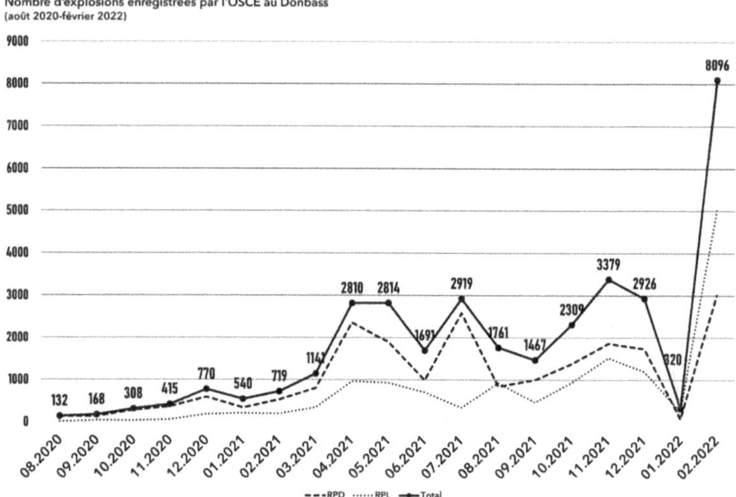

Figure 48 - The number of explosions in the Donetsk and Lugansk People's Republics (DPR and LPR) and the civilian casualties of the Ukrainian army firing on its own population do not attract the attention of any Western media. Their sudden increase in February 2022 indicated the imminent start of a large-scale operation. [Sources: OSCE, International Crisis Group]

Explosions recorded by OSCE monitors (14 February - 22 February 2022)

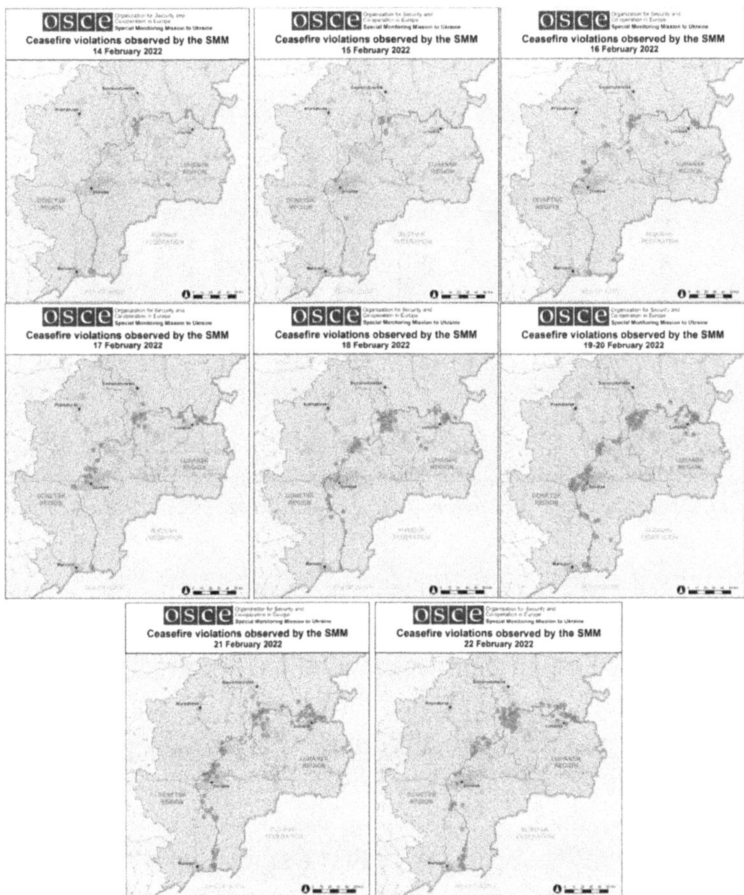

Figure 49 - The number of explosions and ceasefire violations increases dramatically from 15 February. The locations of the explosions, which are not very visible on these black-and-white maps, clearly indicate the interior of the Donetsk and Lugansk republics. [Source: OSCE monitors' daily reports]

Number of explosions recorded by OSCE monitors between 14 and 22 February 2022

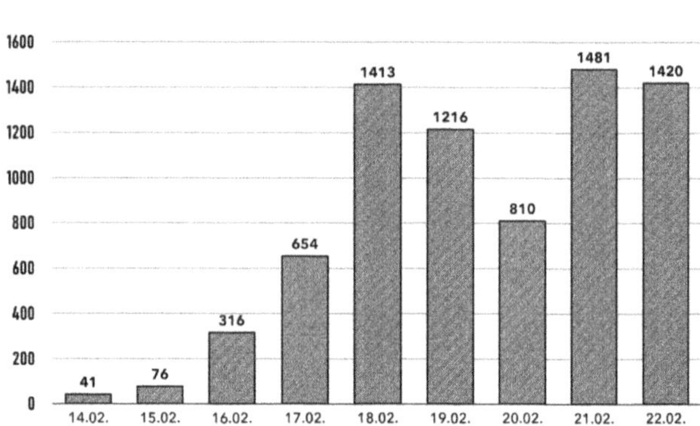

Figure 50 - Number of explosions recorded by OSCE monitors on both sides of the Line of Contact. However, examination of the maps shows that the bulk of these explosions affected the population of the Donbass. Source: OSCE monitors' daily reports

All the indicators of impending conflict were thus present since March 2021. Western diplomacy chose to ignore them, proving that, despite their declarations, neither our diplomats nor our media feel any compassion for Ukraine. The arguments that «you don't negotiate with a dictator» were used as a screen for a policy that sought to weaken Russia rather than help Ukraine.

Of course, the invocation of Article 51 can be seen as a legal device to justify the operation against Ukraine, but what about the Western interventions in Afghanistan, Iraq or Syria, which were only justified by invoking - in a false way - national interests, in defiance of international law?

Neither in 2014 nor in 2021 did Vladimir Putin intend to attack or invade Ukraine. Those who claim this have difficulty articulating an objective for a possible attack. The situation is obviously very different in early 2022, but so far none of the accusations made by the West have been confirmed by Western intelligence services. The idea that Vladimir Putin is trying to «reclaim» Ukraine and that, unable to do so, he is trying to hinder its development[320] has no reality.

320. Pascal Boniface in the programme «C dans l'air» of 25 January 2022 («Ukraine: Russian or American one-upmanship? #cdanslair 25.01.2022», France 5/YouTube, 26 January 2022 (15'50")

5. Operation Z

5.1. The issues

5.1.1. Ukrainian issues

The stakes of a conflict with Russia are many for Ukraine and Western action. First, on the economic front, in May 2014, the International Monetary Fund warned Ukraine that it would not get its $17 billion loan if it did not regain control of the east of the country:

> *If the central government loses effective control of the East, the programme will have to be rethought.* [321]

This is what is pushing Kiev to relaunch its offensive against the Donbass. Ukraine receives a first tranche just

321. Catherine Boyle, «IMF warns Ukraine on bailout if it loses east», CNBC, 1 May 2014 (updated 21 May 2014) (https://www.cnbc.com/2014/05/01/ukraine-gets-17bn-bailout-russian-risks-remain.html)

after the events in Odessa[322]. There is therefore international pressure to push Ukraine to re-establish its sovereignty over the entire territory. However, this pressure does not a priori exclude a negotiated solution to the conflict. But this is not the path chosen by Kiev.

Ukraine's main stake is its accession to NATO, which it sees as a guarantee of its independence and survival. It knows that this objective will remain unattainable as long as the conflict in Donbass is not resolved. However, the Ukrainian authorities do not want a political solution as foreseen in the Minsk Agreements, i.e. involving the autonomy of the country's regions. Ultra-nationalists see this as the beginning of the country's decomposition.

They want a «pure Ukraine». They therefore need to push the Russian speakers out of the borders, which means a confrontation with Russia that is likely to last as long as Russia is able to support the Russian speakers in the Donbass. Therefore, a decisive victory over Russia must be achieved. Oleksei Arestovich, advisor and spokesman for President Zelensky, explains this in an interview with Ukrainian channel Apostrof TV on 18 March 2019:

> *Oleksei Arestovich: With a 99.9% probability, our price for joining NATO is a big war with Russia. And if we don't join NATO, Russia will absorb us completely within 10-12 years. That is the whole range we are in. Now go and vote for Zelensky!*
>
> *A': And if you could choose, what would be best?*

322.»Ukraine receives first $3.2 bln from IMF programme -central bank», Reuters, 7 May 2014

O.A.: Of course, a big war with Russia and the move to NATO following the victory over Russia.

A': And what would a big war with Russia be like?

O.A.: Well, it could be a big offensive air operation. Invasion by the Russian army, with the units established on our border. The siege of Kiev. An attempt to encircle the troops that are in the Donetsk and Luhansk regions, an attack across the Crimean isthmus, access to the Novokakhovsk reservoir in order to give water to Crimea. An offensive from the territory of Belarus. The creation of new people's republics. Sabotage. Strikes on critical infrastructure. And so on. An air assault. This is a full-fledged war. And it has a 99% probability of happening.

A': When?

O.A.: 2021 to 2022. Well, from 2020 to 2022. The most critical period. And then the most critical period is 2024 to 2026. And the next one is 2028 to 2030. There could be three wars with Russia.

A' : And what about 2024 to 2028... If there is such a big war, then new people's republics will be proclaimed?

O.A.: Of course! As soon as the Russian saboteurs and paratroopers enter in front of the Russian tanks, they will proclaim the people's republics of Kharkov, Soumy, Chernihiv, Odessa, Kherson. And so on. The People's Republic of Zaporozhie. But the price of joining NATO is, in all likelihood, a full-scale conflict with Russia. A larger conflict with Russia than we have today. Or a series of such conflicts. But in that conflict we will be very actively supported by the West. Weapons. Equipment. Assistance. New sanctions against Russia. Most likely, the introduction of a NATO contingent. A no-fly zone, and so on. In other words, we won't lose it. This is a good thing.[323]

Thus, convinced by Western rhetoric about Russia's military and economic weakness, the Ukrainians felt that a decisive victory against it would be possible. They therefore deliberately risked sacrificing their country to obtain a defeat of Russia as a condition for joining NATO.

In fact, Ukraine and the West have been prisoners of their narrative about the situation in Donbass. By claiming that Russia was militarily involved in the Donbass, to justify their military defeats in 2014-2015, the Ukrainians trapped themselves. NATO is unlikely to welcome a country in open conflict with Russia. The Ukrainians were then pushed into a kind of headlong rush. With the guarantee of Western support to wreck the Russian economy and to bring about a catastrophic situation leading to regime change in Moscow, Ukraine began to hope for a victory over Russia.

323.»UKRAINE 24: Ukrainian Nostradamus who predicted war with russia in 2019 with stunning accuracy», YouTube, 3 April 2022 (https://www.youtube.com/watch?v=RZ3GsYPRkv4)

This is why the Russian intervention had to be provoked. As Pope Francis expressed it in the Milanese daily Il Corriere della Sera:

> *NATO's barking at Russia's doorstep, prompted the head of the Kremlin to react and wage war on Ukraine. I don't know if this anger was provoked, but it helped the anger to rise.*[324]

5.1.2.Russian issues

For Russia, the issue is more complex. It has a domestic political dimension and a geostrategic dimension. It is a question of maintaining the country's stability while improving its national security.

Domestically, the Russian government cannot afford to have a Russian minority abroad attacked by its government. As was the case in Georgia, the Russian population strongly supports Russian intervention in these situations.

In geostrategic terms, Russia sees Ukraine's possible accession to NATO as a matter of national security. The problem is not membership itself, but the possibility that the United States could install weapons - even nuclear weapons - in the immediate vicinity of its border. That is why it made proposals to NATO and the United States in mid-December 2021. That said, Russia knew that, because of the conflict in Donbass, Ukraine's entry into NATO was not on the agenda for many years to come.

At the beginning of 2022, the Russians understand the imminence of the offensive that the Ukrainians have been preparing since 2021 against the Donbass with the complicity of the

---

324. https://www.marianne.net/monde/europe/la-colere-de-poutine-et-les-aboiements-de-lotan-le-pape-francois-se-confie-sur-la-guerre-en-ukraine

Americans. They know that their intervention, whatever the scale, will be accompanied by a shower of sanctions. Therefore, they can kill two birds with one stone: annihilate the Ukrainian military capacity and force Ukraine - and therefore NATO - into neutrality.

It is therefore the situation in the Donbass that is the trigger for the Russian offensive, whose objectives are clearly associated with the security of the Russian-speaking population. But this could allow Vladimir Putin to use his success in Ukraine as a lever to achieve other objectives. One could even imagine that, as the European economic situation deteriorates, Russia will exploit this situation to reinforce its geostrategic position.

5.2.Planning

The state of Russian military planning is unknown until the start of the Russian offensive. In any case, until mid-February 2022, Western services do not see any of the indicators that are usually observed before such an operation. It can be concluded that, until February 2022, Russia did not intend to attack Ukraine. This explains the doubts of US officials in the Washington Post about a possible offensive[325].

On the other hand, it is more than likely that it has prepared planning for military intervention in the event that Ukraine launches a decisive offensive to seize the Donbass by force. As in many countries, the Russian General Staff is constantly working on alternative planning to respond to unexpected situations. This is what is known as contingency planning («contingency plan» in NATO, and «reserved decisions» in Switzerland). On RTS, Marc

325.Souad Mekhennet, Karoun Demirjian, Ellen Nakashima, John Hudson & Shane Harris, 'Zelensky rips the West for inaction as shelling makes Russia-Ukraine war seem increasingly imminent', The Washington Post, 19 February 2022

Allgöwer, the channel's deputy editor-in-chief, claims that the Russian offensive was planned by the FSB's 5th directorate and that, after the operation's poor results, its director was imprisoned and then (inexplicably) released before the GRU, the military intelligence service, took over its responsibilities[326]. This is pure conspiracy, as the channel is wont to do: facts are created from hypotheses, then assembled in order to spread rumours about dysfunctions in Russian governance.

In reality, the operation was planned by the Russian General Staff (GSS). This is the task of its Main Operations Directorate (GOU), while intelligence on the situation in Ukraine was provided by the Main Intelligence Directorate (GRU). The GRU has close contacts with the military intelligence of the Donetsk and Lugansk republic forces. It is not clear why the GRU would have turned to an external structure - the FSB - which has a different remit.

In the spring of 2021, Western chancelleries note a renewed level of activity by Russian forces in the Southern Military District. The Americans raised the spectre of a Russian offensive in Ukraine. In fact, as early as March 2021, two events attracted Russia's attention:

a) On 24 March, President Volodymyr Zelensky issued a decree to retake Crimea by force[327], which presupposes the neutralisation of the Donbass. He is starting to deploy troops in the south of the country. Naturally, no Western media reports on these Ukrainian troop movements observed in mid-March[328] and early April[329], while Twitter closes accounts showing Ukrainian tank transports to the Donbass...

---

326. https://www.rts.ch/play/tv/redirect/detail/13086647?startTime=1092
327. https://www.president.gov.ua/documents/1172021-37533
328. https://twitter.com/theragex/status/1371009926395494402
329. https://twitter.com/worldonalert/status/1377691126149349382; https://twitter.

b) Simultaneously, NATO launches the DEFENDER EUROPE 21 series of exercises, which take place between March and June 2021 in the vicinity of the Russian border between the Baltic and Black Seas[330]. The Russians note that NATO reconnaissance flights on the Ukrainian border and in the Black Sea are increasing alarmingly[331]. From bases in Waddington in Britain, Sigonella in Italy or Souda Bay in Crete, the RC-135 Rivet Joint electronic reconnaissance aircraft, the RQ-4 Global Hawk strategic UAVs of the US Air Force, and the ARTEMIS aircraft of the US Army carry out missions along the Crimean coast[332].

The Russians do not expect a NATO attack. Instead, they know that the US, Britain and France share intelligence with Ukraine. This intensification of reconnaissance missions could be the prelude to a Ukrainian offensive. This situation explains the Russian army's exercises in spring 2021. Russia is testing the operational readiness of its troops and showing that it is following the evolution of the situation. The manoeuvres are ostensibly intended to be a deterrent, what the Americans call a show of force. However, there is no indication that Russia intends to intervene in Ukraine. In fact, it is not intervening!

Six months later, on 30 October 2021, the Washington Post reported an unusual deployment of Russian troops on the Ukrainian border[333]. The next day, the US media outlet Politico

---

com/AmbranderB/status/1378773857142706181

330. https://www.europeafrica.army.mil/DefenderEurope/

331.Tim Ripley, «US, UK surge surveillance flights over Ukraine and Black Sea», janes.com, 12 April 2021 (https://www.janes.com/defence-news/news-detail/us-uk-surge-surveillance-flights-over-ukraine-and-black-sea)

332. https://www.itamilradar.com/2022/01/25/busy-sky-over-black-sea-2/

333.Paul Sonne, Robyn Dixon & David L. Stern, «Russian troop movements near Ukraine border prompt concern in U.S., Europe», The Washington Post, 30 October 2021

published satellite photos of troops stationed 'near the Ukrainian border'[334].

The images are being shown around the world, but they are deceptive. They show vehicles parked in Yelnia, Smolensk Oblast, which is on the Belarusian border and 250 km from the Ukrainian border. Moreover, these close-up photos suggest that they are temporary parking lots awaiting engagement. However, some of this equipment was stored after the ZAPAD 2021 exercise which has just ended. They are to be reused during joint exercises in Belarus in early 2022. Furthermore, it can be seen on Google Maps that these parking lots are associated with permanent installations and troops whose deployment has been known for a long time. At this stage, it does not appear that the Russians had any intention of conducting an offensive in Ukraine.

On 12 February 2022, in an interview on the channel of the major daily Neue Zürcher Zeitung (NZZ), Thomas Süssli, head of the Swiss Army, stated without much conviction that the Russians were waiting for the ground to be frozen before launching their offensive[335]. He is not the first to try to explain why the Russians are not doing what our strategists imagine they might do. Yet a quick look at the weather forecast for Ukraine at this time shows that the predicted temperatures are rising, proving - once again - that this strategic 'calculation' is fanciful.

Indeed, on 1 November, the Ukrainian Ministry of Defence denied that Russian forces had been deployed on its borders[336]. The next day, Oleksiy Danilov, secretary of the Ukrainian

334.Betsy Woodruff Swan & Paul Mcleary, «Satellite images show new Russian military buildup near Ukraine», Politico, 1er November 2021

335.Andreas Breitenstein, «Stell dir vor, es ist Krieg - und die Schweiz mit drin», nzz.ch, 12 February 2022

336. «Ukraine Denies Report of Russian Troop Buildup Near Its Borders, US News/Reuters, 1er November 2021

National Security and Defence Council (NSDC), confirmed the denial[337]. His opinion was validated by American military experts (real ones... not the ones from « C dans l'air») from the Institute for Study of War (ISW), who concluded that «Russian military movements are probably not preparing for an imminent offensive against Ukraine»[338]. The next day, these same experts published their conclusions in the Kyiv Post under the title «It is unlikely that the Russian army is preparing for an imminent offensive»[339].

Also on 2 November, CIA Director William Burns travelled to Moscow to meet his Russian counterpart Nikolai Patrushev, Director General of the FSB (security service)[340] and Sergei Naryshkin, Director General of the SVR (foreign intelligence). He also has a telephone conversation with Vladimir Putin, the exact content of which has not been revealed. It is therefore not known whether they discussed the Ukrainian issue, but it would seem likely. In any case, it seems that the US government is not really alarmed by the situation.

On 3 November, the Ukrainian government confirms that there are no Russian troops on its border[341].

Everything leads us to believe that the affair will quickly «deflate». But this is without counting on the desire of conspiracy media to see a Russian offensive. This was the case in Le

---

337.»Danilov denied Western media statements about the concentration of Russian troops near the borders of Ukraine», uatv.ua, 2 November 2021

338. Mason Clark, George Barros, "Russian Military Movements Unlikely Preparing for Imminent Offensive against Ukraine but Still Concerning", Institute for the Study of War (ISW), 2 November 2021

339.Mason Clark & George Barros, «Russian military unlikely preparing for imminent offensive», Kyiv Post, 3 November 2021

340.Vladimir Isachenkov, «Russian security chief meets with CIA director in Moscow», AP News, 2 November 2021

341.Ukraine Denies Russian Military Buildup on Border as Defense Minister Quits, The Moscow Times/AFP, 3 November 2021

Monde, three weeks later, which revived the thesis of an imminent offensive and did not hesitate to write that «the reaction of the Ukrainian authorities, on the other hand, is confusing»[342]. It seems to be a pity that the main party concerned - the Ukrainian government - is providing some rationality.

As Western rhetoric hardens, the Ukrainian government appears to be under pressure. At the beginning of November, Andrei Taran, Minister of Defence, Oleksiy Lyubchenko, Minister of Economy, Oleg Urusky, Deputy Prime Minister and Minister of Strategic Industries and Oleksiy Reznikov, Minister of Reintegration of Temporarily Occupied Territories, resigned[343].

On 3 December 2021, the Washington Post headlined: 'Russia plans massive military offensive against Ukraine involving 175,000 troops, US intelligence warns'. The newspaper published a map prepared by US intelligence showing the deployment of Russian forces in the Ukraine region[344].

Commentators use the figure of 175 000, but the US service map is less definitive. It indicates that only 70,000 troops are actually present in the region near Ukraine and in Crimea. The rest of the troops are described as «expected». In other words, they are not there. Among the absentees are 100,000 reservists, who are part of a project launched in the second half of 2021 and still experimental, to replace the conscription system. Similarly,

342.Faustine Vincent, «Aux frontières de l'Ukraine, 'c'est juste un nouveau jour de guerre'», Le Monde, 22 November 2021 (updated on 24 November 2021)

343.»Міністр із питань стратегічних галузей Уруський подав заяву про звільнення,» thepage.ua, 1er November 2021 (https://thepage.ua/ua/politics/uruskij-podav-zayavu-pro-zvilnennya); «Міністр оборони Таран подав заяву про звільнення,» thepage.ua, 3 November 2021 (https://thepage.ua/ua/politics/taran-jde-z-minoboroni)

344.Shane Harris & Paul Sonne, «Russia planning massive military offensive against Ukraine involving 175,000 troops, U.S. intelligence warns», The Washington Post, 3 December 2021

the 100 Battle Groups (BTGs) are only a guess. Russia has only 168 of them on its entire territory. Thus, the scenario suggested by the US intelligence services would engage 60% of Russia's total capacity. In the end, Russia will attack Ukraine in February with a force far inferior in number to that of Ukraine.

At this stage, the Kiev authorities believe that the equipment detected by the Americans was merely «troop movements after exercises»[345]. This is consistent with Russia's withdrawal of the equivalent of one division (10,000 troops) from the region at the end of December 2021[346].

It seems that the Americans are trying to raise the tension with Russia. In doing so, they are creating tension within the Atlantic Alliance, as Germany and its intelligence services seem to have a different analysis of the situation. Joe Biden sent William Burns, the CIA director, to parley with Scholz and Bruno Kahl, director of the Bundesnachrichtendienst (BND), the strategic intelligence service, because, as Spiegel reports, he remains sceptical about the quality of American intelligence[347].

Chancellor Olaf Scholz is reluctant to meet with Joe Biden, and Germany is vetoing the supply of arms to Ukraine[348]. This is why Britain is sending arms to Ukraine bypassing German airspace, for fear that Germany will close it. This speaks volumes about the trust between NATO allies.

On 23 January, the announcement of the withdrawal of some American and British diplomatic personnel from Kiev irritated

---

345.Faustine Vincent, «Aux frontières de l'Ukraine, 'c'est juste un nouveau jour de guerre'», Le Monde, 22 November 2021 (updated on 24 November 2021)

346.»Russia announces withdrawal of 10,000 troops after drills near Ukraine», France 24, 26 December 2021

347.Markus Becker et al, «Germany Has Little Maneuvering Room in Ukraine Conflict», der Spiegel, 21 January 2021

348.Michael R. Gordon & Pancevski, «Germany Blocks NATO Ally From Transferring Weapons to Ukraine», The Wall Street Journal, 21 January 2022

the Ukrainian government. The Ukrainians see that the risk of war brandished by the West - but which they have always denied - is taking on proportions that could affect the country in the long term.

Indeed, BBC News Ukraine reports that «the Ukrainian hryvnia has plummeted and investors have started to panic». They are shunning Ukraine, whose economy is faltering. Oleksiy Danilov, who heads the National Security Council, blames the West:

> *When this case started on 30 October last year with a publication in the Washington Post, I had a conversation with a journalist from that publication. He ignored what I told him*[349].

For Danilov, Russia remains a threat, but the threat has not increased. Instead, he believes that the US and British statements are making the situation worse. When asked by the journalist why these big statements are coming now, Danilov links them to the US difficulties with China, political changes in Germany and the French presidential elections. He suspects that the West is stirring up tensions for domestic political reasons. Moreover, the Americans and the British, who raise the spectre of a war that Boris Johnson promises will be «bloody», are not rushing to take concrete measures. It is claimed that «Biden wants to strike hard (...). The Pentagon is mobilising 8,500 soldiers ready to join the 40,000 men of the Military Alliance already on the ground»[350]. But

349.Oksana Torop, «Some of our partners are contributing to the panic. This is beneficial for Russia - Danilov» («Деякі наші партнери сприяють паніці. Це вигідно Росії - Данілов»), BBC News Ukraine, 24 January 2022 (https://www.bbc.com/ukrainian/features-60112868)

350.Programme «C dans l'air» of 25 January 2022 («Ukraine: Russian or Ameri-

the reality is more nuanced: they have not been 'mobilised', but their level of preparation has been raised from 10 days to 5 days; as for their deployment, no decision has been taken[351].

5.3.The situation in the Donbass

In his speech on 24 February, Vladimir Putin triggered the disapproval of the Western community by using the term «genocide» in relation to the situation in Donbass. In fact, as is often the case with Vladimir Putin, the term is not chosen at random.

Since 2014, Ukraine has been under the influence of far-right activists, who want to see a return to a «pure Ukraine», in other words, free of Russian speakers. This is the «Idea of Nation» expressed by the Wolfsangel and explained by a far-right activist in Maïdan on the BBC: «The idea of a Nation», that is to say the idea of «a nation, a people, a country (...), a pure nation, (...) not like under Hitler, but in our own way only a little bit like that. Ukraine must be for Ukrainians». [352]

For example, on 1 July 2021, the Ukrainian Parliament adopted the «Law on Indigenous Peoples of Ukraine»[353]. It defines who the indigenous peoples of Ukraine are and what rights they enjoy. On the face of it, there is nothing very bad about this, except that it does not mention Russians[354] (or Ukrainians, for that matter). Even

---

can one-upmanship? #cdanslair 25.01.2022', France 5/YouTube, 26 January 2022 (11'05")

351.Barbara Starr & Jeremy Herb, «US places up to 8,500 troops on alert for possible deployment to Eastern Europe amid Russia tensions», CNN, 25 January 2022

352.»Profile: Ukraine's ultra-nationalist Right Sector», BBC, 28 April 2014 (https://www.bbc.com/news/world-europe-27173857)

353.»Принят Закон «О коренных народах Украины»», rada.gov.ua, 1er July 2021 (https://www.rada.gov.ua/ru/news/Novosty/Soobshchenyya/211516.html)

354. https://zakon.rada.gov.ua/laws/main/2494-12#Text

the Russian opposition website Meduza notes that the rights of Russian-speaking citizens are different from those of Ukrainians[355]. Oleg Seminsky, a deputy from the presidential party, explains:

> *After the adoption of the Law on Indigenous Peoples, Ukrainian citizens of Russian nationality will not have the same constitutional rights as the representatives of the Ukrainian nation, the Crimean Tatar nation, as well as the Karaites and the peoples of Crimea.* [356]

The law has shocked democrats around the world, who note its similarity - proportionately - to the Nuremberg racial laws of the 1930s, granting different rights to Ukrainian citizens according to their ethnic origin.

The law goes unnoticed by the complacent media, but not in Russia. It prompted Vladimir Putin to write an article entitled «On the historical unity of Russians and Ukrainians», published on 12 July 2021 on the websites of the Foreign Ministry[357]. In it he explains that ethnic Russians and Ukrainians are equal and have the same right to live on Ukrainian territory.

On France 5, Isabelle Mandraud, concludes that Vladimir Putin considers that Ukraine «is a country that does not exist and that he does not recognise the existence of Ukraine as a country»[358].

355.»Why Ukraine's legislation on 'indigenous peoples' doesn't include Russians», meduza.io, 9 July 2021 (https://meduza.io/en/cards/why-ukraine-s-legislation-on-indigenous-peoples-doesn't-include-russians)

356.»Нардеп від «Слуги народу» Семінський заявив про «позбавлення конституційних прав росіян, які проживають в Україні»,» AP News, 2 July 2021 (https://apnews.com.ua/ua/news/nardep-vid-slugi-narodu-seminskii-zayaviv-pro-pozbavlennya-konstitutciinikh-prav-rosiyan-yaki-prozhivaiut-v-ukraini/)

357.Article by Vladimir Putin «On the historical unity of Russians and Ukrainians», belgium.mid.ru, 12 July 2021

358.»Putin dreams of the USSR, Ukraine under tension #cdanslair 11.01.2022»,

It shows his «desire for annexation»[359] and his determination to unite the two countries by force[360]. This discourse is now widespread in France, but it is disinformation.

In fact, in his article, Vladimir Putin not only unambiguously acknowledges the existence of Ukraine by defining it as a «free state», but he also clearly refers to Ukraine's «sovereignty». His point is not to suggest a reunification of Russia and Ukraine, but to make it clear to Ukraine - without addressing it directly - that it has no reason to treat its ethnic Russians and Ukrainians differently.

5.4.The Ukrainian system

Between 2015 and 2018, the Ukrainian armed forces were conducting an Anti-Terrorist Operation (ATO) in the Donbass, led by the Security Service of Ukraine (SBU). This was then an internal security operation, where the autonomist populations were considered terrorists[361].

From 30 April 2018, the operation turns into a military operation, designated as Operation of the Joint Forces (Операція Об'єднаних Сил) (OOS) and placed under the command of the General Staff of the Armed Forces. Its task is «the liberation of temporarily occupied territories». We can already see the beginnings of a «reconquest» of the Donbass. With the help of military

France 5/YouTube, 12 January 2022 (08'55")

359.Axel Gyldén, «Russians and Ukrainians are one people»: what Putin's writings say about his aims», L'Express, 3 February 2022

360.Paul Gogo, «L'inquiétant article de Vladimir Poutine sur l'Ukraine», La Libre, 16 July 2021 (updated 18 July 2021)

361.»Old war, new rules: what comes next as ATO ends and a new operation starts in Donbas?», Ukraine Crisis, 4 May 2018 (https://uacrisis.org/en/66558-joint-forces-operation)

advisors from NATO countries, the OOS forces bring together all security and military forces under one command.

By the end of 2021, this force has about 120,000 men, 500 battle tanks, 1,500 armoured vehicles, 550 multiple rocket launchers, 2,000 pieces of artillery, about 100 combat aircraft and about 40 combat helicopters. In addition, there are the National Guard forces, which are essentially paramilitary forces, deployed in the cities, for a total of 450,000 men according to the National Review[362] (although this figure seems a bit excessive).

The OOS is articulated in two Operational Tactical Groups (OTGs):

- OTG North (Lugansk operational area), comprising two armoured brigades, one mechanised infantry brigade, two air assault brigades and one artillery brigade; and
- OTG East (Donetsk Operational Zone), comprising two armoured brigades, one mechanised infantry brigade, one marine infantry brigade, one air assault brigade and artillery.

The OOS concept was to conduct the offensive against the Donbass after artillery preparation along the line of contact, in order to decimate the first line of defence of the DPR and the LPR. The aim was then to surround and isolate the cities of Lugansk, Gorlovka and Donetsk with mechanised forces, and then push rapidly towards the Russian border to prevent a Russian reinforcement. OWG North also had the function of flanking the OWG South offensive.

By February 2022, Ukraine had numerical superiority in all areas, plus electronic and aerial reconnaissance and intelligence support from the United States and NATO.

362.Robert Zubrin, «NATO Needs Ukraine», National Review, 15 February 2022 (https://www.nationalreview.com/2022/02/nato-needs-ukraine/)

From the very first days of the Russian offensive, Ukrainian weaknesses became apparent:

- Overconfidence in the ability of the West to intervene decisively in the conflict.
- A quantitative (capability) approach to combat, understood in terms of what can be done and not what is intended (this is the approach that Westerners have developed over the last quarter of a century, based on wars that had the characteristics of colonial wars, against a fragmented and ill-equipped opponent).
- A command of operations that is essentially political in nature, even in opposition to the military's planning.
- The obsession, encouraged by Western discourse, with 'holding' the ground, at the expense of preserving combat capability.
- The belief - also generated by Western discourse - in a general uprising of the populations and the emergence of popular resistance in the Russian areas of operation.

Thanks to its numerical superiority and the prospect of Western support, Ukraine neglected the importance of manoeuvre in its operations from the outset. Paradoxically, it was certainly the encouragement of the West and the total absence of Western criticism that pushed the Ukrainians to persevere in a path that could only lead to defeat.

For their part, the West, convinced of the short-term effectiveness of their sanctions and political action, seriously underestimated Russia's capabilities. This is why Russia did not need to resort to counter-sanctions to put pressure on them. One can even imagine that Vladimir Putin played on Western overconfidence.

5.4.1. The *political* context

In Ukraine, as the Russian advance continues, the political situation is becoming more tense. Since his election, Volodymyr

Zelensky has been under pressure from extremists - and Western countries - to refuse any dialogue with Russia on the issue of the Minsk Agreements. For example, in May 2019, a month after his election, he was openly threatened in the Ukrainian media by Dmitry Yarosh, leader of the Praviy Sektor troops, in case he fulfilled his campaign promises:

> *he would lose his life. He will be hanged from a tree on [Khreshchatyk Avenue], if he betrays Ukraine and the people who died during the Revolution and the War. And it is very important that he understands this.* [363]

Volodymyr Zelensky is under constant threat from extreme right-wing movements. During a visit to troops deployed in the Donbass, Zelensky was attacked by fighters from the AZOV movement[364]. The video went viral and his campaign promise to reach an agreement with Russia was quickly forgotten.

In early March 2022, Zelensky claimed that Russia had sent a hit team to eliminate him[365]. Of course, no evidence is put forward to support the

363.Лилия Рагуцкая, «Ярош: если Зеленский предаст Украину - потеряет не должность, а жизнь», Obozrevatel, 27 May 2019, (https://incident.obozrevatel.com/crime/dmitrij-yarosh-esli-zelenskij-predast-ukrainu-poteryaet-ne-dolzh-nost-a-zhizn.htm)

364.Oksana Grytsenko, «I'm not a loser: Zelensky clashes with veterans over Donbas disengagement», Kyiv Post, 28 October 2019 (https://www.kyivpost.com/ukraine-politics/im-not-a-loser-zelensky-clashes-with-veterans-over-donbas-disengagement.html?__cf_chl_tk=SbolmTBS6QnjMnPJLiQEsivGNnuW6T4o-d28tzMOrEM0-1646110945-0-gaNycGzNCJE)

365.»A team of elite Chechen special forces sent to assassinate President Volodymyr Zelensky has been eliminated, according to the head of the National Security and Defense Council, Oleksiy Danilov», The Kyiv Independent, 1er March 2022 (https://kyivindependent.com/uncategorized/a-team-of-elite-chechen-special-forces-sent-to-assassinate-president-volodymyr-zelensky-has-been-eliminated-according-to-the-head-of-the-national-security-and-defense-council-oleksiy-danilov) accusation, but all the Western media relay it without batting an eyelid. In fact, the Russians have nothing to gain from his elimination: since 25 February he has indicated his interest in a negotiated solution, and this is what the Russians are looking for. On the other hand, the Western countries and the neo-Nazi forces within the state apparatus are trying to prevent any form of negotiation. This is the same discourse that can be heard on the French airwaves and in Switzerland. This is why it is possible that Zelensky was threatened in early March, but probably not by the Russians: by the Ukrainians themselves.

At the same time, with the blessing of Western countries, those in favour of negotiations were eliminated. This was the case of Denis Kireyev, one of the Ukrainian negotiators, assassinated on 5 March by the Ukrainian secret service (SBU) because he was considered too favourable to Russia and a traitor[366]. The same fate befell Dmitry Demyanenko, former deputy head of the SBU's main directorate for Kiev and its region, who was murdered on 10 March, also for being too favourable to an agreement with Russia. He was shot dead in his car by members of the special Mirotvorets («Peacemaker») battalion, created on 9 May 2014 within the department of internal affairs of the Kiev region[367].

Figure 51 - Logo of the Mirotvorets battalion, which carries out extrajudicial killings (eliminations) for the Ukrainian government.

366. https://www.timesofisrael.com/ukraine-reports-claim-negotiator-shot-for-treason-officials-say-he-died-in-intel-op/
367. https://www.youtube.com/watch?v=ZWHpVnrwfLY

This militia is associated with the Mirotvorets website, which publishes a list of «enemies of Ukraine», with their personal data, address and telephone numbers, so that they can be harassed or even eliminated. The Ukrainian singer Oleg Vinnik was put on the Mirotvorets list[368] for calling for peace between Ukrainians and Russians in September 2019, after the election of Zelensky[369].

The practice is punishable in many countries[370] but not in Ukraine[371]. In October 2019, the UN and some European countries called for the closure of[372], but this was refused by the Rada[373].

In May 2022, following the World Economic Forum in Davos, where he spoke in favour of a negotiation process between Ukraine and Russia as the only reasonable solution to the conflict in Ukraine, Henry Kissinger was blacklisted by Mirotvorets.

---

368. https://myrotvorets.center/criminal/vinnik-oleg-anatolevich/

369.»Олег Винник попал в «чистилище» базы «Миротворец»», zn.ua, 27 September, 2019 (https://zn.ua/CULTURE/vinnika-popal-v-chistilische-bazy-mirotvorec-331067_.html)

370. https://www.mirror.co.uk/news/world-news/dark-website-lists-russian-spies-26051893

371. https://www.refworld.org/docid/58ec89ad13.html

372.»В ООН настаивают на закрытии сайта «Миротворец»» («UN insists on closing down 'Peacemaker' site»), zn.ua, 16 October 2019 (https://zn.ua/UKRAINE/v-oon-nastaivayut-na-zakrytii-sayta-mirotvorec-332863_.html); Tetiana Popova, «Benjamin Moreau, deputy head of UN Human Rights Monitoring Mission to Ukraine», Diplomat, 16 February 2019 (http://diplomat.media/en/2019/02/16/benjamin-moreau-deputy-head-of-un-human-rights-monitoring-mission-to-ukraine/); 'UN demands to close down «Mirotvorets» calling for persecution of UOC', Union of Orthodox Journalists, 17 October 2019, (https://spzh.news/en/news/65761-v-oon-potrebovali-zakryty-mirotvorec-prizyvavshij-k-gonenijam-na-upc)

373.»Разумков ответил на призыв ООН закрыть сайт «Миротворец»» («Razumkov responded to UN call to shut down 'Peacemaker' site»), zn.ua, 17 October, 2019 (https://zn.ua/UKRAINE/razumkov-otvetil-na-prizyv-oon-zakryt-sayt-mirotvorec-332952_.html)

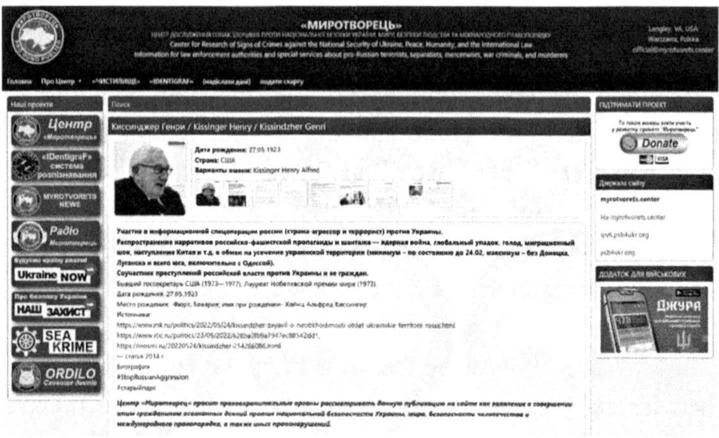

Figure 52 - Henry Kissinger blacklisted by Mirotvorets for suggesting negotiations with Russia at the WEF, 23 May 2022.

5.4.2. Respect for human rights

Despite claims that Vladimir Putin attacked Ukraine because he was jealous of Ukraine's democratic model and could not «tolerate a democracy on its borders», Ukraine's democratic record remains very modest, to put it mildly.

The US State Department's website on human rights in Ukraine speaks volumes on this subject.

> *Significant human rights problems included credible reports of unlawful or arbitrary executions, including extra-judicial killings by the government or its agents; torture and cruel, inhuman or degrading treatment or punishment of detainees by law enforcement officials; difficult and life-threatening conditions of detention; cases of arbitrary arrest or detention; serious problems with the independence of the judiciary; serious abuses in the context of*

the Russian-led conflict in the Donbass, including physical violence or punishment of civilians and members of armed groups held in detention centres; severe restrictions on freedom of expression and the media, including violence or threats of violence against journalists, unjustified arrests or prosecution of journalists and censorship; severe restrictions on Internet freedom; refoulement of refugees to a country where their lives or freedom would be threatened; severe acts of government corruption; lack of investigation and accountability for gender-based violence; crimes, violence or threats of violence motivated by anti-Semitism; crimes involving violence or threats of violence against persons with disabilities, members of ethnic minorities, lesbian, gay, bisexual, transgender, homosexual or trans-sexual persons; and the existence of the worst forms of child labour.[374]

Shortly after Zelensky's decision to recover Ukraine's territorial integrity by taking back Crimea and Donbass, he attacks Russian-speaking parties and media. The aim is to avoid a mobilisation similar to the one in 2014 when the whole south of the country rose up. Actions are multiplying: the arrest of Viktor Medvetchouk, leader of the main parliamentary opposition party («Opposition Platform - For Life»)[375] ; the closure of three Russian-speaking TV channels; the banning of pro-Moscow Ukrainian media[376].

374. https://www.state.gov/reports/2021-country-reports-on-human-rights-practices/ukraine/

375. «Ukraine opposition leader and Putin ally under house arrest after being charged with treason", euronews/Associated Press, 13 May 2021

376. «Ukraine: President bans opposition media Strana.ua and sanctions editor-in-chief", European Federation of Journalists, 26 August 2021

On 20 March 2022, the National Security Council banned eleven political parties (Opposition Platform - For Life, Sharij's Party, Nashi, Opposition Bloc, Left Opposition, Union of Left Forces, Derzhava, Progressive Socialist Party of Ukraine, Socialist Party of Ukraine, Socialists, and Volodymyr Saldo Bloc)[377].

In addition, the Ukrainian government is used to «blacklists» of individuals to be removed or banned. For example, in July 2022, in addition to the Mirotvorets list, the Ukrainian government drew up a blacklist of international actors who «promote narratives in line with Russian propaganda», which includes members of the US Congress, politicians, journalists, ex-Western intelligence officers and... the author of this book[378]. These lists, which seek to eliminate any opinion that deviates from the official Ukrainian discourse, are characteristic of totalitarian regimes. Above all, it is an admission of weakness.

377.»NSDC bans pro-Russian parties in Ukraine», Ukrinform, 20 March 2022 (https://www.ukrinform.net/rubric-polytics/3434673-nsdc-bans-prorussian-parties-in-ukraine.html)

378. https://cpd.gov.ua/reports/спікери-які-просувають-співзвучні-ро/

Western personalities blacklisted by Ukraine

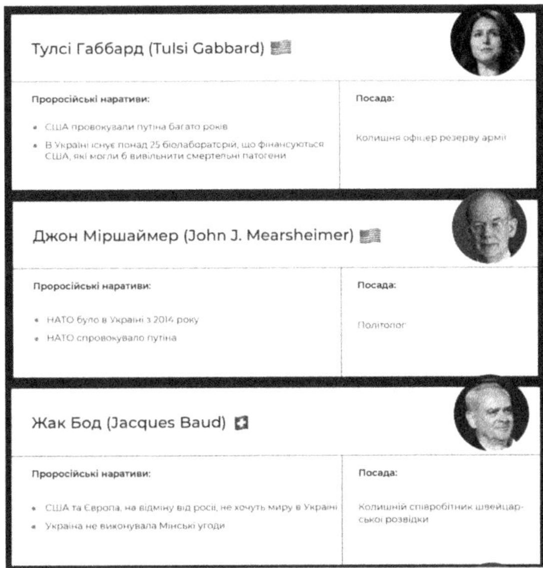

Figure 53 - The Ukrainian government's blacklist includes some 70 international figures critical of Western policy. The list includes the excellent Tulsi Gabbard, a Democratic member of the House of Representatives and unsuccessful US presidential candidate, and Professor John Mearsheimer of the University of Chicago. It also features various political and academic figures from the left and the right.

6. The conduct of operations

6.1.Russia's objectives

On 24 February 2022, Vladimir Putin surprised the world by stating the two objectives of his operation: «demilitarisation» and «denazification». He chose the first two of the four objectives formulated by the Allied Control Authority in July 1945 at the Potsdam Conference for Germany.

One of the many peculiarities of the Ukrainian conflict is that the West has attributed objectives to it without listening to what the Russians themselves have said. In fact, the West has favoured narrative over reality on the ground. The main consequence was that their reaction (and the advice they gave to Volodymyr Zelensky) was based on rhetoric and not on the operational situation.

Russia's objectives are not linked to a fixed element (territory, city, etc.), but to a dynamic element (force destruction). This means that anything that can change this dynamic element also changes the way the objective is achieved. Evolution of the definition of Russian objectives.

	Event in Ukraine/West	Adapting Russia's objectives
24/02/2022		In the speech explaining his decision to attack Ukraine, Putin clearly stated the two objectives of his operation: «demilitarisation» and «denazification» of the threat against the Russian-speaking population of Donbass. He then clarified that he was not aiming to take control of the whole of Ukraine.
25/02/2022	Zelensky hints that he is ready to negotiate with Russia379.	
27/02/2022	The EU then arrives with a 450 million euro arms package to encourage Ukraine to fight380.	
07/03/2022		While the goal of demilitarisation and denazification is almost achieved and negotiations with Ukraine have made no progress, Russia adds the recognition of the return of Crimea to Russia and the independence of the two Donbass republics to its list of demands. It states that its position could change if Ukraine does not wish to negotiate.
21/03/2022	Zelensky makes an offer that goes in the direction of Russia381.	

379. Olga Rudenko, «Ukraine ready to negotiate with Russia», The Kyiv Independent, 25 February 2022 (https://kyivindependent.com/national/ukraine-ready-to-negotiate-with-russia/)

380. Maïa de La Baume & Jacopo Barigazzi, «EU agrees to give €500M in arms, aid to Ukrainian military in 'watershed' move», Politico, 27 February 2022 (https://www.politico.eu/article/eu-ukraine-russia-funding-weapons-budget-military-aid/).

381. «Russia, Ukraine 'close to agreement' in negotiations, says Turkey', Aljazeera, 20 March 2022 (https://www.aljazeera.com/news/2022/3/20/turkey-says-russia-ukraine-close-to-agreement); 'After rejecting ultimatum, Zelensky insists 'meeting' with Putin needed to end war', The Times of Israel, 21 March 2022 (https://www.timesofisrael.com/liveblog-march-21-2022/).

	Event in Ukraine/West	Adapting Russia's objectives
23/03/2022	As in February, the EU returns two days later with a package of 500 million euros for arms purchases. Britain and the US put pressure on Zelensky to withdraw his offer. The Istanbul negotiations stall382.	
25/03/2022		Colonel General Sergei Rudskoy, Head of the GOU, announces that the objectives of Phase I have been achieved383.
27/03/2022	The content of Volodymyr Zelensky's proposal to Russia is revealed. Ukraine commits to - to be neutral with international safeguards and to remain free of nuclear weapons; - not to take back the territories of Crimea and Sevastopol by force, and to declare that this is only possible through negotiations. The Donetsk and Lugansk regions are considered «separate zones»; - not to join military alliances; - renounce the deployment of foreign military bases and contingents, as well as the conduct of military exercises on its territory without the consent of guarantor states, including Russia384 397.	

382. «Ukraine: EU doubles military aid to €1 billion - as it happened», dw.com, 23 March 2022 (https://www.dw.com/en/ukraine-eu-doubles-military-aid-to-1-billion-as-it-happened/a-61226171; https://p.dw.com/p/48tit)
383. Nathan Hodge, «Top Russian general claims military efforts now centered on eastern part of Ukraine», CNN, 25 March 2022.
384. «Zelensky says Ukrainian neutrality on the table ahead of fresh talks with Russia in Turkey', France 24, 27 March 2022 (updated 28 March 2022) (https://www.france24.com/en/europe/20220327-live-kyiv-accuses-russia-of-destroying-fuel-and-food-storage-depots-in-ukraine); 'Ukraine ready to discuss adopting neutral status in Russia peace deal, Zelenskiy says', Reuters, 28 March 2022 (https://www.reuters.com/world/europe/ukraine-prepared-discuss-neutrality-status-zelenskiy-tells-russian-journalists-2022-03-27/)

	Event in Ukraine/West	Adapting Russia's objectives
28/03/2022		Russia is interested in Zelensky's proposal. With the capture of Mariupol, it considers that the objective of 'denazification' has been achieved. It removes it from its objectives for negotiations385. It does not oppose Ukraine's desire to join the EU386.
29/03/2022		After the Ukrainian proposals, Russia offers to reduce its presence around Kiev387.
08/04/2022	In a tweet, Josep Borrell, the EU's foreign minister, said: «500 million in additional EU aid is being released. Arms deliveries will be tailored to Ukraine's needs. This war must be won on the battlefield.388	
09/04/2022	During an impromptu visit to Volodymyr Zelensky, Boris Johnson brings him two messages: «Putin is a war criminal, he should be pressured, not negotiated with. And secondly, if you are ready to sign guarantee agreements with him, we are not.»389 402	

385. «Russia no longer requesting Ukraine be 'denazified' as part of ceasefire talks», Financial Times, 28 March 2022.
386. Joe Walsh, 'Russia-Ukraine Peace Talks: Russia Willing To Let Ukraine Join EU If It Stays Out Of NATO, Report Says', Forbes, 28 March 2022 (https://www.forbes.com/sites/joewalsh/2022/03/28/russia-ukraine-peace-talks-russia-willing-to-let-ukraine-join-eu-if-it-stays-out-of-nato-report-says/).
387. Jonathan Spicer & Gleb Garanich, 'Russia pledges to reduce attack on Kyiv but U.S. warns threat not over', Reuters, 29 March 2022 (https://www.reuters.com/world/europe/ukraine-sets-ceasefire-goal-new-russia-talks-breakthrough-looks-distant-2022-03-29/).
388. https://www.courrierinternational.com/article/vu-de-russie-l-ue-veut-sweeping-diplomacy-for-profit-war-esteem-moscow
389. Роман Романюк, « Від «капітуляції» Зеленського до капітуляції Путіна. Як ідуть переговори з Росією», pravda.ua, 5 May 2022 (https://www.pravda.com.

	Event in Ukraine/West	Adapting Russia's objectives
22/04/2022		While no progress has been made in the negotiation process, the Russians are adapting their objective. The Ministry of Defence announces that the new objective is to take control of the southern part of Ukraine up to Transnistria, where the Russian-speaking minority is mistreated.

Figure 50 - Evolution of operational objectives and their impact on Russian strategic objectives in Ukraine.

Russian objectives are therefore adjusted as the situation evolves. Even what look like concessions are part of a more general plan. For example, the withdrawal of troops from around Kiev, announced on 29 March 2022 as a goodwill gesture in the framework of the Istanbul negotiations, was most likely planned a long time ago. It served to withdraw troops from an area of secondary importance to Moscow in order to strengthen its position in the Donbass area, where its primary objective lies. The Russians also seek to exploit their operational successes into strategic successes. Thus, the creation of a corridor between Donbass and Crimea was probably not the initial objective of the operation. But the 'demilitarisation' of the Ukrainian threat (i.e. the destruction of forces) gradually led to the establishment of this corridor. It is likely that if the EU and the Ukrainian far right had let Zelensky negotiate with Russia on 25 February, as he had wanted, Russia would not have been able to establish the corridor. Western self-persuasion that Russia's defeat was inevitable helped Ukraine lose the southern part of the country.

ua/articles/2022/05/5/7344096/); Abdul Rahman, «Ukrainian news outlet suggests UK and US governments are primary obstacles to peace», Peoples Dispatch, 9 May 2022 (https://peoplesdispatch.org/2022/05/09/ukrainian-news-outlet-suggests-uk-and-us-governments-are-primary-obstacles-to-peace/)

As Sergei Lavrov reminded us in his interview with several Russian media on 20 July 2022, Russia's objectives are not geographical or territorial. As Vladimir Putin said on 24 February, it is to «demilitarise», in other words to neutralise the military threat to the Donbass. This obviously means an advance on the ground, but the ground is not the objective. As Lavrov says, if the West provides missiles with a range of 300 km to Ukraine, to achieve their objective, Russian forces will have to advance 300 km to destroy these missiles or have a 300 km buffer zone[390]. Lavrov is merely repeating what Vladimir Putin said in early July 2022: «The longer the conflict goes on, the more difficult the negotiations will be.[391]

In October 2022, General Surovikin, newly appointed Commander of the Joint Task Force in the area of the special military operation in Ukraine, explains the Russian strategy:

> *We have a different strategy. [...] We do not seek a high speed of progress, we spare each of our soldiers and methodically «crush» the advancing enemy[392].*

The problem is that our 'experts' and TV generals have a very Western view of the conduct of war. For them, the

390.»Foreign Minister Sergey Lavrov's interview with RT television, Sputnik agency and Rossiya Segodnya International Information Agency, Moscow, July 20, 2022», Embassy of the Russian Federation in Germany, 21 July 2022 (https://russische-botschaft.ru/de/2022/07/21/foreign-minister-sergey-lavrovs-interview-with-rt-television-sputnik-agency-and-rossiya-segodnya-international-information-agency-moscow-july-20-2022/)

391.»Putin warns negotiations will get harder longer conflict in Ukraine continues, Radio New Zealand, 8 July 2022 (https://www.rnz.co.nz/news/world/470559/putin-warns-negotiations-will-get-harder-longer-conflict-in-ukraine-continues)

392. «Суровикин: российская группировка на Украине методично «перемалывает» войска противника», TASS, 18 October 2022 (https://tass.ru/armiya-i-opk/16090805)

objective is always material (oil, land, industries, etc.). So we saw the Iraq war motivated by oil and the Afghanistan war by gas pipelines... But, contrary to appearances, these are rarely the real objectives of a war, and they are sometimes collateral gains: there are many cheaper and less risky ways to appropriate wealth. But Westerners find it hard to see military objectives in anything other than quantitative terms. In Ukraine, our armchair military is making exactly the same mistake. The Russians have defined a qualitative objective: the disappearance of a threat. This can only be achieved in two ways: negotiation or the total annihilation of this threat.

In November 2022, spurred on by the impending failure of the mid-term elections, the American government seems to have understood this dynamic[393] and encourages Volodymyr Zelensky to negotiate. Unlike the European authorities and media, he believes that war leads nowhere. On 14 September, in her State of the Union address, Ursula von der Leyen declared that «this is a time for determination, not appeasement»[394].

6.2.Two ways of waging war

It is difficult to get a clear picture of the course of the conflict in Ukraine. From the outset, there were two distinct ways of conducting operations:

393. Missy Ryan, John Hudson & Paul Sonne, «U.S. privately asks Ukraine to show it's open to negotiate with Russia», The Washington Post, 5 November 2022 (https://www.washingtonpost.com/national-security/2022/11/05/ukraine-russia-peace-negotiations/)

394. «State of the Union Address 2022 by President von der Leyen, European Commission, 14 September 2022 (https://ec.europa.eu/commission/presscorner/detail/fr/speech_22_5493)

- Russia is fighting a conventional war of a military nature. Decisions on the ground are clearly taken by the military staff. Vladimir Putin seems to be following the advice of the military. For a careful - and objective - observer of the course of operations, this gives an impression of coherence between the operational and strategic levels.
- Ukraine is waging a political war. Its field of action is the infosphere: it is not a question of physical victory, but of giving the impression that one is victorious. As Oleksei Arestovich explained in March 2019, the objective is not really to preserve Ukraine: it is to defeat Russia.

The actual outcome of the Ukrainian operations is at odds with the rhetoric in the West. Hence the prohibition on troops retreating (rather like in the First World War). During Phase 1 of the Russian operation, the garrisons were surrounded one after the other. They will be fought in Phase 2, often deprived of command and with their logistical lines cut off. On the one hand, we have the methodical conduct of Russia, which communicates very little about its operations. This is explained by the principle of operational security (OPSEC), which aims to avoid endangering the conduct of operations by divulging details. It also avoids creating false expectations and allows for a more flexible conduct of operations. On the other hand, we have a more Western communication, punctuated by the media appearances of Volodymyr Zelensky. We are in the culture of 'storytelling', where the substance is more in the packaging than in the content. This is the technique of the used car salesman. The Russians do not have this culture. Their communication is more direct, but also more spartan. Less attractive but more factual, the Russian way has the advantage of being more credible. Our media, such as France 5, LCI or RTS, have systematically based their information on - unverified - declarations from Ukraine, systematically dismissing information from Russia as disinformation. However, with the benefit of hindsight, we can see that these media systematically misled their audience, and that the information given by Moscow was much more reliable. If our media had applied the Munich Charter, Ukraine would probably have suffered less...

6.3.Russian conduct

6.3.1.Russian military doctrine

The Russians have always attached particular importance to doctrine. More than in the West, they have understood that «a common way of seeing» - as Marshal Foch said - allows for infinite variations in the conception of operations. Military doctrine is a sort of «common core» that serves as a reference for designing operations.

The problem with the vast majority of our so-called military experts is their inability to understand the Russian approach to war. We have seen this phenomenon with the terrorist attacks: the adversary is demonised to such an extent that we do not understand his way of thinking. Unscrupulous journalists, together with media that reflect their image, contribute to stirring up hatred and increasing our vulnerability[395]. Under these conditions, it is impossible to find rational and effective solutions to the problem!

395. https://oumma.com/jacques-baud-lancien-espion-qui-aimait-poutine/

Based on an article written by Valery Gherassimov, Chief of the Russian General Staff, in 2013, entitled «The Value of Science in Foresight»[396], Westerners have imagined the concept of «hybrid warfare» as part of Russian doctrine. Dubbed the 'Gherassimov doctrine', hybrid warfare is supposed to bring together cyberwarfare, terrorism, clandestine warfare, conventional warfare and information warfare. The magazine Le Point even claims that this doctrine has been «validated by Vladimir Putin» himself[397]. This is disinformation.

Mark Galeotti, a Russia specialist, who initially suggested the existence of this 'Gherassimov doctrine' and the Russian concept of hybrid warfare[398], realises that he was wrong. In 2018, he apologised, and with courage and intelligence wrote an article in Foreign Policy magazine, entitled «I'm sorry I created the Gherassimov doctrine»[399] :

I was the first to write about Russia's infamous high-tech military strategy. One small problem: it doesn't exist.

Observation of the operations in Ukraine shows that they are taking place in a very conventional manner. Western armies have prepared for a type of war that does not exist.

Russian military doctrine is divided into three main components: tactics (taktika), operative art (operativnoe iskoustvo) and strategy (strategiya). While tactics is considered to be an activity

---

396.Герасимов Валерий, «Ценность науки в предвидении», vpk-news.ru, 26 February 2013 (https://vpk-news.ru/articles/14632)

397.Marc Nexon, «Gerasimov, le général russe qui mène la guerre de l'information», Le Point, 2 March 2017

398. Mark Galeotti, "The "Gerasimov Doctrine" and Russian Non-Linear War", inmoscowsshadows.wordpress.com, 7 June 2014

399. Mark Galeotti, "I'm Sorry for Creating the 'Gerasimov Doctrine'", Foreign Policy, 5 March 2018

with an essentially technical character and strategy an essentially intellectual activity with a political character, 'operative art' is the art of designing operations.

Operational art is neither a type of operation (as some experts have stated) nor a way of waging war, but the part of military doctrine that governs the level of conduct between the tactical and strategic levels. It is the general framework within which military operations are designed. It should be noted that it is an 'art', i.e. an activity where imagination and creativity are encouraged, as the Russian Military Encyclopaedia points out[400].

In the West, the terms 'operational' and 'operative' are often confused. This is because the word 'operative' does not exist in English, where it is translated as 'operational'. In Russian terminology, the word «operational» expresses a technical state (e.g. operational equipment), while «operative» refers to a level of conduct. In NATO terminology, the word «operational» covers both aspects.

Since the mid-1990s, Westerners have fought only wars that were almost exclusively fought at the tactical level. This has resulted in two conceptual weaknesses that now affect NATO armies and thus the Ukrainian army in the way it conducts operations:

- the inability to develop strategies, with a tendency to see strategy as the juxtaposition of tactical actions; and
- the inability to think about the conduct of war in operational terms.

400. https://encyclopedia.mil.ru/encyclopedia/dictionary/details.htm?id=13724@morfDictionary

The Russians saw operative art as a multiplier of tactical action to achieve strategic objectives. This is why, from the very beginning, the Russian offensive bore the seeds of victory.

The Western propaganda media like to use the term «Blitzkrieg» to create an analogy between today's Russia and Nazi Germany. However, very few of the experts and strategists of the day who frequent our television sets know what they are talking about. In France, the term «Blitzkrieg» is associated with anti-German propaganda and tends to designate a brutal way of waging war. A way of justifying France's operational errors in 1940...

In fact, 'blitzkrieg' is not a way of waging war, but a way of conducting operations by engaging a numerically superior adversary with less manpower. It is a dynamic approach to operations that combines the synergies of mechanised ground forces and air forces. Theorised by Sir Basil Liddell Hart in the 1920s and 1930s, then taken up by the Germans, it inspired General Mikhail Tukhachevsky in the 1930s, who developed the Russian concept of «operation in depth», used extensively by the Red Army during the Second World War.

One of the «secrets» of Russian success is their ability to use their assets in a synergistic way. This is the concept of «inter-blade operation» (общевойсковая операция) which is one of the foundations of their operative art but which the West, in thirty years of colonial-type wars, has totally forgotten.

The Russians are masters of the operative art. The forces they deployed for their February offensive were inferior to those of Ukraine from the start.

Thus, according to the Western notion of 'balance of power', the Russians were not winning. On the other hand, according to the Russian notion of 'correlation of forces' (соотношение сил), the Russians had the advantage, despite their numerical inferiority. This is the second 'secret' of Russia's success: manoeuvre.

To attack a force with inferior numbers, they manoeuvre their troops to achieve limited superiorities in time and space, sufficient to gain the advantage, before redeploying troops to create another local superiority in another sector. This is the modern version of Tukhachevsky's concept: the Operational Manoeuvre Group (OGM) (Група оперативного маневра - Gruppa operativnovo manevra)

Often confused with the notion of 'operative art' by some 'experts'[401], the LDA is an ad hoc, highly mobile force that pushes into the depths of the enemy's position according to the 'flowing water' principle: its support points and major localities are bypassed without any real fighting. In fact, the objective of the LDA was not to destroy the enemy, but to gain favourable positions for the continuation of operations.

6.3.2. The Russian operative concept in Ukraine

On 24 February 2022, Russia launches its 'special military operation' (Spetsial'naya Voyennaya Operatsiya - SVO) in Ukraine 'at short notice'. It communicates little about its planning. Nevertheless, observation and study of its military doctrine allow us to sketch the broad outlines of its operational thinking.

According to Pentagon figures, the Russians have committed about 80 Battle Groups (BTGs), totalling about 65,000-100,000 men[402], plus the DPR and LPR militias. The Ukrainian forces then

401. https://www.rts.ch/info/monde/13135499-bernard-wicht-le-succes-de-loperation-russe-cest-davoir-reussi-a-mystifier-tout-le-monde.html

402. «Senior Defense Official Holds a Background Briefing, April 18, 2022», defense.gov, 18 April 2022 (https://www.defense.gov/News/Transcripts/Transcript/Article/3002867/senior-defense-official-holds-a-background-briefing-april-18-2022/)

totalled 200,000 to 250,000[403] men. In May 2022, the Russian coalition (Russia, DPR and LPR) will have 100,000-190,000 troops and Ukraine will have 700,000[404].

From these figures, it can be seen that the Russians started their operation with a force three to four times smaller than that of the Ukrainians. In the Donbass, taking into account the forces of the Donetsk and Lugansk People's Republics (DPR and LPR), the ratio of forces can be estimated at 1-2 to 1 in favour of the Russian coalition.

As in Syria, Russia rigorously applies one of the key principles of warfare: economy of force. This principle has implications for the way operations are conducted. Indeed, it seems to contradict the rules of military art, as it is generally accepted that an attack requires a superiority of 3 to 1 for it to be successful. To reconcile this principle with an attack carried out with lesser numbers than the Ukrainian army, the Russians relied on highly mobile battle groups that could be moved quickly to create local superiorities.

6.3.2.1 Phase 1

In accordance with Russian military doctrine, the SVO is articulated in two thrusts:

- a main thrust directed towards the south of the country in the Donbass region and along the Azov Sea coast. It is led by a coalition (Z) consisting of Russian forces from the Southern

403. Prasanta Kumar Dutta, Samuel Granados & Michael Ovaska, «On the edge of war», Reuters, 26 January 2022 (https://graphics.reuters.com/RUSSIA-UKRAINE/dwpkrkwkgvm/)

404. «700,000 soldiers defending Ukraine now, Zelenskyy says, as battles rage in the Donbas», Euronews/AP/AFP, 21 May 2022 (https://www.euronews.com/2022/05/21/live-sievierodonetsk-shelling-brutal-and-pointless-zelenskyy-says-as-russia-continues-offe)

Military District through Kharkov and Crimea, with - in the centre - forces from the Republics of Donetsk and Lugansk, as well as a contribution from the Chechen National Guard for fighting in the urban area of Mariupol; and

- a secondary push on Kiev, led by Russian forces from Belarus (V) and Russia (O).

Summary concept of the Russian operation (Phase 1)

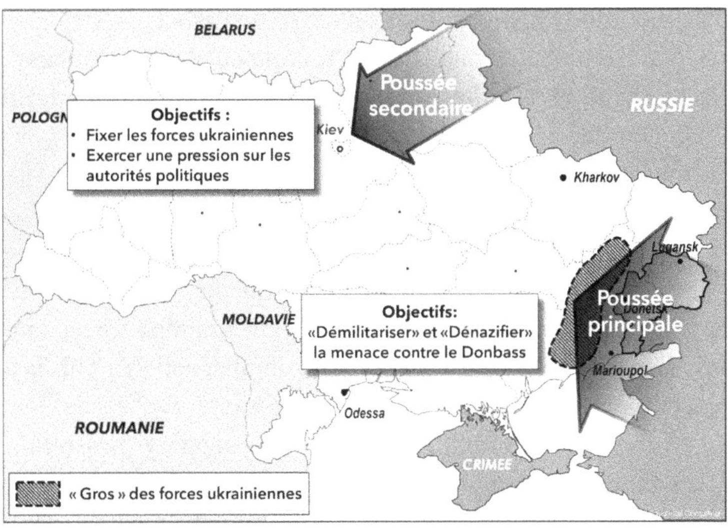

Figure 54 - The general mechanics of Russia's special operation follows its operational doctrine. It is articulated in a main thrust and a secondary thrust. The role of the secondary thrust is to create favourable conditions for the main thrust to unfold.

6.3.2.1.1. The objectives

The sequence of operations follows the objectives set out by Vladimir Putin in his televised address on 24 February. The intention of Phase 1 is to create favourable conditions for Phase 2, which will be the «pièce de résistance» of what the Russians call «Special Military Operation» (Специальная военная операция) (SVO).

The mechanics of the operation stem from the fact that the Russian coalition forces are attacking with an overall smaller force than Ukraine. To achieve their objectives, they must be able to create limited superiorities in space and time. This can only be achieved by preventing Ukrainian forces in the west of the country from reinforcing the main force in the Donbass.

The final objective of the SVO can be broken down into two objectives along the main thrust axis: to neutralise

- the Ukrainian armed forces regrouped in the Donbass in preparation for the offensive against the DPR and LPR («demilitarisation» objective), and
- the ultra-nationalist paramilitary militias of Mariupol (objective of «denazification»).

It is therefore necessary to push very quickly in depth towards Kiev during Phase 1, in order to 'fix' the Ukrainian forces in the capital sector and hold them back with combat actions. This is the objective of the secondary push towards Kiev.

Did the Russians anticipate that this secondary thrust would attract more Western attention than the main thrust? We don't know. Nevertheless, the Western reaction and the media coverage of the Ukrainian defence centred on Zelensky made the Russians' task easier.

Phase 1 of the operation (24 February - 30 March 2022)

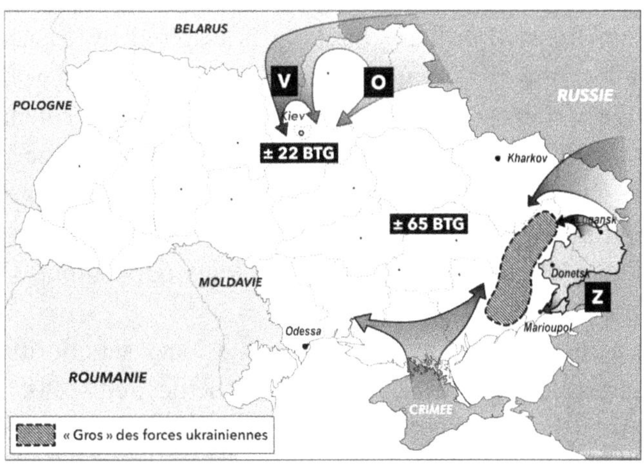

Figure 55 - Phase 1 of the Russian operation from 24 February to 30 March 2022. The number of troops committed by Russia shows that the capture of Kiev was never an objective. With 22 battle groups (about 20,000 men) it was impossible to take the city. [Figures: US Department of Defense]

With Ukrainian forces massed in the south of the country in preparation for an offensive against the Donbass, the Russian-Ukrainian border was virtually undefended. The V and O forces and the northern grouping of the Z force were able to advance fairly easily and quickly towards Kiev.

Listening only to their prejudices, Western pseudo-experts and politicians got it into their heads that Russia's objective was to take over Ukraine and overthrow its government. This is what the West has systematically sought to do in the wars it has waged. Trained and advised by NATO experts, the Ukrainian general staff predictably applied the same logic. They attributed to Russia the objective of regime change in Kiev and thus saw the city as the Russians' primary objective.

Vladimir Putin's speech was unambiguous: he wants to eradicate the threat to the Russian-speaking population of Donbass, full stop. Russian military thinking is inspired by Clausewitz, who defined the «centre of gravity» (Schwerpunkt) as the primary objective of a strategy. The 'centre of gravity' is the element from which a belligerent derives its strength and capacity for action. For the Russians, in the context of the Donbass, the Ukrainian centre of gravity is the ensemble of its military and paramilitary forces that threaten the Russian-speaking population. This is therefore the priority objective.

On a more technical level, to create local superiority, it is necessary to bring sufficient force into the desired sector, while preventing the opponent from reinforcing his position. This is the role of «shaping operations» (in American terminology). The aim of shaping operations is to draw or fix the enemy's forces in certain areas, leaving the way clear for decisive operations, i.e. those that allow the objectives to be achieved. In Phase 1 of the SVO, the action in the Donbass is a 'decisive operation', while the actions around Kiev and in the south towards Zaporozhie are 'shaping operations'.

The Russian Ministry of Defence explains this mechanism in a press release published on 30 March[405].

On 28 March, with the encirclement of the last square of neo-Nazis in Azovstal, the objective of 'denazification' was considered to have been achieved and removed from the list of Russian objectives, as reported by the Financial Times[406].

At this stage, the Russians have received a written proposal from Zelensky in the framework of the Istanbul negotiations.

405. https://z.mil.ru/spec_mil_oper/news/more.htm?id=12415372@egNews

406. «Russia no longer requesting Ukraine be «denazified» as part of ceasefire talks, Financial Times, 28 March 2022 (https://www.businessinsider.com/russia-nazi-demand-for-ukraine-dropped-in-ceasefire-talks-2022-3?r=US&IR=T)

It contained elements that were considered positive but, under Western pressure, Zelensky withdrew his proposal. The fighting therefore continued and the Russian position was strengthened.

The capture of Mariupol allows the Russians to withdraw forces from this area to move on to Phase 2 and concentrate their efforts on the objective of «demilitarisation» in the Donbass. Now in a position of superiority in its decisive area of operation, Russia withdraws its troops from the Kiev sector in order to strengthen its position in the south of the country. It passes off as a gesture of goodwill what is in fact the regrouping of its forces in the Donbass. For its part, Kiev passes this withdrawal off as a victory - which is, so to speak, a good thing - but which also has a perverse effect, because the West sees it as a tangible sign of a defeat that has been announced. This encourages them to supply Ukraine with even more weapons, which will lead to the death of thousands of Ukrainian soldiers, without improving the military situation.

In May 2022, Claude Wild, the Swiss ambassador in Kiev, declared on RTS that the Russians had «lost the battle of Kiev»[407]. This shows that the West has been unable to overcome its prejudices to intervene constructively in the political resolution of the conflict.

Conversely, the Russians sought to transform their operational successes into strategic successes. They understand war from a Clausewitzian perspective: war is the pursuit of politics by other means. This is why they move from one to the other in a fluid manner by adapting their operational objectives to the changing military situation. In the case of Ukraine, their objectives evolve with their

---

407. «No one would have bet a franc on such resistance, says Swiss ambassador to Ukraine», RTS Info, 24 May 2022 (https://www.rts.ch/info/monde/13121067-personne-naurait-parie-un-franc-sur-une-telle-resistance-estime-lambassadeur-suisse-en-ukraine.html)

operational successes in order to encourage the Ukrainian side to engage in a negotiation process.

6.3.2.1.2. Russian failure or success?

Success is determined by whether or not the objectives are achieved. The Western media are happy to talk about defeat based on objectives that were not formulated by Russia but by themselves! Having determined the objectives ourselves, we can now say that Putin has not achieved them! Thus, the «experts» on our TV sets assured us that Vladimir Putin was trying to take over Kiev. On 2 March 2022, on RTS, a Swiss military expert stated that «if Kiev has not fallen in the next 48 hours, there will be a 'rotting' of hostilities»[408].

However, the Russian coalition never tried to take Kiev. From the beginning of the offensive, Zelensky was willing to negotiate with Russia. It was the European Union that scuppered the first attempts at the Belarus border on 25 February. The Russians know that Zelensky is under the influence of neo-Nazi elements in his entourage, but that he is interested in negotiating. They therefore have no interest in trying to overthrow him, quite the contrary. According to the Pentagon, the Russians have deployed only about 20,000 to 25,000 troops in the Kiev area. By comparison, it is estimated that they deployed about 40 000 troops to take Mariupol, a considerably smaller city.

On 9 May 2022, Marc Allgöwer of RTS explains that Vladimir Putin is reluctant to launch a general mobilisation despite the lack

408. «Alexandre Vautravers: «Russia has a weapon just as cruel as chemical weapons», RTS.ch, 2 March 2022 (https://www.rts.ch/info/monde/12906989-alexandre-vautravers-la-russie-dispose-dune-arme-tout-aussi-cruelle-que-larme-chimique.html)

of resources in Ukraine, because it would jeopardise his credibility[409]. This is disinformation.

In reality, Vladimir Putin never said he wanted to take Kiev. He never said he wanted to take the city in two days. He never said he wanted to overthrow President Zelensky. He never said he wanted to take over the whole of Ukraine[410]. He never said he was aiming for a victory on 9 May. He never said that he wanted to announce this victory at the May 9 parade. He never said that he wanted to «declare war» on 9 May so that he could trigger a general mobilisation[411].

Our «journalists» do not analyse anything: they invent!

The Western discourse on a stalled Russian offensive with little success is part of the information war. For example, the sequence of maps of the operations published by Libération between 24 February and 18 March shows practically no difference from one day to the next[412]. On 23 March, on France 5, journalist Élise Vincent estimated the territory taken by the Russian coalition as the equivalent of Switzerland or the Netherlands (i.e. about 41,000 km2)[413].

Officially, Ukrainian counter-offensives followed one another and the Russian coalition forces kept retreating. However, at the beginning of June 2022, Volodymyr Zelensky admitted that

---

409. https://www.rts.ch/emissions/infrarouge/13079683-guerre-en-ukraine-la-russie-dans-limpasse.html

410. https://www.rts.ch/play/tv/redirect/detail/13086647?startTime=790

411. https://www.rts. ch/info/world/13066001-putin-takes-risk-of-declaring-general-mobilization-on-9-May.html

412. Julien Guillot & Alice Clair, «Guerre en Ukraine: la carte de l'évolution des bombardments et de l'avancée russes», Libération, 24 February 2022 (updated on 18 March 2022) (https://www.liberation.fr/international/europe/guerre-en-ukraine-la-carte-des-bombardements-russes-20220224_BULDIVVKBVGS5CBDLTMWWSVPO4/)

413. https://youtu.be/ThzBH5cbH0A?t=1372

Russia controlled 20% of Ukrainian territory (i.e. approximately 120,000 km2)[414].

Self-convinced that the Russian offensive is aimed at the occupation of Ukraine and the overthrow of power in Kiev, Western experts have quite logically concluded that a) the Russians are stalling and b) their offensive is doomed to failure because they will not be able to hold the country in the long term.

In this concert of errors and lies, some honest observers note that Russia is on the road to success. For example, in April, The Times of London noted that Russia was on its way to defeating[415].

This does not prevent Jens Stoltenberg, on 15 May 2022, from declaring that Ukraine can still win the war[416].

The «military experts» who parade around on our television sets seem to have forgotten what a second lieutenant should know: «Know your enemy! And not as you would like him to be, but as he is!

A typical example is the hearing of Colonel Michel Goya by a French Senate committee on the lessons of the war in Ukraine. Without any knowledge of Russian military doctrine or the functioning of alliances, he analyses the war in terms of what a French soldier would do! His approach is to think that the war can only be waged in a French logic. This is precisely what had led France to engage in the First World War, to ignore the German threat

414. «Russia controls 'about 20 percent' of Ukraine, says Zelensky», France 24, 3 June 2022 (https://www.france24.com/en/video/20220603-russia-controls-about-20-percent-of-ukraine-says-zelensky)

415. George Grylls, 'Ukraine war: Revitalised Russia can still win, western intelligence warns', The Times, 21 April 2022 (https://www.thetimes.co.uk/article/ukraine-war-revitalised-russia-can-still-win-western-intelligence-warns-fvwc-9cz0n)

416. «Ukraine 'can win' war, says Nato secretary general», RTS.ch, 16 May 2022 (https://www.rts.ch/info/monde/13095545-lukraine-peut-gagner-la-guerre-selon-le-secretaire-general-de-lotan.html)

in 1940 and which was at the origin of the wave of terrorism in France in 2015-2016. In this context, one is astonished by the lack of hindsight and the poor level of knowledge of the senators who hear our 'expert'.

Furthermore, it should be noted that Ukrainian forces do not appear on any situation map presented in our media. Thus, while the Ministry of Defence map gives a slightly more honest picture of reality, it carefully avoids mentioning Ukrainian forces in the Donbass area.

In fact, Ukrainian forces are never shown on our maps, as this would show that they were not deployed on the Russian border in February 2022, but were regrouped in the south of the country in preparation for the offensive, the preparatory phase of which began on 16 February. This confirms that Russia was only reacting to a situation initiated by the West, through Ukraine, as we shall see. Today, it is these forces that are surrounded and methodically fragmented and neutralised little by little by the Russian coalition.

The vagueness about the situation of Ukrainian forces in the West has other effects. First, it maintains the illusion of a possible Ukrainian victory. Thus, instead of encouraging a negotiation process, the West seeks to prolong the war. This is why the European Union and some of its member countries have sent weapons and are encouraging the civilian population and volunteers of all kinds to go and fight, often without training and without any real command structure, with deadly consequences.

We know that in a conflict, each side tends to provide information to give a favourable image of its action. But the picture we have of the situation and the Ukrainian forces is based exclusively on data provided by Kyiv. It masks the profound deficiencies of the Ukrainian leadership, even though it is trained and advised by NATO troops.

Thus, military logic would have dictated that the forces caught in the Donbass should have withdrawn to a line at the Dnieper, for example, in order to regroup and carry out a counter-offensive; but they were forbidden by President Zelensky to withdraw. Already in 2014 and 2015, a close examination of the operations showed that the Ukrainians were applying 'Western-style' schemes, totally unsuited to the circumstances, in the face of a more imaginative, flexible opponent with lighter leadership structures. The same phenomenon is occurring today. Finally, the partial view of the battlefield given to us by our media has made us unable to help the Ukrainian leadership make the right decisions. It has led us to believe that the obvious strategic objective was Kiev, that «demilitarisation» was aimed at Ukraine's accession to NATO, and that «denazification» was aimed at overthrowing Zelensky. This legend was fuelled by Vladimir Putin's call for disobedience to the Ukrainian military, which was interpreted (with great imagination and prejudice) as a call to overthrow the government. The call was directed at the Ukrainian forces deployed in the Donbass to surrender without fighting. The Western interpretation caused the Ukrainian government to misjudge Russian objectives and misuse its potential to win.

You don't win a war with prejudice: you lose it, and that is what is happening. For example, the Russian coalition has never been «on the run» or «stopped» by heroic resistance: it has simply not attacked where it was expected to! We did not want to listen to what Vladimir Putin explained to us very clearly. This is why we (i.e. our media and politicians) have thus become - volens nolens - the main architects of the Ukrainian defeat that is taking shape. Paradoxically, it is probably because of a few self-proclaimed experts and occasional strategists on our TV sets that Ukraine is in this situation today!

6.3.2.1.3. The conduct of the fight

The analyses presented in our media come either from politicians or pseudo-military experts, who explain the war from their own experience in totally different contexts, and who end up relaying the Ukrainian propaganda.

These 'studio strategists' are clearly trying to overdramatise the situation in order to rule out any negotiated solution[417]. This development is prompting some Western militaries to speak out and offer a more nuanced judgment. Thus, in Newsweek, an analyst from the Defense Intelligence Agency (DIA) - the American equivalent of the Direction du Renseignement Militaire (DRM) in France - notes that

> *In 24 days of conflict, Russia carried out some 1,400 strikes and launched nearly 1,000 missiles (by comparison, the United States carried out more strikes and launched more missiles on the first day of the Iraq war in 2003).* [418]

While the West 'prepares' the battlefield with intensive and prolonged strikes before sending their troops on the ground, the Russians prefer a less destructive but more troop-intensive approach. On France 5, journalist Mélanie Tarvant presents the

417. «War in Ukraine: Vladimir Putin «does not want to negotiate anything, he wants to exterminate Ukraine», says a specialist in Europe, franceinfo, 12 March 2022 (https://www.francetvinfo.fr/monde/europe/manifestations-en-ukraine/guerre-en-ukraine-vladimir-poutine-ne-veut-rien-negocier-il-veut-exterminer-l-ukraine-affirme-un-specialiste-de-l-europe_5006026.html)
418. William M. Arkin, «Putin's Bombers Could Devastate Ukraine But He's Holding Back. Here's Why,» Newsweek, 22 March 2022 (https://www.newsweek.com/putins-bombers-could-devastate-ukraine-hes-holding-back-heres-why-1690494)

death of generals on the battlefield as evidence of the destabilisation of the Russian army[419]. Apart from the fact that she evokes rumours that have already been debunked, she shows a profound ignorance of the traditions and operating methods of the Russian army. While commanders in the West tend to lead from the rear, their Russian counterparts tend to lead from the front. In the West, they say, «Forward!» In Russia, we say, «Follow me! This explains both the high losses in the upper echelons of command once seen in Afghanistan and the much more rigorous selection of cadres than in the West.

The DIA analyst goes further, noting that «the vast majority of airstrikes take place over the battlefield, with Russian aircraft providing 'close air support' to ground forces. The remainder - less than 20%, according to US experts - target military airfields, barracks and support depots. Thus, the phrase «indiscriminate bombing [that] devastates the city and kills everyone» echoed by the Western media seems to contradict the US intelligence expert who says «if we just convince ourselves that Russia is bombing indiscriminately, or that they are failing to inflict more damage because their personnel are not up to the task or are technically inept, then we are not seeing the conflict for what it is.

In fact, Russian operations differ fundamentally from the Western concept. The West's obsession with having no fatalities in their own forces leads to operations that are conducted primarily by very lethal air strikes. Ground troops only intervene when everything has been destroyed. This is why, in Afghanistan[420] or

---

419. https://youtu.be/KV39YTyQpqQ?t=669

420. Amy Woodyatt & Arnaud Siad, «More civilians are being killed by Afghan and international forces than by the Taliban and other militants», CNN, 31 July 2019 (https://edition.cnn.com/2019/07/30/asia/afghanistan-nato-taliban-intl-scli/index.html)

in the Sahel,[421] the West kills more civilians[422] than the terrorists do. This is why Western countries engaged in Afghanistan, the Middle East and North Africa no longer publish the civilian casualties caused by their strikes. In fact, Europeans engaged in regions that only marginally affect their national security, such as the Estonians in the Sahel, go there to «get their act together». In Ukraine, the situation is very different. One only has to look at a map of linguistic zones to see that the Russian coalition operates almost exclusively in the Russian-speaking zone, thus in the midst of populations that are generally favourable to it. This also explains the statements of a US Air Force officer: «I know the media keeps saying that Putin is targeting civilians, but there is no evidence that Russia is doing it intentionally»[423].

Conversely, it is for the same reason - but in a different way - that Ukraine has deployed its ultra-nationalist paramilitary fighters in major cities such as Mariupol[424]. With no emotional or cultural ties to the local population, these militias can fight even at the cost of heavy civilian casualties. These atrocities, which are now coming to light[425], are still being covered up by

421. Nathanaël Charbonnier, «Les armées régulières seraient tout aussi meurtrières (voire plus) que les terroristes au Sahel», radiofrance.fr, 3 May 2021 (https://www.franceinter.fr/monde/les-armees-regulieres-seraient-tout-aussi-meurtrieres-voire-plus-que-les-terroristes-au-sahel)

422. «Sahel: les populations craignent plus les bavures des forces de protection que les attaques djihadistes», RTBF.be, 14 April 2021 (https://www.rtbf.be/article/sahel-les-populations-craignent-plus-les-bavures-des-forces-de-protection-que-les-attaques-djihadistes-10740544)

423. William M. Arkin, «Putin's Bombers Could Devastate Ukraine But He's Holding Back. Here's Why,» Newsweek, 22 March 2022 (https://www.newsweek.com/putins-bombers-could-devastate-ukraine-hes-holding-back-heres-why-1690494)

424. Roman Goncharenko, «The Azov Battalion: Extremists defending Mariupol», dw.com, 16 March 2022 (https://p.dw.com/p/48aCt)

425. Tim Lister, Celine Alkhaldi, Katerina Krebs & Josh Pennington, «Ukraine promises 'immediate investigation' after video surfaces of soldiers shooting Russian prisoners», CNN, 27 March 2022 (https://edition.cnn.com/europe/live-news/

the French-language media for fear of losing support for Ukraine, as noted by media close to Republicans in the United States[426].

After «decapitation» strikes[427] in the first minutes of the offensive, the Russian operational strategy consisted in bypassing the urban centres to envelop the Ukrainian army «fixed» by the forces of the Donbass republics. It should be remembered that the aim of «decapitation» is not to annihilate the staffs or the government (as our «experts», steeped in French history, tend to understand it), but to cut off the leadership structures to prevent the coordinated manoeuvre of the forces. On the contrary, the aim is to preserve the leadership bodies in order to allow the negotiation of a way out of the crisis.

6.3.2.2. Phase 2

6.3.2.2.1. The objectives

After Phase 1, which consisted of putting forces in place, Phase 2 is devoted to «nibbling» at the Ukrainian position on the borders of the Donbass region.

The objective of Phase 2 is the actual demilitarisation of the threat against the Donbass. In other words, it is the methodical neutralisation of the bulk of the Ukrainian forces, which have been regrouped since 2021 in the south of the country in preparation for the offensive against the Donbass.

---

ukraine-russia-putin-news-03-27-22/h_6e158d3fc5bc5efe7fc3f10b69b7aeee)

426. «Zelenskyy Worried About Western Financial Support After Video Surfaces Showing Ukraine Military Torturing Russian POW's», The Conservative Treehouse, 27 March 2022 (https://theconservativetreehouse.com/blog/2022/03/27/zelenskyy-worried-about-western-financial-support-after-video-surfaces-showing-ukraine-military-torturing-russian-pows/?utm_source=rss&utm_medium=rss&utm_campaign=zelenskyy-worried-about-western-financial-support-after-video-surfaces-showing-ukraine-military-torturing-russian-pows)

427. https://military-history.fandom.com/wiki/Decapitation_strike

Since it is about destroying capabilities, there is no geographically determined objective. Therefore, the Ukrainian strategy of «holding» the ground at all costs and feeding the forces with troops instead of playing with their mobility makes the Russians' job easier.

Phase 2 of the operation (from 31 March 2022)

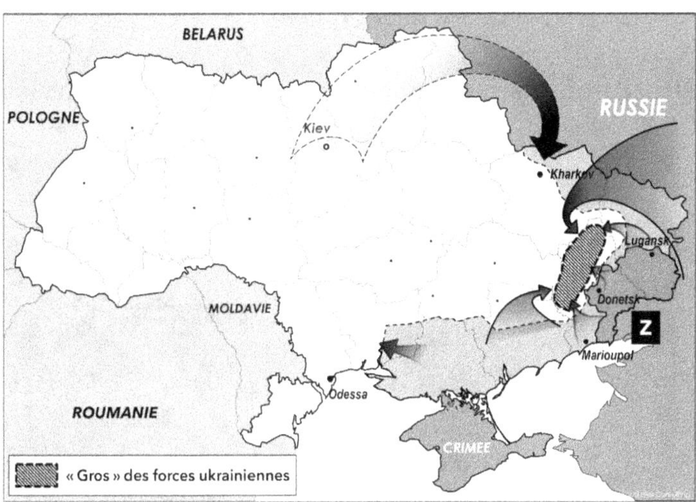

Figure 56 - Phase 2 is the gradual nibbling away of encircled Ukrainian forces in 'cauldrons'. This is done primarily by mechanised infantry forces and largely by militias from the Donetsk and Lugansk Republics.

6.3.2.2.2. The conduct of the fight

The actions carried out in the Donbass constitute the decisive operation. They are carried out by successive «nibbling» of encircled troops in secondary cauldrons, such as Severodonetsk-Lissitchansk, around the main cauldron of Slaviansk-Kramatorsk.

The Russians then applied the same operational scheme as in Phase 1, but limited to the Donbass. They created local superiorities by 'juggling' the BTGs:

- The forces surrounding Kiev in the north and those fighting in Mariupol in the south were redeployed to the Donbass region where most of the fighting was taking place.
- Shaping operations at the extremities of the area of operations (Kharkov in the north and Kherson in the south) prevent any reinforcement of Ukrainian troops in the cauldrons.

Density of Russian coalition forces in southern Ukraine (July 2022)

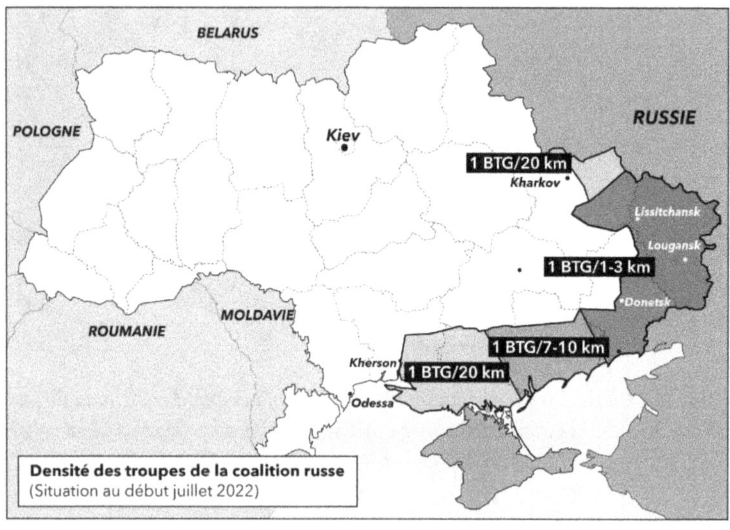

Figure 57 - BTG density is an indication of Russian main efforts. As of 10 June 2022, in the Kharkov and Kherson sectors, the density is 20 km per BTG. In the sector west of Donetsk, the density is 10 km per BTG. But in the Lissitchansk sector, the density is 3km per GRT. In other words, in the Kharkov and Kherson sectors the Russians are carrying out 'shaping operations', defensive operations in the Zaporozhie-Donetsk sector, and a decisive operation in the Lissichansk sector. The capture of Lissitchansk marks the complete takeover of the Lugansk Oblast by the Russian coalition.

The «counter-offensives» claimed by the Kiev authorities - and therefore by our media - in Kharkov and Kherson are in fact only «counter-attacks» of tactical scope. These sectors, described as «strategic», are not strategic for the Russians, at least not in this phase. The density of troops they deploy there is very insufficient to carry out large-scale attacks. In fact, their role is «simply» to fix the Ukrainian forces so that they do not reinforce the troops that the Russian coalition is «nibbling» in the Kramatorsk region. This is exactly the same pattern as in Kiev during Phase 1.

The complexity of this phase seems to be due to the fact that Russia does not want to significantly increase the number of its BTGs in the Ukrainian theatre. Indeed, Russia has only a limited number of these BTGs and obviously the Russian command wants to keep most of this potential as a reserve in case of a possible untimely offensive by a NATO country. This requires it to renew its forces by rotation, without increasing them.

The slowdown in the rate of advance of Russian forces in Phase 2 was due to five main factors.

Firstly, it was a question of dealing with the strong points that the LDAs of the first phase had initially bypassed. A change in the pace of operations was therefore clearly expected by the Russians.

Secondly, these strong points are usually made up of networks of trenches spread out in depth or localities where the defenders are difficult to dislodge. Unlike the West in Afghanistan, Iraq or Syria, which faced a determined but unarmed opponent, the Russian coalition is fighting an opponent of an equivalent nature. The choice of the Ukrainian command to fight for every square metre of land makes it difficult to advance, but also allows the objective to be achieved: to destroy Ukrainian military capabilities in the Donbass.

Thirdly, the Ukrainian troops deployed in the Donbass are highly trained and hardened.

Fourth, much of the fighting is being carried out by DPR and LPR troops, who are local, have acquaintances or relatives in the combat zone and - contrary to what our media claim - seek to avoid civilian casualties.

Fifthly, conversely for the Ukrainians, these populations are not really considered Ukrainian. They fought and bombed them for eight years. For them, they are the enemy. Consequently, they have far fewer scruples about forcing the civilian population to stay in the villages as long as possible.

It is likely that the slowing of the coalition's advance has disappointed some Russian expectations. The Western narrative of a Blitzkrieg is misleading, probably in order to create unreasonable expectations and point to Russian incapacity. In reality, this slowdown does not correspond to a decline in operational capabilities but to the changed nature of the fighting that was anticipated. This does not detract from the vagaries of war and the bravery shown by Ukrainian troops despite the incompetence of their command.

6.3.2.3. Phase 3

The Russian command has not clearly defined the end of Phase 2 and the next steps of its operation. By the end of the summer of 2022, there is a slowdown in Russian coalition operations, and a continuing effort in the Donbass region.

6.3.2.3.1. Ukraine's «deceptive» victory in Kharkov

On 6 September 2022, Ukrainian forces launched an offensive and retook the Kharkov region within days. Western politicians and media relayed Ukrainian propaganda to present this success as evidence of Russia's weakening and the prospect of a final victory soon. The reality is very different, and a closer look at the operations might have prompted Ukraine to be more cautious.

For several weeks now, some Western experts have been questioning the presence of the Russians in the Kharkov area, because clearly they had no intention of fighting in the city. In fact, as we have seen, the Russian coalition forces were maintaining only a minimal presence there, in order to fix the Ukrainian troops and prevent them from going into the Donbass, which is the real operational objective of the Russians. At the beginning of August, the Russian press already mentioned the possibility of a Ukrainian offensive in this sector[428].

The Ukrainians, for their part, had been under pressure since August to achieve success on the ground. Joe Biden needed a success before the mid-term elections in November and Volodymyr Zelensky feared that Western support was running out of steam. The Americans are therefore pushing Ukraine to multiply counter-offensives in the Kherson sector. Disorganised and led by inexperienced troops, they were systematically repulsed and caused enormous losses in the Ukrainian ranks, creating tensions between Zelensky and his staff.

In August, there were reports that the Russians had planned to abandon the Kharkov sector well before the Ukrainian attack began. They therefore withdrew in good order with some civilians who might have been subject to retaliation. For example, the huge ammunition depot at Balaklaya was empty when the Ukrainians discovered it, demonstrating that the Russians had been evacuating all sensitive personnel and equipment for several days. The Russians even left areas that Ukraine did not subsequently attack. Only a few Russian National Guard troops and Donbass militias remained in the area.

428. Алина Корнеева, «»СП»: Президент Украины Зеленский собрал миллионную армию под Харьковом для вторжения в РФ», RK-News, 8 August 2022 (https://rk-news.com/2022/08/08/568521166248.html)

The Russian reaction is limited to strikes against the electrical infrastructure. The aim is to paralyse the delivery of Ukrainian reinforcements by train to the Donbass and thus facilitate the redeployment of the Russian coalition troops. This abandonment of the field without a counter-offensive is interpreted as a weakness by the West.

6.3.2.3.2. Reasons for the Russian withdrawal

In August 2022, the Russians anticipate the outcome of the referenda in Kherson, Zaporozhie, Donetsk and Lugansk oblasts. They realise that the Kharkov region is not directly useful for the achievement of their objectives, and that they are in the same situation as with Snake Island in June: the energy to defend this territory is greater than its strategic importance.

When US intelligence detected the Russians' departure from the Kharkov region, they saw an opportunity for the Ukrainians to succeed and passed the information on. Ukraine thus abruptly decided to attack an area that was already virtually empty.

By withdrawing from Kharkov, the Russian coalition was able to regroup within Russia's future new borders and densify its defence line along the Oskol River. Moreover, the manpower thus freed up was able to strengthen its offensive capabilities in the Donbass. It is thanks to these troops that the Russian coalition was able to make significant progress in Bakhmut, a key point in the Slaviansk-Kramatorsk sector, which is the real operational objective of the Russian coalition.

Busy celebrating the Ukrainian victory around Kharkov, no Western media reported on the Russian advance in the Donbass. Ironically, it seems that the Russian media had been instructed by their authorities not to report on this success in order not to draw Western attention to this key sector, where the front has not stabilised. This is what happened: the Western media did the Russians' job!

The basic reason why Russian coalition forces did not attempt to fight the Ukrainian offensive on Kharkov is that the Russian command is in the process of restructuring.

Indeed, the Special Military Operation (SVO) launched in February 2022 was a joint action between Russian forces and the armed forces of the Donbass republics. As the latter were officially independent, they were not subordinated to the Russian command. Thus, the Russian General Staff only coordinated between the Russian army and the Donbass forces.

After the referendums and the incorporation of the four regions of southern Ukraine, all the forces of the Russian coalition fell under the responsibility of Moscow. A specific command was then created and led since 8 October 2022 by General Sergei Sourovikin.

Conducting complex military operations at the same time as setting up new leadership structures and adapting the entire strategic-operational chain of command was a source of vulnerability. For this reason, the Russian General Staff preferred to withdraw troops from the coalition, in order to preserve the lives of its military (which cannot be replaced), and to cede areas of secondary importance.

Ironically, Western propaganda media such as RTS[429] in Switzerland, Figaro[430] in France, or BBC[431] in the UK, have interpreted

---

429. https://www.rts.ch/play/tv/redirect/detail/13449035

430. «En pleine mobilisation, la Russie limoge le général chargé de la logistique», Le Figaro / AFP, 24 September 2022 (https://www.lefigaro.fr/flash-actu/en-pleine-mobilisation-la-russie-limoge-le-general-charge-de-la-logistique-20220924)

431. Matt Murphy, «Dmitry Bulgakov: Putin fires deputy defence chief amid supply failures», BBC News, 24 September 2022, (https://www.bbc.com/news/world-europe-63021117)

these changes in the leadership of the SVO as a sign of a crisis within the Russian leadership and the «fiasco» of the operation. Once again the conspiracy of our media is turning against Ukraine. Because in reality, it is exactly the opposite. The Russian command is strengthened and has greater freedom of action than before, but the Western analyses These «analyses» only led to underestimating Russian capabilities and to making the Ukrainians lower their guard, which was observed in the following days.

It is noteworthy that none of the European media has picked up on the creation in Russia of the Coordination Council (SK)[432], under the leadership of the Prime Minister, to coordinate all civilian and military resources to meet the needs of the SVO[433]. The creation of the SK indicates that Russia is determined to resolve the Ukrainian issue by force, even if the West were to become more involved in the conflict in some way.

6.3.2.3.3. The results of the Ukrainian offensive

For the Ukrainians, it was a Pyrrhic victory. They advanced into Kharkov without encountering any resistance and there was hardly any fighting. Instead, the area became a huge «pocket of fire» (or «killing zone») («огневой мешок»), where Russian artillery was able to destroy an estimated 4,000-5,000 Ukrainians (about 2 brigades), while the Russian coalition suffered only marginal casualties as there was no fighting.

The Ukrainian losses are in addition to those from the Kherson offensives. According to Russian Defence Minister Sergei Shugu, the Ukrainians lost about 7,000 men in the first three weeks of September. Although these figures are not verified, their order of magnitude

432. «Putin orders creation of special council for military operation needs», Tass, 19 October 2022 (https://tass.com/politics/1524957)
433. http://en.kremlin.ru/catalog/keywords/91/events/69657

corresponds to the estimates of some Western experts. In this hypothesis, the Ukrainians would have lost about 25% of the 10 brigades that had been created and equipped in recent months with Western help. This is a far cry from the million-man army mentioned by the Ukrainian leaders.

From a military point of view, this recapture is a tactical victory for the Ukrainians and an operational/strategic victory for the Russian coalition. To understand this, we need to go back to Vladimir Putin's stated objectives: «demilitarise» and «denazify». They are not about gaining territory, but about destroying the threat to the Donbass. In other words, the Ukrainians are fighting for territory, while the Russians are trying to destroy capabilities. You can always take back land, you can't take back human lives.

From a political point of view, this could be seen as a strategic victory for the Ukrainians, and a tactical loss for the Russians. This is the first time the Ukrainians have taken back so much territory since 2014, and the Russians seem to be losing. The Ukrainians are using this opportunity to communicate their final victory, raising expectations that are probably exaggerated and showing even less willingness to engage in negotiations.

The West sees this as confirmation of their statements since March about a Russian defeat. This is why Ursula von der Leyen declared that the moment «is not one of appeasement»[434].

The problem is not so much that Ukraine is claiming victory, but that the West is convinced that Russia is weak. Thus, this success is a poisoned chalice for Ukraine. It leads the West to overestimate the capabilities of the Ukrainian forces and to push them to carry out further offensives, instead of negotiating.

434. https://www.francetvinfo.fr/monde/europe/manifestations-en-ukraine/guerre-en-ukraine-ursula-von-der-leyen-promet-la-solidarite-avec-kiev-sans-convaincre-tous-les-eurodeputes_5362294.html

In the belief that they are weakening Russia, our media are encouraging the gradual disappearance of Ukrainian society. This is consistent with the way our leaders view Ukraine. They did not react to the massacres of civilians in the Donbass between 2014 and 2022, nor do they mention Ukraine's losses today. In fact, for our media and authorities, Ukrainians are just a kind of «sub-human» whose life is only to satisfy the goals of our politicians. In fact, no Western media is interested in the Ukrainian losses, as this could encourage European countries to promote a negotiated solution to the conflict.

6.3.2.3.4. Referendums in Southern Ukraine

Between 23 and 27 September 2022, referendums are being held in four oblasts in southern Ukraine. But not all the questions asked are the same. In the self-proclaimed republics of Donetsk and Lugansk, which are officially independent, the question is whether the population wants to be attached to Russia. In the oblasts of Kherson and Zaporozhie, which are still officially part of Ukraine, the question is whether the population wants to remain in Ukraine, whether they want to be independent or whether they want to be attached to Russia.

Unsurprisingly, the results of the referendums range from 87% to 99.2%[435]. Naturally, Westerners consider these referendums to be «bogus» and do not recognise their validity. Lawyers will certainly be able to comment on the legal dimension. In human terms, these results are consistent. Since 2014, the newly elected far-right authorities have systematically curtailed the rights and freedoms of linguistic minorities, making them 2nd class citizens.

435. «Ukraine 'referendums': Full results for annexation polls as Kremlin-backed authorities claim victory», Euronews, AP, Reuters, 28 September 2022 (https://www.euronews.com/2022/09/27/occupied-areas-of-ukraine-vote-to-join-russia-in-referendums-branded-a-sham-by-the-west)

Thus, Ukrainian policy has resulted in Russian-speaking citizens no longer feeling Ukrainian. This was even highlighted by the Law on the Rights of Indigenous Peoples in July 2021, which is somewhat equivalent to the Nuremberg Laws of 1935, which give different rights to citizens depending on their ethnic origin[436]. This prompted Vladimir Putin to write an article on 12 July 2021 calling on Ukraine to consider Russian speakers as part of the Ukrainian nation and not to discriminate as proposed by the new law.

Naturally, no Western country has protested against this discrimination, which follows on from the abolition of the Official Languages Act in February 2014, which led to the secession of Crimea and Donbass.

Secondly, in order to fight the Russian speakers who sought to retain their rights, the Ukrainians never tried to win the «hearts and minds» of the insurgents. On the contrary, they did everything to drive them further away by bombing them, undermining their roads, cutting off drinking water, stopping the payment of pensions and salaries or stopping all banking services. This is exactly the opposite of an effective counter-insurgency strategy.

During the September 2022 referendums, no Western media or government protested against the artillery and missile strikes aimed at lines of voters in Donetsk and other cities in the Zaporozhie and Kherson regions to intimidate them from voting[437].

---

436. «Нардеп від «Слуги народу» Семінський заявив про «позбавлення конституційних прав росіян, які проживають в Україні»,» AP News, 2 July 2021 (https://apnews.com.ua/ua/news/nardep-vid-slugi-narodu-seminskii-zayaviv-pro-pozbavlennya-konstitutciinikh-prav-rosiyan-yaki-prozhivaiut-v-ukraini/)

437. «Referendum in Kherson to continue despite deadly Ukrainian shelling», Al Mayadeen English, 25 September 2022 (https://english.almayadeen.net/news/politics/referendum-in-kherson-to-continue-despite-deadly-ukrainian-s)

After the referendums, Kiev promised to severely punish those who had participated in their implementation[438].

So we have a situation where Western countries refuse to recognise these referendums, but have done absolutely nothing to encourage Ukraine to have a more inclusive policy with their minorities. In the end, these referendums show that there has never really been an inclusive Ukrainian nation. Moreover, Western countries have systematically denied the existence of these minorities and the unequal treatment they receive.

On a political-strategic level, these referendums will freeze a situation and make Russia's conquests irreversible. What is interesting is that if the West had allowed Zelensky to continue with the proposal he made to Russia at the end of March 2022, Ukraine would more or less retain its pre-February 2022 configuration. Russia was ready to discuss it, but the EU pushed Zelensky to withdraw it by offering a second package of €500 million for weapons. Then, as Ukraïnskaya Pravda explains, Boris Johnson phoned Zelensky on 2 April[439] and asked him to withdraw his proposal or the West would stop its support. Then, on 9 April[440], during his visit to Kiev, «BoJo» repeated the same thing to the Ukrainian president. Ukraine was therefore ready to negotiate with Russia, but the West does not want negotiations, as 'BoJo' made clear during his last visit to Ukraine in August[441].

438. Isobel Koshiw, «Ukrainians involved in 'referendums' face prison terms, says Kyiv», The Guardian, 27 September 2022 (https://www.theguardian.com/world/2022/sep/27/ukrainians-involved-in-russia-referendums-face-prison-terms-says-kyiv)

439. https://www.gov.uk/government/news/pm-call-with-president-zelenskyy-of-ukraine-2-april-2022

440. https://peoplesdispatch.org/2022/05/09/ukrainian-news-outlet-suggests-uk-and-us-governments-are-primary-obstacles-to-peace/

441. Roman Romaniuk, «Possibility of talks between Zelenskyy and Putin came to a halt after Johnson's visit», Ukrainskaya Pravda, 5 May 2022 (https://www.pravda.

Paradoxically, it is certainly the prospect that there will be no negotiations that has pushed Russia to embark on the path of referendums. It should be remembered that until 2022, Vladimir Putin had always rejected the idea of integrating the southern territories of Ukraine into Russia. Similarly, if the West were so committed to Ukraine and its territorial integrity, France and Germany would certainly have fulfilled their obligations under the Minsk Agreements before February 2022. Moreover, they would have let Zelensky proceed with his proposed agreement with Russia in March 2022.

6.3.2.3.5. Partial mobilisation

As early as February 2022, the Western media tried to present the Russian forces as quantitatively and qualitatively insufficient, thus explaining that they could only lose the war. This is why our «experts» announce a general mobilisation for 9 May 2022[442]... which the Russians have never mentioned.

At the end of August 2022, Vladimir Putin signed a decree authorising the increase of the Russian armed forces by 137 000 men[443]. Our media see this as a sign of Russian inadequacy and weakness. In reality, as the precision of the figure indicates, it was only to authorise the future integration of the Donbass forces after the referenda and the taking of preparatory measures.

On 21 September, Vladimir Putin announced the partial mobilisation of 300 000 reservists[444]. It only concerns soldiers who

com.ua/eng/news/2022/05/5/7344206/)

442. https://www.rts.ch/emissions/infrarouge/13079683-guerre-en-ukraine-la-russie-dans-limpasse.html

443. «War in Ukraine: Vladimir Putin signs a decree to increase the number of army personnel», Euronews / AFP, 26 August 2022, (https://fr.euronews.com/2022/08/26/guerre-en-ukraine-vladimir-poutine-signe-un-decret-pour-augmenter-les-effectifs-de-larmee)

444. https://объясняем. рф/mobilization/

have already served in the armed forces during the previous ten years and who have specialist functions. It is not therefore a matter of troops destined to be sent to the front, but of personnel with a technical function outside the combat zones.

To understand this decision, it should be recalled that Russia intervened in Ukraine with considerably fewer troops than the West considers necessary to conduct an offensive campaign. This can be explained in two ways. Firstly, the Russians rely on their mastery of the «operative art» and play with their operative modules in the theatre of operations like a chess player. This is what allows them to be effective with reduced manpower. In other words, they know how to conduct operations efficiently.

The second reason, which our media deliberately ignore, is that the vast majority of the fighting in Ukraine is being carried out by Donbass militias. When they mention «the Russians», they should (if they were honest) say «the Russian coalition» or «the Russian-speaking coalition». In other words, the number of Russian troops in Ukraine is relatively small. This is compounded by the fact that the Russians keep their troops in the area of operations for a limited period of time only, and rotate their troops more frequently than the West.

In addition to these functional considerations, there are structural consequences. The integration of the four southern Ukrainian oblasts into the Russian Federation extends the Russian border by almost 1,000 kilometres. This implies additional capacities to build a more robust defence system, to construct permanent command and logistic facilities, etc. Contrary to what Western propaganda would have us believe, this partial mobilisation is simply a logical consequence of the referenda.

As for the timing of this partial mobilisation, two important elements explain it. Firstly, some of the Russian military were engaged in the operation on six-month contracts. It was therefore known that at the end of August, some of the soldiers would return to civilian life. This is why some Russian generals had asked for recruitment to take place in June. The second element is that apparently the Russian authorities did not want to take the decision to mobilise more soldiers until they had a clear picture of the impact of the sanctions and the economic situation. At the beginning of the summer, the Russian economy is in convalescence and Vladimir Putin's concern is not to weaken it in this phase. This is why the decision to mobilise was delayed. Indirectly, it shows that the Russian economy is doing better than the West expected.

As for the conduct of the partial mobilisation of 300,000 reservists, our picture of the situation is very imperfect, even caricatured. Certainly, the decision was not unanimous and was criticised, even in the official media. Clearly, not all young people are enthusiastic about going to fight, whatever the cause. Moreover, this problem affects Ukraine much more massively, where a very large part of its mobilisable personnel can be seen in the major European capitals at the wheel of powerful German sports cars... This is why Ukraine had to make a massive appeal to foreign volunteers, including militants from jihadist movements[445] considered as terrorists in the West, such as the Hayat Tahrir al-Sham[446] !...

Russia is certainly no exception and our media focus on the Georgian border to talk about a mass exodus of Russians[447]. This shows that Russian society has wide access to Western media.

445. «Hundreds of Al-Qaeda militants arrive in Ukraine from Syria», The Cradle, 8 March 2022 (https ://thecradle.co/Article/news/7669)

446. https://www.state.gov/executive-order-13224/; https ://www.gov.uk/government/publications/proscribed-terror-groups-or-organisations--2/proscribed-terrorist-groups-or-organisations-accessible-version; https://www.publicsafety.gc.ca/cnt/ntnl-scrt/cntr-trrrsm/lstd-ntts/crrnt-lstd-ntts-en.aspx

447. «Thousands of Russians cross borders to flee mobilisation», rts.ch, 28 September 2022 (https://www.rts.ch/info/monde/13421767-des-milliers-de-russes-tra-

Our media talk about a disaster, but this does not seem to be the case. Indeed, at the beginning of October already 200,000 reservists were directed to training centres in order to support the operation in Ukraine. Moreover, it seems that Vladimir Putin's decision has triggered vocations, as 70,000 volunteers (who are not part of the recalled reservists) have spontaneously announced themselves to participate in the operation in Ukraine. In the end, a total of 370 000 soldiers will join the special operation in Ukraine.

6.3.2.3.6. The attack on the Kerch bridge

On the morning of 8 October 2022, a truck explodes on the Kerch bridge linking the Crimean peninsula to Russian territory. Very quickly, videos from surveillance cameras showing the explosion of a truck circulate. The images are a little too reminiscent of the Islamic State attacks of 2015-2016. This is probably why Radio-Télévision Suisse Romande modestly describes the event as «a major fire broke out on the vast automobile and railway bridge linking the Ukrainian Crimea annexed by Moscow and Russian territory». Obviously, after the attack on journalist Darya Dugina, the attack on the Nord Stream 1 and 2 gas pipelines, and the elimination of Ukrainian politicians in favour of the referendums, the West avoids pointing out that Ukraine and its Western allies resort to terrorism.

This attack shows several things. Firstly, our inability to analyse the situation. The Kerch Bridge was of strategic importance before March 2022. The capture of the southern part of Ukraine by the Russian coalition has changed things. The importance of the Kerch

---

versent-les-frontieres-pour-fuir-la-mobilisation.html); «Russian military call-up sparks major exodus», DW, 24 September 2022 (https://www.dw.com/en/russian-military-call-up-sparks-major-exodus/a-63227879)

Bridge today is mainly due to its railway component, which was not affected by the attack.

Secondly, the attack, which was set up by the Ukrainian SBU special services, according to the Washington Post[448], is a suicide attack modelled on the Islamic State attacks. Exactly as observed in Syria and Iraq, it is possible that the driver of the truck bomb was unaware and that the attack was remotely activated, although apparently there is no evidence of this.

The US investigative media Grayzone has released documents it has obtained which show that the British have at least helped to design and train militants to carry out terrorist attacks, including the Kerch Bridge[449].

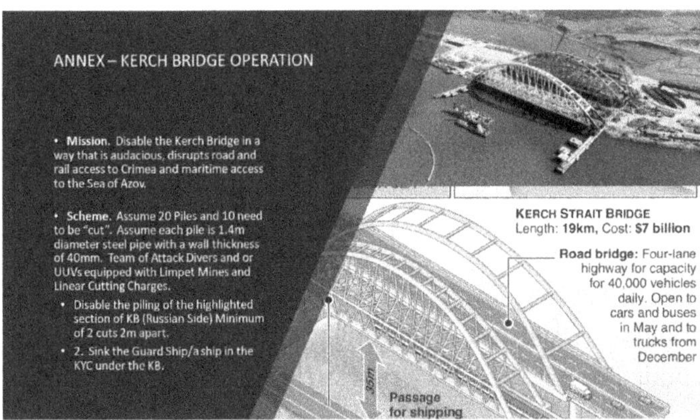

Figure 58 - Slide from a British intelligence presentation in April 2022, showing the involvement of Western countries in organising terrorist attacks [reproduced courtesy of The Grayzone].

---

448. Missy Ryan, Natalia Abbakumova & Kostiantyn Khudov, 'Amid Ukrainian taunts, Russia scrambles to salvage Crimean Bridge after fiery explosion', The Washington Post, 8 October 2022 (https://www.washingtonpost.com/world/2022/10/08/crimea-kerch-bridge-attack-explosion-russia-ukraine/)
449. https://thegrayzone.com/2022/10/10/ukrainian-kerch-bridge/

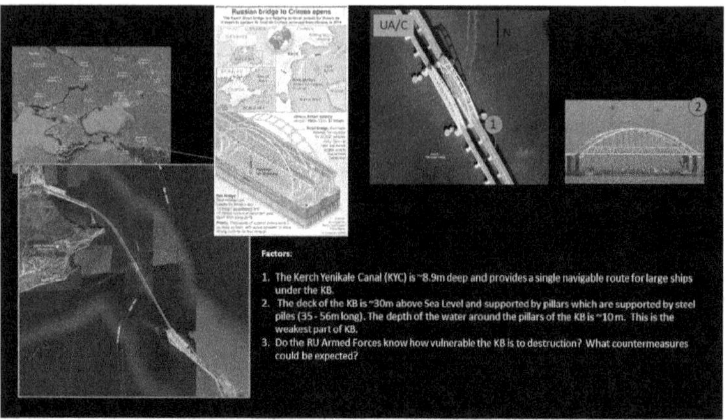

Figure 59 - The aim of the attack was to collapse the suspension part of the bridge, which was considered by the British services to be the most vulnerable part of the structure. The destruction of this part would have caused the interruption of land traffic between Russia and Crimea, but also maritime traffic between the Sea of Azov and the Black Sea. In fact, the suicide truck exploded too early and the damage was limited. [Reprinted courtesy of The Grayzone]

There is no such thing as good terrorism or bad terrorism. Terrorism is a method. We (rightly) dislike it when it is used against us, but we tolerate it - not to say encourage it - when it is used against others. Note that no Western media or government has condemned the method used!

6.3.2.3.7. The withdrawal of Kherson

Since June 2022, the city of Kherson has been the object of a multitude of unsuccessful Ukrainian 'counter-offensives'. Systematically repelled by the Russians, they caused enormous losses to the Ukrainian forces[450]. However, on 8 November 2022, the

450. Jeremy Bowen, «Russia-Ukraine war: At the front line of Ukraine's struggle for Kherson», BBC News, 4 November 2022 (https://www.bbc.com/news/world-europe-63489081)

Russian command announced the withdrawal of its troops from the city, located on the eastern bank of the Dnieper.

The West immediately saw the fruits of the Ukrainian offensives, but Volodymyr Zelensky was more reserved. Indeed, the Ukrainians know what happened in Kharkov two months earlier, whose recapture was extremely costly, despite the absence of fighting. As the saying goes, «once bitten, twice shy». In fact, the analysis of the situation by the Russian general staff is very similar to that of Kharkov. The objective of the Russians was not initially the conquest of territory. The junction between Russian territory and the Crimean peninsula came as Ukrainian forces were destroyed, but the Russians clearly had no intention of engaging in stabilisation operations. In early October, General Surovikin had announced that he was ready to make difficult decisions, implying the evacuation of Kherson. During October, Russian forces evacuated civilians, monuments and works of art reminiscent of Russian history, and moved the remains of Prince Potemkin, who had founded Kherson, for burial in the east.

Unlike the Ukrainians, and as General Surovikin made clear, Russia's priority is to preserve the lives of its fighters. In Kherson in November 2022, the Russians are in the same situation as on Snake Island in June or in Kharkov in August: the energy to defend these areas is greater than the strategic interest in keeping them. What looks like a defeat is simply an expression of a balance between the strategic objective and the cost of achieving it. As we have seen since the beginning of the SVO, the Russian conduct of operations is extremely efficient. The problem is to explain this convincingly to the Russian public.

Apparently, this withdrawal has been the subject of long debates in Russia since late September. The military demanded it, but the politicians were rather opposed to it, for two reasons.

The first is that the territory concerned, even if it only represents 40% of the Kherson oblast, is formally Russian; the second is that the withdrawal would give Ukraine an easy victory that would be exploited by Western propaganda. In the end, the military won the day. Even 'hawks' like Ramzan Kadirov welcomed the withdrawal[451]. On the other hand, the Russians learned the lessons of Kharkov and communicated better on the Kherson withdrawal, which was finally well accepted by the Russian public opinion.

It should be recalled here that no Ukrainian 'counter-offensive' in Kherson succeeded in breaking through the Russian defences. On 10 November, as the Russian forces withdrew, a final Ukrainian counter-offensive was repelled. In fact, the Russians had a very large force in Kherson, which would have been more useful elsewhere. Moreover, by withdrawing to the left bank of the Dnieper, they shortened their front and gained a strong position by the river. This is typically what is known in common parlance as a 'strategic withdrawal'.

This is a withdrawal, not a retreat. A retreat is a movement made under pressure and in constant contact with the adversary. A withdrawal is an operation to regroup forces, close a front line or prepare for further action.

Russia is therefore withdrawing by its own decision and not under pressure from Ukrainian forces. It should be remembered that Russia's objective is not territorial but security, unlike Ukraine, which favours the reconquest of territory over the lives of its men. This makes the withdrawal a victory shared by both sides.

What this withdrawal shows is that the Russian conduct of operations is less political than military and that the military

451. Mark Trevelyan, «Russia's war hawks rally behind decision to abandon Ukrainian city of Kherson», Reuters, 10 November 2022 (https://www.reuters.com/world/europe/russias-war-hawks-rally-behind-decision-abandon-ukrainian-city-kherson-2022-11-09/)

sets the operational and tactical objectives. This contrasts with Ukraine, where the conduct of operations is totally political, which explains the huge losses and inefficiency. This inefficiency (i.e. the amount of resources used to achieve a given objective) is measured by the speed with which the Ukrainians lose the equipment provided by the West.

That said, the Russian decision is not without foreign and domestic political consequences. Externally, Ukraine and the West have obviously been quick to communicate the Ukrainian «victory». The risk is to continue to overestimate Ukrainian capabilities and thus reject the idea of negotiations. On the domestic front, one could expect disappointment in the form of mistrust of the authorities. But the Russian general staff has learned the lessons of the Kharkov withdrawal: instead of explaining the reasons for the decision afterwards, General Sourovikine communicated in advance. Thus, the Russian authorities do not seem to have lost the confidence of the public.

Moreover, even though its troops have left Kherson, Russia still considers Kherson to be Russian territory[452]. A Russian offensive in this area can therefore be expected later.

6.3.3.The final state

By August 2022, the Russian coalition could be said to have achieved the objectives set in February. The Ukrainian army as it was in February no longer exists and has been replaced by less experienced forces whose major equipment has been partially replaced by Western equipment.

452. «Peskov says 'Kherson remains Russian' as Ukrainian forces enter city», The Kyiv Independent, 11 November 11 (https://kyivindependent.com/news-feed/peskov-says-kherson-remains-russian-as-ukrainian-forces-enter-city)

Nevertheless, the West saw in the events of August to October signs of Russia's weakness and its inability to regenerate its forces. Military experts have been appearing on television to explain that Russia lacks missiles, equipment and troops and that the morale of the Russian army is at its lowest.

Thanks to these propaganda-driven analyses and obsessed with a chimerical Ukrainian victory, the West concentrates its arms deliveries on offensive equipment (armour and artillery) and neglects the supply of defence equipment. This is why, after the attacks on Russian infrastructure, Russia retaliates with repeated brutal missile attacks that destroy much of Ukraine's energy infrastructure. These attacks demonstrate two things.

Firstly, that this infrastructure had not been destroyed before, thus underlining that the Russians' original aim was the destruction of the forces, not of Ukraine. Secondly, that the determination of Ukraine and the West to prolong the war is only pushing Russia to increase its pressure.

The nature of the objectives set for the Russian operation makes it impossible to determine precisely on a map what Ukraine will look like at the end of the combat actions. Given the constant adjustment of objectives to the changing situation and the absence of a negotiation process, it is difficult to say where the Russian coalition forces will end up. It is also difficult to say what image of the end state of the war Vladimir Putin on the one hand and Volodymyr Zelensky on the other have in mind.

It is quite clear that, for Vladimir Putin, the advance will stop when the military threat is physically neutralised or as a result of an agreement. From this perspective, territorial gains are not decisive. For Volodymyr Zelensky, it is more difficult to imagine what final state he is seeking. It is certainly easy to imagine that he would like to see the Russians disappear from Ukrainian territory and thus regain his entire territory, but the idea of a total victory over Russia that he and his entourage evoke seems unrealistic.

Possible state at the end of hostilities

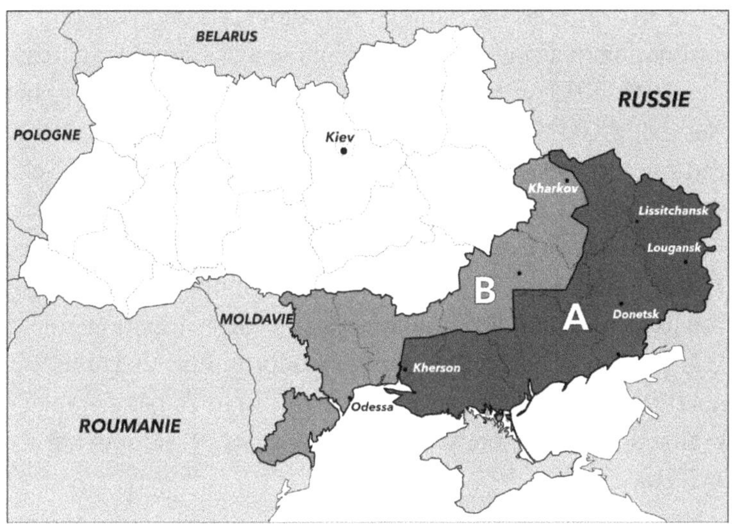

Figure 60 - One can imagine that the final state of the conflict on the ground could be a territory that extends from Zone A (the situation of Russian forces in August 2022) to Zone B (the extension of areas with high Russian-speaking representation). It is unlikely that the Russians would have considered going beyond Zone B. But in reality we do not know. The supply of long-range weapons by the West could push the Russians beyond Zone B.

The problem is that the Ukrainian leadership seems to be focused on the idea of a Russian defeat, without really having a vision for Ukraine in the - likely - event that it is cut off from part of its territory.

6.4.Ukrainian conduct

6.4.1.Popular resistance

When talking about 'resistance', we have to distinguish between two things: the structures of resistance and the will to resist.

The first are the institutional instruments for conducting and coordinating resistance activities against an armed aggressor. Since 2014-2015, although no Russian military training has been observed in Ukraine, and Ukrainian forces have not - therefore - faced any, resistance structures have been established. Praviy Sektor even established a «National Liberation Movement» (NVR).

The second is essentially the determination of the people to resist external aggression. From the beginning of the Russian offensive, our media applauded the determination of the Ukrainian people. The Swiss ambassador in Kiev, Claude Wild, even declared on RTS that «no one would have bet a franc» on Ukraine's ability to resist the Russian army[453]. He has not read Sun Tzu!

> *If you know the enemy and you know yourself, in a hundred battles you will never be in trouble.*

> *If you don't know the enemy but you know yourself, your chances of winning or losing are equal.*

453. «No one would have bet a franc on such resistance, says Swiss ambassador to Ukraine», RTS Info, 24 May 2022 (https://www.rts.ch/info/monde/13121067-personne-naurait-parie-un-franc-sur-une-telle-resistance-estime-lambassadeur-suisse-en-ukraine.html)

If you don't know the enemy or yourself, you are certain to fail in every battle.[454]

A more nuanced and less partisan view is therefore needed.

First of all, Ukraine is a complex country. Contrary to Western rhetoric, there is no Ukrainian nation, only Ukrainians. In their desire to make the Mayan revolution the revolution of the entire Ukrainian people, the West has erased the ethnic and cultural difference between the western and central part of the country on the one hand and the south-eastern part on the other. They have swept the racist character of the new authorities under the carpet. However, the various polls on relations with NATO or Russia illustrate this division[455]. The south-eastern part of the country is predominantly Russian-speaking and in favour of improved relations with Russia. It was therefore foreseeable that, in the event of an invasion, the different regions would behave differently.

With the 2014 coup, forces came to power that do not seek to unify the Ukrainian nation but to drive out non-Ukrainians to make it an ethnically homogeneous country. They do not seek national unity through cooperation but through purification[456]. This is very different. This explains two things. First, the categorical refusal of the various Ukrainian governments to implement the Minsk Agreements that would have granted some autonomy to the Donbass and other linguistic communities in the country.

454. Defense Technical Intelligence Center (https://apps.dtic.mil/sti/citations/ADA440962)

455. «Attitudes towards Ukraine's accession to the EU and NATO, attitudes towards direct talks with Vladimir Putin and the perception of the military threat from Russia: the results of a telephone survey conducted on December 13-16, 2021», Kyiv International Institute Of Sociology, December 2021 (https://www.kiis.com.ua/?lang=eng&cat=reports&id=1083&page=1)

456. «Profile: Ukraine's ultra-nationalist Right Sector», BBC, 28 April 2014 (https://www.bbc.com/news/world-europe-27173857)

Secondly, the deployment of ultra-nationalist volunteer militias in the south of the country and in the Donbass region, and their abuses against the mainly Russian-speaking population.

The election of Zelensky seemed to show that Ukraine had overcome this division: his programme was to resolve the dispute between Ukraine and Russia. But for various reasons he did not succeed. The main reason was that neo-Nazi or 'ukro-fascist' forces prevented him from carrying out his programme[457].

This is why, in the south of the country, the Russians tend to be seen as liberators[458] and why there is no resistance movement. This is also the reason why Ukrainian forces continue to bomb civilian populations such as Donetsk. This is to show them that the Russians are not able to protect them and thus change their attitude towards them.

This also explains why, on 17 July 2022, Volodymyr Zelensky ordered some 651 investigations for 'treason and collaboration with the enemy' against officials and members of the security forces[459]. Among those charged are many officials of regional administrations.

In fact, the myth of this Ukrainian resistance is based on reporting from the western and central part of Ukraine, because our journalists do not travel to the Russian-speaking area. And

457. Лилия Рагуцкая, «Ярош: если Зеленский предаст Украину - потеряет не должность, а жизнь», Obozrevatel, 27 May 2019, (https://incident.obozrevatel.com/crime/dmitrij-yarosh-esli-zelenskij-predast-ukrainu-poteryaet-ne-dolzh-nost-a-zhizn.htm)

458. Siobhán O'Grady, Serhii Korolchuk & Anastacia Galouchka, «In Slovyansk, conflicted loyalties as Russian forces approach», The Washington Post, 18 June 2022 (https://www.washingtonpost.com/world/2022/06/18/ukraine-slovyansk-divided-loyalties-russia/)

459. Max Hunder, «Ukraine's President Fires Spy Chief and Top State Prosecutor», Reuters/US News, 17 July 2022 (https://www.usnews.com/news/world/articles/2022-07-17/ukraines-president-fires-security-service-chief-and-prosecutor-general)

when they do, they are penalised, like the German journalist Alina Lipp[460] or the British freelance journalist Graham Philipps[461].

6.4.2. The conduct of operations

Ukrainian staffs have been trained by NATO for eight years to respond to a Russian offensive. The axes of penetration used by Russian forces in February 2022 were the same as those trained in NATO exercises. Yet the Ukrainian army was unable to contain the Russian offensive. This failure was due to two factors:

- An inadequate strategy. Ukraine was prepared to attack the Donbass, which is why the bulk of its forces were gathered in this area, and why they could be surrounded so easily.
- The way its forces are conducted. While the Russians conduct operationally, Ukrainian conduct is divided into political conduct of operations and tactical conduct on the ground. There is no real operative conduct.

In practical terms, this means that the conduct of the war is split between the work of Volodymyr Zelensky in managing the perception of the international community and the work of the soldiers fighting on the ground. Staff work and manoeuvring are not part of the equation.

In 2014-2015, the authorities in Kiev legitimised the fight against the insurgency in the south of the country by the presence of Russian forces. This narrative may have worked well for the

---

460. Lars Wienand, «Behörden ermitteln wegen Kriegspropaganda gegen Alina Lipp», t-online.de, 16 June 2022 (https://www.t-online.de/nachrichten/ausland/id_92326694/putins-deutsches-sprachrohr-alina-lipp-behoerden-ermitteln-wegen-kriegspropaganda-.html)
461. Matt Mathers, «British vlogger accused of being 'Kremlin mouthpiece' sanctioned by UK over work in Ukraine», The Independent, 27 July 2022 (https://www.independent.co.uk/news/world/europe/graham-phillips-sanction-russia-ukraine-b2131509.html)

Western community, but it could not work against the rebels who knew that there were no Russian troops. In other words, the government made it impossible to build trust with insurgents who were not even trying to separate from the country! This shows an inability to conduct the war at the operational level. In 2022, as in 2014, the Ukrainian leadership is trapped between the strategic and tactical levels.

The absence of the operative level in Ukrainian military thinking is largely explained by the fact that Ukrainian military staffs were trained by NATO. Satisfied with military successes that were more verbal than operational, the West did not hide the importance of the training given to the Ukrainian military:

> *But one of the components of their success on the battlefield is that they were trained to fight to NATO standards! This was done both by the Alliance and by individual allies - Canadians, British, Americans, Poles, Romanians, etc.* [462]

In fact, for more than 20 years, NATO armies have been fighting tactical-level adversaries. In other words, their wars have been fought at the tactical level, but not really at the operational level. As a result, the Ukrainian conduct of combat focuses on the engagement of small tactical units, with an emphasis on protection and no real capacity for manoeuvre. The Ukrainians have made the same mistakes as in 2014 and 2015 before the defeats that forced them to conclude the Minsk Agreements. Today, they are in a similar situation to the French army in 1940, facing a

462. «Deputy Secretary General of NATO Responded to Kyiv's Criticism - We Taught You NATO-Style Solutions», European Pravda, 27 June 2022 (https://www.eurointegration.com.ua/eng/news/2022/06/27/7142077/)

German army that is not always more powerful, but considerably more mobile.

The Russian military intelligence service (GRU) clearly understood this Ukrainian weakness. This is why the first phase of the offensive consisted of large thrusts into the depths, bypassing the strong points of the Ukrainian defence, without lingering on them.

Vladimir Putin's stated objectives on 24 February 2022 made it clear that the priority of the Russian coalition would be the destruction of forces, not the capture of territory. This is a Clausewitzian approach to warfare: the destruction of opposing forces before the conquest of territory.

By burying themselves and resisting in fortified positions and localities, the Ukrainians associated the Russian objective with the capture of territory.

Symptomatically, on France 5, Pierre Haroche, from the Strategic Research Institute of the Military School, sees the war in Ukraine as a kind of competition in the number of artillery projectiles exchanged, the objective of which is to «inflict pain on the Russians» and to be «able to hold out»[463]. This is exactly the same thinking that the generals of the First World War had! This is exactly what the Ukrainian leaders are saying.

Instead of leading dynamically and using operational mobility, Ukraine - and in particular Zelensky - asked his troops to hold the ground at all costs. This is the equivalent of the German army's 'Durchhaltebefehl', which was given by Hitler to Field Marshal von Paulus, commander of the German 6th Army in Stalingrad. It was an example of incompetence at the time and it remains so today in Ukraine...

---

463. «Ukraine in Europe: what will Putin do? #cdanslair 25.06.2022», France 5/ YouTube, 25 June 2022 (10'54") (https://youtu.be/Rgy2Bbe3HYE?t=654)

This way of conducting the war explains the high losses of the Ukrainian forces. The West is reluctant to talk about it, because it is necessary to maintain the illusion of a victory against Russia, which justifies the delivery of arms. Thus, at the beginning of June 2022, President Zelensky mentions daily losses of 60 to 100 men[464]. On 9 June, Mykhailo Podoliak, Zelensky's adviser, declared on the BBC that Ukrainian forces were losing 100 to 200 men a day[465]. In mid-June, David Arakhamia, Zelensky's chief negotiator and close adviser, spoke of 200-500 deaths per day and mentioned a total loss (dead, wounded, captured, deserters) of 1,000 men per day[466]. It is not clear whether these figures are accurate. On the one hand, experts close to the intelligence services believe that these figures are far below the reality. On the other hand, the Ukrainian figures are higher than the estimates given by the Russian army. Some claim that Ukrainian forces have suffered 60,000 dead and 50,000 missing. According to Business Insider, Ukraine has lost the equivalent of the entire British infantry. In reality, we don't know, but these estimates illustrate the questioning in Anglo-Saxon military circles[467].

From the end of April 2022, in order to make up for these losses, the Ukrainian command began deploying territorial units from the west of the country to the Donbass front. With

464. Mazurenko Alona, «Подоляк: Щодня гине 100-200 українських захисників», Ukrayinska Pravda, 9 June 2022 (https://www.pravda.com.ua/news/2022/06/9/7351600/)

465. «У війні гине 100 - 200 українських військових щодня - Офіс президента», BBC News, 9 June 2022 (https://www.bbc.com/ukrainian/news-61752749)

466. Dave Lawler, «Ukraine suffering up to 1,000 casualties per day in Donbas, official says», Axios, 15 June 2022 (https://www.axios.com/2022/06/15/ukraine-1000-casualties-day-donbas-arakhamia)

467. Katie Anthony, «Ukraine has lost more troops during the Russian invasion than there are infantry in the British army, defence expert says», Business Insider, 28 June 2022 (https://www.businessinsider.com/ukraine-has-lost-more-troops-than-there-are-in-the-british-army-expert-2022-6?r=US&IR=T)

very rudimentary training and no real experience, these fighters are not capable of containing the Russian offensive. The result is demonstrations by mothers and wives of these soldiers. The Western myth of Ukrainian unity behind its government is slowly crumbling, but the phenomenon is attributed to Russian disinformation[468].

According to some, the proportion of professional soldiers in the Ukrainian army has fallen to 20% in a few weeks. This is unverifiable, but reports from the front tend to confirm this qualitative shift in the Ukrainian forces[469].

A key difference between Ukraine and Russia is that in Ukraine, operations are directed by the political leadership, whereas in Russia they are the business of the military. Thus, in June 2022, David Arakhamia, a majority deputy and close adviser to Zelensky, justified the need for a counter-offensive to regain lost territory:

> *Our negotiating position is actually quite weak, so we don't want to sit at the table if we are in that position. We have to reverse it somehow.* [470]

Thus, gaining ground against the Russians is simply to have a better position to negotiate with them later. This is a strictly political conduct of the war, without regard for the lives of the soldiers. An approach that is supported by Western countries and

468. Paul Waldie, «In the small Ukraine city Khust, a rare public display of dissent over war with Russia,» The Globe and Mail, May 2, 2022 (https://www.theglobeandmail.com/world/article-russia-ukraine-war-conscription-protest/
469. Alexander Savitsky, «On the front line: The volunteers defending Kyiv», dw.com, 26 March 2022 (https://p.dw.com/p/49553)
470. Dave Lawler, «Ukraine suffering up to 1,000 casualties per day in Donbas, official says», Axios, 15 June 2022 (https://www.axios.com/2022/06/15/ukraine-1000-casualties-day-donbas-arakhamia)

our diplomats, but which is also the source of Ukraine's military failure.

6.4.3.Durchhaltebefehl

In mid-April 2022, Mariupol is almost entirely in the hands of the Russian coalition. Only the 36th Marine Infantry Brigade in the Azovmash industrial complex and the fighters of the Azov Regiment in the Azovstal complex are still holding out.

In Azovstal, the resistance of the OZSP AZOV symbolises the heroism of the Ukrainian resistance to the Kiev regime. While the entire city has fallen, the Russian coalition offers the fighters to surrender[471].

Volodymyr Zelensky addresses Ukrainians:

> *A difficult day. But this day, like all the others, is precisely about saving our country and our people. As far as the situation in Mariupol is concerned. Thanks to the action of the Ukrainian military - the Armed Forces of Ukraine, the intelligence services, the negotiating team, the International Committee of the Red Cross and the United Nations, we hope to save the lives of our men. Among them, there are seriously wounded, they are receiving medical help. I want to emphasize: Ukraine needs living Ukrainian heroes. This is our principle. I think any reasonable person will understand these words.*[472]

471. «Kyiv refuses demands to surrender Mariupol», NBC News, 21 March 2022 (https://www.nbcnews.com/news/world/blog/ukraine-russia-war-live-updates-kyiv-refuses-demands-surrender-mariupol-n1292442); Anna Myroniuk, «Defenders of besieged Mariupol plead for help, criticize commandment», The Kyiv Independent, 11 April 2022 (https://kyivindependent.com/national/defenders-of-besieged-mariupol-plead-for-help-criticize-commandment)

472. https://t.me/V_Zelenskiy_official/1671

The response was not long in coming. On Twitter, the Azov fighters expressed themselves:

This man [the commander in Mariupol] who is defending our motherland, Ukraine, and who is ready to give his life for it and who has already been shot in the arm (...), he is completely furious about the way they - our defenders - are being treated by the people who run us, I mean, by our government. He angrily asked me to tell Arestovich, and I can't personally, but I can like this: «If the surviving fighters of the Azov Regiment who hear all the bullshit, all the nonsense that comes out of his little mouth, if they manage to get out of there and meet him», and I quote: «They're going to smash his face, they're going to smash his face. So, guys...[473]

On Telegram, an activist explains how they will clean up Kiev after defeating Russia:

And then we will «clean up the swamp». That's for sure. No one today, so you can understand, is counting on the fact that we'll just kick them [the Russians] out, and then you corrupt officials will rob us. No. We are going to kill you all. You understand, nobody will give up their weapons, we will clean up your place. Do you understand? We will clean everything from you. That's what I think, you corrupt officials, and all those who have stolen from us for years. You better run. You better run. [474]

473. https://twitter.com/Ukraine66251776/status/1526292915433230337
474. https://t.me/UkraineHumanRightsAbuses/3922

In Ukraine, such surrenders are considered treason. This is why, at the end of April 2022, the commander of the 36th Marine Infantry Brigade, entrenched in the Azovmash complex in Mariupol, agreed to surrender on condition that he be transported to a third country[475].

From mid-May 2022, and especially after the surrender of the Azov regiment in Mariupol, many Ukrainian army units mutinied and refused to fight. Strangely, the format of their announcement always seems to follow the same pattern: on a video showing a group of armed soldiers, the leader of the unit reads a proclamation, in which he declares that the conditions are no longer right to continue fighting and that their command has left them behind.

In fact, they follow a protocol precisely described in leaflets disseminated in artillery shells by Russian troops and which gives the procedure to follow in five points:

1. Abandon your position and leave the combat zone. This should be done with your formation. The more, the better. An individual soldier can be charged with treason, but not a unit.
2. Isolate nationalists and SBU snitches.
3. Record a video message to your command in Ukraine. On this video there should be all the personnel of the military formation who decided to abandon their positions. This should avoid the accusation of individual servicemen and prove that it is an abandonment by the whole unit.
4. In the video, say that you have been abandoned by your commanders, that you have run out of ammunition and fuel, that you have many wounded, that you can no longer receive

475. «Ukrainian troops in Mariupol ask to be evacuated to a third country», A News, 20 April 2022 (https://www.anews.com.tr/world/2022/04/20/ukrainian-troops-in-mariupol-ask-to-be-evacuated-to-a-third-country)

orders from your superiors, that morale and psychological conditions no longer allow you to continue fighting. Under these conditions you are forced to abandon your positions and leave the combat zone, in order to save yourself and your formation as a combat unit.

5. Come in compact formation, without collective weapons but with your personal weapons that show that you are a fighting unit. Be careful not to run into nationalists whose task is to prevent you from surrendering or retreating by executing you.

In July 2022, the inability of the Ukrainians to effectively contain the Russian offensive tended to cause fatigue in the United States. This is why the Biden administration pushed Zelensky to impose a «Durchhaltebefehl» on the Ukrainian troops and to lead a vast counter-offensive in the Kherson sector. The situation is being dramatised so as not to lose political support...

6.4.4. A different perception of the battlefield

Unlike the Russians, the Ukrainian leadership is more concerned with portraying the war than fighting the war itself. This explains, on the one hand, the 'Durchhaltebefehl' seen above and, on the other hand, the tensions between the country's political leadership and the armed forces' general staff.

6.4.4.1. Protection of civilians

Our media never misses an opportunity to mention - often without proof - the savagery of Russian forces towards the civilian population. Informed observers note, however, that the Russians are proceeding with caution and avoiding civilian casualties[476] for two main reasons.

- Firstly, it tends to be forgotten that the «Russian forces» are in fact a coalition and that the troops fighting in the Donbass cities are mainly from the self-proclaimed Donbass republics. In other words, not only do they know the inhabitants of the towns and villages, but they are often friends or family. There is no incentive for savagery.
- Secondly, the southern and eastern part of Ukraine is mainly Russian-speaking. It is in this huge region that the Russian coalition has the most support. Therefore, it has no interest in alienating the civilian population. Moreover, there are no rebellion movements against the coalition.

In contrast, since 2014, Ukrainian forces have made extensive use of volunteers and political extremists, often foreign, and now troops from the western part of Ukraine, who have no empathy for the people of Donbass and brutally repress them. Moreover, the authorities in Kiev, although they claim the territory of Donbass, have never considered its inhabitants as full Ukrainians. Between February 2014 and February 2022, the conflict in Donbass is estimated to have resulted in the deaths of 13,000-14,000 people, but not only civilians. The Ukrainian authorities are rather stingy with figures and international organisations are reduced to making estimates: 'At least 3,350 civilians, about 4,100 members of Ukrainian forces and about 5,650 members of armed groups'[477]. This means that - according to these

476. William M. Arkin, «Putin's Bombers Could Devastate Ukraine But He's Holding Back. Here's Why,» Newsweek, 22 March 2022 (https://www.newsweek.com/putins-bombers-could-devastate-ukraine-hes-holding-back-heres-why-1690494)
477. https://www.ohchr.org/Documents/Countries/UA/29thReportUkraine_

estimates - the Ukrainian government has killed at least 9,000 of its citizens. A government no more concerned about its citizens than its military, since in 2018 about 2/3 of them died outside combat actions, as we have seen.

This is hardly surprising since the Ukrainian counterinsurgency strategy has never sought to create an inclusive nation. On the contrary, it has sought to exclude citizens who do not fit the 'Idea of Nation'. Instead of encouraging people to remain loyal to Kiev, it has sought to punish them for supporting the rebels. The Ukrainians are fighting against their fellow citizens of Donbass like the Israelis are fighting against the Palestinians. This is the opposite of the counter-insurgency strategies applied by the British in the 1950s in Asia, or by the Americans at the beginning of the Vietnam conflict, where they tried to win the «hearts and minds» of the local population in order to dissociate them from the insurgents.

Our media are very discreet about this aspect of the war, which would undermine the narrative they cynically serve us. For many journalists and media, the end justifies the means: denouncing Russia's exactions is fine, but evoking these same misdeeds when it is a Western country or one of its allies, out of the question! This is an ethic of variable geometry, which does not bend to the minimisation of the crimes of the extreme right-wing militias[478]. However, information on war crimes committed by Ukraine since 2014 abounds[479] and has multiplied since the beginning of the Russian offensive[480]. As for the

---

EN.pdf

478. https://www.hrw.org/news/2022/04/03/ukraine-apparent-war-crimes-russia-controlled-areas

479. https://www.osce.org/files/f/documents/e/7/233896.pdf

480. Rasmus Tantholdt & Mikkel Secher, «Russiske krigsfanger bliver henrettet i Ukraine, fortæller dansker», TV2, 7 April 2022 (https://nyheder.tv2.dk/

systematic elimination and mutilation of prisoners of war by the Ukrainians, this has long been documented[481].

Since 2022, the Russian intervention seems to have changed the nature of the conflict that Ukraine had been conducting until then. The victims seem to affect the military more than civilians. Peter Maurer, president of the International Committee of the Red Cross (ICRC), declared in March 2022 in the Swiss magazine Die Weltwoche:

> *We note that there are genuine efforts on both sides not to allow this conflict to degenerate completely. There are precautionary measures against the civilian population.*[482]

The Russians are accused of practising a scorched earth strategy[483] or using civilians as «human shields». Strategies that are used by defenders are attributed to Russian forces: destroying abandoned facilities to prevent the attacker from using them, and exploiting the presence of civilians to prevent an attacker from using their weapons.

---

udland/2022-04-07-russiske-krigsfanger-bliver-henrettet-i-ukraine-fortaeller-dansker)

481. Haley Willis, «Video shows Russian prisoners of war in Ukraine being beaten and shot in their legs», The New York Times, 28 March 2022

482. «Peter Maurer, President of the Roten Kreuzes, says: «The Ukraine war marks a trend. Das humanitäre Völkerrecht werde wieder stärker beachtet. The role of the neutral authorities remains unchallenged. Friede sei nur durch Gespräche möglich», Die Weltwoche, 7 October 2022 (https://weltwoche.ch/daily/praesident-des-roten-kreuzes-peter-maurer-sagt-der-ukraine-krieg-markiert-eine-trendwende-das-humanitaere-voelkerrecht-werde-wieder-staerker-beachtet-die-rolle-des-neutralen-vermittlers/)

483. «The future strategy of the Russian army in Ukraine analysed by experts», rts.ch, 24 April 2022 (https://www.rts.ch/info/monde/13040980-la-strategie-future-de-larmee-russe-en-ukraine-analysee-par-des-experts.html)

In fact, Ukrainian forces are trying to compensate for their tactical inferiority by placing their troops near or in the centre of civilian targets. As William Schabas, Professor of International Law at Middlesex University in London, states:

> *I am very reluctant to say that Ukraine is responsible for civilian casualties, because Ukraine is fighting to defend its country against an aggressor, but to the extent that Ukraine brings the battlefield into civilian areas, it increases the danger to civilians*[484].

In Mariupol, it was known that the Ukrainians were preventing civilians from leaving the city through the humanitarian corridors set up by the Russians[485], but the appeals for help from the population of Donbass remained totally ignored by our media[486].

In Kherson, as soon as they entered the city, the Ukrainians began a purge[487]. Lists of «collaborators» were drawn up[488], including those who had helped set up the September referendum. The hunt is on, with the support of the Western media, who keep silent about Ukrainian exactions and crimes.

---

484. Sudarsan Raghavan, 'Russia has killed civilians in Ukraine. Kyiv's defense tactics add to the danger,» The Washington Post, 28 March 2022 (https://www.washingtonpost.com/world/2022/03/28/ukraine-kyiv-russia-civilians/)
485. https://youtu.be/kdYUbVaFNRw
486. https://www.youtube.com/watch?v=f4qAXEjHCZA
487. Louise Callaghan, «Russian 'collaborators' rounded up as Ukraine reasserts control over tense, divided region», The Sunday Times, 13 November 2022 (https://www.thetimes.co.uk/article/russian-collaborators-rounded-up-as-ukraine-reasserts-control-over-tense-divided-region-d3r28vkgj)
488. https://t.me/s/Kherson_kolaborant

La base des traîtres à Kherson et dans le sud de l'Ukraine

Collaboration
Moraire Olena Oleksandrivna
29/04/1999
Elle a travaillé à l'école n ° 36 de Kherson en tant qu'enseignante-organisatrice.
Actuellement, sous les autorités d'occupation, il occupe un poste au "Ministère de la Santé de la Région de Kherson". Sur la photo, avec Saldo et d'autres collaborateurs, le 22 juin, elle était à l'événement près de la flamme éternelle à Slavy Park.

https://www.facebook.com/profile.php?id=100022327162142
https://instagram.com/k_m_lena
https://vk.com/kimlena29
https://vk.com/id230001708 (https://archive.ph/P5My3)

@Kherson_kolaborant
Kherson

12.8K 11:38

Figure 61 - Extract from the database of 'traitors and collaborators', which went online immediately after the arrival of Ukrainian troops in Kherson. Like its big sister Mirotvorets, this database aims to point out to the public journalists, teachers, civil servants and others who are accused of helping Russia. In Switzerland, no state media (such as RTS) or traditional media have condemned these practices and passed them over in silence... (automatic translation) [Source: https://t.me/s/Kherson_kolaborant]

6.4.4.2. The notion of victory

Operations in Ukraine tend to have an asymmetric aspect. Russia understands victory as the destruction of the military («demilitarisation») and paramilitary («denazification») threat against the populations of Donbass. Ukraine associates victory with maintaining and regaining its territorial sovereignty. In other words, Russia seeks to destroy capabilities, while Ukraine is fighting for territory.

This explains why Ukraine does not conduct its operations in a dynamic manner and «hangs on» to the ground at the cost of enormous losses. Conversely, Russia, which intervened with fewer troops than Ukraine, is trying to preserve its human resources, just as it is trying to spare the local population, which is Russian-speaking. You can recover land, not people.

A second fundamental difference is that Ukrainian political leadership seems to attach more importance to Vladimir Putin's defeat than to its own victory[489]. This is why sanctions are so important to the West, even if it is hoped that they will have medium-term effects at best, while in the short term the Ukrainian military is dying. Volodymyr Zelensky's statement at the end of September 2022 that he would only agree to negotiate with Russia if Vladimir Putin was no longer in power illustrates this quasi-millennialist vision[490]. This statement reinforced popular support for Vladimir Putin by confirming what the Kremlin has been saying for years.

489. David J. Kramer, «Defeating Putin in Ukraine Is Vital to the Future of Democracy», Journal of Democracy, May 2022 (https://www.journalofdemocracy.org/defeating-putin-in-ukraine-is-vital-to-the-future-of-democracy/)
490. «Ukraine Will Not Negotiate With Russia As Long As Putin Is In Power: Zelensky», Barron's/AFP, 30 September 2022

In Ukraine and in the West, people remain attached to chi-metric objectives that have very little chance of being achieved[491], whereas on the Russian side the objectives are very concrete and already largely achieved.

The result of this perception gap is an asymmetrical situation in which the more the West pushes Ukraine to continue the war, the more it encourages Russia to consolidate its position and the weaker Ukraine becomes. This is the paradox of the weapons supplied by the West to Ukraine: they encourage Russia to continue its methodical destruction of Ukrainian forces.

491. Shahin Berenji, «Arms Alone Cannot Win the Peace in Ukraine», The National Interest, 2 August 2022 (https://nationalinterest.org/feature/arms-alone-cannot-win-peace-ukraine-203913)

7. The information war

War is a theatre of combat in physical space but also in informational space (infosphere).

Since the dawn of time, the protagonists of a conflict have sought to valorise their actions and denigrate those of their adversary. This can be done to explain defeats, to valorise victories, to legitimise actions vis-à-vis one's own side or third parties, or even the enemy.

Several tools exist:

- propaganda, which highlights a positive point about oneself or a negative point about the opponent;
- misinformation, which aims to mislead an adversary or friend; and
- Concealment, which seeks to hide a weakness or disguise an intention.

Contrary to the claims of outfits like Conspiracy Watch, not all misinformation is intended to be misleading. In the heat of battle and the confusion of combat, our picture of the battlefield may be fragmentary or even distorted because sensors are imperfect or there is not enough time for verification. This is what Clausewitz called the 'fog of war'.

7.1.Communication

From the beginning of the offensive, Russia's communication shows fundamental differences with that of Ukraine.

- Ukraine's focus is on glorifying its actions and maximising Russia's losses.
- Russia focuses its communication on manifestations of «Russophobia» and the absurdity of Western sanctions.

Generally speaking, Ukrainian communication is essentially offensive. It is based on Zelensky's omnipresence, with a dress code and a tone that mark the will to fight and determination. In contrast, Russian communication is less 'Western', more sober and more defensive.

In terms of content, however, Ukrainian communication seems less solid: its aim is to shape minds rather than to inform. Zelensky appears to be the keystone of the communication system.

On the Russian side, communication is more conventional, more academic, but more factual and reliable. Communication of an operational nature is given by the military, while communication of a political and strategic nature is the responsibility of the presidential team.

Generally speaking, in a conflict, both sides communicate according to their interests. Exaggerations, cover-ups and misinformation are practised by both sides and this conflict is certainly no exception. We know this. Yet our media inform exclusively on the basis of Ukrainian sources: Russian losses, Ukrainian «counter-offensives», strikes against civilian targets, etc., systematically reflect the Ukrainian discourse.

The two countries have a very different approach to war: Zelensky fights in informational space; Vladimir Putin fights in material space. Zelensky seems to think that convincing the international community that you are winning is enough to win. Reading our media, we can see that he is not completely wrong. However, there is a point where the word and the reality come into contact, and that is where the difficulty lies. After so much talk about Ukraine winning this war, the accumulating defeats that are «consuming» more and more men are creating tensions between the military and the political leadership, i.e. Zelensky. This is what we observe at the beginning of July 2022 and which explains - in part - the purges carried out in the Ukrainian administration.

7.2.Cyberwarfare

On 15 February, the media reported a denial-of-service cyber-attack that targeted major Ukrainian banks and institutions[492]. The next day, in 'C dans l'air', Alain Bauer, a criminologist (but clearly not a strategist), explained a complex strategy of 'small steps' by which Vladimir Putin would seek to wage war without waging war, and that the attack was a message that the war would be waged both on the ground and in cyberspace[493]. Yet on the day of the attack, Reuters notes:

> *Cloudflare, a leading denial-of-service security firm based in San Francisco, said it had seen no evidence of «significant*

492. Maggie Miller, «Ukrainian Ministry of Defense websites hit by cyberattack», politico.com, 15 February 2022
493. Alain Bauer, in the programme «C dans l'air» of 16 February 2022 («Ukraine: mais à quoi joue Poutine? #cdanslair 16.02.2022', France 5/YouTube, 18 February 2022) (16'45")

denial-of-service activity» in Ukraine against its data centres or customers there. [494]

These doubts are also raised by Tatyana Bolton, policy director of the R Street Institute's Cybersecurity and Emerging Threats team, that «there is no direct indication that Russian entities are responsible»[495].

In support of these allegations, Tatiana Kastouéva-Jean, researcher and director of the Russia Centre at IFRI, gives the example of the Colonial Pipeline, an oil pipeline that in May 2021 was subject to a cyber-attack in Texas with a ransom demand. However, on 10 May 2021, Joe Biden stated: «There is no evidence that the Russian government was involved in the Colonial Pipeline ransomware attack»[496]. The FBI attributed the attack to «DarkSide, a group of criminal hackers based in Eastern Europe»[497]. Our so-called experts have therefore constructed a fictitious reality. This raises questions about the quality of research in France...

What our pseudo-experts are not telling us is that the information war began immediately after the Russian intervention on 24 February, but on the Ukrainian side, not the Russian. Researchers at the University of Adelaide (Australia)[498] found

---

494. «Ukraine defence ministry website, banks, knocked offline», Reuters, 15 February 2022

495. Mark Pomerleau, «Experts urge caution in assessing Ukraine cyberattacks», C4ISR.net, 16 February 2022 (https://www.c4isrnet.com/cyber/2022/02/16/experts-urge-caution-in-assessing-ukraine-cyberattacks/)

496. Lauren Egan, «Biden says no evidence Russian government was involved in pipeline hack», NBC News, 10 May 2021

497. Sara Morrison, «How a major oil pipeline got held for ransom», Vox, 8 June 2021

498. Bridget Smart, Joshua Watt, Sara Benedetti, Lewis Mitchell & Matthew Roughan, '#IStandWithPutin versus #IStandWithUkraine: The interaction of bots and humans in discussion of the Russia/Ukraine war', The University of Adelaide,

that in the first few weeks of the intervention, 80% of the tweets about the war came from «bots», fake accounts generated as part of an underground propaganda campaign. They also found that 90.2% of the 5 million tweets (real and bot) studied came from pro-Ukrainian accounts, while only 7% came from pro-Russian accounts.

From the start of the Russian operation on 24 February, the hashtag #IS-tandWithUkraine was used in 38,000 tweets per hour, peaking at 50,000 tweets per hour on the third day of the war. It was only after a week that 'pro-Russian' tweets began to appear at the rate of a few hundred per hour[499]. While the Ukrainian cyber operations appear to have been prepared for a long time, the Russian ones «that we have seen are not prepared for a long time and seem rather haphazard», according to Dr Lennart Maschmeyer of the Center for Security Studies at the Swiss Federal Institute of Technology in Zurich[500].

The intensity of cyber activity immediately after the Russian offensive began suggests the existence of a carefully prepared machinery. This tends to confirm the idea of a provocation by Ukraine in order to push Russia to intervene, and then to provoke its collapse through massive sanctions. There is then a decrease in the activity of these bots, probably due to the Russian strikes. The Australian researchers also note that the activity of the Russian bots never reached the level of the Ukrainian bots.

15 August 2022 (updated 20 August 2022) (https://arxiv.org/abs/2208.07038)

499. Peter Cronau, «Massive Anti-Russian 'Bot Army' Exposed by Australian Researchers», Declassified Australia, 3 November 2022 (https://declassifiedaus.org/2022/11/03/strongmassive-anti-russian-bot-army-exposed-by-australian-researchers-strong/)

500. Dan Milmo, «Russia unleashed data-wiper malware on Ukraine, say cyber experts», The Guardian, 24 February 2022 (https://www.theguardian.com/world/2022/feb/24/russia-unleashed-data-wiper-virus-on-ukraine-say-cyber-experts)

Use of #IStandWithUkraine and #IStandWithRussia

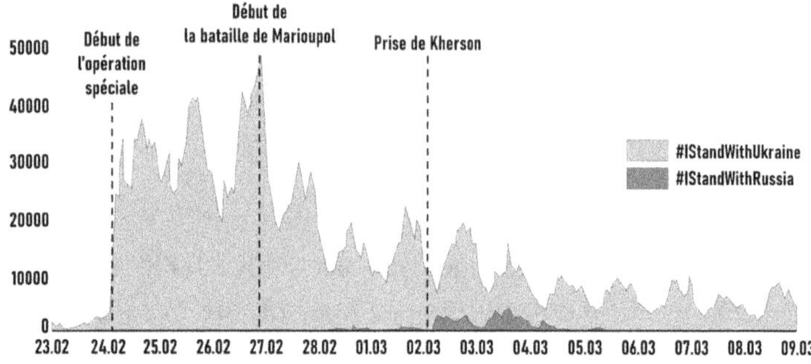

Figure 62 - Twitter bot activity by hour during the first week of the Russian offensive. We can see that the #IStandWithUkraine bots started immediately on 24 February with more than 30,000 hits per hour. The pro-Russian bots only intervene very late after a few days with only a few hundred hits per hour. [From the University of Adelaide School of Mathematics report (https ://arxiv.org/abs/2208.07038)]

Finally, it can be seen that cyber warfare seems to play only a modest role in Ukraine. There is a very large number of actions on computer networks, but they are carried out by non-state actors, groups of individuals or isolated individuals, who participate on both sides in the war in their own way. More spectacular than effective, these actions do not seem to affect the course of the fighting. They essentially play a role for influence. With the complacent assistance of the media, which reproduce without verification the information coming from Kiev, actions in cyberspace have contributed to making sanctions acceptable and to mobilising Western public opinion in favour of a war against Russia. These findings show that war remains - unfortunately - an essentially concrete phenomenon, made of blood, sweat and tears. This illustrates the fact that the threat of a «hybrid war» (the content of which no one knows) remains a concept so abstract as to be obscure, if not non-existent.

7.3. Disinformation

Free claims

To say that...	... made it possible to say
Ukraine is one people	that Ukraine would stand up as one against Russia. that there was no Ukrainian genocide in the Donbass. that the Russian coalition would not have supporters in the areas it occupies.
The Ukrainian population is unanimous against Russia	that Russia is also fighting against the civilian population in Ukraine.
Russia wants to destroy Ukraine	that Russia is bombing civilian populations.
Vladimir Putin wanted to take over Kiev in two days Russia wanted to win on 9 May 2022	that Ukraine is resisting Russia. that the Russian targets were unrealistic. that Russian intelligence services misjudged the situation.
Vladimir Putin wants to take over Ukraine	that popular resistance should be encouraged and supported. that more weapons must be sent and the conflict must be prolonged.
Vladimir Putin seeks to reconstitute the USSR Putin wants to restore the Russian empire[501]	that the Baltic countries are directly threatened by Russia.
Ukraine is democratic	that Russia envies Ukrainian democracy. that Vladimir Putin hates democracy.
Putin claims that the Ukrainian nation does not exist[502]	that Russia believes it has a legitimate claim to annex it.

Ironically, the claim that Ukraine was winning the war prompted the West to tout the quality of the training it had provided to Ukraine in tactical leadership, operational manoeuvring and conduct of operations. As Pentagon spokesman John Kirby put it in May 2022:

What you see now is not just the effect of the weapons, but the skills and abilities that [the Ukrainians] are exercising on

501. https://youtu.be/Rgy2Bbe3HYE?t=3630
502. https://youtu.be/Rgy2Bbe3HYE?t=3623.

the battlefield. This is not accidental. They have gone from a Soviet-era, Russian-dominated, vertical military system with a rigid doctrine to a much more Westernised system in terms of how they think and act, and encouraging that on the battlefield. Again, this is not an accident but the result of the work of the US and several allies. [503]

Thus, Western disinformation is turning against the West. The West has been so involved in Ukraine, so ostensibly and loudly claiming that Russia would soon fold, that the failure of Ukraine is increasingly seen as the failure of the entire West. After NATO's spectacular failure in Afghanistan, it is an illustration of a West that is no longer capable of acting rationally.

In fact, as revealed by the American media outlet Mint Press News, the Americans have created a network of about 150 public relations firms to shape the narrative against Russia. So the Ukrainian narrative is created, which is then reflected in our media[504].

7.3.1. The nuclear threat

Since the beginning of the Russian offensive, Western propaganda has sought to amplify the Russian nuclear threat and give it a continental dimension. This rhetoric has several objectives:

- justify the scale of the Western response;
- mobilise public opinion against Russia and fuel a narrative of hate;

503. https://youtu.be/v5OanupYl94

504. Dan Cohen, «Ukraine's Propaganda War: International PR Firms, DC Lobbyists and CIA Cutouts», Mint Press News, 22 March 2022 (https://www.mintpressnews.com/ukraine-propaganda-war-international-pr-firms-dc-lobbyists-cia-cutouts/280012/)

- feed the myth of a tougher opponent than expected (on RTS, the 'journalist' Alexis Favre spoke of 40 million resisters[505]) to postulate that nuclear weapons became the only Russian recourse to obtain victory.

At the beginning of March 2022, as Russian troops pushed rapidly towards the Zaporozhie nuclear power plant in order to prevent any act of sabotage with dramatic consequences, an administrative building was hit by fire. Hit by a Russian tank according to some, victim of a Ukrainian sabotage attempt according to others, we don't really know what happened, even if the Russian version seems to be confirmed. But there is considerable excitement. Playing with the event, Volodymyr Zelensky declared:

> *If there is an explosion, it is the end of everything. The end of Europe.* [506]

It is claimed that Vladimir Putin is trying to activate the nuclear threat. France 5 devotes a «C dans l'air» programme to the incident, under the title «Nuclear power stations, gas... Putin's other weapons»[507]. In short, it seems that we are on the eve of the apocalypse... Russia invites the International Atomic Energy Agency to inspect the site but, at the request of Volodymyr Zelensky, the agency refuses the invitation. On 20 July 2022, the plant was attacked by four Ukrainian «kamikaze drones» whose «powerful explosions» were heard throughout the city, injuring «a dozen employees»[508].

505. https://www.rts.ch/play/tv/redirect/detail/12908299?startTime=381
506. «Ukraine nuclear plant: Russia in control after shelling», BBC News, 4 March 2022 (https://www.bbc.com/news/world-europe-60613438)
507. «Nuclear power plants, gas... Putin's other weapons #cdanslair 08.03.2022», France 5 /YouTube, 9 March 2022 (https://youtu.be/8Ub97_37vkg)
508. Nataliya Vasilyeva, «'Kamikaze drones' strike Russian-controlled Zaporizhzhia nuclear power plant», The Telegraph, 20 July 2022 (https://www.telegraph.co.uk/world-news/2022/07/20/ukrainian-kamikaze-drones-strike-russian-

Yet, with the exception of the British Telegraph, no Western media reported the attack. The «end of Europe» was only in March...

In fact, Vladimir Putin did not mention nuclear weapons until after Western officials, and informed experts - and there are some - observe that the use of nuclear weapons is most likely not in the Kremlin's intentions[509].

	Western statements	**Russia's response**
24 February 2022	French Foreign Minister Jean-Yves Le Drian tells Russia that NATO could use nuclear weapons[510].	
27 February 2022	Liz Truss, British Foreign Secretary, talks about the destruction of the Russian military-industrial complex and the possibility of direct confrontation between NATO and Russia[511].	
27 February 2022		Vladimir Putin announces that he has put his nuclear forces on «*special* combat *alert*»[512] and[513].

controlled-zaporizhzhia/)

509. Susan D'Agostino & François Diaz-Maurin, 'Will Putin go nuclear? An updated timeline of expert comments», Bulletin of the Atomic Scientists, 6 June 2022 (https://thebulletin.org/2022/06/will-putin-go-nuclear-an-updated-timeline-of-expert-comments/)

510. Anthony Audureau/AFP, «Ukraine: Le Drian reminds Putin that «the Atlantic Alliance is also a nuclear alliance», BFM TV, 24 February 2022 (https://www.bfmtv.com/international/ukraine-le-drian-rappelle-a-poutine-que-l-alliance-atlantique-est-aussi-une-alliance-nucleaire_AD-202202240685.html)

511. Stephen Mcilkenny, «Liz Truss: Kremlin says decision to put nuclear bases on high alert due to comments made by Foreign Secretary | What did she say about Ukraine crisis?», The Scotsman, 28 February 2022 (https://www.scotsman.com/news/politics/kremlin-says-nuclear-bases-on-high-alert-due-to-comments-made-by-liz-truss-3589463)

512. Andrew Roth, Shaun Walker, Jennifer Rankin & Julian Borger, 'Putin signals escalation as he puts Russia's nuclear force on high alert', The Guardian, 28 February 2022.

513. Runai Tairov, «Путин приказал перевести силы сдерживания в особый режим боевого дежурства», Forbes.ru, 27 February 2022 (https://www.forbes.ru/

	Western statements	Russia's response
28 March 2022	President Biden decides to abandon the no-first-use policy for nuclear weapons [514]	
5 May 2022		Vladimir Putin mentions the risk of a nuclear conflict[516].
24 August 2022	Liz Truss declares herself ready to use nuclear weapons, even if it means «global annihilation»[515].	
21 September 2022		Vladimir Putin warns against the use of nuclear weapons and says that Russia has other very powerful weapons, but does not mention the use of nuclear weapons.[517]

For example, at the end of February 2022, RTS declared that Putin was «clearly brandishing the nuclear threat»[518]. But, as usual, our media use disinformation to create panic. In fact, Rose Gottemoeller, former Under Secretary for Arms Control in the Obama administration, puts things in perspective:

society/457237-putin-prikazal-perevesti-sily-sderzivania-v-osobyj-rezim-boevogo-dezurstva)

514. Daryl G. Kimball, 'Biden Policy Allows First Use of Nuclear Weapons', Arms Control Today, April 2022 (https://www.armscontrol.org/act/2022-04/news/biden-policy-allows-first-use-nuclear-weapons).

515. https://www.independent.co.uk/news/uk/politics/liz-truss-nuclear-button-ready-b2151614.html; https://youtu.be/IvH7cgbdazU

516. Alain Barluet, «Vladimir Putin waves the nuclear threat around as an instrument of his up-to-the-minute strategy», Le Figaro, 5 May 2022 (https://www.lefigaro.fr/international/vladimir-poutine-agite-la-menace-nucleaire-comme-un-instrument-de-sa-strategie-jusqu-au-boutiste-20220505)

517. http://en.kremlin.ru/events/president/news/69390

518. https://www.rts.ch/play/tv/redirect/detail/12908299?startTime=683

Putin's order will only bring «three to six more people» to the nuclear command posts normally staffed by about six people. [519]

Once again, the media and «experts» try to present Vladimir Putin as an irrational individual. According to them, the stalemate of the Russian forces in Ukraine could push him to commit nuclear weapons. At the beginning of May, shortly after the test firing of a Russian RS-28 SARMAT missile[520], our media (again) brandish the threat of an irrational use of nuclear weapons[521].

In fact, what none of the media reported was that in late April 2022, President Joe Biden decided on a major change in US nuclear policy by abandoning the «no-first-use» principle of nuclear weapons. In other words, while the US had previously considered the use of nuclear weapons only for deterrence (the «sole purpose» policy), Biden approved a policy «that leaves open the option to use nuclear weapons not only in retaliation for a nuclear attack, but also to respond to non-nuclear threats[522] «. In other words, the US allows itself to use nuclear weapons at any time.

519. Stephanie Cooke, «Will Putin Use Nuclear Weapons in Ukraine?», Energy Intelligence, 17 March 2022 (https://www.energyintel.com/0000017f-94cd-d81c-a9ff-9ecf7ccf0000)

520. Lateshia Beachum, Mary Ilyushina & Karoun Demirjian, «Russia's 'Satan 2' missile changes little for U.S., scholars say», The Washington Post, 20 April 2022 (https://www.washingtonpost.com/world/2022/04/20/satan-2-icbm/)

521. «Russian nuclear threat: «Putin has already proved that he is capable of illogical and self-destructive decisions», says Mitt Romney», La Libre, 23 May 2022 (https://www.lalibre.be/international/europe/guerre-ukraine-russie/2022/05/23/menace-nucleaire-russe-poutine-a-deja-prouve-quil-etait-capable-de-decisions-illogiques-et-autodestructrices-estime-mitt-romney-XAKAPL257BHALGDTIAA3V423JQ/)

522. Daryl G. Kimball, «Biden Policy Allows First Use of Nuclear Weapons», Arms Control Association, 29 April 2022 (https://www.armscontrol.org/act/2022-

In short, since the end of April, the United States has given itself the right to start a nuclear war. Moreover, in order to achieve its aims, it does not hesitate to adopt measures - such as sanctions - that hurt its allies as much as Russia. This is why the Russian leadership is worried about the change in US doctrine and warns that the use of nuclear weapons would also come at a price for the US.

The Russian doctrine remains unchanged: Russia will not use nuclear weapons first. Once again, it is the concealment of essential information concerning the West, which the less than honest media exploit to make people believe that Vladimir Putin is irrational, and thus generate panic among the population[523].

In contrast to our media, US intelligence seems more confident, with Avril Haines, Director of National Intelligence, telling a congressional hearing: There is no imminent potential for Putin to use nuclear weapons. President Putin would probably only authorise the use of nuclear weapons if he perceived an existential threat to the Russian state or regime.[524]

The ball is therefore clearly in the Western camp.

After Vladimir Putin's speech on 21 September[525], our media talked about the risk of nuclear escalation. Naturally, the conspiracy media (i.e. those who construct narratives from unrelated information), immediately spoke of 'nuclear threats'[526].

In reality, this is not true. If you read the text of Putin's speech, you will see that he did not threaten to use nuclear weapons. In fact, he has never done so since the conflict began in 2014.

04/news/biden-policy-allows-first-use-nuclear-weapons)

523. «Should we fear the nuclear threat?», RTS.ch, 21 May 2022 (https://www.rts.ch/info/suisse/13105385-podcast-doiton-craindre-la-menace-nucleaire.html)

524. https://twitter.com/therecount/status/1524034365075992576

525. http://en.kremlin.ru/events/president/news/69390

526. https://www.rts.ch/info/monde/13410803-les-scenarios-possibles-apres-les-menaces-nucleaires-de-vladimir-poutine.html

Instead, he has warned the West against using such weapons. For example, on 24 August, Liz Truss said that it was acceptable to strike Russia with nuclear weapons, and that she was prepared to do so, even if it led to «global annihilation»[527] ! This is not the first time she has made such a statement, provoking warnings from the Kremlin in February[528].

So clearly, Vladimir Putin is wary of a totally irrational and irresponsible Western behaviour, which is ready to sacrifice its own citizens to achieve objectives guided by dogmatism and ideology. This is what is happening in the field of energy and sanctions at the moment. Putin is certainly worried about the reactions of our leaders who are in increasingly uncomfortable situations due to the catastrophic economic and social situation they have created through their incompetence. This pressure on our leaders could lead them to escalate the conflict just to avoid losing face...

In his speech on 21 September, Vladimir Putin did not threaten to use nuclear weapons, but other types of weapons. He is naturally thinking of hypersonic weapons, which do not need to be nuclear to be effective. Moreover, contrary to what our media say, the use of tactical nuclear weapons has not been part of the Russian employment doctrine for many years now.

In other words, it is Westerners and their erratic behaviour that are the real factors of insecurity...

7.3.1.1. Attacks on the Zaporojie nuclear power plant

In July 2022, the Zaporozhie nuclear power plant (ZNPP) in Energodar was the victim of artillery fire, which the Ukrainians and Russians attributed to the opposing side.

---

527. https://www.independent.co.uk/news/uk/politics/liz-truss-nuclear-button-ready-b2151614.html

528. https://www.itv.com/news/2022-02-28/not-naming-names-but-it-was-liz-truss-minister-blamed-for-putin-nuclear-move

Russian coalition forces have occupied the NPA site since 4 March. The Russian coalition then quickly seized it, in order to prevent it from being caught up in fighting and thus avoid a nuclear incident.

During the capture of the power station, a fire broke out in an administrative building. Hit by a Russian tank according to some, victim of a Ukrainian sabotage attempt according to others, we do not really know what happened, even if the facts seem to confirm the Russian version, which is more likely. At that time, Volodymyr Zelensky's objective was to obtain the establishment of a no-fly zone by the West. He spoke of a danger to Europe[529]. The state media, such as France 5, are adding fuel to the fire by stating that Vladimir Putin is seeking to use the NFZ as a weapon[530]. This is disinformation, because on the same day, at a press conference in Vienna, Rafael Grossi, Director of the International Atomic Energy Agency (IAEA), declared that there were no safety problems in the plant and that it was operating normally[531].

In fact, the Russians immediately deployed units of the National Guard (Rosgvard) to secure the site from sabotage or commando actions. Ukrainian technical staff remained on site and continue to work under the supervision of the Ukrainian operator Energoatom and the Ukrainian Nuclear Safety Agency (SNRIU).

---

529. «Ukraine nuclear plant: Russia in control after shelling», BBC News, 4 March 2022 (https://www.bbc.com/news/world-europe-60613438)

530. «Nuclear power plants, gas... Putin's other weapons #cdanslair 08.03.2022», France 5 /YouTube, 9 March 2022 (https://youtu.be/8Ub97_37vkg)

531. Margaret Besheer, «IAEA Chief: Ukraine's Zaporizhzhia Nuclear Plant Safe After Russian Strike», voanews, 4 March 2022 (https://www.voanews.com/a/iaea-chief-ukraine-s-zaporizhzhia-nuclear-plant-safe-after-russian-strike-/6470760.html)

Everything goes on normally until July. The plant is then hit by US-supplied 'kamikaze' drones, as we have seen.

But at the end of August, artillery and missile fire increased over the NPPZ. The West only listens to the Ukrainians, whose versions change and who claim to be responding to artillery fire from the plant itself. But the Rosgvard units deployed on the site are not combat units and are not equipped with heavy equipment. So this is not true.

Russia is then accused of wanting to put pressure on Europe. To what end? No answer. On French television, a French «expert» says that the Russians are firing on the power station in order to cut off the electricity to Ukraine[532]. Yet the Ukrainians themselves say that there are Russian troops in the vicinity of the site[533] and it is therefore difficult to see why the Russians would bomb a nuclear power plant that is under their control[534].

Firing on the plant could cause a nuclear incident. But it is located in an area where the population is generally sympathetic to the Russians and it is not clear why they would take the risk of nuclear contamination of the area.

On the other hand, the Ukrainians seem to have more serious reasons for creating an incident. First of all, the PNZ is in a Russian-speaking area, occupied by the Russian coalition. The Ukrainians have forcibly evacuated the Ukrainian civilian population and the contamination would only affect the Russian-speaking people whom they consider to be their enemies[535].

---

532. https://youtu.be/KZDbFcYAbVE?t=1578

533. https://theins.ru/en/news/253868

534. https://www.rts.ch/info/monde/13302505-kiev-et-moscou-saccusent-a-nouveau-de-tirs-sur-la-centrale-nucleaire-de-zaporijjia.html

535. «Ukraine's Reintegration Ministry names three more oblasts to be subject to compulsory evacuation», The New Voice of Ukraine, 26 August 2022 (https://english.nv.ua/nation/three-more-oblasts-to-be-subject-to-compulsory-evacuation-50265936.html)

Then, the Ukrainians had to show the West that they were capable of regaining the initiative. In July, they announced a major counter-offensive on Kherson with one million men[536], in order to retake the south of the country, but they were unable to implement it. This is why they carry out numerous counter-attacks, which our media call «counter-offensives», but which systematically end in failure, with enormous human losses.

Secondly, in several Russian-speaking areas taken over by the coalition, the authorities have declared that they want to hold autonomy referenda. Their outcome could be a serious setback for Kiev, as they could show that people in the south of the country do not feel Ukrainian.

A more likely explanation is that the Ukrainians are seeking to demilitarise the NPP area, so that they can regain control and the NPPZ can be returned to Ukraine, which would be a political and operational success for Zelensky. Thus, one could imagine that they seek to deliberately provoke a nuclear incident in order to create a «no man's land» and thus render the area unusable for the Russians.

However, more likely, the Ukrainians are seeking to create tension and generate fighting «around the plant[537] « in order to show that the site is not secure and that the area needs to be demilitarised or an international force sent in. In fact, by bombing the plant, Ukraine seeks to pressure the West to intervene in the conflict[538]. This strategy could explain the raid of about 300

536. «Ukraine attacks Russian-held Kherson, plans counterattack», aljazeerah, 12 July 2022 (https://www.aljazeera.com/news/2022/7/12/ukraine-strikes-russian-held-kherson-as-kyiv-plans-counterattack)

537. https://www.rts.ch/info/monde/13342432-combats-intenses-dans-la-quasi-totalite-de-la-region-de-kherson.html

538. https://www.theguardian.com/world/live/2022/aug/19/russia-ukraine-war-putin-is-losing-information-war-in-ukraine-uk-spy-chief-says-live

Ukrainian commandos who crossed the Dnieper River early in the morning of 1 September, the day the IAEA experts arrived, to attack the NPP. The concept of this attack was reportedly suggested by the British, but this has not been confirmed. Naturally, none of our media mentioned this attack, which could show that Ukraine is blackmailing the Europeans.

The evidence currently available suggests that the attacks on Energodar were Ukrainian. The remnants of projectiles fired from across the Dnieper are of Western origin. They appear to be HIMARS rockets and British[539] projectiles of the BRIMSTONE type[540], which are precision missiles, the firing of which is monitored by the British. Apparently the West is aware of the attacks on the Energodar plant.

The Ukrainians fear that the IAEA will confirm the Ukrainian origin of this provocation. This is why they have done everything to prevent a visit by IAEA experts[541].

7.3.1.2. The «dirty bomb

In October 2022, Ukraine's offensives all end in failure with huge losses. It could therefore seek to escalate the conflict and create a situation where NATO would be obliged to intervene.

On 6 October, information appeared on social networks about the use of a nuclear weapon manufactured in Ukraine and transported by train to Russia to be activated there. Everything indicates that it would be a «dirty bomb». That is, a conventional bomb, the explosion of which would disseminate radioactive material. A dirty bomb is not strictly speaking a nuclear weapon.

539. https://t.me/milinfolive/88735

540. https://mezha.media/en/2022/05/12/brimstone-in-ukraine/

541. https://www.ilfattoquotidiano.it/2022/06/07/energoatom-contro-il-direttore-dellaiea-grossi-mai-invitato-a-zaporizhzhya-vuole-legittimare-la-permanenza-degli-occupanti/6618145/

It does not have the destructive capacity. However, by disseminating radioactive dust, it could have the same effect as the projectiles used in the former Yugoslavia by American M-1 tanks and A-10 ground-support aircraft, which used shells with depleted uranium cores, the debris of which contaminated entire areas. The dirty bomb is a weapon that had already been used by Chechen terrorists[542]. Given the direction of the Ukrainian strategy and its Western allies, and the increase in terrorist attacks on public figures and facilities, Russia's allegations are plausible but unverifiable.

Likely or not, that is what the Russians believe. In an interview reported by the Russian opposition website Meduza, the newly appointed General Sergei Surovikin says he has «information that Kiev may be using illegal methods of warfare»[543].

A few days later, Russian Defence Minister Sergei Shoigu contacted his American, British, Turkish and French counterparts directly. On 24 October, France, the United States and Britain issued a joint statement rejecting the Russian allegations. However, the United Nations sent a delegation to Kiev to clarify the situation[544]. This shows that France, Britain and the United States (FUKUS) have - once again - reacted without knowing the precise state of affairs.

---

542. Jeffrey Bale, «The Chechen Resistance and Radiological Terrorism», Center for Nonproliferation Studies, 1 April 2004. (https://www.nti.org/analysis/articles/chechen-resistance-radiological-terror/)

543. «'We may have to make some difficult decisions in Kherson' Meduza's summary of the first interview given by Russia's new top commander in Ukraine», Meduza, 19 October 2022 (https://meduza.io/en/feature/2022/10/19/we-may-have-to-make-some-difficult-decisions-in-kherson)

544. «IAEA preparing to inspect two sites in Ukraine over 'dirty bomb' claims», Reuters, 25 October 2022 (https://www.reuters.com/world/europe/iaea-preparing-inspect-two-sites-ukraine-over-dirty-bomb-claims-2022-10-24/)

The interesting thing about this joint statement is that it does not condemn the use of a dirty bomb (whoever uses it). Yet the point here was not to condemn Ukraine, but the method. But clearly, Westerners accept an equivalence between the method and the perpetrator. In other words, it shows that the FUKUS, who have not condemned any of the terrorist attacks that have hit Russia or its interests, support terrorism as a method...

On 2 November, France 5, citing a New York Times article, claimed that Russian generals had discussed the use of tactical nuclear weapons in Ukraine[545]. Naturally, the experts present theories based on the idea that Russia losing the war could engage nuclear weapons to 'compensate' for its tactical setbacks. In reality, CNN, an American media outlet, takes a more nuanced look at these claims. According to CNN, «the assessment, written by the National Intelligence Council, is neither a product of great secrecy nor raw intelligence, but rather an analysis»[546]. In other words, it is the result of interpretation, not fact.

Western insistence on attributing to Russia the intention to use tactical nuclear weapons in Ukraine is worrying. The Russians see in this the risk of a false-banner incident, which could be used as a pretext for NATO intervention. An incident caused by a «dirty bomb» could be a step towards creating such a scenario. This is why the Russians immediately contacted their Western counterparts to clarify positions and avoid an escalation caused by a misinterpretation of one or the other.

545. https://youtu.be/fmGQfXwJzsc?t=1131

546. Natasha Bertrand, Katie Bo Lillis and Zachary Cohen, «US officials divided over new intelligence suggesting Russian military discussed scenarios for using nuclear weapons», CNN, 2 November 2022 (https://www.cnn.com/2022/11/02/politics/us-russia-nuclear-weapon-intelligence/index.html)

7.3.2. War crimes

War crimes are unfortunately part of the drama of war. They are committed by both sides, deliberately or not. The difference lies in their exploitation in the media and for military purposes.

The crimes attributed to Russia serve a well-tried communication strategy, according to the principle: «Slander! Slander! There will always be something left». Those attributed to Ukraine are ignored, and posts - on Twitter, Facebook or YouTube - about them are systematically deleted under the pretext of being «hate speech».

In fact, the media treatment of these crimes has become a weapon of war. The West so blindly believes without ever checking the allegations of Ukrainian propaganda, that any war crime is automatically attributed to Russia. Therefore, it becomes very tempting for the opposite side - Ukraine - to use such crimes in order to weaken Russia's position.

From the start of the Russian offensive, despite Western rhetoric, the Ukrainian army failed. Our media would not realise this until four months later, but Zelensky already knew. His air force was destroyed on the ground in the first hours of the offensive and, without it, Ukraine has little chance of regaining the advantage. Zelensky therefore asked the West to establish a no-fly zone over Ukraine, but they were not ready to intervene militarily. The temptation for Ukraine to repeat the Benghazi scenario in Libya was strong. In February 2011, Bernard-Henri Lévy claimed that the Libyan armed forces had perpetrated a massacre there[547]. Based on these allegations, the UN Security Council authorised the establishment of a no-fly zone over Libya, which led to the overthrow of Gaddafi. Predictably, the

547. Steven Erlanger, 'By His Own Reckoning, One Man Made Libya a French Cause', The New York Times, 1er April 2011.

information was false! US intelligence had not observed any massacre in Benghazi, but no politician would listen to them[548]. In March 2022, things did not seem to be going according to plan for the West. In the US, President Biden is being challenged by the economy and his son's laptop scandal; in France, Emmanuel Macron is being targeted by the McKinsey scandal, just before the presidential election, while EU leaders are beginning to feel that their sanctions are backfiring on the European economy.

In Ukraine, in the wake of the Russian advance, videos showing crimes committed by the Ukrainian military are surfacing on social networks. They show Russian prisoners of war being beaten, tortured, mutilated by shooting them in the kneecaps or genitals, or even gouging out their eyes. This unhealthy publicity is applauded by all our media, before being labelled as Russian propaganda. Facebook, YouTube, TikTok and Twitter are hastily reformulating their rules of use: praising a neo-Nazi militia or calling for violence against Russians is now allowed in the context of the war, while pro-Russian content is blocked[549].

But these Ukrainian crimes are real. Zelensky fears that their revelation will call into question Western support[550]. The mention

---

548. Kelly Riddell & Jeffrey Scott Shapiro, «Hillary Clinton's 'WMD' moment: U.S. intelligence saw false narrative in Libya», The Washington Times, 29 January 2015

549. Will Oremus, «Social media wasn't ready for this war. It needs a plan for the next one,» The Washington Post, March 25, 2022 (https://www.washingtonpost.com/technology/2022/03/25/social-media-ukraine-rules-war-policy/)

550. «Zelenskyy Worried About Western Financial Support After Video Surfaces Showing Ukraine Military Torturing Russian POW's», www.theconservativetreehouse.com, 27 March 2022 (https://theconservativetreehouse.com/blog/2022/03/27/zelenskyy-worried-about-western-financial-support-after-video-surfaces-showing-ukraine-military-torturing-russian-pows/?utm_source=rss&utm_medium=rss&utm_campaign=zelenskyy-worried-about-western-financial-support-after-video-surfaces-showing-ukraine-military-torturing-russian-pows)

of a massacre in Boutcha comes at the right time, on 2 April 2022. What exactly happened there? Nobody knows. But some civilians were executed, others appear to have been collateral victims of the fighting. As for who was responsible, Ukraine accuses the Russian army, while Russia claims that it was a falsification.

However, very quickly, certain inconsistencies cast doubt and suspicion on the Ukrainian - and therefore Western - accusations.

Course of events

Date	Event/fact
29 March	The Russian command decides to withdraw the troops west of Kiev to the Donbass, to start Phase 2 of the operation.
30 March	The Russians leave.
31 March	Anatoliy Fedoruk, mayor of Boutcha, announces on Telegram[551] with satisfaction the departure of the Russians. He does not mention any corpses or massacres: «March 31 will remain in the history of our community of Butcha as the day of liberation. The liberation by our armed forces of Ukraine from the Russian «Orcs», the Russian occupiers. So today I declare this day to be a joyous one. Happy, and it is a great victory in the Kiev region! And we will certainly wait until there is a great victory in the whole of Ukraine.»[552]
31 March 1 April	The Ukrainian media *Unian* confirms the departure of the Russian forces and reports the words of the mayor of Butcha, without mentioning the presence of corpses or massacres in the town[553]. Ukrainian forces are combing the area for saboteurs and Russian collaborators (a Ukrainian video shows Ukrainian paramilitaries asking to be allowed to shoot those not wearing blue armbands).
1er April	A video shows bodies in the street that have not been there for three weeks, but whose position is similar to that of the satellite images of 11 March. Some wear white armbands, some have their wrists tied with white cloth, some have Russian aid packages, some were executed in a basement.

551. https://t.me/vityzeva/52988.
552. «Bucha liberated from Russian invaders - mayor», ukrinform.net, 1 April 2022 (https://www.ukrinform.net/rubric-ato/3445989-bucha-liberated-from-russian-invaders-mayor.html)
553. Violetta Orlova, «Мер Бучі підтвердив звільнення міста від російських військ», Unian, 1 April 2022 (https://www.unian.ua/war/bucha-novini-mer-buchi-zayavlyaye-pro-zvilnennya-mista-vid-okupantiv-novini-vtorgnennya-rosiji-v-ukrajinu-11769010.html)

Date	Event/fact
2 April	Ukrainian blogger Dimitry Komarov walks through the city and shows the damage after the departure of Russian troops. He mentions neither corpses nor massacres[554]. On the same day, the Ukrainian news website *Unian* announced that special units had *'cleared the city of saboteurs and collaborators of* Russian *troops'*[555]. The SAFARI unit of the Ukrainian police enters the city to carry out mine clearance and de-mining operations, in case the Russians have booby-trapped the city. The video[556] shot by the unit does not show a massacre, but access to it on YouTube is limited.
3 April	Ukraine accuses Russian forces of committing a massacre in the streets of Butcha. The reports of a mass grave are in fact related to the burial of a previously recorded grave in the churchyard on 13 March.

On 4 April, the New York Times published a satellite photo of the scene, dated 11 March 2022, almost three weeks before the bodies were 'discovered'[557] (the date of which was later changed - without reason - to 19 March). Two facts are surprising: that the Russians kept the bodies on the road for three weeks, while they had taken care to bury other victims in the area during that period, and that the bodies remained strictly in the same position throughout this period.

In addition, we know that the New York Times image was provided by the firm Maxar, which works for the US government. We also know which satellites Maxar uses, we know their trajectory, their position at a given moment and the times they pass.

554. «Буча после ухода русских военныхQ», Kedrov Talks/YouTube, 2 April 2022 (https://youtu.be/72TZbAeKPSE)
555. Violetta Orlova, «У звільненій Бучі розпочали зачистку території від диверсантів та російських пособників», Unian, 2 April 2022 (https://www.unian.ua/war/bucha-u-zvilnenomu-misti-rozpochali-zachistku-teritoriji-vid-diversantiv-ta-rosiyskih-posobnikiv-novini-kiyeva-11770498.html)
556. https://youtu.be/Z7yIyNBMpQY.
557. Carole Landry, 'The Horror in Bucha', The New York Times, 4 April 2022 (https://www.nytimes.com/2022/04/04/briefing/russia-ukraine-war-briefing-bucha-warcrimes.html)

On the basis of these elements, by measuring the shadows cast, it is possible to determine precisely the day on which the photo was taken. A group of independent Russian analysts were able to determine that the photo was taken on 1 April at 11:57 GMT (14:57 local summer time)[558]. This is confirmed by the traces of a violent storm that hit the city on the night of 31 March to 1 April. Curiously enough, Maxar does not provide images of the area for 21 and 23 March, although they are included in the catalogue.

On the other hand, other facts call for caution:

- On 4 April, the Pentagon states that it is unable to confirm Russian responsibility for the Boutcha case[559].
- Ukrainian socialist MP Ilya Kiva[560] reveals on Telegram that the Boutcha tragedy was planned by the British MI6 special services and implemented by the SBU[561].
- In June 2022, the Italian television channel TG24 investigated the killings and crimes against civilians who had allegedly collaborated with Russian forces and found that this had been the case in Boutcha[562].
- Other Maxar images from the same area, taken on a different date, 'weigh' 100MB, while the 'massacre' image contains barely 50MB, suggesting that it has been degraded to hide manipulation.

---

558. https://t.me/rybar/30599

559. «Pentagon can't independently confirm atrocities in Ukraine's Bucha, official says», Reuters, 4 April 2022 (https://www.reuters.com/world/pentagon-cant-independently-confirm-atrocities-ukraines-bucha-official-says-2022-04-04/?-taid=624b43bd3225ef0001288ec4)

560. https://en.wikipedia.org/wiki/Illia_Kyva

561. https://t.me/intelslava/24353

562. Jacopo Arbarello, «Guerra in Ucraina, la questione dei collaborazionisti filorussi», Sky TG24, 7 June 2022 (https://tg24.sky.it/mondo/2022/06/06/guerra-russia-ucraina-filorussi)

All this does not prove anything in itself, but shows that what is presented to us as incontrovertible is far from clear. As Swiss Foreign Minister Ignazio Cassis states:

They are not war crimes until a court of law says so.[563]

It would seem, therefore, that these facts should be the subject of an international, impartial and multi-party investigation, in order to establish with certainty the responsibility for this war crime before sanctions are triggered. However, this is not what happened.

Britain, which held the presidency of the UN Security Council at the time, refused three times to hold a session to request an international commission of enquiry into the crimes of Boutcha[564].

So we will probably never know more about this event, but it doesn't really matter, because its purpose was to be able to bring an accusation against Russia. Because as always, our media do not question the context of this «massacre» and condemn Russia, even before an international commission of enquiry is mandated.

On 12 May 2022, members of the US Congress sent a letter to Meta, Twitter, YouTube, and TikTok, asking them to retain information and metadata about possible Russian war crimes in Ukraine. No mention is made - of course - of possible Ukrainian war crimes[565]. This is the problem: the fight against war crimes

563. «Ignazio Cassis: «These are not war crimes until a court decrees it», rts.ch, 7 April 2022 (https://www.rts.ch/info/suisse/13002882-ignazio-cassis-ce-ne-sont-pas-des-crimes-de-guerre-tant-quun-tribunal-ne-la-pas-decrete.html)

564. «The UN Security Council rejected Russia's request to hold a meeting on the «blatant provocation of Ukrainian radicals in Bucha», Front News Ukraine, 4 April 2022 (https://frontnews.eu/en/news/details/25750)

565. «Oversight and Foreign Affairs Committees Call on Social Media Companies to Preserve Evidence of Possible War Crimes in Ukraine, Committee on Oversight and Reform of the U.S. House of Representatives, 12 May 2022 (https://oversight.

or for human rights cannot be conducted unilaterally. It must be impartial to be credible and successful.

However, since 2014, our media have systematically hidden Ukrainian crimes with the aim of promoting the image of the Russian «bad guy» in an opinion ready to believe anything. This policy of systematically condemning Russia - most often without any proof - has the perverse effect of creating a feeling of impunity among Ukrainians, who know that they can afford any crime and that they will never be worried by the West. So much for our values...

7.3.3.Biological laboratories

In May 2022, Russian authorities released documents that allegedly show research activities for bacteriological weapons in Ukraine. Despite multiple denials, it appears to be true that there were some 30 biological research laboratories in Ukraine in which the US Department of Defense supported numerous research programmes[566]. The question is therefore less the existence of these laboratories than the nature of their research. To what extent they were (or are) related to biological weapons remains unclear.

Thus, in support of the Russian accusations, the deletion of certain documents from the website of the US embassy in Kiev is mentioned. But if the programme was so sensitive - and therefore presumably classified - why were these documents posted online? And if they were online - and therefore presumably harmless - why were they deleted? Documents from the Turkish firm Baykar (which

---

house.gov/news/press-releases/oversight-and-foreign-affairs-committees-call-on-social-media-companies-to)

566. «Fact Sheet on WMD Threat Reduction Efforts with Ukraine, Russia and Other Former Soviet Union Countries, Department of Defense, 9 June 2022, (https://www.defense.gov/News/Releases/Release/Article/3057517/fact-sheet-on-wmd-threat-reduction-efforts-with-ukraine-russia-and-other-former/)

produces the Bayraktar-2 drones used by Ukraine) show that in December 2021, the Ukrainians sought to acquire a drone aerosol spraying capability. Was it for biological or chemical weapons? One can assume so. However, the Bayraktar drones do not appear to have this capability.

However, Victoria Nuland, Under Secretary of State for Political Affairs[567], Richard Burns, Director of the CIA[568], and Avril Haines, Director of National Intelligence[569], when questioned by a Senate Committee, do not give a clear explanation. Victoria Nuland acknowledges that these laboratories contain substances that should not fall into Russian hands, but it is not clear that she knows much more. This is not enough to validly support suspicions.

The funding of bacteriological research by the US Department of Defense in Ukraine is an established fact. However, there is uncertainty about the nature of this research. There are two reasons for this. First, the projects funded were likely to be of interest to the US Department of Defense. Second, while nuclear and chemical weapons are not 'dual-use', there is no way to distinguish a 'military' pathogen from a 'civilian' one. However, it can be argued that they were not 'weapons' per se.

Nevertheless, these laboratories - whose work is believed to be strictly peaceful - are not very transparent about their activities. The United States severely restricts access to them. There could be an explanation.

It seems that these laboratories - or some of them - have been working on projects to determine the extent to which certain genes can prevent the development of pathogens, or - in other words

567. https://youtu.be/ydSf57SRtcQ
568. https://youtu.be/YkGTwArDmFQ
569. https://youtu.be/2lUt6DMfrBg

- whether pathogens have different effects depending on the genetic make-up of the person affected.

This research seems reminiscent of research carried out in South Africa in the 1980s by Dr Wouter Basson, who attempted to develop pathogens that could affect the black population without affecting the white population. Designated "Project COAST" and classified SECRET, it was revealed with the fall of apartheid and became the subject of much controversy[570], and fuelled criticism of Swiss foreign policy at the time, particularly because of Basson's links with the Swiss intelligence service[571]. Similar research appears to have been carried out in Israel, with the aim of obtaining pathogens that attack individuals differently depending on their ethnicity[572].

Such research would not be incompatible with the 'Idea of Nation' as defined - or understood - by those in power in Kiev.

To what extent has Ukraine sought to develop such tools? This is not known. If this was the case, can we link this research to bacteriological *weapons*? These remain questions that we cannot answer at this stage. Assuming that such research was conducted, this would explain Victoria Nuland's admission that certain research products should not fall into Russian hands, while justifying the American denial of biological weapons projects.

570. Miles Jackson, 'A Conspiracy to Commit Genocide: Anti-Fertility Research in Apartheid's Chemical and Biological Weapons Programme', Journal of International Criminal Justice, Volume 13, Issue 5, December 2015, Pages 933-950, 14 November 2015 (https://doi.org/10.1093/jicj/mqv060)

571. NdA: during apartheid, Switzerland was not part of the United Nations and did not apply the embargo decreed by the Organisation, and the Swiss secret services had privileged links with the South African services.

572. Salim Muwakkil, «Double Standards Haunt America's Foreign Policy», Chicago Tribune, 23 November 1998 (https://www.chicagotribune.com/news/ct-xpm-1998-11-23-9811230089-story.html)

In early November 2022, the Russian proposal to investigate "military biological" activities in Ukraine was predictably rejected by the UN Security Council[573]. It is likely that the research being carried out does not meet the strict definition of bacteriological weapons, but involves far more worrying ethical issues. US Ambassador Linda Thomas-Greenfield may one day regret having defended this project...

7.3.4.Rape as a weapon of war

Rape has been and still is practised in all conflicts, by all the forces involved and since the dawn of time. For a long time, it was seen as a kind of «reward» for the victor or as a way of marking the «submission» of the vanquished, depending on the region of the world and the culture.

Rape as a weapon of war» is a different and rather new concept. It is regularly used in the discourse of humanitarian organisations and in Western propaganda rhetoric to highlight a systematic and planned practice. But, as is often the case, it is more a matter of demonising an adversary than dealing with the problem effectively.

For it to be a 'weapon of war', the rape must serve a purpose beyond the mere pleasure of the rapist, and be in response to an order from a higher authority. During the Balkan war, some people talked about this practice in order to cause the disappearance of an ethnic entity by generating children of the victor's 'race'. This is a (rather primitive) scheme of ethnic 'cleansing'. On 24 May 1994, in his letter to the Security Council, Boutros Boutros-Ghali, Secretary-General of the United Nations, stated

573. Edith M. Lederer, «UN Security Council denies Russia call for bio weapons probe», The Washington Post, 2 November 2022 (https://www.washingtonpost.com/world/russia-calls-vote-on-unfounded-ukraine-bio-weapons-claims/2022/11/02/6ed16064-5a6b-11ed-bc40-b5a130f95ee7_story.html)

The practice of so-called 'ethnic cleansing', and the rapes and sexual assaults in particular, have been perpetrated so systematically by some of the parties that they appear strongly to be the product of policy.[574]

Documented cases of «rape as a weapon of war», i.e. with a clear chain of command, were those practised by the United States at Abu Ghraib prison in Iraq, as well as in Europe, with countries that participated in the CIA torture programme (Lithuania, Poland and Romania). The aim was to «break the will» of the interrogated persons by subjecting them to sexual abuse. Countries without honour, which carry the values of Europe high!

In the case of the war in Ukraine, while it is likely that rapes took place, there is no evidence that they were used as a weapon of war, as RTS claims[575]. In fact, the media propagates information that it has not verified. It simply relays the rumour propagated by Lyudmila Denissova, Ukrainian delegate for human rights, as part of a vast propaganda campaign conducted by Ukraine[576].

But in May, after the surrender of the AZOV fighters in Mariupol, the documents found on their mobile phones seem to tell a completely different story. Ukrainian parliamentarians get scared and decide to sack Denissova[577]. The Wall Street Journal notes:

---

574. https://www.icty.org/x/file/About/OTP/un_commission_of_experts_report1994_en.pdf

575. «Rape of civilians is part of the Russian war arsenal in Ukraine», rts.ch, 12 April 2022 (https://www.rts.ch/info/monde/13005321-les-viols-de-civils-font-partie-de-larsenal-de-guerre-russe-en-ukraine.html)

576. «Foreign Minister Accuses Russian Soldiers of Rape in Ukrainian Cities, US News/Reuters, 4 March 2022 (https://www.usnews.com/news/world/articles/2022-03-04/foreign-minister-accuses-russian-soldiers-of-rape-in-ukrainian-cities)

577. Eugenie Loutsenko, «Депутати зібрали підписи за відставку омбудсменки

The unclear focus of Ms Denissova's media work on the many details of «unnatural sexual crimes» and «child rape» in the occupied territories, which could not be confirmed by evidence, only hurt Ukraine. (...)

MP Pavlo Frolov said Denissova was also accused of making rash and unverifiable statements about alleged Russian sex crimes, and of spending too much time in Western Europe during the invasion. [578]

This example brings us back to the case of Boutcha, where all the Western media repeated without any analysis the statements of the Ukrainian authorities...

7.3.5. Snake Island

On 25 February 2022, RTS reported the «massacre» of thirteen Ukrainian border guards on Snake Island[579]. However, they were never killed. The fifty or so border guards from the garrison were captured and brought ashore unharmed by the Russian navy[580].

There is no evidence of fighting to take the island, but presumably overwhelmed by information from all sides on the first day of the Russian offensive, the Ukrainians were misled by rumours they could not verify. The starting point of this incident

Денісової. Вона називає можливе звільнення незаконним», hromadske.ua, 31 May 2022 (https://hromadske.ua/posts/deputati-zibrali-pidpisi-za-vidstavku-ombudsmenki-denisovoyi-vona-nazivaye-mozhlive-zvilnennya-nezakonnim)

578. Peter Saidel, «Ukraine's Parliament Dismisses Human-Rights Chief», The Wall Street Journal, 31 May 2022 (https://www.wsj.com/livecoverage/russia-ukraine-latest-news-2022-05-31)

579. https://web.archive.org/web/20220226004357/https://www. rts.ch/info/world/12895433-russian-army-pursues-its-offensive-in-kiev.html

580. https://t.me/intelslava/20649

was certainly the 'fog of war'. This probably explains the rather candid denial of the Ukrainian General Staff on Facebook on 28 February[581].

Honest media, such as Euronews[582], will mention this Ukrainian rectification, but those who are not - such as RTS[583] - will not report it. The incident has a global impact, and is «swallowed» without batting an eyelid by the acritical Western media. This is probably what gave the Ukrainians the idea that they could take advantage of this false information. A stamp was produced to commemorate the (non-)event.

This totally fallacious myth has become emblematic and continues to feed the narrative of a possible victory for Ukraine, and thus pushes Ukraine to continue the fight against Russia. Thus, on 1 July 2022, on France 5, Bruno Tertrais evoked an «act of heroism» as an example of Ukrainian resistance...

At the beginning of May, Ukraine tried to retake the island. According to the Jerusalem Post[584] and the American media The National Interest[585], it was a communication operation to register a Ukrainian victory on the eve of the 9 May celebrations in Russia. It was a failure. According to the Jerusalem Post, which quotes Russian sources, the Ukrainians lost four fighter planes, a

581. https://www.facebook.com/navy.mil.gov.ua/posts/324444389723150

582. Matthew Holroyd, «Ukraine war: Snake Island border guards are alive and well, says Ukrainian navy», Euronews, 28 February 2022

583. https://www.rts.ch/info/monde/12895433-larmee-russe-poursuit-son-offensive-en-direction-de-kiev.html

584. Aaron Reich, «Russia-Ukraine War: Ukraine tried, failed retaking Snake Island, says Russia», The Jerusalem Post, 11 May 2022 (https://www.jpost.com/international/article-706374)

585. Mark Episkopos, 'Ukraine Fails to Retake Snake Island in New Military Assault', The National Interest, 11 May 2022 (https://nationalinterest.org/blog/buzz/ukraine-fails-retake-snake-island-new-military-assault-202362)

dozen helicopters, three assault boats and more than 50 members of the special forces.

On 30 June, Russia announced that it was withdrawing the troops deployed on the island «as a gesture of goodwill». The last Russian occupants had been withdrawn the day before. As it did with Kiev at the end of March, Russia is turning a simple tactical move into a political gesture.

RTS claims that Russian troops «withdrew on Thursday after being driven out by the Ukrainians»[586]. This is not true. The island was not taken over by Ukraine, which took no action at that time, and Russia withdrew on its own, as it stated.

To give credence to this Russian defeat, it is stated that the island is of strategic importance. But this is not the case. Located 140 km from Odessa and 30 km from the Ukrainian and Romanian coast, the island is of very little interest in preventing a possible attack on Odessa from the sea. Moreover, with its 18 ha surface area and very flat terrain, it does not allow for the safe deployment of sophisticated weapons systems. Previously, the island was occupied by only a handful of Ukrainian border guards, and the Russians did not even have to fight to take it. The Russian capture of the island seems to have been almost more accidental than anything else. In fact, the Russians realised that the vulnerability of a contingent deployed on the island and its logistical support is disproportionate to the strategic benefit of possessing the island. It is too small to accommodate air defence or electronic intelligence facilities and their protection.

In fact, on 30 June, one day after the departure of the small Russian contingent, Ukraine struck the island with its only 155

586. «Ukraine accuses Russians of firing phosphorus bombs on Snake Island», rts.ch, 3 July 2022 (https://www.rts.ch/info/monde/13214212-lukraine-accuse-les-russes-davoir-tire-des-bombes-au-phosphore-sur-lile-aux-serpents.html)

mm 2S22 self-propelled howitzer, the only one with sufficient range[587]. On the same day, the Russian air force dropped two bombs on the island to disable the infrastructure.

Contradicting the claims of the «experts» and other journalists, Ukraine did not take any decision[588] to deploy troops on the island afterwards[589]. This did not prevent Le Figaro[590] and RTS from stating on 4 July 2022 that «the Ukrainian flag is flying again on Snake Island»[591]. Once again, this is disinformation. In reality, Ukraine only dropped a flag on the island from an aircraft, as the Ukrainian media themselves confess[592] ! Further confirmation that our media are nothing but propaganda organs.

---

587. David Axe, «Ukraine's Weirdest Howitzer Drove Russian Troops Off Snake Island», Forbes, 30 June 2022 (https://www.forbes.com/sites/davidaxe/2022/06/30/ukraines-weirdest-howitzer-drove-russian-troops-off-snake-island/)
588. Ivan Boiko, «Звільнення Зміїного: у Генштабі розповіли, коли відправлять війська на острів», unian.ua, 30 June 2022 (https://www.unian.ua/war/ostriv-zmijiniy-u-genshtabi-zsu-rozpovili-koli-vidpravlyat-tudi-viyska-novini-vtorgnennya-rosiji-v-ukrajinu-11885682.html)
589. Marina Pavertaylo, «Українські військові ще висаджувалися на Зміїний. Росіяни могли залишити «сюрпризи» «, 30 June 2022 (https://suspilne.media/255840-ukrainski-vijskovi-se-ne-visadzuvalisa-na-zmiinij-rosiani-mogli-zalisiti-surprizi/)
590. «L'Ukraine affirme avoir remis son drapeau sur l'île aux Serpents», Le Figaro/AFP, 4 July 2022 (https://www.lefigaro.fr/flash-actu/l-ukraine-affirme-avoir-remis-son-drapeau-sur-l-ile-aux-serpents-20220704)
591. https://www.rts.ch/info/monde/13217239-poutine-ordonne-la-poursuite-de-loffensive-russe-apres-la-prise-de-la-region-de-lougansk.html#timeline-anchor-1656936216336
592. «Official: Ukrainian flag dropped on Snake Island but not raised yet», The Kiyv Independent, 4 July 2022 (https://kyivindependent.com/uncategorized/official-ukrainian-flag-dropped-on-snake-island-but-not-raised-yet)

8. Western reactions

8.1. The sanctions

Sanctions are not a new foreign policy tool, but they seem to have become the norm when there is a dispute between two countries. It is a new way of looking at international relations at the expense of traditional diplomatic tools.

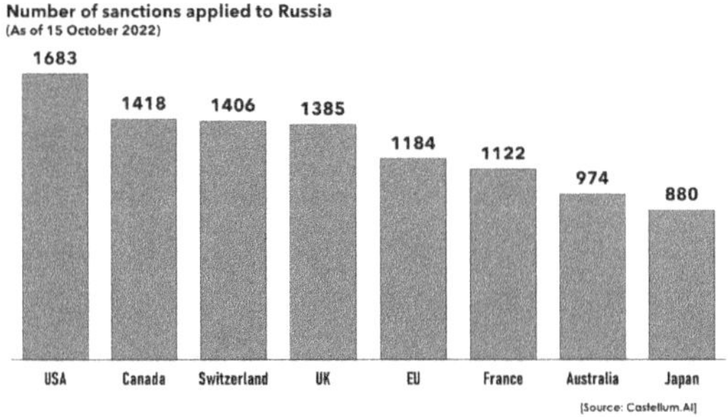

Figure 63 - Number of sanctions against Russia by country. Surprisingly for a neutral country, Switzerland has been the leading sanctioning country for Russia since May 2022. [Source: https://www.castellum.ai/russia-sanctions-dashboard]

They have two main problems. The first is that they do not solve anything. On the contrary, they tend to polarise the situation. The second is that they are endless. Indeed, to be unavoidable, they must include a mechanism forcing third countries to impose them as well. This is why the United States does not hesitate to threaten its own allies when it seeks to implement the treaty with Iran or to complete the Nord Stream 2 project. The international system is no longer dictated by law but by rules imposed by the most powerful country.

In fact, under American pressure, we have moved from a law-based international order to a rule-based international order. In other words, an international order based on rules established by a group of (Western) countries has replaced the international order governed by international law, established at the end of the Second World War.

Sanctions are not intended to 'punish', as is commonly believed, but to 'cause pain'. This is conceptually different. It is about creating an untenable situation for civilian populations, so that they rebel against or even overthrow their government. This principle is clearly described by Richard Nephew, head of sanctions at the State Department under Obama and delegate to Iran under Joe Biden, in a book entitled 'The Art of Sanctions', the spirit of which can be described as repugnant[593]. It is this spirit that animates Bernard Guetta on France 5, when he declares that «the standard of living is constantly falling in Russia partly, but only partly, because of sanctions - or thanks to Western sanctions»[594] ; or Bruno Le Maire who declares that he wants «the

593. Richard Nephew, The Art of Sanctions - A View from the Field, Columbia University Press, New York, 2018

594. Bernard Guetta in « Le 5 sur 5 ! - C à Vous - 03/02/2021», France 5/YouTube, 3 February 2021 (17'10")

Russian people to suffer»[595] (a sentence to which - contrary to official allegations - he has not returned). In short, the Russian population is being held hostage in order to influence Russia's domestic policy.

In terms of strategy of action, sanctions have exactly the same function as the bombing of civilian populations in Germany as early as 1943, in Serbia in 1990, in Iraq in 2003, in Lebanon in 2006, in Gaza in 2014 and - unexpectedly - the Islamic State terrorist attacks in France in 2015-2016[596]. The aim is to inflict suffering on populations so that they revolt against their authorities and incite them to capitulate or stop their military actions. They are also used against Iran, Belarus or Venezuela in order to promote regime change along the same lines.

It is odd that, at the same time as France is applying sanctions against Russia in order to «make the Russian people suffer», it is judging terrorists who have applied the same strategy against it, with different weapons. Sanctions can be deadly: those imposed on Iraq would have caused the death of 500,000 Iraqi children[597]. A figure that does not move Madeleine Albright, then US ambassador to the United Nations in New York, who declared on the CBS channel:

---

595. «War in Ukraine: ''We are going to cause the collapse of the Russian economy'', says Bruno Le Maire, Radio France, 1er March 2022

596. Abu Tayssir al-Faransi in the video «France on its knees», Islamic State, 21 November 2015

597. UN International Children's Emergency Fund figures. «UNICEF - Results of the 1999 Iraq Child and Maternal Mortality Surveys, Federation of American Scientists, (https://fas.org/news/iraq/1999/08/990812-unicef.htm); Jeremy Bowen, «Iraqis blame sanctions for child deaths», BBC News, 12 August 1999. These figures have been debated, with estimates varying between 170,000 and 567,000. According to R. Garfield, the number of children who died as a result of sanctions was at least 227,000 (R. Garfield, Morbidity and Mortality among Children from 1990 to 1998, Assessing the Impact of Economic Sanctions, Occasional Papers Series 16:OP:3. Paper commissioned by the Joan B. Kroc Institute for International Peace Studies at the University of Notre Dame and the Fourth Freedom Forum, March 1999).

I think it's a difficult choice, but we think the price is worth it. [598]

In the same vein, in November 2018, Mike Pompeo introduced the US sanctions by quipping that the Iranian government will have to do the right thing 'if it wants its people to eat'[599].

Apparently, the idea of making a civilian population suffer seems perfectly compatible with our values...

8.1.1.A foolish strategy, decided by fools

The stated logic of the sanctions against Russia is to remove its sources of funding for the war. In reality, it is to collapse the Russian state in order to bring about regime change.

The weakness of the Western strategy is that it is based on the assumption that Russia needs Europe more than Europe needs Russia. This is simply childish. For while Russia certainly needs Europe for consumer goods that it does not produce, Europe needs the raw materials to produce those goods. In the end, it is Europe that depends on Russia. More exactly, Europe depends on the raw materials that Russia provides. For sanctions to work, they must be applied with discretion and - like any weapon of war - must be adapted to the adversary. The Americans had already shown us the ineffectiveness of sanctions in Iraq, Iran and Venezuela, where they strengthened the authority of the governments they wanted to overthrow. In his speech on 17 June 2022 at the International Economic Forum in St Petersburg, Vladimir Putin rightly said:

598. Madeleine Albright, Sixty Minutes, CBS, 12 May 1996

599. ''Interview With Hadi Nili of BBC Persian'', Michael R. Pompeo - Secretary of State, Washington D.C., 7 November 2018; Brendan Cole, 'Mike Pompeo Says Iran Must Listen To U.S. ''If They Want Their People To Eat'', Newsweek, 9 November 2018.

While planning their economic blitzkrieg, they did not notice anything, they simply ignored the reality of how our country has changed in recent years.[600]

The Western narrative of downplaying Russia's performance and ridiculing it has resulted in an underestimation of the Russian economy's capabilities. Experts» who only know numbers and statistics but have no holistic view of the economy compare Russia's economy to that of Italy[601] (or Spain[602]). Based on nominal GDP expressed in dollars[603], they rank Russia as the eleventh largest economy in the world, which seems low for the size of the country.

It is therefore tempting to point the finger at mismanagement, the consequences of corruption or poor strategic choices. Without claiming that the management of the Russian economy is perfect, these sweeping judgements have proven to be wrong, more often than not. Convinced that Russia's economy was as vulnerable as Italy's, the West thought that sanctions would be enough to make it go under very quickly.

However, to get a more realistic view of the Russian economy, it should be compared with that of Western countries, taking into account purchasing power parity (PPP). Indeed, the cost of living is considerably lower in Russia, which is reflected in the purchasing power parity (PPP). Russia is the world's eleventh largest economy in terms of nominal GDP and the sixth largest

600. http://en.kremlin.ru/events/president/news/68669
601. https://youtu.be/Rgy2Bbe3HYE?t=3799
602. Jim Edwards, "Russia's Economy Has Shrunk So Much It's Now Only As Small As Spain", Business Insider, 7 December 2014
603. Philippe Dessertine in the programme «C dans l'air» of 17 October 2021 («Poutine, maître du jeu #cdanslair 17.10.2021», France 5/YouTube, 18 October 2021) (1h47'03")

economy in terms of PPP. Often presented as lower than France or Italy in nominal terms, Russian GDP in PPP terms is about 30% higher than France's and 65% higher than Italy's.

When you only look at your opponent's weaknesses, you don't see his strengths. Russia is one of the least indebted countries in the world. In 2021, the ratio between its debt and its gross domestic product (GDP) is 13.79% (by comparison, it is 99.20% for France and 106.7% for the United States[604]). This probably explains the remarkable stability of the rouble against the dollar, despite fluctuations in the price of hydrocarbons. Since March 2022, the rouble has been so strong that the Russian central bank is trying to lower it. So, unlike Western countries that raise their key interest rates to fight inflation, the Russians are lowering them.

Moreover, Westerners severely underestimate the resilience of its people. It lived in a war economy throughout the Cold War and is culturally used to doing a lot with a little. The sanctions applied to Russia from 2014 onwards have had three major effects:

- encourage Russia to develop an industrial base for consumer products that it did not have,
- push it to develop new links with China, and
- reduce its dependence on foreign capital. The incentive to develop indigenous capacity in many areas has helped to better manage employment.

Today, Russia exports products that it used to import. Moreover, while Russia tends to be seen primarily as a supplier

604. «Debt to GDP Ratio by Country 2021, (https://worldpopulationreview.com/countries/countries-by-national-debt)

of oil products, the share of oil products in its GDP is only about 15%[605], while services account for about 63%.

In other words, the Russian economy is not spectacular, but it is considerably more robust and resilient than that of Western countries. It has become largely self-sufficient in natural resources, technology and defence. Its recent partnership with China - also threatened by sanctions - will most likely contribute to its strengthening.

In Euro Intelligence, Wolfgang Münchau confesses:

> *Western sanctions were based on a formally correct but misleading premise, which I myself believed, at least up to a point: Russia is more dependent on us than we are on it.*

> *(...) Russia is the world's largest exporter of gas, accounting for just under 20% of global exports. Russia is the world's largest exporter of oil, after Saudi Arabia, accounting for 11% of world exports. It is the largest exporter of fertiliser and wheat. Russia and Ukraine together account for almost a third of world wheat exports. Russia is the world's largest exporter of palladium, a metal essential for the production of catalytic converters and fuel cells. Russia is also the world's largest exporter of nickel, which is used in batteries and in the production of hybrid cars. German industry warns that it is dependent not only on Russian gas but also on other essential supplies from Russia.*[606]

605. Charles Kennedy, "Oil & Gas Share Of Russia's GDP Dropped To 15% In 2020", oilprice.com, 13 July 2021

606. Wolfgang Münchau, «The West and the rest», Euro Intelligence, 22 May 2022 (https://www.eurointelligence.com/column/the-west-and-the-rest)

In early May 2022, the British magazine The Economist noted that the Russian economy had returned to normal functioning[607] and was returning to trade surpluses[608].

The exclusion of Russian banks from the SWIFT payment system (which allows faster information exchange between financial institutions) would certainly be dramatic for a European country like France or Switzerland. But Russia has alternatives: its own system (SPFS) denominated in roubles and the Chinese system (CIPS) in yuan, which are smaller than SWIFT. They link 400 and 1,280 financial institutions respectively, which is not much, but the requirement to pay for gas in roubles has increased the credibility of the Russian currency, and the SPFS seems to be gaining in importance. As for Russia's exclusion from the bond market, its low level of sovereign debt makes it much less dependent than its Western counterparts.

In the US, Biden is battling with climate change activists, who want to reduce dependence on oil and gas. But reality demands the opposite and sanctions have created an energy market contraction in the West. Biden is reduced to blaming Putin and the oil companies.

In the end, the sanctions do not seem to have encouraged Russian citizens to overthrow their government, on the contrary! The Western perception that Alexei Navalny, imprisoned for complicity in fraud and corruption in Russia, represents the opinion of the majority of the population against Vladimir Putin is far from the reality. By January 2022, Alexei Navalny's approval

607. «Russia's economy is back on its feet», The Economist, 7 May 2022 (https://www.economist.com/finance-and-economics/2022/05/07/russias-economy-is-back-on-its-feet)

608. «Russia is on track for a record trade surplus», The Economist, 14 May 2022 (https://www.economist.com/finance-and-economics/2022/05/14/russia-is-on-track-for-a-record-trade-surplus)

rating had fallen from 3% to 2%, completely overshadowed by Vladimir Putin's, which rose from 33% in January to 43% in May 2022. Vladimir Putin's popularity rating, which was 65% in December 2021, is 83% in June 2022[609], according to the Levada Centre (considered a «foreign agent» by the Russian authorities).

Vladimir Putin's popularity rating [%] (October 2021 - October 2022)

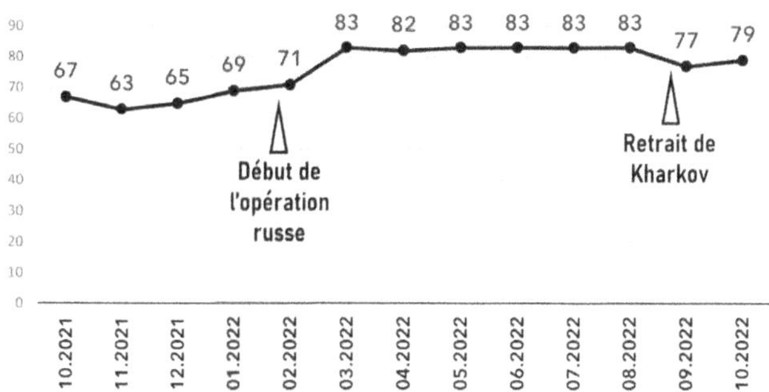

Figure 64 - Vladimir Putin's popularity rating. Overall, the operation in Ukraine was accompanied by an increase in Vladimir Putin's popularity. The poor communication surrounding the withdrawal from Kharkov at the beginning of September caused the curve to bend. [Source: https://www.levada.ru/indikatory/]

Not only that, but the shower of sanctions - including, above all, the most infantile ones - has reinforced the Russian government's long-standing claim that Westerners are irrational and hate Russians. In France, the accounts blocked because of a «Slavic-sounding» name and the acts of vandalism[610], have

609. https://www.levada.ru/en/

610. Angélique Négroni, 'Blocked bank accounts, insults, vandalism... Le quotidien des Russes de France', Le Figaro, 22 April 2022 (https://www.lefigaro.fr/international/comptes-bancaires-bloques-insultes-vandalisme-le-quotidien-des-russes-de-france-20220422)

only strengthened the credibility of the Russian government and gathered the population around Vladimir Putin in a defensive reflex.

When RTS talks about the «vote at the UN General Assembly condemning the Russian invasion»[611], the media is lying to us, because the word «condemn» was precisely rejected by the majority of the member countries of the Organisation. The word «deplore» was preferred, despite the insistence of Western countries[612].

**The international community...
an ethnocentric view of the world**

Figure 65 - Countries that have imposed sanctions on Russia (in grey) are far from representing the entire international community. Those that have not adopted sanctions are less influential than the Western world, but they are nonetheless clients of Russia.

611. «Against Russia, «sanctions are a substitute for armed engagement», RTS.ch, 19 March 2022 (https://www.rts.ch/info/monde/12944278-contre-la-russie-les-sanctions-se-substituent-a-lengagement-arme.html)
612. Hala Kodmani, Léa Masseguin & François-Xavier Gomez, «L'impossible 'condamnation' de la Russie à l'ONU», Libération, 2 March 2022 (https://www.liberation.fr/international/limpossible-condamnation-de-la-russie-a-lonu-20220302_7NJ7K5YS5REAPDPJVC7T225XV4/)

Finally, as Sylvie Bermann, former French ambassador to Russia, noted on BFMTV, «82% of the world population refuses to condemn Vladimir Putin»[613]. Thus, the «international community» that applies sanctions against Russia is limited to... Western countries. At the beginning of June 2022, Vladimir Putin received a visit from Moussa Faki Mahamat, President of the African Union (AU) Commission. A few days later, in order not to leave this exclusivity to Russia, the West provoked a speech by Volodymyr Zelensky at the AU. It took place on 20 June in Addis Ababa and 55 heads of state were invited, but only 4 attended[614]. Clearly, Zelensky is not unanimously supported in Africa!

In short, the opposition that Western chancelleries were capitalising on for regime change does not exist. This shows the inability of Western leaders to overcome their illusions and lead according to the facts. Their wishful thinking has worsened an economic situation that was made worse by the measures taken during the CoViD crisis. By allowing themselves to be guided by dogmatism, by setting objectives at face value, like a chess player who does not think about the next move, Western leaders - and the EU in particular - have put their own economies at risk.

According to Eurostat, the 19 countries sharing the euro recorded a trade deficit, not seasonally adjusted, of EUR 16.4

613. https://twitter.com/Malbrunot/status/1521547132808871938; https://ne-np.facebook.com/Soninkara-TV-24-115045376537305/videos/guerre-russieukraine-82-de-la-population-mondiale-refuse-de-condamner-vladimir-p/1105355363729532/

614. Shifaan Ryklief, «Zelensky says Africa is a 'hostage' of Russia's war on Ukraine», Independent Online, 21 June 2022 (https://www.iol.co.za/news/world/watch-zelensky-says-africa-is-a-hostage-of-russias-war-on-ukraine-e7209002-889f-45cd-a52e-57b98e5d0506)

billion in March 2022, compared with a surplus of EUR 22.5 billion in March 2021[615].

The logic behind sanctions against Russia therefore seems to defy all common sense. I encourage the reader to watch the excellent video by Trouble Fait on YouTube[616].

8.1.2.Strategic materials

Russia is the source of many strategic materials[617], such as scandium, neon (needed to etch microprocessors)[618], titanium (used in aeronautics) and other strategic raw materials[619] which could cripple Western industry[620]. Other more common materials, such as nickel (essential for stainless steel), saw its price rise by 250% in March 2022, affecting a whole range of industrial production[621].

---

615. «Euro zone trade plunges into record deficit in March on energy», Reuters, 16 May 2022 (https://www.reuters.com/world/europe/euro-zone-trade-plunges-into-record-deficit-march-energy-2022-05-16/)
616. Trouble Fact, «[Ukraine] The comical failure of Western sanctions against Russia», YouTube, 16 July 2022 (https://youtu.be/3EDUc7A8QEg)
617. Sharon E. Burke, «Russia is a mineral powerhouse - and its war with Ukraine could affect global supplies», Boston Globe, 9 March 2022 (https://www.bostonglobe.com/2022/03/09/opinion/russia-is-mineral-powerhouse-its-war-with-ukraine-could-affect-global-supplies/)
618. Alexandra Alper, «Exclusive: Russia's attack on Ukraine halts half of world's neon output for chips», Reuters, 11 March 2022 (https://www.reuters.com/technology/exclusive-ukraine-halts-half-worlds-neon-output-chips-clouding-outlook-2022-03-11/)
619. Nick J. Adam, «Striking back: Putin has his own card to play after being hit by sanctions», techilive.in, 23 February 2022
620. Alexandra Alper & Karen Freifeld, «Russia could hit U.S. chip industry, White House warns», Reuters, 11 February 2022
621. Thomas Gualtieri, «Nickel-Price Surge Adds Pressure Onto Stainless-Steel Products», Bloomberg, 17 March 2022 (https://www.bloomberg.com/news/newsletters/2022-03-17/supply-chains-latest-nickel-surge-adds-pressure-onto-stainless-steel-products)

Strategic materials supplied by Russia

Material	Production [t]	Global share [%]
Palladium	2 600 000	40
Neon		30
Scandium		26
Natural gas		17
Titanium	27 000	15
Fertilizers	50 000 000	13
Crude oil		12,1
Gold	3 500	10
Turntable	18,2	10
Nickel	2 700 000	7
Aluminium	3 800 000	6
Coal	400 000 000	5
Steel	76 000 000	4
Cobalt	7 600	4
Copper	920 000	3,5

Figure 66 - Russia's importance in the global strategic materials market[622].

Moreover, Russia, the main supplier of rocket propellants to the United States until February 2022, is far from being a mere 'service station'.

The media has focused on hydrocarbons, but Westerners are also heavily dependent on Russia for the nuclear fuel chain. While Russia extracts only 6% of the world's uranium, it controls 40% of the global market for the enrichment process.

622. «Factbox: Commodity supplies at risk after Russia invades Ukraine, Reuters, 4 March 2022 (https://www.reuters.com/business/commodity-supplies-risk-after-russia-invades-ukraine-2022-03-04/); https://www.statista.com/topics/5399/russian-oil-industry/#dossierKeyfigures

Only the 235 isotope of uranium can be used for energy production (fission). Natural uranium contains only 0.7% of this isotope. Uranium must therefore be enriched to the 3 to 5% U-235 content required to operate nuclear reactors. For this purpose, uranium goes through a process called conversion: raw uranium is crushed into uranium oxide (U3O8) and then processed into a yellow cake, which is then transformed into uranium hexafluoride (UF6), which can then go into the enrichment process. Russia has 40% of the world's conversion capacity and 46% of the world's uranium enrichment capacity. The vast majority of the world's 439 reactors and all American reactors need enriched uranium[623]. Therefore, France, which prides itself on its low dependence on Russian natural gas, may well be concerned by a dependence on other materials.

8.1.3. The blockade of cereal exports

In June 2022, grain prices on the international market are rising rapidly. This was blamed on the Russian war, but it was essentially a political manoeuvre by the Ukrainian government to get the West to help its defeated army. Russia is then accused of blockading Ukraine and preventing ships from leaving the port of Odessa.

Contrary to what our politicians and media say, fertiliser and grain exports are not prevented by Russia, but by European sanctions and... Ukraine.

In theory, maritime transport of grain and fertiliser is not affected by the sanctions. This is not the case for payments, which may be blocked in European or American banks. Buyers

623. Matt Bowen & Paul Dabbar, «What's at risk due to Russia's nuclear power dominance?», The Hill, 12 June 2022 (https://thehill.com/opinion/energy-environment/3519264-whats-at-risk-due-to-russias-nuclear-power-dominance/)

do not trust Western decisions that fluctuate irrationally. For fear of having their payments blocked or seized, they hesitate to place orders. Western sanctions further complicate the game: they prevent both the purchase of grain from Russia by hitting the means of payment, and their delivery by prohibiting insurance and reinsurance companies from covering Russian shipping.

The Black Sea ports on the Russian side are operational, including Mariupol, which has started to resume operations. The port of Odessa is not blocked by Russia, which has left open access corridors for supplies to the city. These corridors are permanently open and their geographical coordinates are communicated at regular intervals on international frequencies.

It was the Ukrainians who, fearing a landing in Odessa, mined the coast themselves with old gold mines. These mines, poorly laid, tend to drift, endangering all maritime navigation[624]. Already in March 2022, the Turkish Navy had to defuse mines that had reached the Bosphorus[625]. Moreover, in mid-June 2022, David Arakhamia, a close adviser to Zelensky, stated that the Ukrainian military «is strongly opposed to the idea of demining Ukrainian Black Sea ports in exchange for allowing grain exports through Russia»[626].

---

624. Hilmi Hacaloglu, Umut Colak & Ezel Sahinkaya, «Amid Russia-Ukraine War, Turkey Worries About Floating Mines in Black Sea», Voice of America News, 8 April 2022 (https://www.voanews.com/a/amid-russia-ukraine-war-turkey-worries-about-floating-mines-in-black-sea/6521222.html)

625. Yoruk Isik & Azra Ceylan, «Turkey defuses mine after Russia warns of strays from Ukraine ports», Reuters, 26 March 2022 (https://www.reuters.com/world/middle-east/turkey-finds-mine-like-object-floating-off-black-sea-2022-03-26/)

626. Dave Lawler, «Ukraine suffering up to 1,000 casualties per day in Donbas, official says», Axios, 15 June 2022 (https://www.axios.com/2022/06/15/ukraine-1000-casualties-day-donbas-arakhamia)

This did not stop RTS from writing on 27 June that «transport ships have been stuck in port since February because of sea mines and Russian warships off the coast»[627].

For the Ukrainian military, the allegations about a Russian blockade seem to have the sole purpose of justifying a possible Western intervention in the Black Sea, as reported in the Washington Post[628]. For Ukrainian politicians, it is a question of using this argument to weaken the Russians in future negotiations. For the West, this crisis is used to put pressure on African countries in order to drag them into their sanctions policy, as explained by Laurent Burkhalter, a journalist with RTS[629]. Our media are thus participating in a criminal enterprise, whose sole objective is to make a diplomatic solution impossible.

For Ukraine could consider exporting its grain by rail. The problem is that the transhipment stations at the Ukrainian border (due to different track gauge standards) are saturated and that, in order to unload them, it would be necessary to allow the transport of these goods through Belarus. However, this would require the lifting of sanctions against Belarus, which the West refuses to do! We are falling from Charybdis into Scylla...

In July 2022, BBC News reported that Western grain farming was in poor shape, partly because of weather conditions, but also because of access to fertiliser. A study by EarthDaily, based on

627. https://www.rts.ch/info/monde/13202280-un-missile-russe-touche-un-centre-commercial-du-centre-de-lukraine-faisant-craindre-un-lourd-bilan.html

628. Karoun Demirjian, Alex Horton & Stefano Pitrelli, «Russia's grain blockade may require U.S. intervention, general suggests», The Washington Post, 26 May 2022 (https://www.washingtonpost.com/national-security/2022/05/26/russia-ukraine-grain-blockade/)

629. https://www.rts.ch/info/monde/13202280-un-missile-russe-touche-un-centre-commercial-du-centre-de-lukraine-faisant-craindre-un-lourd-bilan.html

infrared satellite images, estimated the level of harvests in 2022 and compared them with the average for the previous five years[630].

Variation in the expected cereal harvest in 2022 with the average of the previous five years [%].

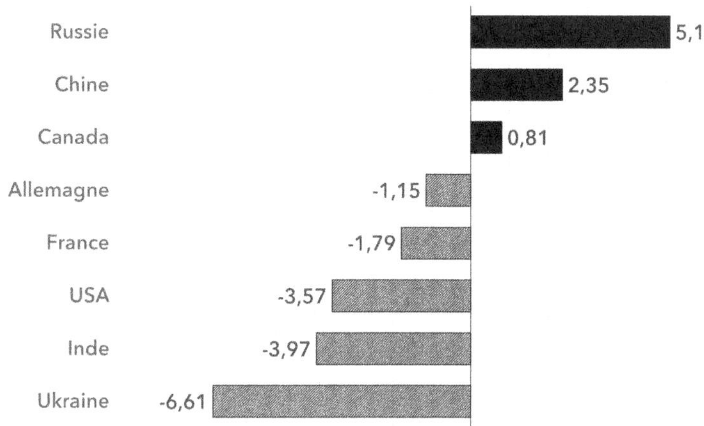

Figure 67 - Only Russia and China (and, to a lesser extent, Canada) will have an increasing harvest compared to the average for the period 2016-2021. [Source: BBC News]

The satellites and the numbers seem to prove Vladimir Putin right when he says that the coming food crisis is essentially the result of mismanagement of our resources.

So this is a situation that has been totally created - once again - by the West, long before the war in Ukraine. What the EU failed to foresee and see, the non-Western world has identified very clearly. Despite the pressure, it tends to side with Russia. The artificial exploitation of the food crisis to blame Russia tends to undermine Western credibility. As Josep Borrell noted at the G20 meeting in July 2022:

630. Stephanie Hegarty, «Satellites give clues about the coming global harvest», BBC News, 15 July 2022 (https://www.bbc.com/news/world-62149522)

The G7 and other like-minded countries are united in condemning and sanctioning Russia and trying to hold its regime to account. But other countries, and we can say here that the majority of countries in the 'Global South', often have a different position. The global battle of narratives is in full swing and, for the moment, we are not winning it. [631]

The West is not winning the battle of the narratives because it is lying. After accusing Russia of being the cause of food shortages in the world, we see that the «corridors of solidarity» set up by the EU stop... in Europe[632].

Then, pushed by the reality of the situation, the EU had to acknowledge that the supply difficulties were indeed caused by its sanctions. This is why, on 19 July 2022, it is quietly considering «amending its sanctions» on grain and fertiliser exports[633]. Clearly, Western state media, such as France 5, or pure propaganda media, such as LCI, have served up a deceptive rhetoric.

Moreover, our media cheat with the figures. On 23 July 2022, for example, RTS reported the signing of an agreement on the resumption of grain exports between Russia and Ukraine. The media states that the signatories represent «30% of the world wheat trade between them» and

631. Aparna Shandilya, «Josep Borrell Says EU Is «not Winning Global Battle Of Narratives» On Ukraine», republicworld.com, 11 July 2022 (https://www.republicworld.com/world-news/russia-ukraine-crisis/josep-borrell-says-eu-is-not-winning-global-battle-of-narratives-on-ukraine-articleshow.html)

632. Yaroslava Bukhta, «Ukrainian grain barely reaches countries in need via 'solidarity lanes', Commission says», EURACTIV.com, 12 July 2022 (updated 13 July 2022) (https://www.euractiv.com/section/agriculture-food/news/ukrainian-grain-barely-reaches-countries-in-need-via-solidarity-lanes-commission-says/)

633. «EU to ease sanctions on Russian banks to facilitate food trade, Reuters, 19 July 2022 (https://www.reuters.com/article/ukraine-crise-ue-alimentation-idFRKBN2OU0ZJ)

that the agreement will make it possible to «take out some 25 million tonnes piled up in Ukraine's silos»[634]. As usual, the media misinforms.

Firstly, on 22 July, not one, but at least two agreements were signed in Istanbul, aimed at facilitating the export of cereals, notably through the creation of a maritime corridor. The first is a memorandum valid for 3 years, which lifts certain sanctions applied to Russia for the export of Russian grain and fertiliser. It is not mentioned by RTS because it shows that the difficulties in supplying grain and fertiliser were caused by Western sanctions. But the memorandum goes further and also concerns the transport of oil to third countries, as well as the supply of spare parts for civilian airliners.

The second agreement, valid for 120 days, aims to facilitate the exit of grain through Ukrainian-controlled ports. It is also a Russian success, as it requires Ukraine to clear its ports of mines (which it had previously refused to do). It establishes a joint control mechanism for ships to ensure that they do not bring weapons to Ukraine, and Turkey guarantees the free passage of ships through the Bosporus.

Secondly, the figures given by RTS are misleading. Firstly, according to the World's Top Exports website, Russia accounts for 13.1% and Ukraine for 8.5%, giving a total of 21.6% of the grain trade, not 30%[635]. Secondly, the specialist website World-Grain.com gives very different figures for Ukrainian grain exports. For the 2021-2022 marketing year, Ukraine exported 47.2 million tonnes of wheat as of 5 June 2022, while it planned to export 63.7 million tonnes, a difference of 16.5 million

634. https://www.rts.ch/info/monde/13261947-washington-annonce-une-nouvelle-aide-militaire-de-270-millions-de-dollars-a-lukraine.html

635. Daniel Workman, «Wheat Exports by Country», World's Top Exports, May 2022 (https://www.worldstopexports.com/wheat-exports-country/)

tonnes[636]. Given that it exported 2 million tonnes in June, which represents its monthly capacity in the current crisis[637], it can be estimated that it has exported between 3 and 4 million tonnes since 5 June. Thus, the stock of wheat then outstanding in Ukrainian silos can be estimated at 12.5-13.5 million tonnes, or half the figure reported by RTS.

This figure is important because if Ukraine manages to export 2-3 million tonnes per month, this means that it will have exported its entire production in 4 months, or 120 days. This is the time frame that Russia apparently insisted on setting in the agreement. Why? Perhaps because it is planning an offensive in the Odessa area between the end of 2022 and the beginning of 2023. It is also for this reason that in July 2022, the ODESSA Brigade was formed. It is one of 16 brigades composed of citizens of southern Ukraine, formed since March 2022 and destined to be operational in September, with the ambition of 'liberating' the cities from Nikolayev to Odessa.

In short, these two agreements are a remarkable success for Russian diplomacy. This is probably why our media is so quiet about them. The EU had already quietly admitted that its sanctions were inadequate and ill-considered.

This episode shows the deleterious role played by our media in our perception of the Ukrainian crisis. Switzerland is the country that has imposed the most sanctions on Russia (as of mid-July 2022). The role of RTS, as a state media, is obviously to support the government's political action. In the issue of

636. John Reidy, 'Ukraine grain exports reach 47.2 million tonnes so far for 2021-22', world-grain.com, 6 June 2022 (https://www.world-grain.com/articles/16997-ukraine-grain-exports-reach-472-million-tonnes-so-far-for-2021-22)
637. Natalia Zinets, «Ukraine's grain exports to reach 2 mln tonnes in June - deputy minister», Reuters, 20 June 2022 (https://www.reuters.com/article/ukraine-crisis-grain-export-idUKL8N2Y7470)

grain exports, our media have in a way taken the population of the southern hemisphere hostage in order to spread hatred of Russia. This is the problem that the West has at the moment. The countries of the «rest of the world» have understood perfectly well that the West is waging an irrational war that serves their interests to the detriment of the rest of the planet. After Joe Biden's visit to Saudi Arabia, the Americans are beginning to understand that they are losing their footing. This is why the West is cautiously retropedalling.

But on 29 October 2022, the problem re-emerges with a Ukrainian attack on the port of Sevastopol. It was carried out by a swarm of 9 aerial and 7 naval drones, which were destroyed by the Russian defence, causing apparently minor damage, according to the Russian authorities. The attack was carried out under the surveillance of a US RQ-4B Global Hawk drone (codename FORTE10), cruising at high altitude off Crimea.

Whether the attack can be described as «terrorist», as the Russian authorities claim, is open to debate. The fact remains that the aerial drones were allegedly fired from commercial ships, which used the maritime corridor guaranteed by the July agreement for their approach. The Ukrainians had therefore not respected the terms of the agreement, which is why Russia was suspending its participation.

It is important to clarify that Russia has never blockaded Ukrainian ports and its withdrawal from the July agreement does not imply a restriction on the movement of Ukrainian commercial vessels. The Russian decision «simply» means that Ukrainian maritime traffic will be able to continue, but that the Russian navy will be able to intervene in the maritime corridor, in order to inspect suspicious vessels or even fight them.

It should be recalled here that the grain market is mainly dominated by Russia and that the Istanbul agreement was also supposed to facilitate the transport of grain and other agricultural products to Russia. However, despite Western promises, nothing has been done. It was only on 21 September 2022 that the London-based shipping insurance company Lloyds received clarification on the application of EU and US sanctions on Russian shipping[638]. Although the EU has not formally sanctioned grain and fertiliser shipments, problems arise when third parties (countries, companies or financial institutions) may be affected by US sanctions. Westerners have not been able to harmonise their sanctions, creating chaos in international trade, which contributes to the overall increase in costs.

Russia was obviously accused of using the «weapon of hunger». In reality, we can see that the vast majority of Ukraine's exports are destined for Europe and high-income countries, according to the UN nomenclature.

638. Michelle Wiese Bockmann, «UK amends sanctions guidance on Russian food and fertiliser exports», Lloyd's list, 21 September 2022 (https://lloydslist.maritimeintelligence.informa.com/LL1142305/UK-amends-sanctions-guidance-on-Russian-food-and-fertiliser-exports)

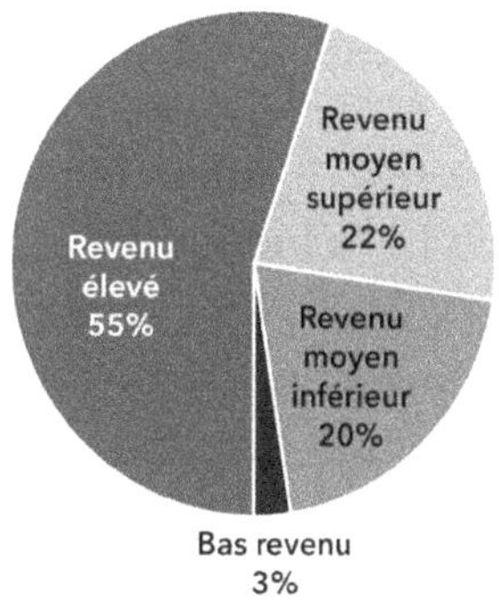

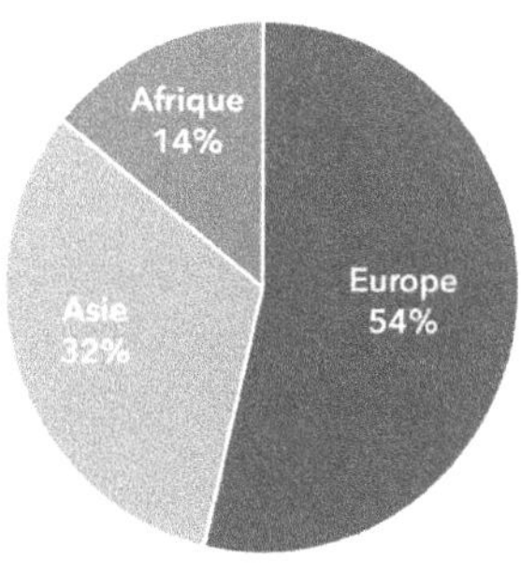

a) Part des tonnages en fonction du revenu des pays destinataires

b) Part des tonnages en fonction des continents destinataires

Figure 68 - Maritime transport between 2 August 2022 and 30 October 2022 from Ukraine. [Source: https://www.un.org/en/black-sea-grain-initiative/vessel-movements]

In fact, because of the inflation caused by the various sanctions, and because of their financial capacity, Western countries have been able to divert the flow of raw materials and cereals initially destined for developing countries to themselves.

8.1.4. The Kaliningrad «blockade

On 17 June 2022, Lithuania announced, with effect from 18 June, that it was closing its border to rail transport between Russia and its Baltic Sea enclave of Kaliningrad to goods placed under EU sanctions[639].

639. «Lithuania enforces EU sanctions on goods to Russia's Kaliningrad», Ajazeera, 18 June 2022 (https://www.aljazeera.com/news/2022/6/18/lithuania-enforces-eu-sanctions-on-goods-to-russias-kaliningrad)

In the first instance, the EU applauds. In the second stage, it reflects.

After trying to cover it up for a while by claiming that it had implemented Brussels' directives, the EU acknowledges that Lithuania has interpreted the word «transit» extensively and gone beyond the sanctions, with the risk of triggering a major crisis. On 23 June, Josep Borrell, the EU's foreign affairs chief, retrograded[640] by stating that «we [the EU] do not want to block or prevent traffic between Russia and Kaliningrad»[641]. The EU is attempting a U-turn, without disowning Lithuania or losing face[642]. In fact, the EU sanctions aim to «effectively reduce Russia's ability to continue its aggression[643] «. This means limiting the import and export of certain goods from and to the EU, as well as goods in transit to other countries (China, USA, etc.). The word «transit» referred to exports to third countries and not to intra-Russian traffic, which is obviously not affected by these sanctions. The text explaining the sanctions on the EU website also states that «this measure does not concern postal services and goods in transit between the Kaliningrad Oblast and Russia».

---

640. Jakob Hanke Vela, Luanna Muniz & Suzanne Lynch, «European officials scramble to douse Kaliningrad tensions», politico.eu, 23 June 2022 (https://www.politico.eu/article/europe-official-scramble-de-escalate-tension-kaliningrad-russia-lithuania/)

641. «EU aims to de-escalate tensions over Russian trade to Kaliningrad, Financial Times, 23 Jun 2022 (https://www.ft.com/content/dcbb1dbd-5e43-4822-a58f-4d301b6f5b0b)

642. Jakob Hanke Vela, Luanna Muniz & Suzanne Lynch, «European officials scramble to douse Kaliningrad tensions», politico.eu, 23 June 2022 (https://www.politico.eu/article/europe-official-scramble-de-escalate-tension-kaliningrad-russia-lithuania/)

643. https://www.consilium.europa.eu/en/policies/sanctions/restrictive-measures-against-russia-over-ukraine/sanctions-against-russia-explained/

The EU and Germany express their dissatisfaction with Lithuania's action[644], but Lithuania refuses to reverse its decision, revealing that European unity is only a façade. On 13 July, the European Commission confirmed that intra-Russian transit was not affected by the sanctions[645]. In the end, this measure is just another hostile act by Lithuania towards Russia. This is not really surprising. In fact, the Lithuanian leadership is blinded by a Russophobia that has been added to their traditional antisemitism. For like Ukraine, Lithuania has a long history of criminal collaboration with Nazi Germany[646], which it tends to glorify today. This is the reason why it was occupied by the USSR in 1945, as were the other two Baltic countries.

The problem is that the «experts», who are supposed to enlighten us in understanding sometimes complex events, do not speak according to the facts, but according to their beliefs. They prefer to lie, rather than admit that there was a mistake in the functioning of the EU, and that Russia was right. Thus, on 25 June, in the programme «C dans l'air», Pierre Haski, a columnist for France Inter and L'Obs, declared that it was not an individual Lithuanian initiative, but that there was «obviously a concerted action»[647]. However, for at least two days, we knew that this was not the case!

644. «Sanktionen gegen Russland Brüssel und Berlin wollen Transitverbot nach Kaliningrad beenden», Der Spiegel, 30 June 2022 (https://www.spiegel.de/ausland/bruessel-und-berlin-wollen-transitverbot-nach-kaliningrad-beenden-a-4b6663c0-4a99-4eed-aa63-cbaacbfb610b)

645. «EU says Russia can transit sanctioned goods to Kaliningrad by rail», dw.com, 13 July 2022 (https://p.dw.com/p/4E4dE)

646. Article «Lithuania», The Holocaust Encyclopedia (https://encyclopedia.ushmm.org/content/en/article/lithuania)

647. «Ukraine in Europe: what will Putin do? #cdanslair 25.06.2022», France 5/YouTube, 25 June 2022 (38'42") (https://youtu.be/Rgy2Bbe3HYE?t=2322)

8.2.Weapons supplies

8.2.1.Well-fitting contracts and ill-fitting weapons

The United States is supplying arms to Ukraine under the Lend-Lease Act of 2022, passed - very conveniently - on 19 January 2022, which

> *authorizes the United States Government to lend or lease defence articles to the Government of Ukraine or to the governments of Eastern European countries affected by the Russian Federation's invasion of Ukraine, in order to help strengthen the defence capabilities of those countries and to protect their civilian populations against a potential invasion or ongoing aggression by the armed forces of the Government of the Russian Federation*

The Western weapons supplied by the West to Ukraine are largely obsolete or obsolete weapons. They are not likely to make a difference on the battlefield. Moreover, the few units sent will not replace the thousands of equivalent Ukrainian weapons already destroyed. Instead, they provide an incentive for Ukraine to continue fighting and sending troops to be destroyed. It should be remembered here that Russia's aim is not to take territory but to «demilitarise», i.e. to destroy Ukrainian military capabilities. In a way, the West facilitates the achievement of this goal: the Russians do not need to go looking for troops to destroy, they come to them.

When the weapons supplied to Ukraine are more modern, they are not always adapted to the nature of the fighting. This is the case with the American M777 towed howitzers, acclaimed by the Western media. Firstly, they were not designed for this type of war, but for conflicts such as Afghanistan, where the Americans developed the concept of «sniping artillery», which uses artillery pieces in isolation for precise firing. Secondly, designed to be handled by the US military, they are ill-suited to be used by the roughly trained military. According to Brigadier-General Volodymyr Karpenko, head of logistics for the Ukrainian land forces, the M777s are very fragile and subject to frequent disruption. 30% of them have to be systematically removed from the battlefield after being engaged[648].

The same phenomenon is observed for Javelin missiles, presented by our media and seen by Ukraine as the «Wunderwaffen» dear to their masters. Testimonies from Ukrainian soldiers[649] mention frequent breakdowns and their inability to properly use weapons that are too complicated, designed for professional soldiers and very long training cycles. Poorly trained, Ukrainian soldiers are nevertheless entitled to manuals that are obviously not written in Ukrainian, which forces them to translate them with Google Translate to understand them[650] !

This is compounded by the fact that these weapons are supplied 'as is', without spare parts or personnel capable of repairing them close to the battlefield[651].

8.2.2.Weapons with an uncertain fate

648. Stew Magnuson, «Ukraine to U.S. Defense Industry: We Need Long-Range, Precision Weapons,» National Defense Magazine, 5 June 2022 (https://www.nationaldefensemagazine.org/articles/2022/6/15/ukraine-to-us-defense-industry-we-need-long-range-precision-weapons)
649. https://t.me/HersonVestnik/5489
650. Thomas Gibbons-Neff & Natalia Yermak, «Potent Weapons Reach Ukraine Faster Than the Know-How to Use Them», The New York Times, 6 June 2022 (https://www.nytimes.com/2022/06/06/world/europe/ukraine-advanced-weapons-training.html)
651. Alex Horton, «For Ukrainian troops, a need arises: Javelin customer service», The Washington Post, 14 June 2022 (https://www.washingtonpost.com/national-security/2022/06/14/ukraine-javelin-assistance/)

The EU's decision to supply arms to Ukraine at the start of the Russian offensive is causing concern among experts. They are being distributed unchecked to the Ukrainian population in the west of the country, as it is expected that Kiev will be taken over. Very quickly, they are found to be in the hands of criminal individuals and organisations and are already beginning to pose a security problem for the Kiev authorities themselves. Not to mention that the weapons that are touted as effective against Russian aircraft could eventually threaten our military and civilian aircraft... No real analysis of the situation has been made, and it is clear that Russia will not attack Kiev. The population knows this and weapons are sold very quickly.

The fact is that the weapons delivered to Ukraine are not reaching the frontline fighters. There are several reasons for this.

First, some of the weapons that arrive in Poland and are then shipped to Ukraine are diverted on European soil. For example, the FGM-148 Javelin anti-tank missiles, which carry the hopes of the West[652] against Russian forces, are sold on the darknet for US$30,000 each[653] by elements of the Ukrainian government. NLAW anti-tank missiles can also be found for US$15,000 and Switchblade 600 suicide drones for US$7,000.

Secondly, there is no real mechanism for distributing these weapons, the best of which are given to units in the west of the country, to the detriment of fighters at the front.

Third, Ukrainian stocks are rapidly falling into Russian hands. The Russians have recovered considerable quantities of FGM-148 Javelin anti-tank missiles and handed them over to the Donbass

652. https://www.rts.ch/audio-podcast/2022/audio/le-meme-de-la-sainte-javelin-permet-de-recolter-1-500-000-francs-pour-l-ukraine-25819753.html

653. Boyko Nikolov, «Location Kyiv: Javelin ATGM is sold for $30K on the darknet», bulgarianmilitary.com, 2 June 2022 (https://bulgarianmilitary.com/2022/06/02/location-kyiv-javelin-atgm-is-sold-for-30k-on-the-darknet/)

militias, where they are now stocked[654]. According to the French lawyer Régis de Castelnau[655], two CAESAR artillery systems donated by the French government to Ukraine have made their way to the Russian factory Uralvagonzavod. The French army staff denied the information. Sold at a low price to the Russians or captured by Russian special forces, the details of this operation are neither known nor confirmed... The fact remains that, around mid-July 2022, an American HIMARS multiple rocket launcher system also found its way to Russia: it was sold by Ukrainian «officials». The information was not confirmed at the time, but a few days later, on 17 July, Volodymyr Zelensky suspended Ivan Bakanov, head of the SBU, and Iryna Venediktova, Prosecutor-General of Ukraine, from their posts and launched investigations against 651 people for «treason and collaboration with the enemy»[656].

It is not clear whether these individuals are linked to the HIMARS transfer (if it is found to be true), but the case is the last straw in undermining Western confidence in the Ukrainian regime. This is the case for the Americans. While they had planned to supply four MQ-1C Gray Eagle drones, they backed out in June 2022. The reason given? The risk of technology leakage[657]. They fear that members of the Ukrainian establishment might sell one

654. Linda Kay, «Russia to Hand Over Western Weapons seized in Ukraine to Donetsk and Lugansk Militias», Defense World, 11 March 2022 (https://www.defenseworld.net/2022/03/11/russia-to-hand-over-western-weapons-seized-in-ukraine-to-donetsk-and-lugansk-militias.html)

655. https://twitter.com/R_DeCastelnau/status/1538841005612572674

656. Matt Murphy, «Ukraine war: Zelensky suspends security chief and top prosecutor», BBC News, 18 July 2022 (https://www.bbc.com/news/world-europe-62202078)

657. Inder Singh Bisht, «Pentagon Postpones Armed MQ-1C Drone Sale to Ukraine», The Defense Post, 21 June 2022 (https://www.thedefensepost.com/2022/06/21/pentagon-postpones-mq1c-drone-ukraine/)

to the Russians. This would tend to confirm that the Russians were able to acquire Western equipment thanks to corrupt Ukrainians.

The problem is that even US intelligence services do not know where the weapons delivered to Ukraine are going[658]. This situation alarms Juergen Stock, Secretary General of Interpol, who fears that these weapons are going to criminal organisations[659]. This is happening with the complicity of Western governments who refuse to put in place safeguards and verification mechanisms[660] on the distribution and use of these weapons[661]. It is likely that such mechanisms would expose the deep level of corruption in the Ukrainian apparatus.

Western arms were supplied for a popular guerrilla war against the Russian occupation army, which does not seem to be developing. But the weapons remain.

In July 2022, the Financial Times sounded the alarm. Weapons supplied by the West are being shipped to Poland, from where they are supposed to be transported to Ukraine in private cars. The problem, as the Financial Times points out, is that there is no way of tracking the arms. No one knows where they arrive[662]. As

---

658. Katie Bo Lillis, Jeremy Herb, Natasha Bertrand & Oren Liebermann, 'What happens to weapons sent to Ukraine? The US doesn't really know», CNN, 19 April 2022 (https://edition.cnn.com/2022/04/19/politics/us-weapons-ukraine-intelligence/index.html)

659. «Interpol Warns of Flood of Illicit Arms After Ukraine War», thedefensepost.com/AFP, 2 June 2022 (https://www.thedefensepost.com/2022/06/02/interpol-illicit-arms-ukraine/)

660. Andrew Desiderio, Lara Seligman & Connor O'Brien, «Pentagon vs. Congress tension builds over monitoring billions in Ukraine aid», Politico, 2 June 2022 (https://www.politico.com/news/2022/06/02/congress-pentagon-ukraine-aid-oversight-00036463)

661. Dave DeCamp, «Pressure Mounts on Pentagon Over Lack of Oversight for Ukraine Military Aid», antiwar.com, 2 June 2022 (https://news.antiwar.com/2022/06/02/pressure-mounts-on-pentagon-over-lack-of-oversight-for-ukraine-military-aid/)

662. «Nato and EU sound alarm over risk of Ukraine weapons smuggling, Finan-

videos on Twitter show, some of the weapons end up in the hands of Albanian organisations...[663]

Our media explains these anomalies by Russian disinformation. In August 2022, CBS News ran a report claiming that only 60-70% of Western-supplied weapons arrived on the battlefield[664], but after protests from Ukraine, the incriminating passages were quickly removed the next day[665].

In early November, Superintendent Christer Ahlgren of the Keskusrikospoliisi (KRP), the Finnish security service, confirmed that some of the weapons delivered to Ukraine had found their way to Sweden, Denmark and the Netherlands to supply criminal gangs[666]. The KRP states in a press release that these weapons have not (yet) been observed in Finland[667].

In fact, the RAND Corporation's 2019 report already warned the US government and predicted that «there is also some risk that weapons supplied to the Ukrainians will end up in the wrong hands[668] «. This statement is based on a study conducted by the

---

cial Times, 12 July 2022 (https://www.ft.com/content/bce78c78-b899-4dd2-b3a0-69d789b8aee8)

663. https://twitter.com/i/status/1547041520963960832

664. Adam Yamaguchi & Alex Pena, «Why military aid in Ukraine may not always get to the front lines», CBS News, 7 August 2022 (https://www. cbsnews.com/news/ukraine-military-aid-weapons-front-lines/)

665. Sinéad Baker, «CBS partially retracts documentary that outraged Ukraine by claiming that US weapon shipments were going missing», Business Insider, 8 August 2022 (https://www.businessinsider.com/cbs-partially-retracts-ukraine-documtnary-alleging-missing-us-weapons-2022-8?r=US&IR=T)

666. «NBI suspects arms sent to Ukraine might be in criminal hands», Yle News, 30 October 2022 (modified 31 October 2022) (https://yle.fi/news/3-12670239)

667. «NBI has no evidence on donated weapons delivered to Finland», poliisi.fi, 1 November 2022 (https://poliisi.fi/en/-/nbi-has-no-evidence-on-donated-weapons-delivered-to-finland)

668. James Dobbins, Raphael S. Cohen, Nathan Chandler, Bryan Frederick, Edward Geist, Paul DeLuca, Forrest E. Morgan, Howard J. Shatz, Brent Williams, «Extending Russia: Competing from Advantageous Ground», RAND Corporation, 2019, p. 101

think tank at the request of the Ukrainian government in 2016[669]. In other words, the West was well aware that there is a significant risk of diversion by supplying arms to Ukraine...

8.2.3. Deficient Western capacity

In addition to these distribution problems, there is the problem of the West's capacity to support this supply effort. In March 2022, on France 5, Sylvie Matelly, deputy director of IRIS, explained that Russia was not in a position to compete with Western industrial capacities[670]. In fact, she is reciting Ukrainian propaganda. In June, the Royal United Services Institute (RUSI), a think tank affiliated to the British government, published a very different analysis, which attests that the West does not have the industrial capacity to sustain the Ukrainian conflict[671]. It uses the example of Javelin anti-tank missiles. The US produces 2,100 per year while Ukraine uses 500 per day[672] ! In other words, not only has the US delivered a third of its own stockpile to Ukraine, but its annual production capacity is only enough for four days of combat! Even assuming that the Ukrainian figures are exaggerated, Western industrial capacity was sufficient to fight the Taliban, but not to fuel a conventional conflict.

---

669. Olga Oliker, Lynn E. Davis, Keith Crane, Andrew Radin, Celeste Gventer, Susanne Sondergaard, James T. Quinlivan, Stephan B. Seabrook, Jacopo Bellasio, Bryan Frederick, et al, «Security Sector Reform in Ukraine», RAND Corporation, 2016 (https://doi.org/10.7249/RR1475-1)
670. «War in Ukraine: the turning point? #cdanslair 25.03.2022», France 5/YouTube, 26 March 2022 (10:25) (https://youtu.be/g5SHrW_QPtc?t=625)
671. Alex Vershinin, «The Return of Industrial Warfare», Royal United Services Institute, 17 June 2022 (https://rusi.org/explore-our-research/publications/commentary/return-industrial-warfare)
672. Zachary Cohen & Oren Liebermann, «Ukraine tells the US it needs 500 Javelins and 500 Stingers per day», CNN, 24 March 2022 (https://edition.cnn.com/2022/03/24/politics/ukraine-us-request-javelin-stinger-missiles/index.html)

RUSI notes that US ammunition production capacity can only keep up with Russia's pace for 2-3 weeks, even though it is engaged in the Ukrainian theatre alone with relatively limited forces!

In fact, the Ukrainians are losing their materials much faster than the West expected. Western inventories have literally melted away in support of Ukraine, and by the autumn of 2022, the West finds that it can no longer supply Ukraine without endangering its own capabilities[673].

The modern equipment supplied to Ukraine at the beginning of the Russian offensive is gradually giving way to old equipment designed in the 1960s, which the West can no longer use because it is unsuitable or obsolete. This is the case of the MIM-23 HAWK anti-aircraft missiles, which the Americans have not used since 2002 and which they must upgrade in order to send them to Ukraine[674].

8.2.4.A weak operating result

Strategically, the Russians have repeatedly stated that their objective is the «demilitarisation» of the threat to the Donbass, not the conquest of territory. By continuously supplying arms, and by inciting the Ukrainians to fight, the West and our media have led the Russians to pursue their objective. Thus, the West is logically prolonging the conflict, as Colonel General Sergei Rudskoy stated in March 2022[675]. As a result, the prolongation

673. «Sabrina Singh, Deputy Pentagon Press Secretary, Holds a Press Briefing», US Department of Defense, 10 November 2022 (https://www.defense.gov/News/Transcripts/Transcript/Article/3216785/sabrina-singh-deputy-pentagon-press-secretary-holds-a-press-briefing/)

674. Valerie Insinna, «Refurbished Soviet tanks, HAWK missiles and more Phoenix Ghost drones coming soon to Ukraine», Breaking Defense, 4 November 2022 (https://breakingdefense.com/2022/11/refurbished-soviet-tanks-hawk-missiles-and-more-phoenix-ghost-drones-coming-soon-to-ukraine/)

675. «Speech of the Head of the Main Operational Directorate of the General Staff

of the war is certainly to the detriment of Russia, but also, and to a much greater extent, of Ukraine. Russia has had to adjust its objectives as it has succeeded, as we have seen. If their objective had been expressed in terms of territory, an end to their intervention could be determined, but the strategic objective of 'demilitarisation' has been made flexible by the flow of Western arms. The problem is that, while weapons can be renewed in some way, human resources cannot. Thus, the Ukrainians are exhausting their own human potential.

Added to this is the fact that Western weapons are used to strike civilian populations. This is the case of the CAESAR guns[676] and the American kamikaze drones against the Zaporojie nuclear power plant[677].

The weapons supplied by the West are only about one tenth of what the Ukrainians had in February and which were destroyed. To think that Ukraine will be able to turn things around with weapons that are difficult to maintain, whose ammunition depends on logistical lines that are difficult to protect, and which are served by military personnel who have to translate the instructions with Google is just plain stupid. For example, France Info claims that the US-supplied HIMARS missile launchers will be a «game changer» in Ukraine. Apart from the fact that one might be surprised that there is a need to «change the game» when the French state media keeps repeating that Ukraine is winning, one wonders by what miracle this would

---

of the Armed Forces of the Russian Federation Colonel General Sergei Rudskoy, Russian Ministry of Defence, 25 March 2022 (https://eng.mil.ru/en/special_operation/news/more.htm?id=12414735@egNews)

676. https://lecourrierdesstrateges.fr/2022/06/14/guerre-dukraine-jours-106-109-les-canons-caesar-et-leurs-munitions-livrees-par-la-france-a-larmee-ukrainienne-tuent-des-civils-ukrainiens-a-donetsk-et-gorlovka/

677. https://www.telegraph.co.uk/world-news/2022/07/20/ukrainian-kamikaze-drones- strike-russian-controlled-zaporizhzhia/

be the case. Ukraine has received 20 systems. In May, Poland ordered 500[678], to combat a possible invasion by Russia (whose army has already lost almost all its major equipment in Ukraine, according to Western propaganda!)

We are in total incoherence. All this shows that Western leaders have been more interested in «scoring points» against Russia than in finding a solution to the conflict. By starting out very quickly and very strongly, the West has found itself without any capacity to escalate the conflict, apart from a military intervention that it is not in a position to carry out. Moreover, at no time did the European Union get involved in a diplomatic process. From the very first days of the conflict, the EU has been involved in supplying arms to the conflict. There was no objective reason to do so, however, since the Ukrainian army was intact at the time and even had more equipment than the Russian attacker.

8.3.Natural gas

8.3.1.The problem

While the crisis between Russia and Ukraine has been developing since 2014, another source of tension has been added to it and is probably what precipitated the events of February 2022. Already in 2019, the completion of the Nord Stream 2 (NS2) gas pipeline triggers the anger of the Trump administration, which raises the risk of energy dependence on Russia. The United States ordered Germany to withdraw from

678. Jaroslaw Adamowski, «Poland eyes 500 American rocket launchers to boost its artillery forces», Defense News, 27 May 2022 (https://www.defensenews.com/global/europe/2022/05/27/poland-eyes-500-us-himars-launchers-to-boost-its-artillery-forces/)

the project and abandon its commissioning, threatening it with sanctions[679]. However, neither Russia nor the USSR ever used their gas supply as a means of pressure on the West. It was the West that used gas and oil as a means of pressure against Russia. Moreover, it should be noted that, even since the beginning of its offensive, Russia has never stopped passing its gas through Ukraine and paying it «royalties», thus contradicting Western propaganda, which claims that its objective was to «destroy» Ukraine. It is indeed the West that has been militarising energy since 2019 in an attempt to weaken Russia.

In fact, since the Cold War, the United States has believed that Europe's energy ties with Russia could affect the willingness of Germany and the Europeans to fight the USSR in the event of a conflict[680]. This was stated in a Special National Intelligence Estimate presented to President Ronald Reagan in 1982, which was the basis for an executive order authorising the CIA to sabotage gas pipelines in the Soviet Union.

This idea is a constant in US foreign policy. In May 2014, Condoleeza Rice, then former US foreign secretary, declared[681] :

> *In the long term, we simply have to change the structure of energy dependence. We need to depend more on the North American energy platform, on the tremendous wealth of oil and gas that we find in North America. We need pipelines that don't go through Ukraine and Russia. For years we have been trying to get the Europeans to look at different pipeline routes. It is time to do it.*

679. https://www.state.gov/imposition-of-further-sanctions-in-connection-with-nord-stream-2/
680. «The Soviet Gas Pipeline in Perspective», Special National Intelligence Estimate, SNIE 3-11/2-82, Central Intelligence Agency, 3 September 1982
681. https://youtu.be/btk_Ldd3NF0

First of all, it should be remembered that Europe is not dependent on Russia but on energy. Economic ties in this area were built when the Soviet regime was much more terrible than Russia, in a climate of much more serious tension than today. So it is the Western point of view that has changed.

Initially, after the Russian offensive was launched, the Europeans were reluctant to impose sanctions against their main source of energy. Faced with the threat of having the proceeds of its gas sales confiscated by the West, Russia imposed payment in roubles. This mechanism does not change anything for Western buyers, as we shall see, but Poland decides that it will not pay, and Gazprom therefore ceases deliveries to Poland through the Yamal pipeline.

The irony of this story is that Poland had a long-term contract with Gazprom, based on a floating average gas price. At a time when gas prices were very low, the price Poland paid was higher than the market price. In 2019, following a court case, and on the recommendation of the EU, Poland gets to pay the market price for Russian gas[682]. But then the price of hydrocarbons rises dramatically, and Poland finds itself 'captive' to the market, whereas its previous contract would have protected it from these increases. In 2022, after Gazprom stops delivering gas to Poland, Poland buys gas from Germany, which it pays less for (because the Germans have a long-term contract with Gazprom). The problem is that this gas is taken from the reserves that Germany thought it would have before the winter of 2022...

In April 2022, the German government decided to confiscate Gazprom's subsidiary in Germany and to create a new company,

682. «Arbitration Gazprom/PGNiG: the Polish gas company claims victory and asks for 1 .5 billion dollars», Le Figaro /AFP, 30 March 2020

Securing Energy for Europe GmbH (SEFE)[683], which was activated in June 2022. The problem is that taking over Gazprom's terminals does not give access to energy sources! For example, India had a contract with Gazprom's subsidiary to deliver 2.5 million tonnes of LNG per year at a price of $500 per 1,000 m3. But since May, no LNG has been delivered to India[684], which is therefore obliged to buy on the spot market and pay $1,350 per 1,000 m3. This situation is leading to a diplomatic tug of war between Germany and India[685]. The paradox is that the West is increasing the pressure on India not to buy Russian oil and gas[686]!

Volodymyr Zelensky, who seeks at all costs to provoke direct Western involvement in Ukraine. In early May 2022, he ordered the closure of the Soyuz pipeline, one of two that run through Ukraine, cutting off about 30% of Europe's gas resources[687].

In May, the Europeans decided to follow the example of the United States and cut their gas imports from Russia[688]. After a

683. https://www.sefe-group.com/en/company.html

684. Joseph P Chacko, «India faces shortage as Germany diverts GAIL LNG shipments from Russia», Frontier India, 3 August 2022 (https://frontierindia.com/india-faces-shortage-as-germany-diverts-gail-lng-shipments-from-russia/)

685. «Germany, India in escalating tussle over canceled LNG supply», Bloomberg/The Economic Times, 12 November 2022 (https://economictimes.indiatimes.com/industry/energy/oil-gas/germany-india-in-escalating-tussle-over-canceled-lng-supply/articleshow/95467334.cms)

686. Frédéric Grare, «A question of balance: India and Europe after Russia's invasion of Ukraine», European Council on Foreign Relations, 16 May 2022 (https://ecfr.eu/publication/a-question-of-balance-india-and-europe-after-russias-invasion-of-ukraine/)

687. Pavel Polityuk & Susanna Twidale, «Ukraine to halt key Russian gas transit to Europe, blames Moscow», Reuters, 10 May 2022 (https://www.reuters.com/business/energy/ukraine-gas-system-operator-declares-force-majeure-sokhranivka-entry-point-2022-05-10/)

688. Jorge Liboreiro, «What is the EU's grand plan to do without Russian oil and gas?», Euronews, 19 May 2022 (https://fr.euronews.com/my-europe/2022/05/19/en-quoi-consiste-le-grand-plan-de-l-ue-visant-a-se-passer-du-petrole-et-du-gaz-

short period of euphoria, they realised that they could not stop their natural gas imports altogether and decided to reduce them gradually. For their part, the Russians - like the Chinese - are opposed to the principle of sanctions and have not adopted any countermeasures to the European decisions. The EU's closure of the market has pushed up the price of gas, and Russia benefits from the sanctions. But the logistical costs of supplying Europe are becoming significant in relation to the quantity supplied. It is likely that Russia will decide not to renew contracts with European countries, precipitating a halt to deliveries. This will allow Russia to focus fully on the more stable and promising Asian market.

8.3.2. The alternatives

Natural gas is a cheap, relatively climate-friendly energy.

Natural gas is delivered in two possible forms: in gaseous form through pipelines (mainly from Russia) or in liquid form (LNG) by ships from overseas sources. To reach users, LNG requires liquefaction facilities, transportation by special ships, and regasification facilities. This infrastructure is expensive and rare in Europe, which used to receive most of its gas by pipeline.

Year on year, European gas demand is 400 bcm, of which 45% was supplied by Russia (2021). About 26% of this gas is used for power generation, 23% is used directly by industry, while about 50% is used for heating. Currently, 320 bcm is delivered in gaseous form (mainly from Russia), while 80 bcm is delivered in liquefied form (LNG).

Replacing Russian natural gas with LNG in Europe means that LNG would have to cover 33 billion m3/month year in, year out.

russes)

However, the US and Qatar can currently only supply 7 bcm/month, with the rest of their production going elsewhere in the world.

The solution is therefore to increase LNG production capacity. But this requires the construction of multi-billion dollar liquefaction facilities. However, the uncertainties of the long-term energy market - especially with the commitment of European countries to green energy - make investors reluctant to consider new facilities.

Furthermore, LNG involves the construction of regasification facilities in Europe. Germany is the main importer of natural gas with 140 billion m3 per year, exclusively in gaseous form. It therefore has no infrastructure to receive LNG and has had to order regasification ships from Norway and Greece that will only supply 55% of its annual gas needs.

In addition, 25% of the LNG imported into Europe is transported by the US company Freeport. In June 2022, one of its terminals in the Gulf of Texas exploded. It will not be operational again until the end of the year. As we can see, Europe's supply alternatives are very fragile.

For these reasons, the EU has shaped its sanctions packages and maintained gas and oil purchases so that its members' economies are not overly affected. In other words, the excuse of not wanting to finance the war in Ukraine is just a pretext. Therefore, on 4 June 2022 at the GLOBSEC 2022 Bratislava Forum, Subrahmanyam Jaishankar, India's Minister of External Affairs, responds to the moderator's accusation that he is financing the war in Ukraine by buying Russian oil:

> *I don't want to sound like I'm arguing, but tell me, isn't the purchase of Russian gas financing the war? I mean, why is it*

only Indian money and oil coming into India that is financing the war, but not gas coming into Europe? [689]

Intelligence is definitely not European...

On 15 June 2022, Ursula von der Leyen proudly announces that she has signed an agreement to access natural gas through the EastMed pipeline[690]. She tweets:

With this agreement, we will work towards a stable supply of natural gas to the EU from the Eastern Mediterranean.

This will contribute to our energy security.[691]

At first glance, this seems like a solution to an intractable problem. However, according to Wikipedia, «in January 2022, the United States announced that it was withdrawing its support as the project was not considered economically viable or environmentally sound, which means that the project is likely to be cancelled»[692].

In fact, the predictable consequence of the European decision to do without Russian gas is an increase in the price of natural gas and liquefied natural gas (LNG). It is therefore very surprising to see

689. «If You Can Be Considered To Yourself»: Jaishankar Slams EU Criticism Over India's Russian Oil Imports», News18.com, 4 June 2022 (https://youtu.be/ZWi9t-JX_VU?t=2009)

690. «Putting an end to the EU's dependence on Russian fossil fuels: Gas agreement with Israel and Egypt», La Libre Éco / AFP, 15 June 2022 (https://www.lalibre.be/economie/conjoncture/2022/06/15/mettre-un-terme-a-la-dependance-de-lue-aux-energies-fossiles-russes-protocole-daccord-gazier-avec-israel-et-legypte-4KPCAH2JYNFUPO2U3ZBRCAVOQE/)

691. https://twitter.com/vonderleyen/status/1536984358619435008

692. https://en.wikipedia.org/wiki/EastMed_pipeline

Europeans, led by France and Germany[693], complaining about the 3-4 times higher price the Americans are charging for their LNG[694].

But the real problem is that LNG is only available in limited quantities and insufficient to cover Europe's energy needs. The result is a race for energy, which leads to higher prices on the spot market, which Third World countries are no longer able to pay. In other words, Western countries are draining the energy resources intended for poor countries... This is one of the factors that explains the growing distrust of the «rest of the world» towards the West, which is slowly sawing off the branch on which it is sitting.

8.3.3. The turbine case

On 14 June 2022, Gazprom reduces the flow of gas to Germany by 40%. RTS reports that «Russia is increasingly using the gas weapon to put pressure on the Europeans»[695]. Pressure for what? The media obviously does not specify this, nor does it explain the reason for this reduction. The point is to show that Russia is waging an economic war against the West, in order to «tighten the raw materials market and raise prices».

What the Swiss media is hiding is that Siemens, the company responsible for the maintenance of the Nord Stream 1 (NS1) gas pipeline turbines, had to have one of these turbines repaired in one of its workshops in Canada. The problem is that Canada refuses to return the turbine to Germany because of the sanctions

693. Holly Ellyatt, «German minister criticises U.S. over 'astronomical' natural gas prices», CNBC, 5 October 2022 (https://www.cnbc.com/2022/10/05/german-minister-criticizes-us-over-astronomical-natural-gas-prices.html)

694. Steven R. Miles & Anna Mikulska, «Who's To Blame For Exorbitant Natural Gas Prices In Europe? Hint: Maybe Not Who You Think», Forbes, 26 October 2022 (https://www.forbes.com/sites/thebakersinstitute/2022/10/26/whos-to-blame-for-exorbitant-natural-gas-prices-in-europe-hint-maybe-not-who-you-think/)

695. https://www.rts.ch/info/monde/13181278-le-robinet-de-gaz-russe-pour-leurope-est-progressivement-coupe.html#timeline-anchor-1655470920416

against Russia. Without the turbine, Gazprom cannot operate the pipeline normally and reduces its capacity by 40% for technical reasons[696]. In other words, not only is Canada imposing sanctions on Germany, but the reduction in Russian supplies is - once again - the result of problems within the Western camp. The Swiss media is therefore lying.

Finally, following lengthy negotiations, in mid-July Canada agreed to Germany's request to return the turbine, which provoked the ire of Zelensky, who summoned the Canadian ambassador to admonish him[697]. But the problem did not end there. Despite the Canadian agreement, the turbine was late in arriving, and the Russians had no guarantee that they would see it again. The problem remains for the other turbines, which must undergo maintenance work. Therefore, on 14 July 2022, Gazprom sent a letter to the German authorities announcing that it could invoke «force majeure» after the maintenance work planned on NS1 between 11 and 21 July. In fact, it seems that the Russians fear that the Canadians will sabotage the turbine before returning it. For this reason, they have asked Siemens to provide all the documentation on the work carried out, before reinstalling the turbine in the compressor station. In the absence of this documentation, Russia is not allowing the turbine to be returned. The problem

696. «Russia lowers gas flows to Europe with part stuck in Canada», The Associated Press, 14 June 2022 (https://apnews.com/article/russia-ukraine-canada-business-baltic-sea-8558b02f065d79bd5d9f725188239c98); Huileng Tan, «Russia is cutting 40% of one key pipeline's natural-gas supply to Germany because a piece of equipment is stuck in Canada due to sanctions», Business Insider, 15 June 2022 (https://www.businessinsider.com/russia-cuts-gas-supply-germany-siemens-equipment-stuck-canada-sanctions-2022-6?r=US&IR=T)

697. «Canadian ambassador to Kiev summoned after 'unacceptable' turbine transfer», Le Figaro / AFP, 11 July 2022 (https://www.lefigaro.fr/flash-actu/l-ambassadeur-du-canada-a-kiev-convoque-a-la-suite-du-transfert-inacceptable-de-turbines-20220711)

with this turbine is obviously not isolated, as other turbines are due to undergo maintenance in Canada from the end of July 2022 and Russia has no guarantee of seeing them again.

The Russians are rightly suspicious. In January 1982, President Ronald Reagan approved a CIA plan to sabotage gas pipelines in Russia[698]. The management software of a turbine in the Brastvo (Brotherhood) pipeline was modified to cause it to overheat and explode.

8.3.4. The sabotage of Nord Stream 1 and 2

On 26 and 27 September 2022, after a series of explosions, leaks are detected on the Nord Stream 1 and 2 gas pipelines near the Danish island of Bornholm.

A consensus is rapidly building in the West to condemn an act of sabotage[699]. The question is who did it. Despite the lack of facts, all eyes are on Russia. On the French television channel LCI, the French general Michel Yakovleff even asserts that Russia could have sabotaged its own gas pipelines, which were no longer of any use anyway, in order to demonstrate that it was capable of doing so[700] ! The reasoning is silly: why, then, did the Russians not destroy the Soyuz pipeline in Ukraine, shut down by Zelensky in May? To think that the Russians are as stupid as we are is a mistake: this general would do well to re-read Sun Tzu.

This line of reasoning illustrates the conspiracy mentality that prevails in the West.

Firstly, Russia has never used its gas deliveries as leverage since the 1960s. In 1982, the Americans had already sabotaged

---

698. Roman Kupchinsky, "Analysis: The Recurring Fear Of Russian Gas Dependency", Radio Free Europe/Radio Liberty, 11 May 2006

699. «Nord Stream leaks: Sabotage to blame, says EU", BBC News, 28 September 2022 (https://www.bbc.com/news/world-europe-63057966)

700. https://youtu.be/EMD47FFBvTs

the Russian gas pipeline Bratsvo[701]. Forty years later, it was the West that announced that it wanted to stop importing Russian gas and oil products, so as to no longer be dependent on its neighbour. In March, Canada's refusal to return a turbine for Nord Stream 1, followed by its refusal to give guarantees for the return of other turbines, forced Russia to stop deliveries.

Secondly, if it wanted to put pressure on the West, it could play with the tap to control the market and thus impose its will. This is the principle of blackmail: to be able to back out. By destroying the gas pipelines, it automatically excludes itself from any capacity to act and blackmail the European countries. So there is absolutely no point. The accusation against Russia is all the more absurd in that Russia and Turkey have announced that they want to create an «energy hub» to supply gas to Europe[702].

On a more technical level, the island of Bornholm is located in the middle of the strait between Sweden and Poland. Since the Cold War, it has been used to monitor the passage of Russian nuclear submarines between the Baltic Sea and the North Atlantic. Called BALTAP in NATO terminology, the strait is covered by the highest density of underwater electronic sensors and electronic listening devices in the Baltic. It is hard to imagine that Russian submarine actions could have taken place so close to Bornholm without raising an alarm. Russia would have had neither the interest nor the possibility to commit such a sabotage.

Among the other possible culprits, we can probably exclude Germany. The Nord Stream 1 pipeline was built at the request of Gerhard Schröder, and Nord Stream 2 at the request of Angela Merkel, in order to move away from nuclear power and coal.

701. Roman Kupchinsky, "Analysis: The Recurring Fear Of Russian Gas Dependency", Radio Free Europe/Radio Liberty, 11 May 2006

702. https://www.reuters.com/business/energy/erdogan-says-he-agreed-with-putin-form-natural-gas-hub-turkey-2022-10-19/

Moreover, Germany is the country that suffers most from Western sanctions on fossil fuels.

On the other hand, the US and Poland have shown opposition to the Nord Stream project from the start. In February 2022, President Biden said that in the event of a Russian offensive, «there will be no more Nord Stream 2». When asked how this would be done, he replied «I promise you we will be able to do it[703] «. During the construction of the pipeline, the Polish navy repeatedly interfered in a dangerous and irresponsible manner with the Russian ships responsible for the construction site[704]. The Poles have shown since the beginning of the Russian operation a very immature political conduct, which is why many Anglo-Saxon military analysts believe that Poland is involved in this attack.

Already in 2015, the Swedish Navy intercepted an underwater drone loaded with explosives in the vicinity of the Nord Stream 2[705]. The Swedish authorities did not specify the nationality of the underwater vehicle, but it seems to be of Western construction. Moreover, as this event took place just after the Ukrainian crisis and given the atmosphere of the moment, it is very likely that if the underwater vehicle had been Russian, Sweden would have said so!

Between April and October 2022, the US Navy deployed the USS Kearsarge and its amphibious group[706], which conducted a

703. «If Russia invades Ukraine, there will be no Nord Stream 2, Biden says", Reuters, 8 February 2022 (https://www.reuters.com/business/energy/if-russia-invades-ukraine-there-will-be-no-nord-stream-2-biden-says-2022-02-07/)

704. «Poland Denies 'Provocative' Naval Maneuvers Near Nord Stream 2», The Maritime Executive, 2 April 2021 (https://maritime-executive.com/article/poland-denies-provocative-naval-maneuvers-near-nord-stream-2)

705. Mark Iden, "Explosive-Laden Drone Found Near Nord Stream Pipeline", Pipeline Technology Journal, 13 November 2015 (https://www.pipeline-journal.net/news/explosive-laden-drone-found-near-nord-stream-pipeline)

706. Staff Sgt. Brittney Vella, "22nd MEU Returns from Seven-Month Deployment," marines.mil, 11 October 2022 (https://www.marines.mil/News/News-Display/Article/3184121/22nd-meu-returns-from-seven-month-deployment/)

series of exercises (with sabotage and underwater demolition units) over a six-month period in the Baltic Sea[707]. The websites ads-b.nl and Flightradar24 have in their database the movements of US helicopters in the Baltic Sea and show numerous movements of US helicopters of the MH-60S type in the area of the sabotage a few days before the observed leaks[708].

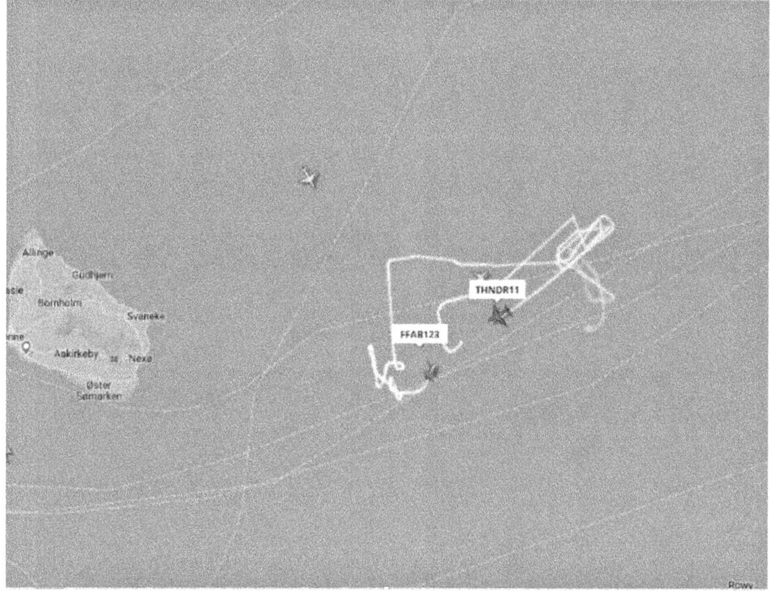

Figure 69 - US air movements in the area where the pipeline sabotage took place.

707. https://www.fehmarn24.de/fehmarn/us-navy-passiert-fehmarnbelt-grosser-flottenverband-der-91809308.html

708. https://www.moonofalabama.org/2022/09/whodunnit-facts-related-to-the-sabotage-attack-on-the-nord-stream-pipelines.html

Figure 70 - Aerial movements off Bornholm Island, with MH-60 helicopters, equipped to spot underwater objects, including gas pipelines, exactly in the areas where the sabotage was observed.

The hypothesis of American responsibility is gaining ground in European intelligence circles and in Anglo-Saxon intellectual circles. An analysis by economist Jeffrey Sachs[709], of Columbia University, is described as a «conspiracy theory» by the Neue Zürcher Zeitung (NZZ), a formerly respectable Swiss daily,

709. https://youtu.be/nbt-CsSRJl8?t=6695

which accuses without any factual basis[710] ! In fact, the NZZ is based on an article published the day before[711] by the Center for European Policy Analysis, (which is funded by the US arms industry, the National Endowment for Democracy (NED), the US and Estonian governments). A source that is both judge and jury, which shows that the NZZ does not work according to the principles of the Munich Charter...

Moreover, it is interesting to note that the NZZ attributes the attack to Russia, while neither the United States, nor the European Union, nor Germany have attributed the sabotage to Russia or any other country! A conspiracy media that denounces a conspiracy theory...

The NZZ covers what has all the hallmarks of a terrorist attack, without providing any factual information. It is true that only circumstantial evidence allows conclusions to be drawn at this stage. The neutralisation of Nord Stream 2 has been a major focus of US foreign policy for almost a decade and especially under Donald Trump's term in office.

In addition to Joe Biden's statements, which can be interpreted in different ways, it is certain that such sabotage could not have taken place without the knowledge and approval of Denmark and Sweden, which have technical control over the underwater space there. It is also certain that such sabotage could not have taken place without the political approval of the United States.

---

710. Lia Pescatore, „Nord-Stream-Lecks: kaum Fakten, dafür umso wildere Spekulationen", NZZ, 18 October 2022 (https://www.nzz.ch/amp/wirtschaft/nord-stream-lecks-kaum-fakten-dafuer-umso-wildere-spekulationen-ld.1706600)

711. Mary Blankenship & Bill Echikson, "Conspiracy Theorists, Right-wing Politicians Fuel Nord Stream Disinformation", Center for European Policy Analysis (CEPA), 17 October 2022 (https://cepa.org/article/conspiracy-theorists-right-wing-politicians-fuel-nord-stream-disinformation/)

Moreover, the context in Germany would tend to confirm the hypothesis of American responsibility. The sabotage comes at a time when the German parliamentary left is calling on the government to enter into negotiations with Russia and encouraging the population to take to the streets to demand the reopening of Nord Stream[712], which Germany (not Russia) has closed.

Since the beginning of September, there have been increasing demonstrations in Germany[713] to demand an end to sanctions against Russia and the restoration of natural gas supplies[714]. They are not reported by the European media, which seeks to maintain a state of tension. At the same time, Germany is conducting secret negotiations with Russia to find solutions[715].

A German shift towards 'normalisation' with Russia was therefore possible. Therefore, the US would have sought to make the current situation irreversible. Apparently, the CIA warned the German authorities of possible sabotage of the gas pipelines[716]. It is difficult to interpret this warning, but it seems that the US agency was opposed to such sabotage, which could have endangered NATO's cohesion. In any case, it seems that the BND, the German strategic intelligence service, was not informed... Thus,

712. Sevim Dagdelen, „Sturm statt Burgfrieden", Junge Welt, 5 September 2022 (https://www.jungewelt.de/artikel/433948.sturm-statt-burgfrieden.html)
713. «Thousands march in eastern Germany to protest soaring energy prices", aa.tr, 27 September 2022 (https://www.aa.com.tr/en/environment/thousands-march-in-eastern-germany-to-protest-soaring-energy-prices/2696034)
714. Philip Oltermann, "Germany's Die Linke on verge of split over sanctions on Russia", The Guardian, 19 September 2022 (https://www.theguardian.com/world/2022/sep/19/germanys-die-linke-on-verge-of-split-over-sanctions-on-russia)
715. Pepe Escobar, "Who profits from Pipeline Terror?", The Cradle, 29 September 2022 (https://thecradle.co/Article/Columns/16307)
716. https://www.spiegel.de/politik/nord-stream-gasleitungen-cia-warnte-bundesregierung-vor-anschlag-auf-ostsee-pipelines-a-3ab0a183-8af6-4fb2-bae4-d134de0b3d57

everything looks like an operation carried out by some NATO countries against Germany.

Russia requested to be included in the Joint Investigation Team (JIT) on the incident, which was to be set up by Denmark, Sweden and Germany. Predictably, its request was denied. Then, on the basis of a preliminary investigation, Sweden refused to participate in a JIT on the grounds that it could not share its information with Germany because of the classification level. On 6 October, the Swedish police announced that they had completed their investigation and concluded that there was «serious sabotage»[717], but refused to share their findings for reasons of «national security». This was the content of the German government's response to the parliamentarians' question. At the end of October, the Swedish government announced a further investigation by the Swedish armed forces.

At the same time, Russia accused Britain of involvement in the sabotage.

Clearly, if the investigation had confirmed Russia's responsibility, there would have been a succession of emergency meetings in Europe and within NATO. But this was not the case. It is not clear who actually carried out the attack, but the Germans know that it was not Russia and that it was one of their NATO allies...

Add to this the fact that Anthony Blinken, the US Secretary of State, called the attack an «incredible opportunity»[718], which certainly no Westerner would have said after the September 2001 attacks, and you get a picture of the special status of this sabotage.

On 13 October 2022, while Russia was proposing to Turkey the creation of an «energy hub», an attempt to sabotage the

717. https://sakerhetspolisen.se/ovriga-sidor/nyheter/nyheter/2022-10-06-starkt-misstanke-om-grovt-sabotage-i-ostersjon.html

718. https://www.state.gov/secretary-antony-j-blinken-and-canadian-foreign-minister-melanie-joly-at-a-joint-press-availability/

TurkStream gas pipeline was intercepted[719]. The perpetrators of this attempt are not known to us, but we can assume that it is part of the same project, which is to isolate Russia completely and irreversibly.

All these elements are not factual evidence, but circumstantial evidence of the involvement of the United States in these sabotages, with the complicity of European countries. This raises the question of the substance of relations between Western countries: are these relations based on the permanent blackmail of the use of force, even terrorism?

These sabotages illustrate the fact that Western intelligence is struggling to integrate and continues to serve national interests or interests that are not necessarily in their favour[720]. Already in 2021, Denmark was pinned down for having authorised the American services to spy on its NATO and EU partners[721] !

But it also questions the substance of German democracy, whose leaders accept being presented with faits accomplis by their own allies and against their own people. What are the values that Germany stands for? If Germans accept such authorities, they should not complain about the economic disaster that threatens them...

8.3.5.Economic suicide

There is talk of Russian 'blackmail' but in reality Russia has never used or threatened to use its gas exports to pressure Europe.

---

719. https://www.aa.com.tr/en/politics/several-arrested-after-attempt-to-blow-up-turkstream-pipeline-russia/2710880

720. Charlie Duxbury, "Nord Stream investigation tests EU intelligence sharing around the Baltic", Politico, 28 October 2022 (https://www.politico.eu/article/sweden-denmark-germany-nord-stream-investigation-tests-eu-intelligence-sharing-around-the-baltic/)

721. Charlie Duxbury & Laurens Cerulus, "Vestager dodges tough questions on US spy scandal", Politico, 3 June 2021 (https://www.politico.eu/article/margrethe-vestager-unsolved-spy-mystery-nsa-surveillance-edward-snowden/)

In 2022, it is the convergence of two Western determinations that create the problem: that of the US to weaken Russia and that of the Europeans who seek to implement unpopular environmental policies. Europe is then led by left-wing and 'green' governments, such as in Germany, who see an opportunity to exploit the war in Ukraine to impose sanctions and thus force the European economy to meet its climate targets, as noted in a report by the International Energy Agency (IEA)[722]. This is a way of blaming Russia for the unpopularity of the measures.

It is quite surprising that this abundant and cheap energy, which had allowed Europe to prosper, while maintaining its international competitiveness, particularly in the face of China, is now being replaced in a completely voluntary manner by an energy that is more expensive and more difficult to deliver.

The cost to Europe will not allow it to regain the competitiveness needed to compete with Asia, as the Wall Street Journal notes[723].

8.3.6.Natural gas sales in roubles

The sanctions adopted against Russia provided for the blocking of Russian accounts in European banks. Thus, Russian gas would be paid into Gazprom accounts in European banks; the sums would then be blocked until the West wanted them. The Russians would respect the contract by delivering the gas; the Westerners would respect their payment obligations but would reserve the right to take back what they had paid. This is a form of

722. Dr Fatih Birol, «Coordinated actions across Europe are essential to prevent a major gas crunch: here are 5 immediate measures», International Energy Agency, 18 July 2022 (https://www.iea.org/commentaries/coordinated-actions-across-europe-are-essential-to-prevent-a-major-gas-crunch-here-are-5-immediate-measures)
723. Matthew Dalton, «Some European Factories, Long Dependent on Cheap Russian Energy, Are Shutting Down», The Wall Street Journal, 13 June 2022 (https://www.wsj.com/articles/some-european-factories-long-dependent-on-cheap-russian-energy-are-shutting-down-11655112927)

theft. No more and no less. Moreover, with the confiscation (not freezing) of Russian sovereign reserve funds in Western banks, the prospect of confiscation of gas sales proceeds was a real risk.

Russia therefore undertook to transfer financial transactions to a Russian jurisdiction in order to eliminate the risk of payment interruptions and account blockages. Therefore, in March 2022, following Western sanctions on dollar and euro transactions, Russia announced that it would no longer accept payment for natural gas in these currencies. It demands payment in roubles. This measure took Western chancelleries by surprise.

The EU initially objected, stating that this would be a violation of the sanctions[724].

In fact, under the Foreign Exchange Control Act, Russian hydrocarbon export companies were required to exchange a portion of their revenues into rubles. The share that had to be converted into rubles varied at different times. Vladimir Putin's decree of 28 February 2022[725] «On the application of special economic measures in connection with the unfriendly acts of the United States of America and foreign states and international organisations that have acceded to it» sets this share at 100%.

The mechanism defined by Russia is quite simple, and - in fact - does not change much from the one that was in place before the Western sanctions:

---

724. «EU Says Pay for Russian Gas in Euros to Avoid Breaching Sanctions, Reuters/US News, 22 April 2022 (https://money.usnews.com/investing/news/articles/2022-04-22/eu-says-gas-payments-may-be-possible-under-russian-roubles-proposal-without-breaching-sanctions)

725. Указ Президента РФ от 28.02.2022 N 79 (ред. от 23.05.2022) «О применении специальных экономических мер в связи с недружественными действиями Соединенных Штатов Америки и примкнувших к именостранных государств и международных организаций» (http://www.consultant.ru/document/cons_doc_LAW_410417/)

The buyer is requested to open two accounts with Gazprombank: a first account denominated in euros or dollars and a second account denominated in roubles.

2. at the time of purchase, he/she shall pay the agreed amount in euros or dollars into his/her first account.
   He then orders the transfer of this sum to his ruble account.
   He then pays Gazprom.

Once this last operation is completed, the transaction is completed.

The advantage of this system for Russia is twofold. Firstly, it prevents the proceeds from its sale from being sanctioned or even confiscated, as is regularly the case with Western banks. Secondly, it creates a demand for roubles which contributes to the appreciation of the Russian currency.

Faced with the choice of applying the mechanism defined by the Russians or not receiving any more natural gas, the European Union, caught at its own game, asks its members to pay the sums into the first account and then transfer them to the other account, without giving the order to convert them into roubles and then declare the transaction completed[726]. This is exactly the process required by the Russians, except that the Westerners do not specify that the money has been converted into roubles. In reality, this is done automatically without any order, with the change from the first to the second account. The EU is reduced to this trick to try to save face with a schoolyard exercise...

726. Ewa Krukowska & Alberto Nardelli, «EU Drafts Plan for Buying Russian Gas Without Breaking Sanctions», Bloomberg, 14 May 2022 (https://www.bloomberg.com/news/articles/2022-05-14/eu-drafts-plan-for-buying-russian-gas-without-breaking-sanctions)

Difference between the Russian process and that advocated by the EU

	Process decided by the Russian authorities	Process recommended by the EU
1	The buyer shall open with Gazprombank: an account denominated in euros or dollars, and an account denominated in roubles.	Same as
2	The buyer pays the agreed sum into his account in euros or dollars.	Ditto, but the buyer issues a statement that it considers the transaction to be completed.
3	This sum is transferred to his account in roubles and thus automatically converted.	Same as
4	The converted amount is then transferred to a Gazprom ruble account.	Same as
5	The transaction is then deemed to be completed by Gazprom.	Same as

This system also allows Russia to control the rouble exchange rate and thus make a profit on the transaction. It is therefore to be expected that, in time, foreign importers will gradually abandon the use of their euro or dollar accounts and pay roubles directly. It can also be expected that other commodities will be sold using this system.

According to Bruno Le Maire, the French Minister of the Economy, the Western strategy was to provoke a massive depreciation of its currency in order to create catastrophic inflation in Russia and thus cause the collapse of the Russian economy[727].

727. «War in Ukraine: «We are going to cause the collapse of the Russian eco-

The Russian decision, which had clearly not been anticipated by the West, very quickly restored confidence in the rouble and stabilised it. So much so that, in March, the rouble was the best performing currency on the market[728], and the financial media Bloomberg called it «currency of the year[729] «! Whereas it was trading at 80 roubles per dollar before the Russian offensive, it is trading at 60-63 roubles per dollar in May 2022 and 59-60 in July.

8.4.The Russian oil embargo

The West took its sanctions against the advice of the economic world, notably the US Fed, and the financial world, basing their judgement on the idea that Russia was just a petrol station whose hydrocarbon trade should be prevented.

In April 2022, Janet Yellen, former Fed boss and now Treasury Secretary under Joe Biden, warned the Europeans not to impose an embargo on Russian oil in order not to unbalance the market.

According to the EU, the sanctions are intended to reduce the ability to finance the Russian offensive in Ukraine. In reality, preventing Russia from selling its oil and gas in the West creates a decrease in supply which has two consequences: a relative increase in demand and the use of more expensive alternative sources. Thus, thanks to the closure of the European market, Russia's revenues have increased significantly. According to

nomy», says Bruno Le Maire», Radio France, 1er March 2022

728. Krishna Kant, «Ruble becomes best-performing currency in March; soars to 83 to the dollar», Business Standard, 29 March 2022

729. Davison Santana, «Ruble Surpasses Brazil's Real as Year's Best-Performing Currency», Bloomberg, 11 May 2022 (https://www.bloomberg.com/news/articles/2022-05-11/russian-ruble-surpasses-brazilian-real-as-world-s-best-currency)

Business Insider, they increased by 50% in May 2022[730]. In June 2022, according to Oilprice.com, Russia expects an additional revenue of $6.4 billion[731].

Two conclusions can be drawn from this. First, the sanctions are not intended to reduce Russia's military capabilities and thus improve the situation in Ukraine, but to disconnect Russia from Europe. Secondly, the West seems to have ignored the fact that, unlike some manufactured goods for which the market has a finite dimension, energy commodities have a very dynamic market. What does not go to Europe quickly finds a buyer elsewhere. Western sanctions would make sense if the «international community» were not limited to the West! This is why the Americans have tried to put pressure on China[732] and India[733] by threatening them with sanctions.

In July 2022, the International Energy Agency (IEA) report shows that, despite a drop in oil exports of 250,000 barrels/day, Russia's revenues have increased by $700 million to $20.4 billion for June 2022[734].

---

730. Brian Evans, «Russia is earning $20 billion per month in oil sales as higher crude prices lift export revenue 50%, says IEA», Business Insider, 12 May 2022 (https://markets.businessinsider.com/news/commodities/russian-oil-sales-20-billion-month-export-revenue-jumps-iea-2022-5)

731. Tsvetana Paraskova, «Russia Sees Extra $6.4 Billion Oil Revenue In June As Prices Rally», oilprice.com, 3 June 2022 (https://oilprice.com/Energy/Oil-Prices/Russia-Sees-Extra-64-Billion-Oil-Revenue-In-June-As-Prices-Rally.html)

732. Michael Martina, «U.S. says China could face sanctions if it supports Russia's war in Ukraine», Reuters, 6 April 2022 (https://www.reuters.com/world/us-says-china-could-face-sanctions-if-it-supports-russias-war-ukraine-2022-04-06/)

733. «US Warns India of «Consequences» Over Avoiding Sanctions On Russia, NDTV.com, 1er April 2022 (https://www.ndtv.com/india-news/us-warns-india-of-consequences-over-avoiding-us-sanctions-on-russia-2855569)

734. «Oil Market Report - July 2022», iea.org, 7 July 2022 (https://www.iea.org/reports/oil-market-report-july-2022)

The equation is simple. By imposing an embargo on the purchase of Russian oil, the Europeans have caused a reduction in supply, which creates a price increase. The European sanctions therefore defeat their purpose, which was to remove Russia's sources of funding for the war in Ukraine. For this to work, there would have to be global unanimity against Russia, but this does not exist. The other oil-exporting countries are rubbing their hands together because they are also benefiting from this windfall.

As for China, it knows that, whatever the outcome of the conflict in Ukraine, it is next in the sights of the West. It therefore has absolutely no interest in aligning itself with the West. The same is true for India, which is under strong US pressure to align itself with Western sanctions[735].

Thus, while the West blames Russia for influencing Ukraine's security policy, it is trying to impose its foreign policy on the rest of the world by force. This has been very badly perceived by the 'rest of the world'. Countries such as Saudi Arabia know that the West is not living up to its commitments and are ready to declare those who refuse to align themselves with their policies as «enemies».

The magnitude of the sanctions against Russia has had collateral effects that the West did not expect. In particular, it has shown the other countries of the world that they are not protected by international law. It made them realise that their economic stability depends exclusively on the goodwill of Western countries. In other words, they have to slowly free themselves from their dependence on the West. This is why

735. Mujib Mashal, «As World Rebukes Russia, India Tries to Stay Above the Fray», The New York Times, 1er March 2022 (https://www.nytimes.com/2022/03/01/world/asia/india-russia-united-states-ukraine.html)

Saudi Arabia, Brazil and India have begun to move closer to China and Russia.

An important event, but one that has received little attention in our media, is Saudi Arabia's decision to sell its oil in yuan. It seems insignificant, but it could mean the end of the petrodollar and thus have - in the long run - huge repercussions on the US economy.

The «petrodollar» is a system developed by the Americans and imposed on Saudi Arabia (in exchange for military protection) and then on all the oil-producing countries, from 1975 onwards, so that oil is paid for exclusively in dollars. At that time, the Americans were no longer able to finance their war in Vietnam and were forced to increase their money supply, with the risk of inflation. The 'petrodollar' system forced other countries in the world to buy dollars to pay for their oil. This increases the demand for dollars, allowing the US to 'print money' without getting caught in an inflationary loop. It is a «Ponzi scheme»[736] whereby the US economy - which is essentially a consumer economy - is supported by the economies of other countries around the world. The demise of the petrodollar would be a major setback for the US economy, if not its collapse, as Republican Senator Ron Paul has warned[737].

After the failure of sanctions against Russian natural gas, the EU is changing its tune and proposing an embargo on Russian oil. Janet Yellen, US Treasury Secretary, warns Europeans that such an embargo would destabilise the market and cause a prohibitive

736. Wikipedia: A Ponzi scheme is a fraudulent financial arrangement in which clients' investments are paid for primarily by funds provided by new entrants.

737. Addison Wiggin, 'No Iran Deal, No Petrodollar', The Daily Reckoning, 18 August 2015. (https://dailyreckoning.com/no-iran-deal-no-petrodollar/)

rise in crude oil prices[738] with disastrous consequences for the world economy.

Western attempts to influence the price of oil by imposing a price cap or demanding an increase in production have been very badly received in the non-Western world. European propaganda explains this as a desire to take advantage of the crisis in the West and «make more money», but this is a bit simple.

OPEC is a cartel that decides on production levels according to the market and the interests of its members. Western - and American in particular - attempts to influence the organisation's decisions are nothing more than a way to manipulate the market. Capping the price for Russia alone allows it to buy oil at a lower price and then sell it at the market price. This is not only a manipulation against the rules of the market, but also a way of bypassing OPEC and trampling on its interests.

In response to rising energy prices, Germany decided to release €200 billion to help households pay their bills. We are therefore in a situation where supply is reduced by sanctions and demand is stimulated by subsidies. This is exactly the opposite of what should be done to curb inflationary pressure.

Western sanctions against Russia have been added to those against Iranian and Venezuelan oil. The West - and the Europeans in particular - have trapped themselves. They expect OPEC to come to their rescue when they have taken decisions that circumvent the rules of the market, and they demand that the Americans supply them with gas at a price below the market price resulting from the shortage created by the sanctions!

738. Sylvan Lane, «Yellen: European ban on Russian energy may do more harm than good», The Hill, 21 April 2022 (https://thehill.com/policy/finance/3275829-yellen-european-ban-on-russian-energy-may-do-more-harm-than-good/?rl=1)

8.5.Ukraine in the EU

On 23 June 2022, the EU officially - and noisily - grants candidate member status to Ukraine. The victorious tone of the announcement is reminiscent of the film Le Dîner de cons, when François Pignon (Jacques Villeret) proudly exclaims: «We have the rights! You do something that has no impact on the resolution of the crisis, and that you know in advance will lead to nothing; but you see it as a victory. In fact, the aim of this approach is to consolidate Russia's isolation rather than to move Ukraine forward.

A rather strange aspect of the European reaction since 2014 is the belief that Russia is trying to prevent Ukraine's accession to the EU. Yet it is well documented that in 2013 it was the EU that vetoed the possibility of a solution that would have accommodated the interests of the EU, Ukraine and Russia simultaneously. Imposed on Ukraine by José-Manuel Barroso, this dilemma led it to delay the decision of the Yanukovych government, which was the trigger for the Mayan events.

In 2019, Ukraine had written into its constitution the goal of joining the EU[739]. As early as February 2022, the EU is using Ukraine's membership as a form of retaliation to the Russian offensive. However, as Reuters notes, Russia has no problem with this[740].

In fact, the Association Agreement between the European Union and the European Atomic Energy Community (EAEC), which was negotiated in 2013 and finally entered into force in 2017, was not favourable to Ukraine. There are two main reasons

739. «Ukraine president signs amendment on NATO, EU membership, AP News, 19 February 2019 (https://apnews.com/article/cb742d45ae394798bbc7891d30e-faa71)
740. «Putin says Russia has «nothing against» Ukraine joining EU Access, Reuters, 18 June 2022 (https://www.euronews.com/2022/06/18/uk-ukraine-crisis-eu-russia)

for this. The first is that the EU is not equipped to partner with countries whose economies are in such a state. Its tools «were designed for advanced market economies to form a single market, rather than for countries trying to modernise their economies and governance, such as Ukraine»[741]. As has been seen since 2017, the EU is unable to address institutional and structural challenges, such as an incapacitated administration, weak rule of law, corruption and a weak economy[742]. In 2020, Ukraine is the only country of the former USSR with a lower GDP than in 1991! In February 2021, according to a poll by Interfax Ukraine, almost 70% of Ukrainians believe that the country is on the wrong track[743].

The second is that the Comprehensive Free Trade Agreement (CFTA), which is part of the EAEC, affects the north of the country differently from its industrial and traditionally Russian-oriented south. This is the case for the jewels of Ukrainian industry, such as the aircraft manufacturer Antonov, which was linked to the Russian aeronautical industry[744], or the Nikolaïev shipyards on the Black Sea, which went bankrupt[745]... In fact, the EAEC has resulted in a gradual deindustrialisation of Ukraine. This is one

---

741. Balázs Jarábik, Gwendolyn Sasse, Natalia Shapovalova & Thomas de Waal, «The EU and Ukraine: Taking a Breath», The Carnegie Endowment for Peace, 27 February 2018 (https://carnegieendowment.org/2018/02/27/eu-and-ukraine-taking-breath-pub-75648)

742. Timothy Ash, Janet Gunn, John Lough, Orysia Lutsevych, James Nixey, James Sherr & Kataryna Wolczuk 'The Struggle for Ukraine', Chatham House, 18 October 2017 (https://www.chathamhouse.org/2017/10/struggle-ukraine#european-integration)

743. «Some 69% of Ukrainians call economic situation bad, 32% expect it to deteriorate - poll", Interfax-Ukraine, 9 February 2021

744. Article «Antonov (aeronautics)», Wikipedia

745. «Ukraine has lost the shipyard that built the corvette "Vladimir the Great", metallurgprom.org, 29 June 2021 (https://metallurgprom.org/en/news/ukraine/8859-ukraina-poterjala-sudostroitelnyj-zavod-kotoryj-stroil-korvet-vladimir-velikij.html)

of the reasons why the south of the country did not agree with the signing of an agreement with the EU in 2014.

Since 2014, Vladimir Putin has understood that the objective of the Europeans was not to develop Ukraine, but to keep it away from Russia. Forced to restructure its economy by Western sanctions, Russia no longer has economic ties with Ukraine. The products it used to buy from Ukraine are now produced there. In other words, it does not care about Ukraine's ties with the EU[746].

In fact, Ukraine is a poisoned chalice for the EU. With a GDP per capita that is the second lowest in Europe[747], Ukraine is a net cost to the EU. It is a country that has been losing its population since 1991, and the process is likely to accelerate, pushing the country further into the doldrums. This is why Denmark and the Netherlands had expressed their disagreement with Ukraine's EU application[748]. But apparently, politics decided before the economy, fiscal policy, the fight against corruption[749] or the respect of human rights...

746. Elena Teslova, «Russia not worried about Ukraine's EU candidate status: Putin», aa.com.tr, 17 June 2022 (https://www.aa.com.tr/en/world/russia-not-worried-about-ukraines-eu-candidate-status-putin/2616606)

747. https://statisticstimes.com/economy/european-countries-by-gdp-per-capita.php

748. Anastasia Kalatur, «Bloomberg: Данія і Нідерланди проти кандидатства України на вступ в ЄС», Ukraïnska Pravda, 10 June 2022 (https://www.pravda.com.ua/news/2022/06/10/7351618/)

749. «EC Set To Back Ukraine's EU Candidate Status Despite Objections from Denmark, Netherlands», Radio Free Europe/Radio Liberty, 10 June 2022 (https://www.rferl.org/a/ec-set-to-back-ukraine-eu-candidate-status-despite-objections/31892207.html)

8.6.Swedish and Finnish membership in NATO

In mid-May 2022, in the emotion and frenzy triggered by the Russian offensive in Ukraine, Sweden and Finland declared their intention to apply for NATO membership soon.

In the early 1990s, when Switzerland was considering membership of NATO's Partnership for Peace (PfP), one of our first visits was to Moscow to gauge their perception of Swiss neutrality in this new situation.

In 2022, Turkey's opposition shows the incredible dilettantism of the Swedish and Finnish leaders who totally neglected to consult the various members of the Alliance - and Turkey in the first place - to gauge their support.

On 26 May 2022, at the end of the talks in Ankara, the Turkish representative stresses that Sweden and Finland must resolve the issues related to terrorism in order to join NATO. He states that the process of Sweden and Finland joining NATO will not continue until Turkey's demands are met. These include:

- the extradition to Turkey of PKK members suspected of terrorism; and
- the immediate removal of restrictions on the supply of products to the defence industry.

Finally, in order to obtain Tayyip Erdogan's consent, Sweden will have to extradite 73 people whom Turkey considers to be terrorists for their links with the PKK terrorist organisation and the Gülen network. They were under the political protection of Sweden, which did not consider them as terrorists and had until then rejected all extradition requests.

This is a paradoxical situation, to say the least, where a «democratic» country hands over to an «autocratic» country individuals to whom it has granted protection in the name of fighting autocracy! This shows the importance that Sweden attaches to its «values», which it has lost by selling its soul to the devil.

Strategically, the decision of Sweden and Finland highlights the analytical weakness of their and the Europeans' governing bodies. For these «Generation X» governments are making the same mistake as the former Eastern Bloc countries in thinking that American nuclear power would protect them in the event of conflict. They are making two mistakes in their thinking.

Firstly, they are based on the idea that Russia seeks to attack its neighbours without reason. This is obviously false, as we have seen. Russia's decision to intervene in Ukraine is far from irrational, even if one disagrees with it. Our unfortunate habit of not listening to what the Russians tell us and substituting our own reasoning has systematically led us to the wrong decisions.

Secondly, they do not take into account the US nuclear strategy. The US will not sacrifice its own national soil by striking Russian soil for the sake of Sweden or Finland. In other words, these two countries, which met the criteria of neutrality that Russia would want for its direct neighbours, have deliberately put themselves in Russia's nuclear crosshairs. For Russia, the main threat comes from the Central European theatre of war. In the event of a hypothetical conflict in Europe, Russian forces would be engaged primarily in Central Europe, and could use their theatre nuclear armies to «flank» their operations by striking the Nordic countries, with virtually no risk of a US nuclear response.

In June 2022, the Ukrainian media ZN,UA stated:

Some NATO allies may misinterpret the lessons of this war, given the long-term prospects for European security. Russia will not disappear as a strategic rival, and its army is not as «Potemkin» as it seems. [750]

Our pseudo-experts like to recall the example of the Russo-Finnish war of 1939-1940 to explain that Ukraine could very well defeat Russia. As The Economist reminds us, Finland successfully resisted the Soviet attack at the time. But it is generally overlooked that the German command at the time failed to learn the relevant lessons for its attack on the USSR in 1941, which was the cause of its defeat[751].

At the end of October 2022, the Finnish government is drafting a bill authorising the deployment of nuclear forces on its territory[752]. This law still needs to be approved by the parliament. Given the political climate in 2022, it is likely that this law will be accepted. In this case, Finland is making a historic decision, as it increases the risk of being caught in a nuclear conflict, without significantly improving its strategic posture in case of a conflict in Europe...

---

750. «The Economist: Україні вдається борися з армією Росії, але це не означає, що НАТО теж зможе», ZN,UA, 10 June 2022 (https://zn.ua/ukr/WORLD/the-economist-ukrajini-vdajetsja-borisja-z-armijeju-rosiji-ale-tse-ne-oznachaje-shcho-nato-tezh-zmozhe.html)

751. «NATO should avoid learning the wrong lessons from Russia's blunder in Ukraine, says Michael Kofman», The Economist, 7 June 2022 (updated 9 June 2022) (https://www.economist.com/by-invitation/2022/06/07/nato-should-avoid-learning-the-wrong-lessons-from-russias-blunder-in-ukraine-says-michael-kofman)

752. Lauri Nurmi, «Hallituksen esitys Nato-jäsenyydestä: ei rajoituksia ydinaseille Suomessa», Iltalehti, 26 October 2022 (https://www.iltalehti.fi/politiikka/a/79b81501-689d-4ad8-bf69-c6aabab71985)

9. Ridicule does not kill

9.1. Vladimir Putin's illnesses

In May 2022, Sir Richard Dearlove, former head of the Secret Intelligence Service (SIS), the British foreign intelligence service (also known as MI-6), said that Vladimir Putin's condition would require him to be hospitalised in a sanatorium in 2023[753].

The list of illnesses from which Vladimir Putin is said to be suffering seems to grow longer by the day. Every photo of the Russian president is scrutinised by journalists who would probably have been better off putting the same energy into the Minsk Agreements. Every tremor, every change in skin colour, every gesture is a pretext for a new medical diagnosis. After two years of pandemic where our media incited us - with reason - to «follow science», they have become the Diafoirus of politics.

753. David Propper, «Putin will land in sanatorium and lose power by 2023: ex-MI6 head», The New York post, 22 May 2022 (https://nypost.com/2022/05/22/putin-will-be-sent-to-sanatorium-by-2023-ex-mi6-chief/)

The RTS sees a «paranoid megalomaniac»[754] who certainly has «thyroid cancer»[755]. In reality, this is just conjecture used for propaganda purposes. In July 2022, at the Aspen Security Forum, CIA Director William Burns said that Putin is «too healthy»[756] and that there is «no intelligence to suggest that he is in poor health»[757].

These are the same media that call others conspiracy theorists!

9.2.The fate of Marina Ovsyannikova

On 14 March 2022, Marina Ovsyannikova provoked international applause by interrupting the Russian First Channel news programme with a sign calling for an end to the war in Ukraine[758]. She was arrested and fined US$280.

France offers her political asylum. She refused and preferred to stay in Russia[759]. This shows two things: that the French government

754. «Megalomaniac, on cortisone, paranoid: Vladimir Putin's mental health analysed by a psychiatrist», rts.ch, 19 March 2022 (https://www.rts.ch/info/monde/12951473-megalomane-sous-cortisone-parano-la-sante-mentale-de-vladimir-poutine-analysee-par-un-psychiatre.html)

755. «According to an investigation, Vladimir Putin has thyroid cancer, but should recover», rts.ch, 13 June 2022 (https://www.rts.ch/info/monde/13162992-selon-une-enquete-vladimir-poutine-aurait-un-cancer-de-la-thyroide-mais-devrait-en-guerir.html)

756. Nahal Toosi, «CIA director: Putin 'too healthy'», Politico, 20 July 2022 (https://www.politico.com/news/2022/07/20/cia-putin-health-00047046)

757. Gordon Corera & George Wright, «Ukraine war: CIA chief says no intelligence that Putin is in bad health», BBC News, 21 July 2022 (https://www.bbc.com/news/world-europe-62246914)

758. Pjotr Sauer, «They're lying to you»: Russian TV employee interrupts news broadcast», The Guardian, 14 March 2022 (https://www.theguardian.com/world/2022/mar/14/russian-tv-employee-interrupts-news-broadcast-marina-ovsyannikova)

759. Richard Luscombe, «Marina Ovsyannikova, Russian TV protester, de-

does not have a clear understanding of the situation in Russia, and that it cannot understand the journalist's approach. Because she is campaigning against the war, not against Russia. This is the same ethnocentrism that countries like Mali rightly accuse her of.

However, Marina Ovsyannikova accepts an offer from the German newspaper Die Welt for a job in Germany[760]. Until then, everything seems to remain in the realm of the rational. But things change quickly. In Berlin, pro-Ukrainian activists are demonstrating to get the newspaper's editorial staff to abandon its collaboration with the Russian journalist[761]. The media outlet Politico even suggests that she might be a Kremlin agent[762].

So she expatriates once again and goes to Odessa, her hometown, where she resides since the beginning of June 2022. Finally safe in a real democracy!

But there, instead of the recognition she could legitimately expect, she was threatened by nationalists and neo-Nazi militants, who considered her an enemy of Ukraine. In turn, she was blacklisted by the Mirotvorets website, where she was accused of treason, «participation in the Kremlin's special information and propaganda operations» and «complicity with the invaders»[763]. Thus, Ukrainian neo-Nazi extremists apply exactly the same

cries Putin propaganda», The Guardian, 20 March 2022 (https://www.theguardian.com/world/2022/mar/20/marina-ovsyannikova-russian-journalist-refuses-france-asylum)

760. «Marina Ovsyannikova: German outlet hires Russian protester, BBC News, 11 April 2022 (https://www.bbc.com/news/world-asia-61071163)

761. https://twitter.com/dw_ukrainian/status/1514860587393720323; «Украинцы в Берлине требовали от издания Die Welt не сотрудничать с Овсянниковой», European Pravda, 15 April 2022 (https://www.eurointegration.com.ua/rus/news/2022/04/15/7137880/)

762. Zoya Sheftalovich, 'The Mysterious Case of Marina O.', Politico, 1er May 2022 (https://www.politico.com/news/magazine/2022/05/01/the-mysterious-case-of-marina-o-00029150)

763. https://myrotvorets.center/criminal/ovsyannikova-marina-vladimirovna/

logic as Western media, such as Heidi.News or Conspiracy Watch, which accuse those who try to provide more balanced, less polarised and more dialogue-friendly information without taking sides against Russia, of conspiracy.

Not very surprising...

9.3.Prohibition of the letter Z

In fact, the use of the letter 'Z' in a combination that could be reminiscent of Nazi-era abbreviations has long been banned on German number plates. With the start of the Russian offensive in Ukraine, some Länder went further and banned the conspicuous use of the letter 'Z'[764].

In April, Lithuania banned the display of the letter «Z» as well as the Orange and Black Ribbon of St. George[765], considered as incitement to «military aggression, crimes against humanity and war crimes»[766]. Latvia[767] and Moldova[768] have also banned the use of the letters «Z» and «V».

764. Rachel Treisman, «German states outlaw displays of the letter 'Z' a symbol of Russia's war in Ukraine», npr. org, 28 March 2022 (https://text.npr.org/1089229499)
765. «Lithuania bans using letter «Z» in protest over Russia's war in Ukraine, Reuters, 19 April 2022 (https://www.reuters.com/world/europe/lithuania-bans-using-letter-z-show-support-russias-war-ukraine-2022-04-19/)
766. Matthew Holroyd, «Lithuania's parliament approves ban on Russian military 'Z' symbol», Euronews, 19 April 2022 (https://www.euronews.com/2022/04/19/lithuania-s-parliament-approves-ban-on-russian-military-z-symbol)
767. «Latvian parliament approves ban on Russian military symbols «V» and «Z», Euronews, 31 March 2022 (https://www.euronews.com/2022/03/31/latvian-parliament-approves-ban-on-russian-military-symbols-v-and-z)
768. «Moldovan President Signs Law Banning Symbols Of Russia Aggression; Lithuanian Parliament Passes Similar Ban», rferl.org, 19 April 2022 (https://www.rferl.org/a/moldova-bans-russian-symbols-sandu-ukraine/31811318.html)

Even if it is a ban on the use of letters in a way that is ostensibly favourable to the Russian offensive, it is difficult to understand the logic of such decisions in democratic countries, as they have led to aberrations.

«Z» is not the name of the operation. The West has made it a symbolic name, but it is not used by official Russian bodies. Those who saw a connection with «zapad» (west) or «Zelensky» obviously did not think that the letter «Z» does not exist in the Cyrillic alphabet and that these words are written with the letter «3», which in German, for example, is translated as the letter «S».

In fact, the Russians used the letters «O», «V» and «Z» to identify the different components of their offensive and to distinguish between Russian and Ukrainian equipment. The choice of these letters was probably due to the fact that the Ukrainian army had been trained by NATO instructors, so the Russians could expect it to use the markings seen in Western operations: the «V-inverted», «>» and «<».

But our insistence on fighting Russia on all fronts has certainly made the letter 'Z' a symbol - to the point of absurdity. For example, in March 2022, the Swiss insurance company Zurich changed its logo (a 'Z') to show that it does not support the war in Ukraine[769].

The same goes for the Japanese airline Zipair (a subsidiary of Japan Air Lines). It has decided to change the «Z» on the vertical tail of its aircraft so as not to appear «pro-Russian»[770] !

---

769. «Zurich Insurance removes Z symbol after letter used to show support for Ukraine war», Reuters, 26 March 2022 (https://www.reuters.com/world/europe/zurich-insurance-removes-z-symbol-after-letter-used-show-support-ukraine-war-2022-03-26/)

770. «Japanese airline Zipair ditches «Z» logo to avoid pro-Russia misunderstanding», Japan Today, 16 June 2022 (https://japantoday.com/category/national/ja-

For its part, the Ukrainian army uses white crosses to identify its tanks, like the Wehrmacht did between June and October 1939, for the invasion of Poland!...

9.4.Trees and Russian cats banned

The New York Times notes that «even trees are political now!Russian trees have been banned from the European «European Tree of the Year» competition[771]. The same goes for Russian cats, banned from international cat shows[772] !

Among the dozens of sanctions applied by private institutions, these are particularly emblematic of the atmosphere that currently reigns and is encouraged by our governments. On the one hand, they illustrate the Western desire to affect the entire Russian population and «make them suffer», as the Minister of the Economy, Bruno Le Maire, wishes. On the other hand, it reinforces the idea that there is a latent «Russophobia», which goes far beyond politics. For how can one imagine that these sanctions could lead to the overthrow of Vladimir Putin? In fact, they reinforce his oft-repeated assertion that the West does not like Russia, thus demonstrating that he is far from being a liar...

---

panese-airline-ditches-z-logo-to-avoid-misunderstanding)

771. Jenny Gross, 'Even Trees Are Political Now', The New York Times, 24 March 2022 (https://www.nytimes.com/2022/03/24/world/europe/european-tree-of-the-year-russia.html)

772. Marlene Lenthang, «International Cat Federation bans Russian felines from competitions», NBC News, 3 March 2022 (https://www.nbcnews.com/news/us-news/international-cat-federation-bans-russian-felines-competitions-rcna18595)

9.5.Art

Art is usually seen as a bridge between cultures and societies. For Westerners, this is not the case: it is a weapon and an instrument of domination.

In early April 2022, the National Gallery in London decided to rename the painting by Egdar Degas (1834 - 1917) «Russian Ballerinas» to «Ukrainian Ballerinas»[773].

From the beginning of the offensive, Russian artists in the West were banned from certain events and institutions[774]. In Milan, the University of Milano-Bicocca removed the study of the Russian writer Fyodor Dostoyevsky from its curriculum[775]. The filmmaker Michel Gondry, was forced to retitle his film Coupez! when it was originally supposed to be called Z (for Z)[776]...

The dismissal of certain artists deemed to be 'close to Putin', without it being clear what this means[777], is a signal of a worrying development in society. Firstly, it is a way of politicising art[778].

773. Paul Bérat, «National Gallery renames Edgar Degas's 'Russian Dancers' to 'Ukrainian Dancers'», Le Journal des Arts, 5 April 2022 (https://www.lejournaldesarts.fr/actualites/la-national-gallery-renomme-les-danseuses-russes-dedgar-degas-en-danseuses-ukrainiennes)

774. Ève Beauvallet, «Boycotts - Russian artists: boycotts to the point of absurdity?», Libération, 12 March 2022 (https://www.liberation.fr/international/artistes-russes-des-boycotts-jusqua-labsurde-20220312_XYWLMFY6PFDNPG2ZIVB3WZPLOU/)

775. Alexandre Plumet, «Guerre en Ukraine: Milan censures Dostoyevsky's study and, in Florence, they want to take down his statue», Le Figaro, 9 March 2022 (https://www.lefigaro.fr/culture/guerre-en-ukraine-milan-censure-l-etude-de-dostoievski-et-a-florence-on-veut-deboulonner-sa-statue-20220309)

776. https://www.masculin.com/culture/500767-coupez-critique/

777. Gaby Reucher, «Are bans against Russian arts targeting the right people?», dw.com, 3 March 2022 (https://p.dw.com/p/47xCR)

778. «The Metropolitan Opera says it won't work with pro-Putin artists», CNN, 4 March 2022 (https://edition.cnn.com/style/article/metropolitan-opera-putin-supporters-ukraine-cec/index.html)

Secondly, it is a way of imposing - or forbidding, which amounts to the same thing - a political choice on an artist[779]. Finally, it is the expression of a very current temptation among our journalists[780] with extremist tendencies: the «cancel culture[781]. In other words, they try to erase everything they do not like.

In May 2022, Ukraine began 'cleaning' its libraries by removing Russian and Russian-published books. The Ministry of Culture and Information Policy (MCPI) issued an ordinance on 'de-Russification, de-communisation and de-colonisation'. It restricts access to books in Russian or published in Russia and calls for the destruction of books that could harm Ukraine. The purge is aimed at «works that promote war and the liquidation of the Ukrainian state, glorify those who led armed aggression against Ukraine, and books whose authors publicly support the war in Ukraine»[782]. The problem is that - according to the World Socialist Web Site (WSWS) - among the approximately 100 million books affected (i.e. 70% of the books in Ukrainian libraries), the authors affected are also Pushkin or Dostoyevsky, who predate the war in Ukraine[783]. It is therefore a gigantic auto-da-fé - which no country or traditional Western media has condemned - that recalls the dark hours of our history.

---

779. Richard Morrison, 'Ban Valery Gergiev and Anna Netrebko, but don't cancel all Russian artists', The Times, 8 March 2022 (https://www.thetimes.co.uk/article/ban-valery-gergiev-and-anna-netrebko-but-dont-cancel-all-russian-artists-896mpl577)

780. Antoine Hasday, 'On RT France, Jacques Baud ticks all the boxes of geopolitical conspiracy', Conspiracy Watch, 7 September 2020.

781. G. Fernández, «Destruction & Cancellation - The Cultural Disasters of War», theartwolf.com, 13 March 2022 (https://theartwolf.com/art-essays/ukranian-war-art-risks/)

782. https://www.stopfake.org/ru/manipulyatsiya-iz-bibliotek-ukrainy-izymut-russkuyu-literaturu/

783. David Walsh, «Ukrainian government plans book banning on massive scale», wsws.org, 14 June 2022 (https://www.wsws.org/en/articles/2022/06/15/ooyj-j15.html)

As usual, events that could affect Western political support for Ukraine are immediately countered by a similar event concerning Russia. By the end of May, images of Ukrainian books allegedly burned by the Russian army appeared on social networks. Carl Bildt, former Swedish prime minister, tweeted pictures of burning books, commenting that «Putin has made it clear that he wants to erase the [Ukrainian] nation»[784]. He is lying. In reality, he is not[785] : it is simply disinformation to divert attention from another crime that is being committed at the same time. Moreover, no one in the West is thinking of condemning the cultural genocide that has been taking place in Ukraine since 2014.

784. https://archive.ph/4IFzv

785. «Désintox. Non, l'armée russe n'a pas organisé d'autodafé lors de son invasion de l'Ukraine en 2022», franceinfo, 27 May 2022 (updated 31 May 2022) (https://www.francetvinfo.fr/monde/europe/manifestations-en-ukraine/desintox-non-l-armee-russe-n-a-pas-organise-d-autodafe-lors-de-son-invasion-de-l-ukraine-en-2022_5159122.html)

10. Conclusions

The first question that comes to mind is: why is this conflict more condemnable, more sanctionable than previous conflicts started by the West?

It is the answer to this question that explains everything that has happened since the beginning of 2022, and probably since 2014. As it had done in previous conflicts, the West has aligned itself with US policy, largely under the threat of sanctions... A facade of unity that Europe will no doubt pay dearly for in the coming years.

10.1.What happened?

During Barack Obama's presidency, the Americans realised that their most important rival was going to be China. They began their «pivot» towards the Pacific zone, which was continued by Donald Trump. In this context, the «return» to Europe and Ukraine appears to be more the result of a combination of circumstances than of an elaborate strategy. One of the factors of this change was undoubtedly the influence of Anthony Blinken (of Ukrainian origin) and his Under Secretary of State Victoria Nuland (also of Ukrainian origin).

Nevertheless, the Americans have long had a plan to isolate Russia and banish it from the international community, as the Washington Post confesses[786]. Since 2007, this idea has become more specific, with the aim of provoking a regime change. Based on the idea that the Russian economy was comparable to that of Italy and that a majority of the Russian population was opposed to Vladimir Putin, the American «strategists» estimated that, under a rain of sanctions, Russia's economy would quickly collapse. The resulting surge in inflation, similar to what Germany had experienced in 1929, would create a momentum for political change.

This required a trigger. To this end, the idea was to push Russia into a conflict with Ukraine, in order to back it up with sufficiently powerful rhetoric to prompt the international community to impose sanctions. Of course, Ukraine would suffer as a result, but in exchange for Russia's defeat, it would be offered membership of NATO. This was the scenario explained in detail by Zelensky's adviser Oleksei Arestovich in March 2019.

The West therefore knew full well that Ukraine and its people were being sacrificed in order to overthrow power in Russia. The leaders of the West, the European Union, Switzerland and other neutral countries, as well as the media who refused to alert the international community, are criminals.

The problem is that these criminals are not only ill-intentioned: they are above all cowards. Not daring to confront Russia, they

786. David Ignatius, 'The secret planning that kept the White House a step ahead of Russia', The Washington Post, 26 May 2022 (https://www.washingtonpost.com/opinions/2022/05/26/biden-white-house-secret-planning-helped-ukraine-counter-russia/)

send Ukrainians to their deaths for them, as Dutch Prime Minister Mark Rutte confessed in June 2022:

> *In terms of armaments, we all agree that it is crucial that Russia loses the war (...). And since we cannot have a direct confrontation between NATO troops and Russia, what we have to do is to make sure that Ukraine can fight this war, that it has access to all the necessary weaponry.* [787]

Thus, the objective is not a victory for Ukraine, but a defeat for Russia. For the West fears a direct confrontation with Russia. This vision is very close to that of Ursula von der Leyen who proudly proclaims[788] :

> *Ukrainians are ready to die for the European perspective.*

Andrés Manuel López Obrador, President of Mexico, sums up NATO and EU policy towards Ukraine in a very lucid way:

> *We provide the weapons, you provide the bodies! This is immoral!* [789]

It should be remembered here that it is not necessary to have read the Washington Treaty and its Article 5 in order to come to the military aid of an attacked country. Article 51 of the UN Charter allows military intervention on behalf

---

787. «NATO needs greater readiness, more weapons -military alliance chief», Euronews/Reuters, 15 June 2022 (https://www.euronews.com/2022/06/15/us-ukraine-crisis-nato)
788. https://twitter.com/vonderleyen/status/1537739940942991360
789. «Mexican president slams NATO policy in Ukraine», AP News, 13 June 2022 (https://apnews.com/article/russia-ukraine-mexico-caribbean-nato-b9aaddc8e3da3ad2b2cc013a6e8ff4bb)

of another country. It was this article that Vladimir Putin invoked on 24 February 2022. The West could have done the same, or even invoked the «responsibility to protect» (R2P), but they did not...

On 24 February 2022, Vladimir Putin clearly stated his objectives. It was to demilitarise the threat to the Donbass. But the West did not want to understand this and translated it as «taking over Ukraine». In other words, while Russia sought to destroy capabilities, they encouraged Kiev to defend ground. What logically should have happened is that Ukraine is sending its men to «hold» untenable positions that are being destroyed on the spot, thus reducing the country's future prospects.

For his part, Volodymyr Zelensky deliberately sacrificed his country for NATO membership, knowing that Ukraine would not be a member of the Alliance, as he told CNN[790]. It thus appears that Ukrainians have been deliberately manipulated by a small, deeply corrupt and value-free Western «elite».

With economies at half-mast and inflation showing no signs of abating, the West is heading for a recession whose roots predate the war in Ukraine, but which has been exacerbated by sanctions against Russia. After the failure of Afghanistan, the failure of Ukraine is looming. Public opinion is beginning to tire of a conflict in which their governments have already spent the equivalent of Russia's defence budget in six months for a defeat.

It seems that the West is trying to make a kind of «last stand» by pushing the Ukrainians to fight, so that their heroism will serve as political support for our leaders. They have become so involved in Ukraine that they have ended up directly influencing

790. Chandelis Duster, «Zelensky: «If we were a NATO member, a war wouldn't have started», CNN, 20 March 2022 (https://edition.cnn.com/europe/live-news/ukraine-russia-putin-news-03-20-22/h_7c08d64201fdd9d3a141e63e606a62e4)

its political decision-making process. In the end, Zelensky became so dependent on Western aid that he lost any ability to solve the problem according to the programme he had announced in 2019.

10.2. The absence of Western intelligence

Contrary to what the self-proclaimed experts on our television sets claim, no one anticipated the conflict. The scenarios mentioned before 24 February 2022 were not the result of an analysis of the indications gathered by the American intelligence services but of a reflection on the possible course of an invasion. In fact, by early November 2021, the White House had set up a small group of «experts» to develop possible scenarios for a possible Russian offensive. Under the responsibility of the Secretary of State, this Tiger Team imagines scenarios based on staff exercises. It is these thoughts that feed into the White House's speech at the beginning of 2022. Moreover, as the White House itself acknowledges, the threat of an «imminent» attack is totally hypothetical[791].

It must be emphasised here that this work of a Tiger Team is not intelligence work, but only a scenario that is only an aid to planning. While an intelligence service develops analyses based on facts, the work of the Tiger Team is only a modelling based on thoughts.

On LCI, Ruth Elkrieff questions General Christophe Gomart, former director of the Military Intelligence Directorate (DRM) on Russian intelligence in the Ukrainian crisis. Her questions are

791. Ellen Nakashima & Ashley Parker, «Inside the White House preparations for a Russian invasion», The Washington Post, 14 February 2022 (https ://www.washingtonpost.com/national-security/2022/02/14/white-house-prepares-russian-invasion/)

edifying. They betray his lack of knowledge, they shed light on the ease of creating implausible narratives, and they reveal the credulity of the media apparatus. As for the answers, they show that a former national-level intelligence director apparently does not know that the FSB is an internal security service (like the DGSI in France), and compares it to the French DGSE[792], whose Russian equivalent is the SVR.

In reality, in the Ukrainian crisis, it seems that only the Russians are working with intelligence, anticipating action and basing it on a solid analysis of the operational and strategic situation.

For nearly thirty years, Western military intelligence has not confronted manoeuvring adversaries: it has only considered targets. In these cases, there is no need for analysis, it is enough to detect. Hence its weakness today. The Ukrainians, intensively trained by NATO, are not able to anticipate the action either. Westerners analyse the situation largely on the basis of their prejudices, intuitively, without any real ability to make their observations consistent with a possible course of action, as NBC News[793] notes. The Westerners probably have significant technical means, which allow them to easily acquire targets. But that is all.

In June 2022, in two different articles, the New York Times revealed two seemingly contradictory pieces of information. On 8 June, the journalist states that American intelligence services have less information on their Ukrainian allies than on the Russians[794]

---

792. https://youtu.be/Wrgk6TPSwSI?t=252

793. Ken Dilanian, Courtney Kube, Carol E. Lee & Dan De Luce, «In a break with the past, U.S. is using intel to fight an info war with Russia, even when the intel isn't rock solid», NBC News, 6 April 2022 (https://www.nbcnews.com/politics/national-security/us-using-declassified-intel-fight-info-war-russia-even-intel-isnt-rock-rcna23014)

794. Julian E. Barnes, «U.S. Lacks a Clear Picture of Ukraine's War Strategy, Officials Say», The New York Times, 8 June 2022 (https://www.nytimes.

! And on 25 June, the same journalist states that it is CIA special services that are coordinating the action in Ukraine[795].

In reality, the contradiction is only apparent. The analysis of the military situation in Ukraine is done by the Defence Intelligence Agency, DIA, while the clandestine activities carried out by the CIA have nothing to do with Defence. The divide between these two branches of intelligence is relatively tight, especially on the civilian side, i.e. the CIA.

As evidenced by the two stars added in May 2022 to the wall of its fallen operatives at Langley, the CIA is conducting operations in Ukraine[796]. These operations are clearly cloaked in secrecy, as they could justify the US being considered a party to the conflict by Russia.

The decisions taken by the EU authorities and members show a total inability to anticipate the consequences of their decisions and to foresee the 'next move'. Clearly, decisions from Brussels are 'shot from the hip': without much thought and with a sketchy picture of the opponent. What is surprising is that Westerners have not been able to foresee the consequences of the situation they have created. Such is their inability that even Bruno Kahl, president of the Bundesnachrichtendienst (BND), the German intelligence service (arguably the best service in the world), was surprised in Kiev by the Russian offensive on 24 February and had to be rushed out by his special services[797].

---

com/2022/06/08/us/politics/ukraine-war-us-intelligence.html)

795. Eric Schmitt, Julian E. Barnes & Helene Cooper, «Commando Network Coordinates Flow of Weapons in Ukraine, Officials Say», The New York Times, 25 June 2022 (https://www.nytimes.com/2022/06/25/us/politics/commandos-russia-ukraine.html)

796. «CIA Honors Fallen Officers in Annual Memorial Ceremony», CIA, 23 May 2022 (https://www.cia.gov/stories/story/cia-honors-fallen-officers-in-annual-memorial-ceremony/)

797. «Special forces evacuated German spy chief from Ukraine», Focus magazine/

Whether the intelligence services are unable to get an accurate picture of the situation or are not listened to, in any case our political leaders do not have an honest representation of reality at all levels. They are not helped by a media that overpowers them with information from Ukrainian propaganda and thus prevents a rational response to the crisis.

Combine the intelligence deficit with the inability of our leaders to take a strategic approach to decision-making and we have all the ingredients for failure. So says British General David Richards, former Chief of the British Defence Staff, in The Telegraph.

> *A similar lack of coherent strategy is now apparent in Ukraine. There is, at best, what might be called an incremental strategy, with no prior and decisive synchronisation between objectives, methods and means. It is a «let's see how it goes» type of «strategy», in other words, not really a strategy at all.*

> *(...) I have seen with my own eyes how short-term objectives are prioritised over long-term strategy: unfortunately, the problems I have faced throughout my career are again evident in our approach to the conflict in Ukraine.*

> *(...) Like many politicians, Mr Cameron and French President Nicolas Sarkozy, aided by a strategically detached President Obama, have confused politics, strategy and tactics. They have focused too much on the short term and tactics,*

Reuters, 25 February 2022

and on their respective political needs to be seen as the heroic victors of a war.[798]

Beyond its material consequences, this conflict illustrates the incredible lack of strategic thinking and intelligence of Western leaders. If France and Germany had understood what was at stake in being the guarantors of the implementation of the Minsk Agreements, if they had kept their word and helped Ukraine to fulfil its obligations under the Minsk Agreements, we would obviously not be here...

10.3.Western unity strengthened?

The magnitude of the sanctions against Russia and the unanimity with which they were adopted gave the impression of unity within the international community, but appearances are deceiving.

Firstly, what is called «the international community» is in fact «the Western world».

Secondly, a careful observer can see that Europe is divided. The ex-Eastern countries that seem to have hatred as a basis for foreign policy are the drivers of the acrimony against Russia. This is Donald Rumsfeld's 'new Europe': corrupt and unfamiliar with the notion of democracy. On the other hand, the «old Europe», more democratic but with incompetent leaders, more concerned with their re-election than with spreading the «values» they claim to represent.

---

798. General Lord Richards, «The West is not thinking strategically about the Ukraine war», The Telegraph, 10 June 2022 (https://www.telegraph.co.uk/world-news/2022/06/10/lord-richards-west-not-thinking-strategically-ukraine-war/)

The Western rhetoric of dependence on Russian oil and gas began during the Trump era. It has been slavishly repeated by the Western media and politicians. Rarely is it recalled that the sanctions were decided under the threat of sanctions by the US against its own allies. Inflamed by their own foolishness, European leaders were more royal than the king by going beyond what the American big brother demanded. The fact remains that the facade of unity against Russia was achieved under duress.

In addition to extra-European constraints, there are internal threats. On France 5, Bernard Guetta, a fervent advocate of the European cause, explains that if the Hungarian president Viktor Orban tries to oppose European sanctions, 'he may find himself deprived of his voting rights, deprived of subsidies, deprived of many things within the European Union'[799]. Thus, this defender of the EU shows us that unity is only achieved by the threat of sanctions against its own members. Not very glorious.

In the end, we can see that, since 2014, the EU has failed to play a constructive role in the Ukrainian crisis. Unable to take a step back from the crisis, it has placed itself at the level of the worst and most intransigent, who are also those closest to Washington. It has failed to show that it has something different to offer. The consequence is that its role in the crisis has been minor, but not because Vladimir Putin does not like it, because its contribution is limited to defending American interests and it is not able to bring originality.

The attacks on the Nord Stream pipelines and the attempt on TurkStream show that even the slightest attempts to compromise

799. Bernard Guetta in the programme «C à vous», («Bernard Guetta et Sébastien Chenu - C à vous - 15/06/2022», France 5/YouTube, 16 June 2022) (22'13") (https://youtu.be/48rt7q_5hzI?t=1333)

with Russia are met with attacks. Western unity is partly achieved through the use of force and force. In fact, it seems that Western unity is increasingly resembling an «omertà»!

Western unity is only achieved by accentuating the negative consequences of the war for Russia and masking those affecting Ukraine. The civilian casualties in the Donbass since 2014, which are the cause of the Russian intervention, are considered «negligible quantities» by the media and the governments that support war crimes. By hiding the number of deaths that Ukraine is suffering due to the disastrous management of the fighting and giving the impression that it is victorious. The Western countries thus justify their continued arms deliveries and their refusal of a negotiated solution. The price of this unity is to hide the number of Ukrainian casualties, which some experts estimate at up to 402,000 on the basis of social networks, which is most probably exaggerated. In June 2022, former US General Stephen Twitty estimated Ukrainian army losses at 200,000 men[800]. The real figures are unknown because the Ukrainian government does not disclose them. And for good reason, this would dampen the enthusiasm of Western countries to pro-long the conflict by sending arms. But their intelligence services know...

10.4. Prospective

We are not trying to appease the situation. As the Washington Post said in April 2022:

800. «US-General verwundert: «200.000 Ukrainische Soldaten verschwunden», Exxpress.at, 8 June 2022 (https://exxpress.at/us-general-verwundert-200-000-ukrainische-soldaten-verschwunden/)

For some in NATO, it is better that the Ukrainians continue to fight and die than to achieve peace too soon or at too great a cost to Kyiv and the rest of Europe. [801]

In other words, they don't want peace: they want Russia to be defeated. At any cost. They are not looking for a one-off defeat in terms of a specific strategic objective, but rather «to inflict more losses than the Russian government is prepared to bear»[802].

In October 2022, the general situation in the world is almost word for word similar to what was described in the RAND Corporation's 2019 'Ex-tending Russia' report, which outlined a strategy to destabilise Russia. This suggests that this document has served as a blueprint for US foreign policy since then.

96 Extending Russia: Competing from Advantageous Ground

This chapter describes six possible U.S. moves in the current geopolitical competition: providing lethal arms to Ukraine, resuming support to the Syrian rebels, promoting regime change in Belarus, exploiting Armenian and Azeri tensions, intensifying attention to Central Asia, and isolating Transnistria (a Russian-occupied enclave within Moldova). There are several other possible geopolitical moves discussed in other RAND research but not directly evaluated here—including intensifying NATO's relationship with Sweden and Finland, pressuring Russia's claims in the Arctic, and checking Russia's attempts to expand its influence in Asia.[3]

Figure 71 - Extract from the RAND Corporation's 2019 paper on how to destabilise Russia. This document shows that the United States was aiming for a campaign of subversion against Russia, in which Ukraine was merely an unfortunate instrument.

801. Michael Birnbaum & Missy Ryan, «NATO says Ukraine to decide on peace deal with Russia - within limits», The Washington Post, 5 April 2022 (https://www.washingtonpost.com/national-security/2022/04/05/ukraine-nato-russia-limits-peace/)

802. Michael Brendan Dougherty, 'How to Lose Big in Ukraine', National Review, 24 June 2022 (https://www.nationalreview.com/2022/06/how-to-lose-big-in-ukraine/)

The Western media will be sure to invoke 'conspiracy', but they will not say that the US think tank also predicted that Russia's collapse through sanctions was an 'overly optimistic assumption'.

For example, RAND predicted that military aid to Ukraine would cause Russia to increase its support for the people of Donbass and lead to an intensification of the conflict. It said that such aid «could result in disproportionate casualties, territorial losses, and refugee flows for Ukraine» and that it «could push Ukraine into a disadvantageous peace»[803].

In other words, Western countries were well aware of the risks that their sanctions and policies would pose to Ukraine. For their part, it is very likely that the Russians were able to anticipate what the West was planning against them. Russia was thus able to prepare itself politically and diplomatically for the crisis that they wanted to create. It is this capacity for strategic anticipation that shows that Russia is more stable, more effective and more efficient than the West. This is why I think that if this conflict is going to escalate, it will be more because of Western incapacity than because of a Russian calculation.

Our politicians try to convince us that we are in a war between two visions of society: democracy versus authoritarianism. This vision, which can only end in the annihilation of one or the other, does not allow any way out. This is why they always have in the back of their minds the idea that, by isolating Russia and making life difficult for it, we will push its population to turn against the government and overthrow it. Then Russia can be broken up into micro-states[804]...

803. James Dobbins, Raphael S. Cohen, Nathan Chandler, Bryan Frederick, Edward Geist, Paul DeLuca, Forrest E. Morgan, Howard J. Shatz, Brent Williams, «Extending Russia: Competing from Advantageous Ground», RAND Corporation, 2019, p.100
804. Casey Michel, 'Decolonize Russia', The Atlantic, 27 May 2022

From the perspective of Russia and countries such as China, Iran and even India, the threat of the US seeking to maintain its hegemonic position will continue to grow as these countries inevitably develop.

The desire to isolate Russia on the international stage seems to be a model for a similar crisis with China. In so doing, the West is destroying the trust that the rest of the world had in them. This explains India's or Saudi Arabia's lukewarm attitude towards them and their slow rapprochement towards the emerging Eurasian bloc despite historical disagreements.

The West's unanimous brutality in combating Russia was seen to be in full measure by the rest of the world. The West already had a reputation for not keeping its promises, and it has confirmed this and lost the confidence of the southern hemisphere. The confiscation of Russia's assets (and thus the Russian people's) was certainly a wake-up call for countries that were closer to the West through the force of sanctions than through the aspiration to replicate their model.

This is the case with Saudi Arabia, which has a military cooperation agreement with Russia[805] and receives assistance from China in the production of ballistic missiles, according to US intelligence[806].

(https://www.theatlantic.com/ideas/archive/2022/05/russia-putin-colonization-ukraine-chechnya/639428/; https://www.csce.gov/international-impact/events/decolonizing-russia

805. Ismaeel Naar, «Saudi Arabia, Russia sign deal to develop joint military cooperation», Al Arabiya English, 24 August 2021 (https://english.alarabiya.net/News/gulf/2021/08/24/Saudi-Arabia-Russia-sign-deal-to-develop-joint-military-cooperation)

806. Zachary Cohen, «CNN Exclusive: US intel and satellite images show Saudi Arabia is now building its own ballistic missiles with help of China», CNN, 23 December 2021 (https://edition.cnn.com/2021/12/23/politics/saudi-ballistic-missiles-china/index.html)

For its part, the United States is seeking to prevent Saudi Arabia from falling into the Eurasian camp[807], and to get the kingdom to increase its oil production. To this end, Joe Biden announced an official visit to Mohammed ben Salman (MbS) for 15 July 2022. But symptomatically, on 11 July 2022, four days before, Saudi Arabia applied for membership of the BRICS (Brazil-Russia-India-China-South Africa)[808].

Not only is this a slap in the face to the US and the West, but it indicates that Saudi Arabia is ready to cohabit with Iran[809] (like China and India and probably Turkey with Egypt) in the organisation. This means that international relations based on cooperation and not on confrontation are being approached. In contrast to Western diplomacy, Russian diplomacy works...

As for the increase in Saudi production, our media sees it as a success for Joe Biden[810]. Once again, this is a lie. In fact, MbS promises to increase its production capacity, but not its production. On 21 July, MbS calls Vladimir Putin to confirm that it will stick to OPEC+ decisions[811]. In short: no increase in production.

807. Ruth Michaelson, 'Joe Biden lands in Saudi Arabia seeking to halt shift towards Russia and China', The Guardian, 15 July 2022 (https ://www.theguardian.com/us-news/2022/jul/15/joe-biden-lands-in-saudi-arabia-seeking-to-halt-shift-towards-russia-and-china)

808. Abraham Blondeau, 'Saudi Arabia Abandons the United States', The Trumpet, 11 July 2022 (https://www.thetrumpet.com/25851-saudi-arabia-abandons-the-united-states)

809. Parisa Hafezi & Guy Faulconbridge, «Iran applies to join China and Russia in BRICS club», Reuters, 28 June 2022 (https://www.reuters.com/world/middle-east/iran-applies-join-brics-group-emerging-countries-2022-06-27/)

810. Niels Saelens, 'Saudi Arabia agrees to pump more oil after Joe Biden visit', Business AM, 16 July 2022 (https://fr.businessam.be/larabie-saoudite-accepte-de-pomper-davantage-de-petrole/)

811. «Telephone conversation with Crown Prince of Saudi Arabia Mohammed bin Salman Al Saud», kremlin.ru, 21 July 2022 (http://en.kremlin.ru/events/president/news/69042); Mark Trevelyan, «Putin discusses oil market with Saudi crown prince who hosted Biden last week», Reuters, 21 July 2022 (https://www.reuters.

He will keep his word, as we will see in October 2022. with OPEC+'s decision to cut production by 2 million barrels per day. The US warns that this decision will have consequences. For example, at the end of October, criminal proceedings were initiated by Washington against Mohammed Ben Salmane for the murder of journalist Jamal Khashoggi[812]. Whether MbS is responsible or not is not the point here. The interesting fact is that as long as MbS obeyed Joe Biden's orders, he was not bothered, but the first time he did something wrong, he was sanctioned. We are in a mafia system where international policy is dictated by the threat of force.

Once again the West is hostage to its own arrogance. Russia sells the oil that Europe refuses to buy from it to Saudi Arabia (and other Asian countries) at a reduced price, and the latter sell it to Europe at a high price. The result: Russia continues to sell its oil at a comfortable profit, Saudi Arabia makes a profit by selling it to Europe, and Europeans continue to consume Russian oil... by paying full price!

Since 2014, the problem for the West is that they decide on the basis of a virtual reality made of rumours, propaganda and ideology. The sanctions imposed on Russia certainly affect it, but they are only tactical and short-term successes. Apart from boosting the Russian economy and strengthening the bond between the population and its president, they have created distrust in the rest of the world.

---

com/world/putin-saudi-crown-prince-underline-importance-opec-framework-kremlin-2022-07-21/)

812. Stephanie Kirchgaessner, 'Showdown as Saudi crown prince aims to dodge lawsuit over Khashoggi murder', The Guardian, 24 October 2022 (https://www.theguardian.com/world/2022/oct/24/khashoggi-fiancee-us-saudi-arabia-mohamed-crown-prince)

While the latter probably does not approve of Russia's action in Ukraine, it has lost confidence in a West that does not really know where it is going, that acts more by ideology than by pragmatism, that denies its own values and that does not solve the problems. A more Asian approach to international relations is emerging.

The idea that the China-Russia alliance is merely opportunistic and short-lived is simplistic. Some commentators, such as Pascal Boniface, argue that China is embarrassed by Russia's action in Ukraine, which has led to a strengthening of NATO. But this is less obvious than it seems. First of all, the strengthening of NATO has revealed deep-seated flaws. Sweden and Finland apply for membership without real prior consultation with the allies and are surprised by Turkey's reaction; secondly, Turkey imposes its conditions, which violate the domestic politics of the applicants; and thirdly, it (temporarily) tempers its position because of US sanctions. Moreover, despite its probable new enlargement, and a very vocal presence around the Ukrainian conflict, the Alliance has still not succeeded in giving itself a role for the challenges of the 21st century.

In fact, China should be happy about this because Russia has somewhat distracted US attention - and Western pressure - on Taiwan. True to its foreign policy, China does not judge. Whether or not it agrees with Russian action is a very Western question. China's strength is that, unlike the West, it takes the situation as it is and not as it would like it to be. For example, China has refused to join the Western sanctions, and its trade with Russia has surged: in July 2022, Russia's trade surplus with China reached a record $70.1 billion[813]. As for China, its position allows it to act as a

813. «Russia Current Account Hits Record on Surging Energy Exports», Bloomberg News, 11 July 2022 (https://www.bloomberg.com/news/articles/2022-07-11/

mediator in the Ukrainian conflict. In fact, it was China (along with Turkey and Israel) that Zelensky went to ask for mediation with Russia, before the West killed the idea of a negotiation.

In fact, the West is trying to convince itself that Russia is totally isolated on the international scene. This is far from the truth. The southern hemisphere increasingly feels that the West is ready to «let them go». The example of Afghanistan is very vivid, but Iraq and Libya are examples where the West acted according to national interests that are difficult to identify in the medium and long term. Conversely, Russia and China seem more stable in their approach to problems, and therefore more reliable.

Moreover, the sanctions that allowed the US to influence Russian behaviour have lost their coercive capacity. The barrage of sanctions applied to Russia following the war in Ukraine has been so extensive that new sanctions can only marginally affect Russia's relations with Iran or North Korea. In fact, by no longer having the ability to modulate their sanctions, the West - and the Americans in particular - have trapped themselves.

Another consequence of the West's handling of the crisis is more worrying. So far, Westerners have been able to exploit their prosperity to impose their vision on the rest of the world. Whether this is good or bad is not the point. The point is that our partners in the 'rest of the world' want to arrive at the solutions they think are right for them on their own. They want to do it at their own pace, according to their own cultural specificities, and not according to the timetable determined by the West. For more than twenty years we have been trying to impose our «values» by force, and it seems that our determination and brutality increase with the number of our failures.

---

russian-current-account-hits-record-on-surging-energy-exports#xj4y7vzkg)

German journalist Alina Lipp has been sentenced in absentia to three years in prison by a German court for claiming that Russian troops had «liberated» areas in Ukraine and thus «glorified criminal activities». Her revelations about Ukrainian and Western crimes in the Donbass had already led to her being blacklisted by the Ukrainian website Mirotvorets[814]. Today's German politicians are a credit to their grandparents!

British freelance journalist Graham Philipps, who has worked in the Donbass for several years, was placed on his own country's sanctions list for «producing and publishing media content that supports and promotes actions and policies that destabilise Ukraine and undermine or threaten Ukraine's territorial integrity, sovereignty or independence»[815]. As for Julian Assange, he has served more time in prison than the perpetrators of the war crimes he denounced...

In October 2022, a journalist from a major French daily newspaper told me:

> *The editors forbid us to publish the truth because it could indicate support for Vladimir Putin.*

The world is changing. The epicentre of progress, technological development and prosperity was located in the United States. It seems to be moving to China. Caught in Thucydides' trap, the US is bursting with energy to weaken its competitors. As Joe Biden said in his speech on 31 March 2021:

> *The rest of the world is closing in [on us] and closing in fast. We cannot allow this to continue.*[816]

814. https://myrotvorets.center/criminal/lipp-alina/

815. https://ofsistorage.blob.core.windows.net/publishlive/2022format/ConList.html

816. «Remarks by President Biden on the American Jobs Plan, Carpenters Pitts-

Since 2014, the aim of the United States was to isolate Russia from the international community. In reality, Western countries have isolated themselves from the rest of the world. We have already asked why the Russian intervention was more reprehensible than previous Western-led interventions in the Middle East or North Africa. The answer comes from Josep Borrell, EU foreign affairs chief, speaking in Bruges (Belgium) in October 2022:

> *Europe is a garden, [...] the rest of the world is a jungle, and the jungle could take over the garden.*[817]

This remark did not go unnoticed in Africa, where it was considered - rightly - deeply racist. It is representative of that small coterie of pseudo-intellectual journalists and politicians who, like the totalitarian ideologies they (rightly) castigate, think that they hold the Truth and that it is their job to impose it on the rest of the world.

The consequence is that the rest of the world may be tempted to infer that the US will be a threat as long as it thinks it can dominate others. The logical conclusion is that, to remove the threat, they must remove what makes them feel superior. This means destroying their economic capacity. This would cause a global earthquake, but only for those whose economies are linked to the US. And that is already not the case with Russia...

---

burgh Training Center (Pittsburgh, Pennsylvania), whitehouse.gov, 31 March 2021

817. https://youtu.be/ufAHg6hN4OA

Composition :
Christophe Guinel

w.ingramcontent.com/pod-product-compliance
htning Source LLC
Vergne TN
IW012037160826
678LV00014B/2623